Giving Meaning to Economic, Social,
and Cultural Rights

Pennsylvania Studies in Human Rights
Bert B. Lockwood, Jr., Series Editor

A complete list of books in the series is available from the publisher.

Giving Meaning to Economic, Social, and Cultural Rights

Edited by

ISFAHAN MERALI *and* VALERIE OOSTERVELD

PENN

University of Pennsylvania Press

Philadelphia

10 9 8 7 6 5 4 3 2 1

Published by
University of Pennsylvania Press
Philadelphia, Pennsylvania 19104-4011

Library of Congress Cataloging-in-Publication Data
Giving meaning to economic, social, and cultural rights / edited by Isfahan Merali and
Valerie Oosterveld.
    p. cm. — (Pennsylvania studies in human rights)
  Includes bibliographical references and index.
  ISBN 0-8122-3601-7 (alk. paper)
    1. Human rights. 2. Social policy. 3. Economic policy. 4. Cultural policy. 5. Women's rights.
I. Merali, Isfahan. II. Oosterveld, Valerie. III. Series.
JC571.R396 2001
323—dc21   2001027019

Contents

Introduction

A shift in the conceptualization of international human rights has begun: the international community appears to be more open today to advancing a holistic rights framework than it has ever been in the past. While the Universal Declaration of Human Rights (UDHR), adopted by the General Assembly of the United Nations in 1948,[1] encompasses economic, social, and cultural rights as well as civil and political rights within its text, the subsequently drafted 1966 International Covenants[2] divided rights into two distinct categories—civil and political rights, and economic, social, and cultural rights—with distinct levels of justiciability and requirements for realization. However, more recent international human rights treaties, such as the Convention on the Rights of the Child and the Convention on the Elimination of All Forms of Discrimination Against Women, have rejected a division or hierarchy of rights, giving equal importance to economic, social, and cultural rights, and civil and political rights. Regional treaties, such as the European Social Charter and the African Charter on Human and Peoples' Rights, and treaty bodies, such as the Committee on the Rights of the Child, have been at the forefront of integrating economic, social, and cultural rights within their realm of protection. Nongovernmental organizations (NGOs) working in the field of protecting and advancing economic, social, and cultural rights are also being taken more seriously, and being provided with more support, within the treaty monitoring system and by regional organizations or domestic governments. Moreover, some of the human rights treaty bodies have begun to look at rights in an integrated manner, defining and expanding the content and scope of certain rights in order to deal with them in a logical context. For example, the Committee on the Elimination of Discrimination Against Women's General Recommendation on women and health links women's rights to nondiscrimination and health care, thereby linking a social right to a cross-cutting human right.[3]

Despite these positive developments, a lack of political will to devote needed resources and implement infrastructural change in order to protect and advance economic, social and cultural rights remains apparent today. Within the international system, and at domestic levels, the eloquent statement made by the UN General Assembly in 1948, that economic, social, cultural, civil, and political rights are indivisible and interrelated, has not yet translated into reality. There is therefore still a need to look beyond the bare words of the UDHR and the International Covenant on Economic, Social, and Cultural Rights to give true meaning to these rights. Words on paper alone do little justice to the aspirations inherent in these documents; the rights they contain must be humanized, no mean feat in the face of rampant rhetoric. This means recognizing that, without progress in the realization of economic, social, and cultural rights, an ancient language is lost, families struggle in slums, communities go hungry, women's bodies are exploited, children wait days at clinic doorsteps. Both bodies and spirits die.

It is thus our intention in this book to go beyond the rhetoric. To do so, we envision three steps. The first is to explore conceptualizations of human rights that assist in dissolving the traditional, category-bound approach to economic, social, and cultural rights. The second step is to examine how an integrated approach to rights produces a more meaningful analysis of individual economic, social, and political rights. Craig Scott refers to this as looking "between" rights.[4] The third step is to demonstrate that these rights are justiciable and therefore tangible, whether through domestic, regional, or international fora.

Until recently, the conceptualization of economic, social, and cultural rights was wanting in both clarity and dynamism. The authors in Part I of this volume make concrete suggestions for approaching these rights with a fresh eye. Craig Scott argues that a meaningful understanding of economic, social, and cultural rights will not occur until there is a conscious and radical breaking down of normative boundaries among the categories framed by each of the human rights treaties. As a part of this process, Scott proposes a simple yet fundamental change in the current practice of the six existing UN treaty bodies — he calls for substantive interaction, in order to harness the benefits of integrating diverse perspectives in the juridical construction of economic, social and cultural rights.

Chisanga Puta-Chekwe and Nora Flood make a similar plea for breaking down categories, but frame it in the context of how certain NGOs have recharacterized economic, social, and cultural rights as integral and important "basic human rights." Dianne Otto expands on Scott's proposal to undo human rights categories, reminding us of the cross-cutting nature of women's economic, social and cultural rights, and demonstrates the urgent need for "interactive reformation" in the conceptualization of rights by the UN and by states at the domestic level. Thus, these first three authors outline a conceptual approach to economic, social, and cultural rights whereby these rights are considered to be informed by, and indivisible from, all other human rights, so that they are considered not only justiciable, but also fundamental to our understanding of what rights are.

The essays in Part II approach the practical application of Scott's "breakdown of normative boundaries" through a variety of current themes, including equality rights for women and children; the right to health, and the human rights responsibilities of corporations. Like Scott, these authors propose a "governance responsibility" — as opposed to state responsibility — on the part of all individuals, organizations, governments, and other bodies that can affect the implementation of economic, social and cultural rights.

For instance, both Craig Forcese and Kerry Rittich argue that the neglect of market responsibility has led to detrimental effects on workers. Forcese argues that governments must address the moral implications of globalism, including the link between trade and economic rights. He states: "an assumption that economic development abroad will automatically induce improvements in human rights is not supported by the empirical record. Concrete policies on human rights are required." Rittich describes the rise of the market and the eclipse of the state, linking these developments to the persistent devaluation of women's work. In addition, she identifies the "direct collision between the demands for ever more efficient markets and equity for women" and proposes elements of a solution to this pressing issue, such as specific forms of protection and regulatory interventions.

Rebecca Cook explores the challenge of, and state obligations to, effectively guaranteeing health rights and reducing the tragic rates of maternal mortality around the globe. According to Cook, the key to advancing the right to safe motherhood is through the recognition of legally enforceable duties—an objective that health activists and human rights activists must work toward together. Martha Shaffer approaches the issue of children's poverty through an analysis of the relationship between Canada's international human rights obligations to children and its recent child support guidelines and cuts to social programs. She concludes that these guidelines, which were meant to standardize the amount of child support awarded and reduce child poverty attributable to economic upheaval caused by marriage breakdown, cannot be seen as measures that fulfill Canada's legal obligations under the Convention on the Rights of the Child.

The promises made by the international community to protect and promote economic, social and cultural rights remain only words on paper without, first, a progressive vision of these rights and, second, giving effect to these rights. While advancing economic, social, and cultural rights has traditionally been thought of as the role of domestic courts and legislature, Barbara von Tigerstrom in Part III explores the positive role that national nonjudicial human rights institutions, including ombudsman and human rights commissions, can play in implementing these rights. Leilani Farha explores the roles that NGOs can play in the fast-developing area of international housing rights and demonstrates that housing rights implicate almost all categories of rights. Finally, James Anaya illustrates a dynamic approach to using regional human rights judicial bodies in light of domestic intransigence in order to advance claims for indigenous peoples' rights to cultural integrity, property, and a healthy environment.

While the realization of economic, social, and cultural rights is greatly assisted by a legal framework that defines the content of such rights and provides an enforcement mechanism to protect against their violation, the focus cannot be exclusively legal if progress is to be made. A shift in ideological perspective to one that is more communitarian and egalitarian, both domestically and internationally, is imperative if we are to tackle the funda-mental obstacles to realizing these rights. Indeed, progress will be achieved where there is community and political will for substantive equality, social redistribution, and commitment to the dignity of the human being. It is hoped that this book provides thoughtful reflection on this expanded vision of economic, social and cultural rights.

Part I. Conceptualizing Economic, Social, and Cultural Rights: Dissolving Categories

1
Toward the Institutional Integration of the Core Human Rights Treaties

CRAIG SCOTT

By its nature as a pronouncement of high normative principles, the Universal Declaration of Human Rights (UDHR) did not address the hard questions related to the creation of institutions to begin the process of bridging the gap between statement of ideals and practical realization. However, starting with the grand bifurcation that produced the International Covenant on Economic, Social, and Cultural Rights (ICESCR) and the International Covenant on Civil and Political Rights (ICCPR) as the two institutionally separated offspring of the UDHR, the UN human rights treaty order has evolved in such a way that the UDHR's inclusion of the entire range of then-recognized human rights in one authoritative instrument has become fragmented. We now have six core conventions each with its own treaty body charged with interpreting and monitoring compliance with its own instrument.[1] This chapter builds on works that seek to make a case for a much less category-bound approach to thinking about human rights.[2] The theme which unites these works with the present chapter is the need for a conscious and radical breaking down of the normative boundaries among the categories framed by each of the human rights treaties and for a complementary "interactive reformation" of the treaties' institutional orders in order to harness the benefits achievable through dialogue across diverse perspectives in the juridical construction of human rights knowledge.

The argument in the first work, "Reaching Beyond," was that we must strive to make the original promise of the UDHR — that its human rights represent an integrated bundle of fundamental interests — the overarching premise of the current six-treaty order. An analytical shift is required to enable us to search out ways to approach received categories (economic, social, and cultural rights, women's rights, and so on) with a certain wariness of the aptness of those categories and with an associated willingness to cross to and fro among categories. We must further be prepared to engage in category crossing–and category combining — to the point that we begin to defy the categories themselves by developing our shared sense of when it is awkward, usually unhelpful, and often even harmful to understand a given rights claim or context in terms of existing categories. Harm is exacerbated when we approach a right's content as involving only a single category of rights as contained in the one treaty that is subject to interpretation or application.[3]

In the second work, "Bodies of Knowledge," the context was set by recent recommendations that consolidation of the six treaty bodies into one or two bodies should be on the UN reform agenda. It was argued that harnessing of diversity must be central to any consolidation reforms and that diversity-enhancing initiatives must start immediately with respect to the current six-committee order, in part because practical experimentation with promoting diversity will provide valuable lessons at the institutional design stages of any eventual consolidation project. But the central thrust of the argument was that such an approach was independently desirable quite apart from whether treaty-body consolidation is in the cards. Two premises were — and remain — central. The first is that superior collective judgment is exercised when multiple perspectives are encouraged to interact with each other in coming to grips with any given normative issue or decision. The second is that, in order for diverse perspectives and actors to interact, there must first be a commitment to ensuring diversity within the composition of the membership of collective decision-making bodies. Diversity multiplies perspectives, while the need for decision making necessitates that those perspectives engage each other. Diversity helps oust monological reasoning in favor of dialogical reasoning, making it less likely that reasoning will take place within the four corners of a single person's limited knowledge and more likely that it will take place in the context of the necessity to test one's assumptions and intuitions against those of others. The operative good of a "dialogical universalism" is *knowledge* and the perspectives that adhere to knowledge. In somewhat oversimplified terms, we can think of "social experience" and "disciplinary expertise" as the two main forms of knowledge relevant to the juridical construction of normative knowledge.[4]

"Bodies of Knowledge" noted but bracketed a third form of diversity of knowledge in the human rights treaty context which fuses diversities of expertise and experience, namely, diversity of "normative focus." This term was meant to capture the epistemological perspectives that tend to coalesce around a category of human rights as it gets constructed over time as its own distinct field of knowledge. In this way, we can speak metaphorically, but meaningfully, about the potential of treaty texts to enter into dialogues with one another, dialogues that profit from the interaction of the diverse knowledge(s) each treaty regime has constructed for itself. The present chapter was signaled by the following passage at the end of the introduction in "Bodies of Knowledge":

[A] second proposal . . . could complement [the discussion in "Bodies of Knowledge"]. This is for the human rights committees, through pragmatic acts of institutional co-operation, to consider their six treaties as interconnected parts of a single human rights "constitution" and thereby to consider themselves as partner chambers within a *consolidating* supervisory institution. Through such acts of pragmatic imagination, each committee would be encouraged to place itself within a network of dialogue with the other committees; all would seek to expand their horizons through harnessing the pool of diverse knowledge represented by their large collective membership and the diversity of normative mandates of the six treaties.[5]

The operative assumption of this passage is that, if diversity is seen as an institutional good because of its role in bringing to bear multiple angles of vision on the exercise of judgment, then it makes sense to look at the treaty body order as a whole and ask whether knowledge-enhancing effects can be achieved by reforming the relations of the committees among themselves. It becomes important to think in terms of the normative focus of each committee's constitutive treaty as having only a partial perspective on human rights which would be enhanced by dialogical engagement with the other committees.[6] Such dialogical congress can be organized in terms of at least two broad patterns of interaction.

If, for some purposes or in some contexts, the committees began to interact as a kind of quasi-consolidated committee of the whole, then this would have the effect not only of increasing the overall membership pool (to 97) but also of deepening the pool of knowledge. An analysis that is fuller and normatively richer can — or, can potentially — be achieved than is possible from within a single committee with its more limited membership and its more narrowly categorized normative focus. Here, the treaty bodies (or cross-cutting working groups made up of several members from each treaty body) would interact as some kind of organic or seamless whole, consolidated around a common purpose to the point that the boundaries between the institutions functionally dissolve, even if only temporarily and for limited purposes. So, for example, if the six human rights committees were to meet for two days in a joint plenary session to discuss the draft text of a common general comment on the relationship of social vulnerability to human rights violations, we would speak of the committees (and their members) as consolidated for this purpose.[7]

In other contexts there may not be any actual convening of the members of the committees into some kind of committee of the whole, but rather a more notional or virtual dialogue in which each committee takes note of procedural and substantive developments (some routine and some more experimental) that have taken place in other committees and then makes an independent choice as to whether to emulate what is going on in the other committee(s). On this approach, we would think less in terms of (the members of) the committees interacting as a single consolidated collectivity and more in terms of the committees interacting as autonomous bodies with their own institutional perspectives. Such inter-treaty interaction would be premised on institutional sovereignty (both of jurisdiction and of normative focus) remaining intact in a strong sense. The interaction that takes place is in the form of dialogue across palpable boundaries in which each institution seeks either to persuade or to learn from another institution. Each institution has its separate perspective generated by its normative focus and by its practical experience which it may wish to commend to the other institution(s) or to have enriched by listening to the other institution's perspectives and experience. Jurisdictionally separate institutions are engaging in dialogue (as an *inter-institutional* order), not the membership of the institutions as an amalgamated whole (a *pan-institutional* order).

The first two sections of this chapter discuss various basic possibilities as to *how* such institutional integration could evolve in the near future. The final section then offers some thoughts on what spin-off benefits might be produced by such integration for resituating "economic, social, and cultural rights" in the process of responding to the next generation of monitoring challenges in the rapidly evolving context of economic globalization and transnational reconfigurations in governance structures.

The Role of the Annual Meeting of the Chairpersons in Fostering Evolution of the Human Rights Treaties' Integrated Jurisdictional Order

PICTURING THE SIX-TREATY SYSTEM

A stylized (bordering on caricatured) depiction of the contrast between the state of the current UN human rights treaty order and the as-yet-unrealized potential of institutional integration can be found in Figures 1 and 2. In both diagrams the six treaties are depicted as circles (A–F). Each circle overlaps with the other circles to varying degrees so as to represent the unity of purpose and the shared norms of the treaties as well as the potential for integrated normative analysis to defy the definitional categories of the rights in each treaty. The combined treaty order is shown as embedded in a larger UN human rights system that surrounds the treaties in a cocoon of moral, political, and legal norms. The United Nations Charter and the Universal Declaration of Human Rights are the energy sources for this field. Each treaty has provisions establishing and setting out the authority of its monitoring institution. These provisions are represented as smaller circles located so as to portray each of the six human rights treaty bodies incorporated within its own treaty's normative world. It is with respect to the location of each committee and associated relations with the other committees that Figures 1 and 2 differ.

In Figure 1 (the current treaty order), each committee is shown as lying outside the field of normative overlap. This is suggestive, to an exaggerated extent, of the way each committee has tended to treat its treaty as a self-contained regime relatively unconnected to the other five treaties. Each committee's location on the far edge of each treaty is also suggestive of both its distance from the area of greatest normative overlap (the normative core of the treaty order) and its isolation from the other committees. Six

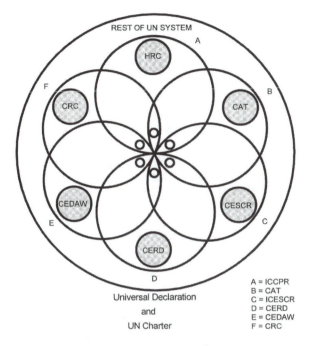

Figure 1. The current core treaty order.

much smaller circles in that area of overlap represent the exception to this Figure 1 state of affairs. These circles represent the chairpersons of the six committees who, as will be discussed in upcoming sections, have been interacting periodically. Except for the occasional individual committee member who may use one or more other treaties as some kind of interactive reference point in the interpretation of her or his own treaty, it is only the chairpersons who currently have the opportunity to participate in a structured pan-institutional context that allows them to view the shared norms of the treaties as fertile ground which is ready for careful cultivation. In contrast, for many of the other members of each committee, this same ground is more likely to be seen as akin to a wild thicket covered in a tangle of branches and thorns — an area to avoid rather than cultivate.

Figure 2 (the potential treaty order) is the diametric opposite to Figure 1. Here, interactive diversity of knowledge is harnessed by mapping institutional arrangements onto the area of greatest normative synergy among the treaties. Not only the chairs (periodically) but also the committees (constantly) interact in such a way that their combined institutional order takes on a shifting amorphous shape. The committees are no longer distinct or distant circles, although the rounded outer curves of this new body are

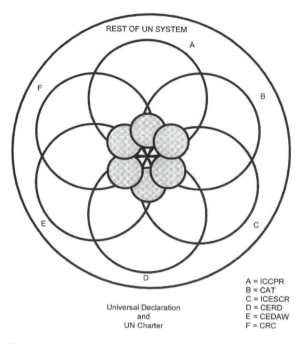

Figure 2. Potential (de facto consolidated) core treaty order.

meant to suggest a certain retention by each committee of considerable ongoing institutional autonomy and of a certain possibility that a given committee can always dislodge (or threaten to dislodge) itself from this consolidated institutional structure if it becomes dissatisfied with how its treaty mandate has fared as a result of the incorporation.

As of 2000, the actual situation has evolved to some point between Figures 1 and 2. A certain, albeit embryonic, institutional integration of the treaty bodies has begun to occur. Much of the cooperation is *inter-institutional* in nature, taking the form of sharing of information and also of tacit emulation, whereby one committee pioneers a procedural innovation and others begin to follow suit.[8] This is of course testimony to the fact that jurisdictional diversity combined with jurisdictional autonomy can foster productive experimentation, something that would be severely hampered by total consolidation of all six existing committees into one committee.[9] At least one committee, CEDAW, has designated committee members to be in charge of liaising with the other committees, one committee member for each other treaty.[10] However, there are nascent, albeit fitful, signs of the possible emergence of an *pan-institutional* order, to which we now turn.

THE ROLE OF THE ANNUAL MEETING OF THE CHAIRPERSONS

The most important form of institutional cooperation among the six human rights treaty bodies is the now annual meeting of the six committee chairpersons. It may be viewed as a forum pushing to become an institution, representing a kind of hybrid of the two forms of institutional interaction described above, the inter-institutional and the pan-institutional. The chairpersons first began meeting in 1984, meeting periodically thereafter until the institution of yearly meetings in 1994.[11] With each subsequent meeting, the range of other significant actors who attend or make presentations to the chairpersons has grown,[12] to the point that some of the more powerful NGOs have not only attended but have also been permitted to make oral presentations to the chairpersons.[13] The meeting's Internet-accessible reports to the General Assembly, along with follow-up reports produced by the UN human rights secretariat in response to recommendations of the previous year's meeting, provide helpful overviews of recent developments in the institutional practices of each of the treaty bodies. The chairpersons' reports, especially those up to the end of 1998, contain many specific recommendations directed to all of the committees, mostly recommendations for procedural reform.[14] There are as many, if not more, recommendations directed to other actors within the system, most notably to the UN human rights bureaucracy.[15] The annual meeting is clearly starting to play a kind of clearinghouse role whereby developments and suggestions from each committee are conveyed by that committee's chairperson to the chairpersons of the other five committees, and then the chairpersons acting as a collectivity feed the most meritorious and/or timely ones back to the committees by way of their annual report. The method by which the chairpersons address the committees varies, taking the form sometimes of simple descriptions of what various committees are doing and sometimes, more ambitiously, of joint recommendations.[16]

By and large, the chairpersons have concentrated until quite recently mostly on procedural and resource issues of common interest to the committees and have not tended to use their meetings as an occasion for substantive normative cooperation. On occasion, however, they have taken a common normative position on matters of substantive law. At least four of these have related to difficult issues of general treaty law: reservations, succession, denunciation, and interpretively implied powers.

On the question of permissibility and the effects of reservations, solidarity among the committees was demonstrated by the chairpersons' support for the Human Rights Committee's General Comment 24 on reservations.[17] This united front is bound to make it easier for the Human Rights Committee to maintain a strong position on reservations in the face of resistance from states like the United States, France, and the United Kingdom who have submitted critical comments on the HRC's reasoning in that general comment.[18]

On the question of state succession to human rights treaties, the chairpersons at their fifth meeting, in 1994, "expressed the view that successor States are automatically bound by obligations under international human rights instruments from the dates of their independence and that respect of their obligations should not depend on a declaration of confirmation."[19] A year later the Human Rights Committee may well have drawn support from this statement when it took the view in its concluding observations on the report of the United Kingdom relating to Hong Kong that human rights treaty obligations devolved with territory such that China would be bound to respect the ICCPR after its takeover of Hong Kong.[20]

On the question of the power to withdraw from human rights treaties, the chairpersons in September 1997 stated their view that a state party cannot withdraw from the ICCPR, a response to the announcement only three weeks earlier by North Korea that it intended to denounce the ICCPR.[21] This view was actually stated *before* the Human Rights Committee itself had had an opportunity to discuss and then pronounce on the subject, which it did two months later in the form of General Comment 26.[22] It is also significant from the perspective of the gradual evolution of the interpretive authority of the Chairpersons that their collective view on denunciation applies not only to the ICCPR but also to the two other treaties which, like the ICCPR, do not contain clauses expressly permitting denunciation, namely the ICESCR and CEDAW.

Finally, on the question of implied powers, the chairpersons have articulated what will probably turn out to be the most significant of their series of views on general treaty law. The specific issue that the Chairpersons were considering was, on the surface, the legal jurisdiction of any of the committees to consider the human rights situation of a state when that state has failed to submit a state report. Two committees, the CESCR and CERD, had adopted a practice of considering situations in states whose state report is long overdue "once all alternative approaches have been exhausted."[23] This is one of the best examples of the benefits of jurisdictional experimentalism within the human rights treaty order in that both the UN Commission on Human Rights and the General Assembly had come to endorse these two committees' initiative. Despite such high level political support within the UN, a number of states (and, it seems, some committee members in other committees) had begun to question whether such an approach "might exceed the legal competence of a committee."[24] This was the context in which the chairpersons weighed in with their view on whether each committee could examine the situation of a state in the absence of a report. The analysis is quite detailed (relative to the usual style found in the chairpersons' reports) and, on the whole, leans heavily toward the view that the practice is within the competence of the committees.[25] However, the significance of the chairpersons' reasoning lies not in their conclusion on the specific interpretive issue (examining states who have not reported) but rather in the general statement of the principles of interpretation that should be applied to resolve claims to implied jurisdictional powers made by the treaty bodies. The chairpersons' reasoning is potentially transformative in that not only does it lay the basis for the evolution of the jurisdictional powers of each committee, but also it points to the legal basis on which a pan-treaty "constitutional" order could itself institutionally evolve:

> The principle which should . . . be applied in responding to a situation which threatened to undermine the entire system for supervising the obligations freely undertaken by States Parties by virtue of their ratification or accession to the relevant treaty was that of ensuring the effectiveness of the regime established by the treaty. In the absence of any provision to the contrary in a treaty, the question was whether or not a particular course of action contributed to the effectiveness of that regime. That approach was analogous to the principle of implied powers, according to which the acceptability of activities not explicitly provided for should be determined in light of the object and purpose of the treaty in question. The International Court of Justice has also noted that, even in the absence of specific enabling powers, an international body may act in ways not specifically forbidden, in order to achieve its purposes and objectives.[26]

As a legal theory of the interpretive acquisition of jurisdictional powers, the above-stated principles will not take root in a vacuum. Parallel processes of political recognition of any powers the committees claim for themselves will operate in tandem with the more forensic processes of interpretation that produce the claims. Yet, in this one tight paragraph, it may not be an exaggeration to say that the chairpersons have sown the seeds for the institutional evolution of an integrated human rights treaty order.

FROM STRUCTURE TO SUBSTANCE: FOSTERING INTEGRATED NORMATIVE ANALYSIS

The just-given examples dealing with the intersection of general treaty law and the evolution of the human rights committees' jurisdictional competence constitute very significant examples of cross-committee coordination. However, with respect to matters of substantive content of human rights guarantees (as opposed to structural treaty law issues), the chairpersons' contribution has, to date, been considerably less far-reaching. The area of "integration of gender perspectives" represents, so far, the major substantive foray of the chairpersons, being the subject of detailed recommendations by the chairpersons in 1995, repeated in 1996 and embellished in 1997. In 1995, the chairpersons endorsed the output of an expert group meeting on women's rights, including that meeting's lead recommendation, which read as follows:

The treaty bodies shall fully integrate gender perspectives into their presessional and sessional working methods, including identification of issues and preparation of questions for country reviews, general comments, general recommendations, and concluding observations. In particular, the treaty bodies should consider the gender implications of each issue discussed under each of the articles of the respective instruments.[27]

The endorsement in the 1995 chairpersons' report seemed to produce some effects within both the conventional human rights order and the nonconventional order.[28] In 1996 the UN Commission on Human Rights adopted a resolution welcoming the chairpersons' recommendation and went on itself to recommend to all the treaty bodies that their reporting guidelines should be amended to reflect a greater emphasis on gender-specific information.[29] During their separate sessions that same year, three committees — the CESCR, CERD, and CRC — signaled that gender perspectives would be a central feature in contemplated revisions of their existing reporting guidelines for state reports.[30] One committee, the Human Rights Committee, announced that it would revise its general comment on article 3 of the ICCPR which deals with discrimination against women.[31] Finally, the secretariat for CEDAW, the Division for the Advancement of Women, "began to develop a methodology by which the treaty bodies might systematically and routinely incorporate a gender perspective in monitoring the implementation of the specific provisions contained in the international human rights instruments."[32] Prior to the chairpersons' 1997 meeting, the secretariat's follow-up report to the 1996 meeting took its cue from the chairpersons to assert that "the equal enjoyment by men and women of all human rights is an overarching principle of the six principal human rights treaties" and to suggest that the chairpersons "may wish to consider inviting an interested organization to convene a round-table or expert meeting to assist with the drafting of general comments on gender equality."[33] At their ensuing meeting, the chairpersons discussed whether another expert meeting such as the one whose conclusions the chairpersons adopted in 1995 and 1996 was desirable. The result of their discussion was an invitation to "the relevant United Nations agencies and secretariats to consider the organization of another such meeting."[34] Meanwhile, another roundtable had already taken place in the preceding year, organized by the United Nations Population Fund (UNFPA) on the theme of human rights approaches to women's health. The chairpersons used this roundtable as a springboard for recommending both that "a gender dimension be incorporated in the revision [by each committee] of general comments/recommendations and [state reporting] guidelines" and that the treaty bodies "consider issuing general recommendations on health."[35] While the chairpersons drew special attention to sexual and reproductive health, their recommendation that health (in general) could be the subject of general comments by all the committees is an important addition to gender as a cross-cutting normative dimension of all six human rights treaties.[36]

THE CHAIRPERSONS AS A COORDINATING AND CATALYZING BODY

It would seem apparent enough that the meeting of the chairpersons is slowly developing and pushing for a role as the coordinating, and to some extent catalyzing, mechanism for the institutional integration of relations among the committees. A good example of the chairpersons serving as institutional catalyst, in a way that combines attention to common substantive concerns and the development of its implied jurisdiction, is the following 1995 recommendation regarding the need for a pan-treaty approach to responding to gross violations of human rights:

The chairpersons encourage treaty bodies to continue their efforts to develop mechanisms for the prevention of gross human rights violations, including early warning and urgent procedures. They consider that coordinated action by the human rights treaty bodies in this regard would increase their effectiveness. To this end, they suggest that any action undertaken by one of the treaty bodies be immediately brought to the attention of the other treaty bodies.[37]

With respect to some of the suggestions (see below) on how consolidation might proceed so as to enhance a diversity-based dialogue, it would seem desirable that the chairpersons act as the institutional hub of the process of consolidation in tandem with whatever political support from the UN political cal bodies and the UN High Commissioner for Human Rights seems appropriate or necessary to secure. The chairpersons have themselves spoken of their role in terms that hint at this function. In the context of discussing reform of the UN human rights treaty system, they spoke of the need to take advantage of "opportunities to promote continuing reform of the working methods of the different committees," ending with the following succinct observation about their own role: "The chairpersons believed that, meeting together, they could play a part in the process of reform. While ensuring that proper account was always taken of the features specific to each of the six treaty bodies, they could identify problems common to different treaty bodies and help them coordinate their responses."[38]

Such a relatively minimal role for the chairpersons is consistent with what appears to be, at present, a lack of support for de jure consolidation of the treaty bodies into one committee.[39] It is also consistent with the kind of process of institutional integration that amounts to a gradual, experimental de facto quasi-consolidation — the subject of this chapter.

Related to the development of the chairpersons' capacity to serve as an institutional hub for the human rights treaties is the chairpersons' repeated recommendation, beginning with their 1994 report, to the General Assembly that some "*sui generis* status" be established for the treaty bodies so that the bodies could interact with the rest of the UN system in a more official capacity.[40] Although this request seems primarily intended to allow *each* treaty body to act independently under the mantle of such status, it would seem just as important from the perspective of integrated institutionalism for the treaty bodies as a collective whole, represented by the chairpersons, to be recognized as having a functional status. Given that it is the meeting of the chairpersons that has begun to take up cudgels on behalf of the treaty bodies as a whole, some recognition needs to be accorded to their meeting as the primary agent in the external relations of the committees.[41] By creating this role in external relations, a dynamic toward enhancing internal cooperation and normative cohesion would thereby also be created. To accomplish this goal, however, some attention arguably needs to be paid to the politics of language. In that regard, the purpose of the next two paragraphs in this subsection is to advance the rather impertinent suggestion that we should consider alternative ways in which to refer to the annual meeting of the chairpersons. This question of the title for the chairpersons' collective must first be situated in the context of the disparity in the official titles as between five of the six treaty bodies and one of them.

This chapter has been using the terms "human rights treaty bodies" and "human rights committees" interchangeably. This is deliberate, motivated by a conviction that a politics of language is an important way to help dislodge systemic biases.[42] This concern extends to the subliminal associations generated by institutional appropriation of the term "human rights."[43] In particular, it has long been a problem that the treaty body overseeing the ICCPR was vested by that treaty with the name "*Human Rights* Committee" while each of the other committees have been given names that simply track the focus in their treaty's title on the set of rights found in that treaty—the "Committee on Economic, Social, and Cultural Rights," the "Committee Against Torture" and so on.[44] There is thus good cause for certain symbolic acts in the realm of language that would try to counteract this linguistic covering of the field by the Human Rights Committee. One option would be to convey to the world at large that, within the current (undesirable) fragmented logic of the multiple treaty system, the "Human Rights Committee" is actually the "Civil and Political Rights Committee." In this somewhat subversive way, we would thereby be trying to encourage a practice of referring to the *six* human rights committees in terms that suggest the unity of purpose of the six treaties taken as a systemic whole and their *shared* claim to be the institutional guardians of human rights. In so doing, the under-inclusiveness of the Human Rights Committee's own "civil and political rights" mandate in relation to its imperial name (at least that mandate as the Human Rights Committee currently interprets it) would be perceived more clearly.[45]

In a similar vein, it is worth noting that the politics of language—

UN-style — seems to have resulted so far in a second class, "lower case" status for the chairpersons' forum. Reports to the General Assembly, the agendas that precede the meetings, and other documents currently refer simply to "the persons chairing the human rights treaty bodies." In view of this practice, the chairpersons might wish to consider pushing the linguistic envelope a bit by referring to themselves in a more symbolically assertive way. At minimum, the annual meeting could be self-styled in capitals as the "Annual Meeting of the Chairpersons of the Human Rights Treaty Bodies," whichever case the UN bureaucracy chooses to use. An even bolder styling could be "Annual Meeting of the Chairpersons of the Human Rights Committees." Perhaps the most radical, but most justified, de facto reform would be for each committee to give its blessing to constituting — linguistically — an overarching body, the name of which would convey the dual idea of integrated normative mandate and cooperative institutional action. Once constituted by collective recognition of the six treaty bodies, the chairpersons could then begin to seek (implicit and eventually explicit) general recognition by states and the rest of the UN system. The chairpersons' forum (encompassing its annual meeting and its inter-meeting activities) could in this way metamorphose into something like the "Coordinating Council of the Human Rights Committees" or the "Council of Chairpersons of the Human Rights Committees" — on either score, the CCHRC.

All this being said, there are reasons to be pessimistic about the likelihood that the chairpersons will evolve to any great extent in this direction without a change in outlook in several quarters. Quite apart from the lack of enthusiasm of some of the chairpersons, any move toward consolidation in the near future is likely to be politically resisted, for reasons that include the opposition of some states to the promotion of more effective UN human rights structures as well as legalistic concerns about treating the six treaties as an "objective" legal order (even an *evolving* one) in a situation where some states have ratified fewer than all six treaties. In this respect, it is worth noting that, while the Commission on Human Rights did respond favorably to the chairpersons' recommendation on cross-treaty integration of gender perspectives, it also added the caveat that "the enjoyment of the human rights of women should be closely monitored by each treaty body *within the competence of its mandate.*"[46] This passage can easily be read as a shot across the bows of the committees.[47]

But pessimism is not fate. Despite the rather sober thoughts in the preceding paragraph, what follows will assume that the chairpersons can come to assume a role as the hub of institutional reform of the treaty body order. The following proposals, then, assume the proactive involvement of the chairpersons. In tandem with the evolution of the chairpersons as a coordinating and catalyzing institution, a number of avenues of intercommittee dialogical engagement will begin to open up. The following brief discussions of some of the more obvious possible initiatives should not be taken as anything but a preliminary endorsement of the merits of any given possibility. Most significantly, the merits of one proposal cannot be assessed in isolation from the other proposals. No claim is being made, at this stage, of the degree of compatibility inter se of the various proposals. The purpose of what follows is merely to put them on the table as candidates for consideration.

Pan-Institutional Dialogue: Further Basic Experiments in Institutional Design

PUSHING FOR UNIVERSAL RATIFICATION AS A COMPLEMENTARY REFORM

A central recommendation of a 1997 report to the UN on enhancing the long-term effectiveness of the UN human rights treaty system is that the goal of achieving universal ratification of all six core treaties should be pursued with renewed seriousness and vigor.[48] In this respect, the report was following up on an earlier recommendation in a 1993 report to make the advent of the millennium the target date for universal ratification.[49] The chairpersons have also been vigorous in endorsing the need for treating universal ratification as a priority for the future treaty system, most recently having referred to universal ratification of the six treaties as "an essential dimension of a global order."[50] This phrasing suggests some awareness that a fully "objective" legal order, which as such would be able to lay claim to a status in the world normative order akin to a constitution, is in constant tension with each state's consent to be bound as the prevailing formal basis for the assumption of treaty obligations qua treaty obligations.

From the perspective of de facto quasi-consolidation of the human rights treaties as a testing ground for a possible formal consolidation of the committees, universal ratification is important, although probably not indispensable. It is important because the closer we get to universal ratification of all six core treaties, the more easily we can treat the treaties as if they were different chapters of the same overall constitutional document and the different human rights committees as if they were chambers of one overall Human Rights Committee.[51] Most significantly from the perspective of cross-treaty dialogue and cooperation among the committees, any perceived problems of formal jurisdictional divisions become less significant in direct proportion to the decrease in the number of states who are not party to all six treaties.[52] At the same time, this evolving unity would be achieved while still retaining both the interactive diversity of knowledge of the six committees' combined membership pool and the ever-present possibility that one or more committees can hold out (more or less explicitly) noncooperation as a way to ensure their treaty's normative focus is taken seriously in the pan-treaty constitutional order.[53]

CONSOLIDATED STATE REPORTS AND TAILORED STATE REPORTS

Perhaps the best example of a reform that commends itself on the basis of both efficiency and effectiveness — but which could cut both ways in terms of diversity — would be the consolidation of the current scheme of sending separate reports to each committee into a scheme centered on a single consolidated report that would address all six treaties and would go to all the committees.[54] A related issue is the proposal that, while a state's first report to any given committee should be comprehensive, its subsequent periodic reports to that committee could be made more focused by having the committee in question signal well in advance (of the reporting deadline) those areas and concerns it wishes to have covered in the state's report.[55] It is not difficult to see how the two proposals could converge into a single report every five years which would be both consolidated and tailored and which could be subject to follow-up scrutiny at the instance of any one of the committees in the intervening five years before the next report is due.

Consolidation and tailoring have been discussed in some detail in the last several sessions of the chairpersons. The current position seems to be one that is not (at least, not yet) in favor of consolidation but that is in favor of tailoring of periodic reports.[56] At the September 1998 meeting, the chairpersons expressed their collective view in the following terms:

> 30. Following the discussion of recent experiences of the respective committees, the chairpersons reiterated their view that it was desirable to strive towards focused periodic reports, adding that account must be taken of the limited scope of the issues covered by some of the treaties.
> 31. With regard to the frequently expressed idea of consolidating reports in a single global report covering all six human rights treaties, no consensus could be reached. As at the eighth meeting, although the chairpersons considered that such an approach would reduce the number of different reports requested of States parties and would serve to underline the indivisibility of human rights by ensuring a comprehensive analysis of the situation, concerns were expressed in relation to problems resulting from different periodicities of reporting under the treaties and, in particular, the risk that the special attention given to groups such as women and children would be lost in a single comprehensive report.[57]

The consolidated report issue is a prime example of the need for reforms to be looked at as a whole so as to ensure that they proceed apace. Adjustments to one reform proposal can provide the necessary correctives to disadvantages feared for another. Reporting periodicity is a technical problem that, with time, can be easily dealt with. Threats to diversity of focus present a more serious concern.[58] In the absence of confidence in the other tracks of institutional reform, it is reasonable to oppose a single consolidated report in favor of ongoing separate reports to each committee. However, the more that institutional integration succeeds in showing that integration not only can but does produce enhancement of normative analysis (that includes bringing the human rights perspectives of less powerful social groups to the center of that analysis) and does not produce the feared (re)marginalization of issues dealing with children, racial discrimination, gender discrimination, and social and economic disadvantage, the more compelling will become the argument for a consolidated pan-treaty report. The achievement of a sustained diversity of experience and expertise within the combined membership of the six committees will be absolutely crucial for such success to be achieved. Also, tailoring of reports could have positive follow-on effects for consolidation; if the committees were collectively to build in principles and procedures designed to ensure nonmarginalization, the kinds of issues on which the committees choose to request focused reporting could alleviate concerns that women's rights or the rights of the poor, for instance, will necessarily be swamped if the tailored reports also become consolidated into a single report. In this respect, in the way they handle the development of *tailored* reports, the committees are in control of their own destiny with respect to the viability and desirability of report *consolidation*.

There is, however, a middle ground possibility that the committees and their chairpersons may wish to consider, perhaps on an experimental basis with a number of willing states. As reflected in the above-quoted conclusions of the chairpersons, it is assumed that tailoring would occur only for *periodic* reports, those subsequent to the initial postratification report of a state party. That initial report would be comprehensive. As for consolidation, the chairpersons seem implicitly to be talking about *all* reports, initial and periodic. However, conceivably, the proposal for consolidated reports could be refined (or clarified) into a proposal that only *periodic* reports be consolidated. In this way, *each* committee would receive a *comprehensive* first report on compliance with its treaty. This approach has the significant benefit of allowing the committee in question (e.g., CEDAW) to develop, as fully as possible, a view of the general situation in each state party with respect to all the rights in its treaty. Such a view would be invaluable in providing a major component of the knowledge base on which that committee can then draw in the future when considering what tailored questions it wishes to put to that state on its consolidated subsequent report(s) to the committees as a whole. A nonconsolidated, nontailored initial report would give each committee a valuable opportunity to prepare the ground for subsequent more focused evaluation of compliance of that state party with the committee's treaty within the larger framework of that state's consolidated, tailored periodic report. Producing a comprehensive initial report for each treaty also has educational benefits for that state. Not only will its officials have to grapple with the full range of its commitments under each treaty but also they will be given the chance to determine for themselves, based on the committee's questions and concluding observations, the areas in which there is a high likelihood that the committee will wish to focus its scrutiny in future.

OVERLAPPING AND COMMON MEETINGS OF THE TREATY BODIES

It seems obvious that placing the committees in closer proximity would assist any efforts at pan-treaty normative dialogue. This means giving consideration to scheduling their meetings in ways that overlap in whole or in part.[59] This seems to already be on the agenda in view of a suggestion contained in the 1997 follow-up report (to the 1996 chairpersons' meeting) written by the (then) Centre for Human Rights:

> In order to enhance awareness of the work of *complementary treaty bodies*, it may be appropriate to reschedule committee sessions so that some of their meetings overlap, for example, the Human Rights Committee with the Committee on Economic, Social and Cultural Rights; the Human Rights Committee with the Committee against Torture; and the Committee on the Rights of the Child with both the Human Rights Committee and the Committee on Economic, Social and Cultural Rights.[60]

It is important to inject a note of caution with respect to the above phrasing by the chairpersons. *Every* committee has some complementary relationship with *every other* committee and, just as importantly, it is impossible to say in advance of actual dialogue the nature or extent of such complementarity. In order to facilitate institutional dialogue, the ideal is that a way eventually be found for an overlap of the meetings of all six treaty bodies for at least part of one session a year. Furthermore, as is implicit in the subsections which follow, an overlap of meeting times should be scheduled not simply in order to facilitate *parallel* meetings but also in order to make possible *common* meetings.

COLLABORATIVE NORMATIVE PRONOUNCEMENTS: GENERAL COMMENTS AND "JOINT STATEMENTS"

One obvious objective of cooperation among some or all of the committees could be the preparation of general comments that benefit from dialogue among the committees. In terms of normative elaboration of the content of rights that would especially benefit from diversity of perspective, there are any number of thematic comments that one could envisage, such as the example given earlier of a hypothetical general comment on the relationship of social vulnerability to human rights protections. The issue of gender is already on the agenda. Presumably, each committee other than CEDAW could draft or revise separate general comments on this issue as it pertains to its understanding of the rights in its treaty. Or, some overarching general comment could be drafted cooperatively by the six committees with each committee then having the option to supplement it with a more detailed comment that applies, as it were, the common general comment to the specifics of its treaty.[61]

Here again the chairpersons have turned their attention to collaborative pronouncements. In September 1998 they had the following to say:

General comments and the possible use of joint statements

34. The chairpersons took note of the fact that some committees were beginning to make reference to the general comments or equivalent statements of other committees. They encouraged the development of that practice, insofar as the pronouncements of other committees appeared to be relevant and appropriate to the situation at hand. . . .

36. It was agreed that a new genre of "joint statements" would be an appropriate means by which to enable the committees to address issues of common concern without taking such matters to the level of general comments, in relation to which joint approaches would always be difficult to achieve. Such joint statements would enable different treaty bodies to work together to address issues of current importance.[62]

Only time will tell whether "joint statements" become general comments by another name or whether they will have a normative status that is not at the same "level" as general comments.

Whatever they are called, the advent of collective committee pronouncements is a significant and welcome development from the perspective of normative and institutional integration of the treaty orders. Here it is important to note that the chairpersons' decision to foster "joint statements" was a direct consequence of a concrete proposal put forward at the meeting by the CEDAW Chairperson, Salma Khan, on behalf of her committee. The proposal was for three committees — CEDAW, along with the HRC and the CESCR — to "consider issuing a joint statement on the indivisibility of rights and the centrality of gender awareness as part of the fiftieth anniversary celebration of the Universal Declaration of Human Rights."[63] Apart from endorsing the general concept of "joint statements," the chairpersons welcomed this specific initiative: "The chairpersons requested the Division for the Advancement of Women to prepare a draft to be considered by the three chairpersons concerned and then to be put to the respective committees."[64]

Given its theme, it is not immediately apparent why this first joint statement, was limited to three of the six committees. Possibly, a strategic decision was made to start conservatively and try to secure cooperation on a smaller scale rather than encounter logistical difficulties by involving all six chairpersons. Such coordination difficulties could easily occur given that an efficient system of intercommittee coordination is not yet in place. These problems should not be underestimated. When the chairperson of the CESCR took the joint statement, as it had been drafted by the chairperson of CEDAW (and, presumably, found satisfactory by the other two chairpersons), to his own committee for its consideration, three CESCR committee members made useful comments about how to improve the joint statement.[65] Given that the committees meet at different times of the year, and given that improvements could be suggested by members of all three committees, the potential for much delay (and time and energy on the part of the three chairpersons) in coordinating the final statement, agreeable to all three committees, is considerable. The CESCR handled the matter with considerable institutional magnanimity by, in effect, delegating authority to their chairperson to produce a final joint comment in consultation with the other two chairpersons that would "duly take into account" their views.[66] The final joint statement, as it appears in the official CESCR records for that same session, contains one change from the draft joint statement, namely the insertion of a paragraph that seems to represent incorporation of the comments which had been made by CESCR member Philippe Texier.[67]

Mention should finally be made of a positive side to having limited the joint statement to a subset of the committees, namely that it signals the possible flexible use of the joint statement in the future. For example, the HRC, CAT, and CERD could join in one that seems particularly relevant to their combined mandates, such as disproportionate police detention of racialized groups in some countries, leading to a higher risk of torture. While it would be undesirable in the long term for themes (such as indivisibility and gender awareness) that profoundly involve the mandates of all six committees to be addressed in a joint statement by fewer than all six, the flexibility to proceed only with a subset of committees would seem to provide useful room for maneuver and experimentation in a transitional period.

COORDINATED SCRUTINY OF STATE REPORTS

Consideration could be given to cooperative scrutiny of state reports, or at least of those aspects of the report with respect to which the committees can see (or come to see) much overlap and thus many benefits flowing from a diversity of committee perspectives. If a given state is due to report to one committee at roughly the same time as it is reporting to another (for example, Canada reporting to the CESCR and to the HRC within a year of each other), the respective committee members in charge of that report could be asked to consult and to coordinate questions to be asked of the state.[68] Common questions could be posed on shared concerns.[69]

If scheduling permits, one committee's member who is responsible for a given state can sit in on the report to the other committee and then take that session into account in preparing for the second report. At minimum, she or he can consult the summary records and concluding observations as well as discuss with the other committee's member what the second committee could most usefully focus on in its dialogue with the state.[70] If reporting can be coordinated enough to allow a state to be reporting to two committees at a time when both committees are meeting in parallel sessions, a decision could be made to have the two committees sit in a joint session for the relevant parts of the report or indeed for the entire report.[71] It is obvious enough that this proposal would be most suitable with respect to states who have decided (or been asked as part of an experimental pilot) to submit consolidated reports, especially if the practice of tailored reports is also adopted for such reports. This would combine the benefits of joint scrutiny with efficiencies produced by the time savings which focused reports should produce as compared to comprehensive reports. Many of the areas of focus for a single tailored report could reflect advance consultation among all the committees to whom the state is reporting.

STANDING CROSS-TREATY THEMATIC WORKING GROUPS

Standing working groups could be set up with a variety of possible tasks, for example, to help foster dialogue on general comments which committees are considering adopting and on joint statements. One could also envisage other kinds of cross-treaty working groups that would be specifically set up to discuss and propose committee action on cross-cutting normative issues. With the proper support from the Office of the UN High Commissioner for Human Rights and training of committee members, these groups could easily be organized using virtual forms of communication, for instance through Internet website discussion boards or, if not all members have access to the Internet, through e-mail listservs. If it were felt that it would be useful to reflect on the health rights of girl children, for example, a working group could discuss this theme, acting as a kind of think tank for the committees as a whole. If a common period of meeting time for the six committees were scheduled and dedicated for intercommittee work and reflection, these working groups could sometimes meet in person in order to pursue discussions, draft proposals that would go to the respective committees, and produce integrated texts (reports, joint statements, and so on) once all committees have made their input.

OVERLAPPING MEMBERSHIP

One of the most direct ways to foster an inter-treaty dynamic would be to create a situation whereby a number of committee members are elected to more than one committee. One treaty, CAT, already expressly provides for the desirability of crossover membership as a consideration for election to its committee.[72] There should, accordingly, be no legal problem with overlapping membership on a wider scale within the human rights treaty system given that the express provision in CAT for shared membership with the Human Rights Committee was not viewed as third-party regulation of the ICCPR. All that would be required would be for states themselves to create overlap through their nomination and voting practice.[73] Each member elected to more than one committee would be a member of each.

There are any number of reasons why overlapping membership would be fruitful from the perspective of inter-treaty dialogue. The basic point would be that overlapping membership would to some extent ensure that human rights issues are examined by each committee from a broader perspective than tends to be the case when the sole mandate of every committee member is one treaty text. One could contemplate any number of axes. For example, a person who is a member of both CERD and CEDAW should be institutionally disposed to inject intersectional issues of race and gender into the deliberations of each committee.

Such shared committee members would in many ways be encouraged to act in a fashion that is a classic example of Georges Scelle's *dédoublement fonctionnel* or "double functioning."[74] Scelle's notion was meant to describe international lawyers, notably legal advisers to states, who have to be normatively faithful both to domestic law and international law, both to the national interest and to the common international interest. In the process, the person who must function in such a double capacity not only becomes skilled at translating one system of legal thought and practice into the terms of the other, but also becomes skilled at mediating the two systems in ways that produce an integrated perspective different from, while still faithful to, both. In the same way, a member of two (or more) human rights committees would have dual (or multiple) normative loyalties which would have to be translated and mediated. In this way, the committee members in question would come to embody a dialogue of treaty texts and the associated normative mandates of those texts.

In relation to the consolidation process, should it ever be desired, a gradual increase in overlapping membership could serve a second function. It could become the primary mechanism whereby de facto consolidation of the six treaty bodies takes place without the need for any formal treaty amendments. By the end of the process, if perfectly coordinated by states in electing the committees (admittedly a remote possibility without a parallel understanding being reached among states that would solve the collective action problems), the total number of committee members would be reduced from the current 97 to 23, which is the number of members on the largest committee (CEDAW). All 10 members of the smallest two committees, CAT and the CRC, would also be members of all five other committees. As for the remaining three committees comprised of 18 members each, there would be a buffer of five CEDAW members (23 minus 18) which would allow some members of the HRC, CESCR, and CERD not to be members of one or more of the other three committees and/or allow some members of CEDAW (statistically, up to five) to be members only of CEDAW.

Benefits of Interactive Integration in Relation to the Next Generation of Monitoring Challenges

The foregoing institutional reform suggestions have been schematic. They also probably fall toward the least creative end of a continuum of reform possibilities, but, for that reason, they also represent practical possibilities. In the various reform studies underway at the UN, these and kindred proposals can presumably be scrutinized with a view to assessing their feasibility as well as elaborating them and sharpening their focus.

What remains to be done in this chapter is to provide a series of concrete examples of how the gradual enhancement of interactive diversity of knowledge through institutional integration of the human rights committees can contribute to the perceptive analysis of the types of human rights problems which the UN human rights order must begin — soon — to get its collective mind around. The following examples are purely illustrative and are virtually randomly chosen. No claim is being made that they represent all the types of next-generation challenges posed for international human rights monitoring, although an effort has been made to identify the key ones.

STRUCTURAL SCRUTINY AND PREVENTIVE REMEDIES

An inevitable feature of the monitoring methods of the treaty bodies has been their reactive nature. That is to say, they by and large look at what has already transpired and pass judgment on whether noncompliance with treaty norms has taken place. However, the state report procedure does — increasingly — have a forward-looking element to the extent that the committees offer recommendations about how structural failures can be remedied. With each passing year, such structural-reform recommendations become more clearly and incisively formulated, at least by several of the committees (notably the CESCR, CRC, and CEDAW). Another way, then, of looking at such structural assessments of past conduct is in terms of their potentially far-reaching preventive function: if carried out, future human rights violations should be avoided. Ideally, the committees must begin to address more directly that aspect of state responsibility which requires states not just to prevent specific harms (notably harms of some nonstate actors by other nonstate actors) that are reasonably foreseeable, but also to organize the entire apparatus of government in such a way that human rights violations are approached as something to avoid and not simply something to repair.[75]

Structural scrutiny and associated preventive remedies involve far-reaching inquiries into the interconnectedness of causes and obstacles. Often enough, no small degree of complexity is involved. As such, the benefits of more integrated normative analysis facilitated by interactive institutionalism among the human rights committees would seem obvious. To illustrate this claim, consider that treaty which most people would, at first blush, see as benefiting the least from a quasi-consolidation of the treaty order due to its seemingly narrow focus: the Convention Against Torture (CAT). Yet a Committee Against Torture that focused only or almost exclusively on what goes on within jail cells and (para)military torture chambers would be missing much that is relevant to torture prevention, even if sophisticated procedural safeguards and mechanisms are necessary ways to prevent torture from occurring in these locales. Here I am assuming that the will to torture is intimately connected to the human capacity to dehumanize and to power structures that nurture and actively exploit this capacity. Take race: how does racism interact with creation and mobilization of the will to torture? Just asking this question is enough to point out how an interface between CAT and CERD should deepen understanding of the "othering" conditions that promote torture.[76] It would be a two-way street if CAT were to use its concrete focus to produce analyses of how structures of racial and ethnic prejudice fuel torture; CERD could then work with these concrete insights in order to assist, in some dialectical manner, its understanding of the larger phenomena that produce the conditions for racial discrimination. Similar interactive advantages could emerge from CESCR-CAT cooperation to the extent that the poor may be hypothesized to be the most vulnerable to certain kinds of torture (notably the "casual" police beating) and to recruitment as the frontline instruments of torture. And when it comes to rape in the context of genocide or ethnocide, CAT and CERD would be less likely to see the gendered dimensions as clearly as they might if CEDAW's perspectives were actively in play (rape as torture and rape-torture as an instrument of genocide). And, beyond these examples, the whole question of the structural dimensions of torture and the preventive measures necessary to modify those structures intimately involves perhaps the most structure-influencing of all human rights: the right to education. As phrased in international human rights instruments, the right to education is nonneutral regarding human rights values.[77] CAT analysis which does not explore education's links to torture would be inadequate from a structural-preventive perspective.[78]

Systemically Implied Rights Protections

It is generally not controversial that rights may be implied even if not expressly provided for in a text. For example, as noted earlier, the Human Rights Committee has implied rights related to health and housing into the ICCPR "right to life."[79] Another example is of the European Court of Human Rights reading a (conditional) right to civil legal aid into the right to a fair trial.[80] A full list of existing doctrinal examples would be quite long.

However, the tendency is to conceive of the process of implication in terms of a given contended-for right. For example, when in *Johnston v. Ireland* the applicants claimed (unsuccessfully) that the right to divorce was protected by the European Convention on Human Rights, they relied on a series of specific articles in turn: article 12 (the right to marry), article 8 (the right to family life), and article 14 (the right to nondiscrimination in relation to other protected rights).[81] They did not rely on *all three rights in combination* to argue for the implied right. Or, if they did argue in this more holistic way, the court did not understand their argument in this way. Rather, the court examined each article in turn, starting with article 12's right to marry.

An alternative way to proceed when assessing whether a right should or should not be implied into a treaty is to look at the issue in terms of the treaty as a whole being the normative touchstone rather than the specific rights in seriatim. The UN Charter provides an interesting analogy. The peacekeeping powers of the General Assembly have often been treated less as having been implied into powers already set out in chapter 4 of the Charter and more as having been imagined as an entirely new chapter located between chapters 6 and 7 — "chapter 6½." That is, they have been systemically implied on the basis of the over-all scheme and purposes of the Charter. On such an approach, implied rights may be found not only *in* given rights but also *between* given rights and in the combined *interstitial zones* of the entire treaty understood as a system of values and interests.[82]

An example of when such an argument has been employed may help. In the case of *Baker v. Canada (Minister of Citizenship and Immigration)*, decided in July 1999 by the Supreme Court of Canada, one issue was whether the Convention on the Rights of the Child protects a child's right not to have the child's parent deported from the child's state of nationality.[83] No provision in the CRC sets out such a right in explicit terms, but two provisions surround the contended-for right. The key provisions within articles 9 and 10 read as follows:

Article 9
1. States Parties shall ensure that a child not be separated from his or her parents against their will, except when competent authorities subject to judicial review determine, in accordance with applicable law and procedures, that such separation is necessary for the best interests of the child. . . .
Article 10
1. In accordance with the obligation of States Parties under article 9, paragraph 1, applications by a child or his or her parents to enter or leave a State Party for the purpose of family reunification shall be dealt with by States Parties in a positive, humane and expeditious manner. . . .

To say that these provisions "surround" the right not to have parents deported is to say that neither one of them *on its own* was completely adequate to the task of serving as the basis of the implied right (a child's right that her or his best interests be given great weight in deciding whether a parent may be deported) that was being argued for. It is with this difficulty in mind that one intervenor in *Baker*, the Charter Committee on Poverty Issues (CCPI), argued that, while neither article 9 nor article 10 is fully apposite when looked at individually, their combined effect is a different story — especially when article 3 of the treaty is taken into account.[84] At one point, the CCPI factum refers to the oblique approach adopted by the CRC, as part of CCPI's attempt to interpretively combine articles 3, 9, and 10:

28. The Committee on the Rights of the Child has interpreted articles 9 and 10 as together recognizing a right of children not to have their parents deported. In 1995, the Committee expressed its regret that "refugee or immigrant children born in Canada may be separated from their parents facing a deportation order." The Com-

mittee also urged that "Solutions should also be sought to avoid expulsions causing the separation of families, in the spirit of article 9 of the Convention."[85]

When paragraph 28 of the CCPI factum refers to articles 9 and 10 "interpreted together," CCPI is in effect saying that the putative implied right lies neither entirely within article 9 nor entirely within article 10. The implied right is justified by viewing the two rights as a mini-system. Put another way, the CRC is looked at as a system whose purposes and textual signals allow for interstitial interpretation such that there should be recognized an implied right *between* article 9 and article 10 — an "article 9½," as it were.

This CRC interpretive example helps make clear how viewing the six treaties as an evolving constitutional whole and the committees as chambers of an integrated institution could produce a much richer tapestry of rights than is possible if each treaty is looked at on its own and if each committee goes about its work in isolation from the others. This is especially the case when we consider the argument that we should constantly draw on the fundamental interests that human rights are meant to protect and thereby engage in interpretation that is more holistic and purposive as opposed to categorical and (unduly) text-bound.[86] Not only would interpretation of the spaces between rights within a given treaty (as between articles 9 and 10 of the CRC) be conducted in light of the normative cocoon provided by the other five treaties but also we could begin to talk about implied rights in the interstitial zones between treaties themselves.

HUMAN RIGHTS ON THE DIAGONAL: BETWEEN *DRITTWIRKUNG* AND INDIRECT RESPONSIBILITY

"Diagonality" (see Figure 3) attempts to capture the idea of (both conceptual and institutional) joinder of the state and relevant private actors in human rights scrutiny.[87] Diagonality looks at human rights in terms of fields of responsibility and power relations that engage the conduct (both acts and omissions) of state and nonstate sectors simultaneously, and then links that analysis to appropriate allocation of both legal responsibility and creative (including joint) remedies. Diagonality analysis offers possibilities for rights-based scrutiny that are more structural and comprehensive than is possible according to a stark either/or division of the applicability of rights into the categories "horizontal" versus "vertical." Rights relations are vertical if they involve the obligation of a governing actor (notably the state) toward nonstate actors and horizontal if they involve the claim that rights are applicable in the "private" sector relations between nonstate actors (an axis of applicability which German legal theory has labeled as *drittwirkung*).[88]

It may be a long time before the committees are recognized as having the implied power to directly scrutinize the activities of private actors given the very state-centered (vertical) orientation of the human rights treaty

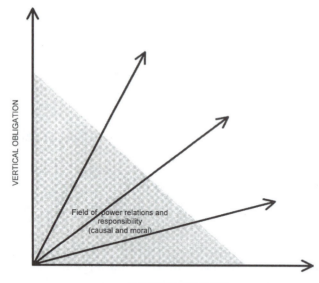

Figure 3. Diagonality vectors representing possible apportionment of shared legal responsibility between public and private actors.

regimes. However, it is a given that the indirect responsibility of states places increasingly onerous obligations on them to regulate the private sector, especially corporate activity given the concentration of power and potential for harm represented by many companies.[89] Within the analysis of the indirect responsibility of states parties to the treaties, it may become desirable for the committees to request that states provide detailed information on the conduct of all companies in given sectors or even on specified corporations — and perhaps even request that states require companies themselves to prepare reports on conduct which affects some or all of the treaty norms. Without actually joining the nonstate actors (for want of the formal jurisdictional nexus on which to do so), the committees could still "notionally" join those actors so as to be able to assess the remedial measures they should recommend *to states*, including the measures they recommend states take vis-à-vis corporations. In a range of situations, the committees could interpret the indirect responsibility of the state to be engaged if it does not regulate certain nonstate actors, notably corporations, in such a way as to place those actors under direct obligations in domestic law to protect certain human rights. With time, one could even foresee the committees encouraging the voluntary appearance of some nonstate actors before the committees in order to enhance the diagonality analysis.

The notion of diagonality may not itself provide a strong reason for institutional interaction among the committees. Rather, it seems only to piggyback on the other reasons for integration already canvassed. However, diagonality analysis *would* seem more achievable in a situation of institutional integration than in one of institutional isolation. The polycentricity quotient of human rights analysis can be expected to go up in diagonality situations where the competing or complementary rights and duties of different persons are being openly addressed. For example, if diagonality analysis under the CRC were to suggest that all schools should be responsible for preventing or repairing certain harms to children (whether or not the schools are state, private, or hybrid), then certain rights of parents, as found for example in the ICESCR or the ICCPR, become relevant to the analysis. Further, if there are reasons to think that placing certain kinds of financially onerous duties on schools will disproportionately affect specific groups such as residentially clustered racial minorities or single mothers, then CERD and CEDAW must be brought into the foreground of the picture.

Another example is brought to mind by the discussion of child support obligations under article 27 of the CRC in Martha Shaffer's contribution to this volume (see Chapter 7). For ease of reference, the relevant portions of article 27 are reproduced below:

1. States Parties recognize the right of every child to a standard of living adequate for the child's physical, mental, spiritual, moral and social development.
2. The parent(s) or others responsible for the child have the primary responsibility to secure, within their abilities and financial capacities, the conditions of living necessary for the child's development.
3. States Parties, in accordance with national conditions and within their means, shall take appropriate measures to assist parents and others responsible for the child to implement this right and shall in case of need provide material assistance and support programmes, particularly with regard to nutrition, clothing and housing.
4. States Parties shall take all appropriate measures to secure the recovery of maintenance for the child from the parents or other persons having financial responsibility for the child, both within the State Party and from abroad. . . .

Article 27 is one of the rare examples of diagonality found on the surface of a treaty text. While article 27(2) places a "primary responsibility" on parents to secure "the conditions of living necessary for the child's development," the state has, by article 27(3), general residual duties (a) to assist parents in ensuring an adequate standard of living for their children and (b) to carry out a classic "social and economic rights" function by "in the case of need[] provid[ing] material assistance and support programmes, particularly with regard to nutrition, clothing and housing."

Of interest in the present example is the relationship between this latter duty and the quite specific recovery duty in the first sentence of article 27(4). Shaffer's coverage of the situation in Ontario reveals that this Canadian province appears to have done much on the side of horizontal responsibility for child support. Not only are a range of adult actors caught by duties to provide child maintenance but also a special enforcement unit has been formed to step in to force a delinquent (separated or divorced) parent to pay court-ordered support payments. Especially as the bulk of persons seeking to enforce support obligations for the care of their children are women, this recent law reform can be viewed as simultaneously combining gains in children's rights and in women's rights.

However, assume as a hypothetical that the Ontario regime does not address, qua child support regime, the transitional period between the default on the support payments and their eventual recovery by the state's enforcement unit. In that period, the custodial parent may have to turn to social assistance. Now assume that the custodial parent may, in some bureaucratic twist, have trouble being accepted as eligible for social assistance until she proves that she has done all she can do to recover the money from the defaulting former spouse. This problem would be easily rectifiable by requiring the state to issue a certificate that would attest to the fact that the state has taken carriage of the recovery efforts and which would be recognized by social assistance authorities; a seamlessness would thereby be created between the child support regime and the safety net of the social assistance regime.

Yet, assume a second problem that cannot so easily disappear through better public/private documentation coordination, namely, that the social assistance rate is likely to be a lesser rate than the support award. The existence of such a disparity in income would suggest that the state, on these assumed facts, has gone too far toward the horizontal end of the field of responsibility. Both gender and child-centered diagonality analyses suggest that a state must, in the transitional period, assume responsibility to continue the support payments rather than leave the shortfall and add to the burden on the mother (by virtue of having to try to access a separate state bureaucracy each and every time the separated or divorced spouse defaults on child support payments). That is to say, in these circumstances, it is the last clause of article 27(3) that should indicate the necessary axis of responsibility. The state's duty to fulfill, as a secondary duty within article 27's structure, kicks in. The state may of course recover the amount paid for the transitional period from the defaulting spouse, but it should not be able to use that spouse's primary responsibility as an excuse to avoid its own duty to provide material assistance and support directly "in the case of need."[90] Furthermore, it takes little effort to see how the effects of a transitional gap are exacerbated to the extent that the state has also adopted policies of privatized responsibility across the range of governmental spheres, including by maintaining social assistance rates at levels that independently violate the duty to avoid and eliminate child poverty. The CESCR's scrutiny of the general (in)adequacy of the state support for economically disadvantaged children and families would thus be a needed third point in a triangle of scrutiny that the CRC, CEDAW, and CESCR could collectively carry out.

INDIRECT EXTRATERRITORIAL RESPONSIBILITY

Indirect state responsibility has been touched upon above, and mention has been made of the special need for regulation of corporate activity in the name of human rights. As economic globalization spreads and deepens, the time is already upon us when the committees should be considering diagonality across borders. The problematic activity especially of overseas oil and mining companies has become a matter of general knowledge and concern in recent years; for example, the conduct of Unocal in Burma and Texaco in Ecuador has resulted in human rights tort litigation in the courts of the United States.[91] The question is: How far should the UN human rights system move toward positive duties on home states of corporations to protect persons in other states from harms caused either by transnational enterprises (TNEs) or by TNEs in association with the foreign state? Here "home state" is used broadly to cover states in which companies are incorporated *or* otherwise have a meaningful presence, such as being the site of the head office or regional decision-making office.

Immediately, of course, the issue of extraterritoriality comes up. It is one thing to hold a state responsible for human rights harm that its own agents cause abroad.[92] Many would view it as quite another thing to extend responsibility to states for failing to regulate private actors that cause the harm. This is not the occasion to take a position on the larger issues involved in placing indirect extraterritorial responsibility on states other than to say that at minimum *some* state responsibility (however it ends up being apportioned between home states and host states) is, as an empirical matter, necessary if transnational corporate conduct is not to continue to fall between the normative cracks of globalization. One area in which there already seems to be emergent consensus on home state responsibility to regulate activity of nationals abroad in the name of human rights is with respect to child sex tourism. While most responses, in countries like Australia and Canada, have been to criminalize the individual conduct of the (ab)users of child prostitutes, it is arguably inadequate if those countries do not also regulate the commercial, and consequent mass-tourism, dimension of travel for sex with children by making it contrary to the law for travel agencies, airlines, and others knowingly to facilitate such tourism. When a leading international lawyer based in a sovereignty-sensitive country like Singapore goes on record as arguing for such extended extraterritorial responsibility, there is good reason to believe that transnational regulation of child sex tourism may well prove to be the Trojan horse for a new paradigm of extraterritorial human rights responsibility.[93]

Take the norm of nondiscrimination as a further example. This is a norm that the human rights treaty bodies have long made clear places positive duties on states with respect to private sector discrimination within their own states.[94] Thus, for example, a country like Japan is under treaty obligations to regulate sex discrimination in private workplaces. Assume the following seemingly fanciful facts.[95] Mitsubishi Corporation, a Japanese company, places advertisements in Japanese newspapers that seek to market Mitsubishi's heavy duty air conditioners by using a double entendre on the idea of "air service." The ads feature a Japanese Airlines (JAL) pilot who is asked an ambiguous question about whether he slept in a room with air conditioning or with one of the (female) JAL cabin crew. The union for JAL pilots launch a protest campaign that includes writing to Mitsubishi to complain that the ad "stereotyped and denigrated the cabin crew profession."[96] After the company dismissed the complaint out of hand, the union approached the Japanese prime minister's office and thus placed the issue on the political agenda. No formal action was taken but, within two weeks, Mitsubishi had agreed to retract the discriminatory ad and to issue a formal apology that was published in full-page ads in four Japanese newspapers and also aired via the broadcast media.

What if neither Mitsubishi nor Japan had acted in response to the complaints and, furthermore, what if there existed no legislative avenue for the JAL employees to seek legal redress for discriminatory treatment by their employer? The nondiscrimination jurisprudence of the Human Rights Committee and of the CESCR (where workplace discrimination is even more central to the treaty's mandate) would clearly be applicable, and Japan's duty to permit freedom of (corporate) expression would be squarely up against the right of female employees not to be discriminated against. Now, assume — crucially for this example — that the above-described events occurred in Thailand, not Japan. The Mitsubishi ad used Thai Airways employees, not Japan Airlines employees; the ads were placed in Thai not Japanese newspapers; and it was the *Thai Prime Minister*'s office that became involved. These three modifications align the example with the facts.[97] As such, the fictionalized situation (all material facts taking place in Japan) is transformed into a situation of extraterritorial responsibility of Japan for Japanese corporate conduct abroad. In asking whether the treaty nondiscrimination norms should require Japan to regulate Mitsubishi's conduct in Thailand no differently than its conduct in Japan, the analysis would clearly benefit from the interactive insights of a number of the committees both on the desirable content of the nondiscrimination norm and on the larger international law question of the extraterritorial scope of human rights treaties. Not only would CEDAW, the HRC, and the CESCR have direct contributions to make, but so also would CERD for whom the central question would be whether Mitsubishi had racialized the Thai women (especially were it to turn out that no such ads run in Japan or that the ads that run in

Japan also use Thai employees and not Japanese employees). Quite beyond the substantive benefits of institutional interaction among the committees, any decision to move toward a paradigm of indirect extraterritorial responsibility for transnational corporate conduct would have its authority enhanced significantly if it could be presented as a decision taken by all six committees in their shared perception that they should promote the evolution of a global constitutional order centered on the UN human rights treaties rather than as a decision of one or two committees who could be condemned by states as acting outside their mandate.

GLOBAL CONSTITUTIONAL MONITORING: ACCOUNTABILITY OF INTERSTATE GOVERNING INSTITUTIONS AND REGIMES

The preceding section ended by broaching the subject of global constitutionalism, but global constitutionalism in the context of the world's evolving political economy cannot rest content with a focus only on apportioning *state* responsibility and on seeking to develop some indirect monitoring of transnational *corporate* conduct. *All governing actors and all governance regimes* within the global(izing) order must also eventually be accounted for in the evolution of the normative functions and authority of the UN human rights committees. Much concern is already being directed in contemporary social and political discourse to the problems of (lack of) human rights accountability of international financial institutions (IFIs) such as the International Monetary Fund (IMF) and the World Bank, for the devastating consequences of recent UN Security Council activity notably in respect of sanctions regimes such as that maintained on Iraq, and on the lack of a human rights counterbalance to the rapidly solidifying hegemony of the World Trade Organization (WTO) regime. To date, the human rights treaty bodies cannot be said to have more than hinted at how they conceptualize their authority to monitor these interstate institutions and regimes.[98]

But it is safe to say, I think, that both ideas and intercommittee solidarity must begin to be generated through a collective articulation of a legal theory of *governance responsibility* (as contrasted to the traditional, and ongoing, focus on "state responsibility") according to which states are no more permitted to escape human rights accountability by configuring governance through delegation to the *interstate* level than they should be allowed to shed human rights through delegation by *privatization*.[99] Given that international organizations and treaty regimes generally retain, at the formal juridical level, their state-centeredness, there should — ultimately — be little doubt about the legitimacy of the human rights committees beginning to address state conduct that takes interstate forms. At minimum, normative pronouncements on human rights violations committed by, for example, the IMF or the Security Council can be presented as preconditions to conclusions about the state responsibility of the states that are members and

decision makers in those institutions. A capacity to focus on global structures and on the human rights obligations of multiple actors represents a
possible constitutional future for the UN human rights treaty system, a
future that will only be possible if the current fragmented treaty order
comes increasingly to be recognized as an integrated (normative and institutional) whole. The trick will be for the UN human rights treaty order to
finesse its own state-centered formal foundations as it moves toward this new
state of affairs.

2

From Division to Integration: Economic, Social, and Cultural Rights as Basic Human Rights

CHISANGA PUTA-CHEKWE AND NORA FLOOD

... may you live, and all your people. I too will live with all my people. But life alone is not enough. May we have the things with which to live it well. For there is a kind of slow and weary life which is worse than death.

— *Chinua Achebe,* Arrow of God

Introduction

More than fifty years ago the Universal Declaration of Human Rights recognized that an individual requires certain civil, political, economic, and social freedoms in order to "live life well." The Universal Declaration did not attach relative values to the rights that it recognized — each right was identified as an essential ingredient of dignified personhood.[1] However, since the adoption of the Universal Declaration the protection of civil and political rights has systematically been given priority over the protection of economic, social, and cultural rights. As a result, the potential of the Universal Declaration to promote the betterment of human existence has not been fully realized. Between one-fifth and one-quarter of the world's population lives in absolute poverty, without adequate food, shelter, and health care. The marginalization of economic, social, and cultural rights has thus served to marginalize further the poorest, most vulnerable groups in society.

Misconceptions about the nature of economic, social, and cultural rights have directly contributed to the diminished respect for these rights in international and domestic arenas. Indeed, such misconceptions influenced the decision to entrench these rights in a covenant distinct from that which entrenches civil and political rights. The existence of a separate covenant has, in turn, served to perpetuate the belief that economic, social, and cultural rights are different both in value and in kind from civil and political rights.

This chapter examines the motivating factors behind the creation of a separate international covenant to protect economic, social, and cultural rights. It demonstrates how the decision to create the International Covenant on Economic, Social, and Cultural Rights (ICESCR)[2] was the product of conflicting political ideologies and misconceptions about the nature of human rights, rather than the necessary consequence of fundamental differences between groups of rights. The chapter illustrates how the protection of economic, social, and cultural rights is as vital to the promotion of human dignity as the protection of civil and political rights. Finally, it summarizes recent efforts to increase respect for, and understanding of, the rights entrenched in the ICESCR and illustrates how one nongovernmental organization, Oxfam International, has attempted to promote respect for these rights through its humanitarian efforts.

The Recognition of Economic, Social, and Cultural Rights From Civil and Political Rights

International human rights law emerged during the latter half of the twentieth century. In the aftermath of World War II, members of the United Nations determined that the protection of human rights should be one of the primary goals of their newly created organization. There was recognition that the political upheavals preceding the war had been spurred by widespread unemployment and poverty.[3] As a result, in addition to recognizing civil and political rights, the United Nations Charter recognized the need to promote economic progress and social development.[4]

In order to promote human rights and fundamental freedoms, the United Nations created the Commission on Human Rights in 1946. The commission's mandate was to draft an "International Bill of Human Rights" that would consist of a nonbinding declaration, a convention, and a document of implementation.[5] On December 10, 1948 the Universal Declaration of Human Rights was adopted by the General Assembly of the United Nations. The Universal Declaration enumerated both civil and political rights and economic, social, and cultural rights and identified *all* of these rights as essential for human dignity and development.[6]

After the adoption of the Universal Declaration, the Commission on Human Rights began drafting a human rights covenant with provisions that would be legally binding on member states. During its fifth session, in 1950, the Commission concluded that additional time was required to define the normative content of economic, social, and cultural rights. The initial draft of the covenant was thus limited to civil and political rights, the content of which could be more easily defined due to the existence of relevant domestic jurisprudence. Viewing the draft as the first in a series, the General Assembly called upon the commission to incorporate economic, social, and cultural rights into the final covenant.[7] The General Assembly noted that the enjoyment of civil and political freedoms, and economic, social, and cultural rights was "interconnected and interdependent."[8]

After adopting 14 articles on economic, social, and cultural rights, the Commission on Human Rights requested that the General Assembly reconsider its requirement of a single covenant, citing "the problems of placing rights and obligations of 'different kinds' in a single instrument."[9] By a vote of 29 to 25,[10] the General Assembly agreed, concluding that the commission should draft two separate covenants to be submitted for approval simultaneously.[11] The General Assembly also specified that the two covenants should contain as many similar provisions as possible.

The International Covenant on Civil and Political Rights (ICCPR) and the International Covenant on Economic, Social, and Cultural Rights (ICESCR) were adopted by the General Assembly on 16 December 1966.[12] The covenants came into force in 1976. Each state party covenanted to submit periodic reports outlining the measures that it had adopted and the progress that it had made in achieving the observance of the enumerated rights. In addition, the ICCPR included an optional protocol, whereby participating states agreed to allow the covenant's monitoring body to hear complaints from individuals who claimed to have suffered violations of their ICCPR rights.

The Hardening of the Line Dividing Economic, Social, and Cultural Rights from Civil and Political Rights

The international covenants placed human rights on the world agenda: "Human rights . . . were no longer abstract principles, but legitimate, tangible goals for which the international community was to strive."[13] The recognition of economic, social, and cultural rights as essential to human dignity, and their entrenchment in the ICESCR, appeared to herald the legitimization of this set of rights. Indeed, as of December 1999, 143 states had bound themselves to protect and promote these rights by ratifying the ICESCR. However, official recognition of the "essential" nature of economic, social, and cultural rights has not resulted in effective protection of these rights in practice. In 1993, the Committee on Economic, Social, and Cultural Rights lamented the fact that while violations of civil and political rights provoke expressions of outrage, massive and direct denials of economic, social, and cultural rights are too often tolerated by the international community.[14]

The existence of separate covenants entrenching civil and political rights and economic, social, and cultural rights has contributed to the assumption that these sets of rights are different both in nature and in value. In reality, the creation of two covenants was motivated in large part by political ideology. Conflicting ideologies in Soviet and Western bloc countries after the war resulted in different conceptions of what constituted a "fundamental" human right.[15] While the Soviet states championed economic, social, and cultural rights, which they associated with the objectives of socialist society, Western states promoted civil and political rights as the foundation of democracy.[16] Western states viewed economic, social, and cultural rights with suspicion because many of these rights required an element of wealth distribution. As such, they represented the very interference with individual liberty that civil and political rights were believed to protect against.

Fearing that Western states would use separation as a means to prevent the adoption of a covenant dealing with economic, social, and cultural rights, Soviet bloc states backed the adoption of a single, comprehensive covenant. Meanwhile, Western bloc states supported the division of rights into two separate treaties, "thus making clear the ideological and political importance the decision was perceived as having."[17] In the end, the expectation that "states that did not want to undertake the obligations arising from social, economic and cultural rights would be willing to ratify a covenant containing only civil and political rights, was one of the motivations for the separation of the two 'sets' of rights."[18]

The rights enumerated in the ICCPR and the ICESCR correspond roughly to the rights that were deemed essential to the postwar political systems of Soviet and Western bloc countries, respectively. The covenants, in turn, follow the traditional dichotomy between "negative" and "positive" rights. A negative right connotes *freedom from* interference and, as such, appears to require mere forbearance on the part of the state. Conversely, a positive right connotes a *right to* something, and is perceived as requiring the (re)distribution of resources by the state. The conception of civil and political rights as negative, and thus "free," has led to the belief that their fulfillment should be absolute and immediate. Meanwhile, the conception of economic, social, and cultural rights as costly has justified a more gradual approach to the protection of these rights.[19]

The wording of the ICESCR acknowledges that the protection of economic, social, and cultural rights is to some extent contingent upon the availability of sufficient resources. Article 2(1) provides, "Each State Party to the present Covenant undertakes to take steps . . . to the maximum of its available resources, with a view to achieving progressively the full realization of the rights recognized in the . . . Covenant by all appropriate means."[20] Certain terminology in this article has been criticized for allowing states too much leeway in the fulfillment of their obligations under the covenant.[21] "To achieve progressively" the rights recognized in the covenant "by all appropriate means" connotes a degree of discretion that is absent from the ICCPR, which obliges states to do everything "within their means" to achieve compliance. Not only does the difference in wording highlight the difference between civil and political rights and economic, social, and cultural rights, but it also suggests that this difference derives from the positive/negative rights dichotomy — that economic, social, and cultural rights require a positive expenditure of money.

Upon closer analysis, the positive/negative rights dichotomy is of little assistance in categorizing human rights. It is possible to identify duties of forbearance with respect to most economic, social, and cultural rights. For example, the right to work, recognized in article 6 of the ICESCR, can be construed to prohibit forced labor.[22] Conversely, it is possible to identify duties of action with respect to civil and political rights. In order to ensure equal access to justice, for example, a state must provide legal aid to those who cannot afford a lawyer. It must also be noted that whether the violation of a human right requires as a remedy the forbearance or the action of the state says nothing about the gravity of the rights violation itself. Acts of commission and acts of omission can result in a human rights violation of the same magnitude.[23]

A newer conception of human rights collapses the positive/negative dichotomy and asserts that a state is obliged to respect, protect, and fulfill every fundamental human right. Identifying human rights obligations in this manner, it is impossible to speak of economic, social, and cultural rights as being solely positive, or civil and political rights as being purely negative.[24] Indeed, the argument that civil and political rights do not require the expenditure of resources "is tenable only in situations where the focus on economic and social rights is on the tertiary level (the obligation to fulfill) while civil and political rights are observed on the primary level (the obligation to protect)."[25]

The precise normative content of most economic, social, and cultural rights is substantially less well understood than that of political and civil rights.[26] Drafters had scant domestic jurisprudence to refer to when defining the nature and scope of ICESCR rights. While it was acknowledged that generally worded provisions could result in conflicting interpretations, it was decided that such wording would in most cases be preferable to restricting the scope of covenant rights.[27] Nevertheless, the vagueness of the covenant has seriously impeded the protection of ICESCR rights. As a result of its lack of precision, even those states that are committed to fulfilling their obligations under the covenant will have difficulty ascertaining what, exactly, their obligations are.[28] Nevertheless, according to Philip Alston, some of the provisions in the ICESCR are no more vague than some of those in the ICCPR. However, "the difference in the extent of elaboration of their normative content . . . is immense."[29] Alston claims that the international community has failed to engage in a meaningful legal analysis of the rights enshrined in the ICESCR in order to clarify the meaning and policy implications of those rights.[30]

The Devaluation of Economic, Social, and Cultural Rights

The failure of the international community to elaborate the content of economic, social, and cultural rights has perpetuated the notion that these rights are less essential to dignified personhood than civil or political rights. Such a view has forestalled the protection of economic, social, and cultural rights on a domestic level. Many of these rights "have yet to be translated in a meaningful way into national laws, and they have not been taken to heart by the people."[31] Indeed, the incorporation of rights into national law and the acceptance of those rights by the people are interrelated concepts. International law is generally applicable to the state. Individuals *within* the state are "more likely to be affected by the terms of domestic law and the availability of local remedies."[32] Hence the most effective way for individuals to develop a sense of entitlement to a right is for that right to be incorporated into the domestic legal system. With regard to the ICESCR, however, even those countries that have incorporated the terms of the covenant into their judicial systems have rarely relied upon them in domestic proceedings.[33]

According to Matthew C. R. Craven, "the lack of national case law directly related to economic, social, and cultural rights has . . . perpetuated the idea that those rights are not capable of judicial enforcement."[34] The method of supervision of economic, social, and cultural rights implemented in the ICESCR has similarly perpetuated the idea that these rights are not justiciable. Respect for the terms of the ICESCR is ensured through the use of a reporting system, whereby states submit periodic reports on the steps that they have taken to promote economic, social, and cultural rights within their jurisdiction. A reporting system forms part of the implementation machinery of several United Nations documents, including the ICCPR. However, in contrast to the ICESCR, which is ostensibly its counterpart, the ICCPR includes an optional protocol which provides for an individual complaints procedure. A state that becomes a party to the protocol recognizes the competence of the Human Rights Committee, established under the ICCPR, to consider communications from individuals who claim that their ICCPR rights have been violated. A complaints procedure allows a treaty's supervisory body to assume a quasi-judicial role by interpreting the provisions of the treaty in light of a fact-specific situation and making recommendations as to how similar situations could be approached in the future. Thus, over time, the normative content of treaty obligations is defined. Proponents of the complaints procedure also note that it generates more public interest than a reporting system. Increased public scrutiny, in turn, motivates states to rectify rights abuses — a phenomenon known as the "mobilization of shame."[35]

It is argued that a reporting system can play a more constructive role in monitoring treaty compliance than can a complaints procedure, which by its very nature is adversarial. Under the ICESCR, for example, a "constructive dialogue" with a state representative is an important aspect of the monitoring body's consideration of the state's report. The result has been to reduce the threat of politicization "and to provide reassurance to states parties to the Covenant that they will be treated fairly."[36] Hence reporting systems may play a more positive role in assessing state compliance with a treaty, and in advising countries as to possible remedial action.

However, as Craven states, "reporting systems are dependent, to a large extent, upon the good faith of the states concerned. They are reliant upon the provision of accurate and relevant information by States parties."[37] It is generally agreed that state compliance with reporting obligations under the ICESCR is relatively poor.[38] Many reports are submitted late, and some are not submitted at all — a violation of a state's obligations under the covenant. This suggests that many parties to the ICESCR do not consider their obligations under the covenant to be important enough to merit the preparation of a comprehensive report.

Mechanisms for Increasing Respect for Economic, Social, and Cultural Rights

Craig Scott proposes the concept of permeability as a means of subjecting ICESCR rights to the quasi-judicial jurisdiction of the ICCPR's optional protocol.[39] He notes that, despite the fact that civil and political rights and economic, social, and cultural rights were separated into two distinct covenants, there was a clear attempt by the United Nations to underscore the interdependence of these rights by creating temporal and material linkages between the two covenants. The covenants were introduced for consideration, approval, and signature simultaneously. In addition, "considerable explicit overlap of substantive rights provisions exists between the Covenants," examples of which include the right to self-determination entrenched in article 1 of both the ICCPR and the ICESCR, and the right to protection of the family, the mother and children in article 24 of the ICCPR and article 10 of the ICESCR.[40] Scott asserts that the links between the two covenants reveal the potential for dynamic interaction between them — interaction that could allow a treaty dealing with one category of human rights to be open to having its norms "used as vehicles for the direct or indirect protection of norms of another treaty dealing with a different category of human rights."[41]

Recently, promoters of economic, social, and cultural rights have stepped up efforts to include an optional protocol within the ICESCR itself. A separate optional protocol would aid, first, in restoring similarity to the structures of the human rights covenants and, second, in laying to rest the notion that economic, social, and cultural rights are not justiciable. Moreover, the introduction of a separate optional protocol would avoid the danger inherent in Scott's "permeability" theory: that making obligations under the ICESCR susceptible to the supervisory mechanisms of the ICCPR will reinforce the idea that economic, social, and cultural rights are merely instrumental — meaningful only insofar as they further civil and political rights. What is necessary is to promote the idea that the rights entrenched in the ICESCR are valuable in and of themselves. As Jack Donnelly states:

Human dignity, the realization of which is the aim of human rights, cannot be reduced to dimensions that can be encompassed by a short or narrow list of "basic" human rights. *All* human rights are "basic rights" in the fundamental sense that systematic violations of *any* human right preclude realizing a life full of human dignity — that is, prevent one from enjoying the minimum conditions necessary for a life worthy of a human being.[42]

Protection of all human rights is necessary in order to assure dignified personhood. This is reflected in the Universal Declaration of Human Rights itself. Article 28 of that instrument provides that everyone is entitled to a social and international order in which the rights and freedoms set forth in the Universal Declaration can be fully realized. Among the rights that the Universal Declaration recognizes are the right to work, the right to education, and the right to a standard of living adequate for health and well-being, including food, clothing, housing, medical care, and social services.[43] The importance of realizing these rights is not qualified in any way: "There is nothing in the language of the Declaration that limits human rights to . . . civil and political rights."[44] It can be argued, of course, that the Universal Declaration is not a legally binding instrument and that it can therefore be the source of neither obligation nor entitlement. However, Pieter Van Dijk points out that the Universal Declaration should be appreciated for what it *is*, rather than for what it is *not*:

The normative values that the Universal Declaration embodies and the normative effects it generates do not depend solely — nor even primarily — on its legal status, but rather on its authority within the international community and within the countries of the world. This authority, in turn, does not depend solely — or even primarily — on legal institutions and legal procedures but rather on people's shared expectations that its norms will be respected and enforced, and on the willingness of the authorities to respect them, and to enforce them where breaches occur.[45]

The Universal Declaration is an elaboration of the commitment to human rights first declared in the United Nations Charter. Due to the influence of the Universal Declaration, politically and morally, its characterization of economic, social, and cultural rights as inherently valuable provides a strong case for increasing respect for these rights.

The task of promoting greater respect for economic, social, and cultural rights has been assumed with vigor by the Committee on Economic, Social, and Cultural Rights, the body charged with monitoring states' compliance with ICESCR obligations. The committee was created in 1985, inheriting the existing procedures of its predecessor, the Sessional Working Group,[46] whose performance during its ten-year existence was widely criticized. According to Philip Alston, dissatisfaction was generated by many aspects of the working group's performance, including its superficial examination of states' reports, its failure to establish standards for evaluation of those reports, and the poor attendance of its members.[47] In such a setting, claims Alston, "it became increasingly difficult to defend the view that the United Nations was taking economic, social, and cultural rights just as seriously as civil and political rights when the institutional arrangements for implementing the former were clearly inferior to those relating to the latter."[48]

The Committee on Economic, Social, and Cultural Rights has been hailed as a significant improvement over the Sessional Working Group: "Not only are the questions and issues raised during the examination of states reports far more inquisitive, insightful and demanding; so too are the Committee's overall analyses."[49] Indeed, while the scant reporting of the Sessional Working Group dealt primarily with procedural matters, since 1989 the Committee on Economic, Social, and Cultural Rights has provided concluding observations for every report it has considered. These reports indicate the extent to which ICESCR rights are protected by a state party, and whether any of the rights entrenched in the covenant have been violated.[50]

An equally significant initiative on the part of the committee has been the preparation of General Comments on the various articles and provisions of the ICESCR. The ICCPR's Human Rights Committee had effectively been using general comments to clarify the normative content of civil and political rights. Thus, in response to a formal invitation by the UN's Economic and Social Council in 1987, the Committee on Economic, Social, and Cultural Rights decided to prepare General Comments.

The General Comments produced by the Committee on Economic, Social, and Cultural Rights have helped to clarify the content of the ICESCR. The committee has aimed to identify the minimum core content of each ICESCR right. According to Alston, this is one of the roles that the drafters of the Covenant intended its supervisory body to play:

The fact that there must exist such a core . . . would seem to be a logical implication of the use of the terminology of rights . . . [T]here would be no justification for elevating a "claim" to the status of a right (with all the connotations that concept is generally assumed to have) if its normative content could be so indeterminate as to allow for the possibility that the rightholders possess no particular entitlement to anything.[51]

Since 1989 the Committee on Economic, Social, and Cultural Rights has issued General Comments that identify the minimum core content of, among others, the right to adequate food and the right to adequate housing. It is the Committee's position that states parties to the ICESCR must ensure the satisfaction of the minimum core content of each ICESCR right, in order to discharge their obligations under the covenant. "Thus, for example, a state party in which any significant number of individuals is deprived of essential foodstuffs, of essential primary health care, of basic shelter and housing, or of the most basic forms of education is, *prima facie,* failing to discharge its obligations under the Covenant."[52]

In its third general comment, the committee acknowledged that an assessment of whether a state party had discharged its duties under the ICESCR had to take into account the resource constraints affecting the state. Indeed, the committee acknowledged that under article 2(1) of the covenant a state is obligated to "achieve progressively" the rights entrenched in the ICESCR. According to the committee, such wording reflects the fact that limited resources prevent the realization of many economic, social, and cultural

rights in a short amount of time. However, the committee identified obligations under the covenant that were of immediate effect:

[The undertaking] in article 2(1) "to take steps" . . . is not qualified or limited by
other considerations. . . . Thus while the full realization of the relevant rights may be
achieved progressively, steps towards that goal must be taken within a reasonably
short time after the Covenant's entry into force. . . . Such steps should be deliberate,
concrete and targeted as clearly as possible towards meeting the obligations recognized in the Covenant.[53]

In addition, the committee asserted that the burden was on the state party
to prove that it had made every effort to use those resources at its disposal to
meet — "as a matter of priority" — its obligations under the ICESCR.[54]

By elaborating the scope and content of ICESCR rights in its general
comments, the Committee on Economic, Social, and Cultural Rights has
dismissed any assumptions that the ICESCR offers states discretion in fulfilling their obligations under the covenant. The committee has highlighted
both the importance and the urgency of satisfying ICESCR obligations.
The committee's position has been echoed by human rights scholars in
subsequent elaborations of the content of the ICESCR. In 1986, a group
of 29 experts in the field of international law met to discuss the nature of
the duty of states parties to the ICESCR. The experts formulated the Limburg Principles on the Implementation of the International Covenant on
Economic, Social, and Cultural Rights, and agreed that the principles reflected the evolution of international law. The principles echoed the opinion of the committee that states parties to the ICESCR have an obligation
to begin immediately to take steps to fulfill their obligations.[55] Moreover,
the Principles held states parties accountable for ensuring protection of
minimum subsistence rights, regardless of the level of the state's economic
development.[56]

Ten years after the formulation of the Limburg Principles, international
legal experts met again, this time to discuss what constitutes a violation of
the ICESCR. The Maastricht Guidelines on Violations of Economic, Social,
and Cultural Rights adopted a modern approach to human rights definition. According to the guidelines, states parties have an obligation to respect, protect, and fulfill each of the rights entrenched in the ICESCR.[57]
Failure to perform any of these obligations violates the covenant. Characterizing the ICESCR as encompassing duties to respect, protect and fulfill minimum core entitlements emphasizes the fact that ICESCR obligations are not
solely positive obligations — states parties are required to *respect* and *protect*
ICESCR rights, in addition to *fulfilling* them. The elaboration of ICESCR
rights in the Maastricht Guidelines thus assisted in collapsing the positive/
negative rights dichotomy, which many had associated with the ICESCR and
ICCPR, respectively. The Maastricht Guidelines have gone some way in dis-

pelling the myth that social and economic rights are different in kind, and more difficult to protect, than "negative" civil and political rights.

Case Study: Oxfam International's Commitment to Promoting the Protection of Economic, Social, and Cultural Rights

According to the Limburg Principles, nongovernmental organizations can play an important role in facilitating the implementation of the ICESCR.[58] Several NGOs have committed themselves to promoting economic and social rights, recognizing these rights as essential to the achievement of dignified personhood. Oxfam International is an example of an NGO that recognizes social and economic rights as equal in importance to, rather than secondary or inferior to, civil and political rights. Formed in 1995, Oxfam International is composed of eleven autonomous nongovernmental organizations, working in partnership to address the structural causes of poverty and oppression. Oxfam International is currently active in more than 120 countries, supporting long-term initiatives to help vulnerable groups increase their self-reliance.[59] As a result of lessons learned during its work, Oxfam launched its "Basic Human Rights Campaign" in 1995 and relaunched it in 1998 to coincide with the fiftieth anniversary of the UDHR. The campaign calls for a reaffirmation of the basic rights which, in the organization's view, are a core set of essential requirements that are fundamental to well-being. These basic rights recognized by Oxfam include the right to a home, the right to enough to eat, and the right to a say in one's future. The core set of rights recognized by Oxfam "represent those which Oxfam believes to be the most basic rights of all — to subsistence and security — without which the other rights are unattainable."[60]

Therefore, Oxfam recognizes that it is effective recognition of a *combination* of civil, political, economic, social, and cultural rights that will lead to human dignity: "Basic rights cannot be looked at in isolation. They are interrelated and interdependent . . . successfully claiming one will make it easier to realize others."[61]

While Oxfam is only one of a number of organizations that currently focus on the promotion within the UN system of economic, social, and cultural rights in tandem with civil and political rights, this was not the case a decade ago. In 1991, Scott Leckie reported that participation of NGOs in sessions of the Committee on Economic, Social, and Cultural Rights remained at a "disappointingly low" level, despite "repeated pleas for greater formal and informal NGO input into the Committee's work."[62] Many obstacles contributed to the low level of NGO participation in the committee's work: lack of funding; greater focus on other bodies such as domestic governments, the IMF and the World Bank; and an overall lower number of NGOs accredited to the United Nations at that time. The United Nations approach to economic, social, and cultural rights also contributed to low NGO participation. The United Nations traditional emphasis on, and provision of, greater avenues of recourse for protecting civil and political rights prompted many NGOs to focus on these rights, in order to invest precious money and time in the manner that promised to be most effective. In 1993, the Committee on Economic, Social, and Cultural Rights formally reiterated its invitation to NGOs to submit in writing, at any time, information regarding any aspect of the committee's work.[63] The committee's invitation revealed an understanding of NGOs' essential role both in disseminating information and in transmitting the concerns and views of various sectors of society to United Nations forums.[64] According to the Vienna Plus-Five Working Group on Effectiveness of and NGO Access to the UN System, there has been a general increase in NGO interaction with the UN since the World Conference on the Environment and Development in Rio de Janeiro in 1992. "Subsequently, global conferences and negotiations saw great participation by NGOs in the [field] of human rights."[65]

Conclusion

Increased participation in the monitoring of UN human rights treaties by nongovernmental organizations has coincided with renewed interest in economic, social, and cultural rights within the United Nations. In recent years, perhaps as a result of more effective monitoring and elucidation of ICESCR obligations by the Committee on Economic, Social, and Cultural Rights, promotion of ICESCR rights within the United Nations has intensified. In 1993, delegates from around the world attended the Vienna World Conference on Human Rights and reaffirmed the indivisible, interdependent, and interrelated nature of all human rights. At the World Summit for Social Development in Copenhagen in 1995, world leaders gathered for the first time to address social development and well-being, and to pledge to give these goals the highest priority in the new millennium. In December 1995, the General Assembly adopted Resolution 50/107, proclaiming the years 1997–2006 the Decade for the Eradication of Poverty. Recent United Nations instruments such as the Convention on the Rights of the Child and the Universal Declaration on the Right to Development have included *both* economic, social, and cultural rights and civil and political rights. The inclusive structure of these documents reinforces the fact that all human rights are equally essential to the protection of human dignity.

Due to the recognition of NGOs like Oxfam International of the interrelated, indivisible nature of human rights, increased NGO participation in the implementation of the ICESCR has the potential to increase respect for economic, social, and cultural rights. Moreover, the capacity of NGOs to generate public interest, combined with their growing participation in United Nations human rights organizations, will help ensure that the recent attention paid to economic, social, and cultural rights within the UN will not be fleeting. For, despite the renewed commitment to these rights that recent conferences and declarations herald, the history of the ICESCR reveals that unless true commitment is demonstrated through *action*, on both international and domestic fronts, the promise of the chance to "live life well" will remain unfulfilled.

3

Defending Women's Economic and Social Rights: Some Thoughts on Indivisibility and a New Standard of Equality

DIANNE OTTO

Even as the post-Cold War era is marked by a heightened emphasis on human rights,[1] the international human rights regime is being downsized as governments divest themselves of the responsibility to provide social services and ensure adequate living and working standards.[2] At the same time as the increasingly powerful international financial institutions are overseeing a transfer of social policy issues from the United Nations to states, governments are under pressure from the same institutions to move previously public responsibilities into the hands of private actors through privatizing, subcontracting, and outsourcing.[3] By definition these private actors, often multinational corporations, sacrifice "community interest" to the dictates of profit and are not bound directly by the existing human rights instruments.[4]

The result is that the new human rights imperative is selective about which rights are promoted. The rights given prominence are those that assist free market economic globalization, in short, certain civil and political rights: freedom of speech and information, minimal forms of representative democracy, the rule of law, and the strengthening of civil society.[5] At the same time, apparently counterintuitively, some developing states resist the spread of even "market friendly" rights by arguing that the right to development must take precedence over any individual rights.[6] I am not suggesting that civil and political rights are unimportant, or that the right to development is not critical. My point is simply that economic and social rights appear to have no place in contemporary free market expansionism or the development agendas of international financial institutions,[7] which leaves the responsibility for addressing issues like poverty, hunger, homelessness, and exploitative working conditions to market forces[8] or, in another view, to transgovernmental networks of powerful professionals.[9]

The way social and economic rights have fallen off the international human rights agenda reflects a precariousness that is similar to that of women's human rights. Both categories of rights are relative newcomers to the human rights heartland, and both are fundamentally important to addressing the rights of the most vulnerable people. This makes these rights more likely to be considered dispensable when structural change takes place.[10] In order to resist this and other erosions of the "organic unity" of the human rights enu-

merated in the 1948 Universal Declaration of Human Rights and its prog-
eny,[11] I suggest adopting an "indivisibility approach." The idea of indivisibility rests on the understanding that all human rights are interdependent and,
therefore, that the displacement of one right or category of rights by another has the effect of reducing the overall enjoyment of human rights.[12] It
suggests that those promoting civil and political rights or advancing the right
to development need to refuse the paradigm of conflict and hierarchy with
respect to each other and economic, social, and cultural rights. Such a
paradigm simply results in reordering rights priorities and legitimates violations of rights that are ranked lower in the order. The goal should not be civil
and political rights, or the right to development at the expense of social and
economic rights. The goal, as I will argue, is to develop practices that recognize the interconnections, as well as the tensions, between different rights
and to foster coalition or indivisibility, rather than hierarchy, in order to
ensure that *all* human rights are enjoyed and to expand the reach of human
rights so that *all* people, including women, are covered.

In this chapter, I develop the notion of an indivisibility approach to human rights and argue that women's human rights struggles are important to
its conceptualization and practice. I begin by outlining three ways in which
the language of indivisibility has been used with respect to human rights: to
reject hierarchical categories within the human rights corpus; to promote
gender inclusivity; and to assert structural linkages between the realization
of human rights and other regimes of power. Second, I examine the indivisibility issues raised during the review by the 1998 Commission on the
Status of Women (CSW42) of progress toward implementation of the Beijing Platform for Action (PFA)[13] chapter on women's human rights. The
CSW42 discussions highlighted intractable political resistance to making
the links that indivisibility advocates claim. Finally, I discuss some of the
strategic possibilities as well as some of the problems associated with the
concept of indivisibility that flow from the CSW42 experience.

The Language of Indivisibility — An Overview

The contention that human rights are indivisible or interdependent is not
new.[14] It has served three main purposes. First, the idea of indivisibility has
been used as a device to challenge hierarchical understanding of the relationship between certain human rights or groups of rights. The most familiar human rights hierarchy, which has a long history in the liberal tradition,
is the prioritization of civil and political rights over economic, social, and
cultural rights.[15] As long ago as 1952, the General Assembly insisted on the
indivisibility of these two categories of rights, as it capitulated to strong
pressure to agree to the codification of the integrated UDHR into two
covenants, corresponding to the two categories.[16] Although the General As-

sembly only reluctantly agreed to this division, and states explicitly affirmed the indivisibility of these two categories of human rights in the 1968 Proclamation of Teheran,[17] it is indisputable that civil and political rights have always received greater emphasis in the UN system.[18] The language of indivisibility has also been used to counter hierarchies by promoting the recognition of interdependencies between the rights covered by the six major human rights treaties (see Chapter 1), highlighting intersectional relationships between human rights categories that have been created to address systemic discrimination,[19] and arguing for the inclusion of third generation rights, such as the right to development, in the human rights heartland.[20]

Since the end of the Cold War, the language of indivisibility has been used in a second sense, to expose and contest hierarchies of a more profound order which results in the *exclusion* of certain rights from the universal register of human rights. Feminists have led the way by asserting the indivisibility of women's human rights in response to the failure of the "neutral" (i.e., masculinist) human rights regime to adequately recognize and protect the rights of women.[21] Similarly, nonnormative sexual minorities have used the language of indivisibility to argue that sexuality rights and protections from discrimination on the basis of sexual orientation also belong in the human rights heartland.[22] As a claim for inclusion, the idea of indivisibility goes to the heart of the concept of universal human rights. In this sense, indivisibility is a rhetorical technique for reasserting the most fundamental premise of the human rights regime — human rights apply equally, without exception, to all human beings.

The series of UN world conferences held during the 1990s called for indivisibility in a third sense, which I will call "structural indivisibility," by stressing interconnections between the political, economic, environmental, and security priorities of the international order and violations of human rights.[23] For example, the PFA links armed conflict and excessive military expenditure to poverty and lack of basic services,[24] and connects unsustainable production and consumption to poverty and environmental degradation.[25] It also clearly catalogs the disproportionate consequences for women flowing from the globalization of capital.[26] This breadth of coverage echoes the preamble to the CEDAW, which links the struggle for the equal rights of women to the establishment of a new international economic order, the eradication of all forms of racism, and the strengthening of international peace and security.[27] These are examples of the visionary statements that have emerged from women's multidimensional experiences of subordination and erasure. The question is how to map these interconnections, so that a single human rights violation can be understood in its full sense as a violation of the rights of an individual and, at the same time, in the context of its interdependency with other human rights and its relationship to larger structures and regimes of power.

The principle of indivisibility in the first sense, as a means of contesting hierarchies between different rights, has remained largely aspirational.[28] The end of the Cold War did seem to open a window of opportunity for shifting, if not erasing, the ideologically fueled hierarchies between civil and political rights on the one hand, and economic, social, and cultural rights on the other.[29] Instead, as I have said, certain civil and political rights have been reprioritized in the rush toward economic globalization, despite continued formal affirmations of the indivisibility of all categories of human rights.[30]

The language of indivisibility in the second sense of promoting more inclusive forms of universality was first embraced by states in 1993 with respect to gender inclusivity. States declared, at the Vienna World Conference on Human Rights, that the human rights of women and girls are an "inalienable, integral and indivisible" part of fundamental human rights.[31] Following the lead of the Vienna conference, the 1995 PFA emphasized that the human rights of women and the girl child are indivisible from "fundamental" human rights and that this indivisibility extends "throughout the life cycle."[32] The Beijing Declaration also stated that "women's rights are human rights."[33] While it may seem redundant to assert that women, as well as men, are equally the subjects of international human rights law, translating this assertion into practices of indivisibility remains elusive. The promotion of gender mainstreaming in the UN human rights system has been met with considerable resistance.[34] Further, many states have been resolute in their opposition to moving beyond rhetorical flourishes with respect to women's human rights, as was demonstrated at CSW42, where there were many attempts to water down the commitments undertaken in Beijing (see below). The unwavering refusal of many states to include women's rights in the category of human rights attests to the fundamental importance of gendered hierarchies in the maintenance of inequitable relations of power globally. It indicates that the masculinist model retains a tight grip and, as a result, many women's human rights violations remain invisible, rather than indivisible.

Progress toward developing practices of structural indivisibility has attracted even less political commitment than that mustered to the project of gender inclusivity. Despite the lip service paid to linking violations of women's human rights to larger economic and security issues in the PFA, the strategic objectives outlined do not challenge the supremacy of free market ideology or the militaristic framework in which international peace and security is negotiated.[35] While there is heightened awareness of the human rights abuses that can accompany free market developments, the activities of the Bretton Woods financial institutions and the World Trade Organization remain functionally distinct from the public law of the UN and continue with virtually no accountability for human rights violations at the local level.[36] In the area of international security, there has been some progress toward acknowledging the violations of women's human rights that occur during armed conflict,[37] yet concern for women's security has not extended to rethinking militaristic justifications for the use of force.[38]

Many argue that the human rights paradigm provides an overarching framework for the PFA, linking all twelve of its critical areas of concern together. But is the human rights framework in its present form really capable of making the linkages involved and effectively resisting the new fragmentations and hierarchies of economic globalization? If it is, why have these many affirmations of indivisibility not been translated into human rights practices? And why are women's economic and social rights among the first to fall off the global agenda in the wake of economic restructuring? If the human rights framework is conceptually inadequate for this task, what must be done to deepen or supplement it in order to make sense of the rhetoric of indivisibility in practice? The discussion at CSW42 of the human rights commitments in the PFA sheds some light on these questions.

The "Indivisibility Approach" at the Commission on the Status of Women

The CSW42 met in New York on 2–13 March 1998. Its main agenda was to continue its role in monitoring the implementation of the strategic objectives and actions adopted by the Fourth World Conference on Women, which included reviewing progress toward implementation of the critical area of concern dealing with the human rights of women.[39] The goal was to reach agreed conclusions that would accelerate implementation of the PFA.[40] Like the PFA, the agreed conclusions are not legally binding. However, the language adopted at UN world conferences and its later interpretation are important secondary sources of customary international law and provide an authoritative guide to the construction of existing legal norms and principles.

Regrettably, the consensus decision-making process adopted at CSW42 opened the way for a weakening of the language in the PFA,[41] particularly as there was no provision for reservations, unlike the PFA. One example of this phenomenon was that CSW42 could not agree to reiterate the important language in paragraph 96 of the PFA, which deals with a woman's right to control her sexuality.[42] During the concluding session, the South African Development Community (SADC) made a statement expressing the frustration of many of the more progressive states and suggesting that CSW should foster dialogue on implementation rather than produce "poorer and watered-down versions" of the PFA.[43] There are serious consequences for the progressive development of international law, if subsequent intergovernmental meetings adopt language that erodes earlier positions. Further, the later adoption of weaker language makes it more difficult to hold states accountable for implementing the commitments they undertook in Beijing.

THE EXPERT GROUP'S REPORT ON THE HUMAN RIGHTS OF WOMEN

In preparation for its review of the PFA, the UN Division for the Advancement of Women (DAW) organized several expert group meetings to provide reports to assist CSW42 in its deliberations.[44] The focus for the expert group that addressed the human rights of women was the promotion of women's economic and social rights.[45] As the expert group's report notes, this focus allowed it to highlight interconnections between human rights and other critical areas of concern in the PFA, particularly those relating to poverty and the economy.[46] In taking this approach, the expert group embraced the view that the human rights paradigm is capable of providing an overarching framework for the PFA.[47]

The focus on economic and social rights was a timely initiative, given the serious erosions resulting from economic globalization and the inadequate framework provided by the PFA.[48] In the PFA's coverage of the critical areas of poverty and the economy there is a paucity of references to rights, and the section on women's human rights is also very weak with respect to promoting economic and social rights.[49] While the PFA does pay considerable attention to certain social and economic rights such as those associated with health, education, social security and the care of female children, many others are not mentioned at all. For example, there is no mention of the right to food, to paid maternity leave, or to the satisfaction of a minimum core of subsistence rights, which the CESCR has advocated so compellingly.[50]

The expert group's report that emerged from this meeting makes many qualitative advances on the PFA. In a nutshell, it stresses that women's human rights will not be realized as a result of general efforts to improve human rights protections, but that they require explicit conceptualization, promotion, implementation, and defense.[51] The report insists that proactive gender-specific measures are necessary because existing human rights standards and mechanisms are disproportionately influenced by the experiences of men and therefore fail to recognize that women are often differently affected. This bias is identified as flowing from the structural imbalances in power between women and men, the absence of women from lawmaking and law-enforcement processes, and the systemic character of discrimination against women.[52]

The report calls for a new standard of equality, acknowledging that women's equality will not be achieved by treating women and men the same, or by adopting measures that protect women.[53] This view is a considerable advance on the PFA, which takes, predominantly, an identical treatment approach to equality.[54] The expert group suggests that the new equality standard should be "based on a reconsideration of current assumptions and a reconceptualization of the meaning of equality from a gender perspective."[55] Although the report does not describe how this new standard of equality for women might look, I will argue that its foundation lies in taking an "indivisibility approach" to human rights. That is, that women's equality depends on developing practices of indivisibility that recognize interdependencies and tensions between different rights and refuse prioritizations that result in reinforcing hierarchies and exclusions.

INDIVISIBILITY AS A REJECTION OF HIERARCHY

The report outlines two strategies that I would describe as promoting indivisibility in the sense of challenging hierarchical relationships between rights. The first is its characterization of the state obligations imposed by economic and social rights as involving three duties — to respect, to protect, and to promote and fulfill.[56] This typology counters the view that economic and social rights are not justiciable and therefore not rights in the true sense. The framework has been embraced by the CESCR[57] and is widely promoted by international human rights scholars.[58]

The importance of this tripartite paradigm lies in its rejection of the conventional wisdom that justifies treating economic and social rights differently from civil and political rights. By insisting that economic and social rights involve negative as well as positive duties, comprise immediate as well as progressively realizable standards, and entail obligations of conduct and of result, the paradigm attests to the justiciability of all human rights. The transformative potential of this paradigm lies in its multidimensional understanding of rights, enabling a common language of conceptualization, standard-setting, and enforcement which is essential to counter the human rights hierarchies that have come to be taken for granted.

Also discernible in the expert group's report is a second strategy which challenges entrenched hierarchies of human rights: that women's equality must be understood as including the "full and equal [substantive] realization of socio-economic rights."[59] While the tripartite typology mandates the identical treatment of economic and social rights as human rights, the deeply embedded hierarchies of the present system require an affirmative strategy that insists on the explicit inclusion of women's economic and social rights. The report recognizes that economic and social rights have a particular significance for women who are "disproportionately affected by poverty and social marginalization" and "especially vulnerable" to economic restructuring.[60] It urges that gender-sensitive definitions of economic and social rights be developed as a priority.[61]

The expert group uses, as examples, women's right to work and their right to an adequate standard of living, neither of which was affirmed by the PFA.[62] This makes the report an important development on the PFA. That certain economic and social rights were omitted from the PFA underscores the expert group's view that women's human rights require explicit conceptualization and attests loudly to the need for women's human rights advocates to review their present conceptualization of women's human rights in order to understand how and why many social and economic rights have come to be ignored when they are crucial to achieving women's equality.

INDIVISIBILITY AS THE PROMOTION OF GENDER INCLUSIVITY

Three strategies emerge from the expert group's report that can be characterized as promoting indivisibility in the second sense of ensuring gender inclusivity. The first of these is that the full realization of women's human rights will require creative interpretation of existing human rights norms. Toward this end, the report implores human rights treaty bodies and other monitoring mechanisms to take up the many opportunities for perceptive responses to women's activities and experiences.[63] As an illustration, the expert group observes that a gender-sensitive formulation of the right to work would include the removal of obstacles such as sexual harassment, discriminatory cultural norms and practices, and the lack of availability of child care services.[64] Other rights identified as urgently requiring gender-sensitive interpretations include the right to social security and safety nets for women living in poverty.[65]

The second strategy lies in the expert group's insistence that creative interpretation may need to be supplemented by *new* rights that take account of the life patterns and experiences of women where they differ from those of men.[66] The expert group's promotion of the need to recognize some new human rights is a significant departure from the approach of the PFA and earlier women's human rights instruments. It firmly opens the equality paradigm to conceptual innovations that move beyond the identical treatment and protective approaches. Some examples of emerging women's human rights are rights associated with reproductive choice, sexual orientation, home work, housing, land, and property, gendered violence, the environment, and disabilities.[67] The position taken by states in Beijing not to recognize any *new* human rights is a deeply gendered and counter-indivisibility position because it forecloses any real possibility of achieving the recognition and inclusion of women's human rights. The argument that efforts should be made to strengthen the existing regime, rather than expanding it further, misses the point that the present system is exclusionary.

The third strategy that reflects the expert group's concern to promote gender inclusivity is its emphasis on mainstreaming a gender perspective in all legislation, policies, and programs. The report warns that gender mainstreaming will, in many cases, require "a fundamental restructuring — a transformation — of institutions and systems such as the labor market, social security systems and the operation of property markets."[68] In taking this position, the expert group reaffirms the emphasis on gender mainstreaming that is a dominant strategy in the PFA and has been a CSW strategy for many years.[69] But the report goes further by recognizing that the strategy will in many instances involve transformative change if women's equality is to be attained, vastly expanding the vision of the PFA.

INDIVISIBILITY AS A MEANS OF ASSERTING STRUCTURAL LINKAGES

The expert group also promotes structural indivisibility by emphasizing that the enjoyment of women's human rights is interdependent with the realization of peace, democracy, and sustainable development.[70] The group points out that the human rights dimensions of achieving economic justice and addressing development needs must be recognized,[71] and thus that human rights are not divisible from structural systems of economic and political power. This approach reflects the contextualized and interconnecting frameworks adopted by both the PFA and CEDAW.

Although the report is remarkably progressive, it does have some shortcomings. In particular, it does not really come to grips with the diversities of women nor with the intersections of gender inequality with other systems of inequality, such as race, which would be indispensable components of a full-fledged indivisibility approach to human rights law. Nevertheless, the report provides a framework for bringing together many of the fragments of women's lives so that they can be understood as an interconnected whole. My point is that the concept of indivisibility links together the strategies proposed by the report, giving them an overall coherence and providing a good starting point for conceptualizing a new model of women's equality. Unfortunately, however, the CSW42 discussions did not rise to this challenge, despite the lead offered by the expert group.

THE CSW42 DISCUSSION

There can be little doubt that the notion of indivisibility in its various guises was placed firmly on the agenda of CSW42. Mary Robinson, High Commissioner for Human Rights, in her address to the Commission, strongly endorsed the indivisibility of human rights and stressed the urgent need, given the reality of the feminization of poverty, to focus on women's economic and social rights and the right to development.[72] Further, contributions from the European Union (EU) and several NGOs highlighted the importance of indivisibility, and three of the four expert panelists who opened the discussion of women's human rights referred directly to the "indivisibility" of human rights.[73]

The dialogue that followed the panel presentations revealed a major split in state's views about women's human rights. Four states, the United Kingdom (for the EU), Canada, Italy, and Namibia referred approvingly to the indivisibility of human rights in the first sense of rejecting human rights hierarchies. On the other hand, Jordan took a more circumspect position saying that while human rights were indivisible as a whole it was necessary to 'establish priorities', and the Swaziland representative expressed hostility to the whole concept of women's human rights, saying that CSW would not need to be discussing women's rights at all if God's teachings were followed.

Even at this early stage the discussion seemed a long way removed from the expert group's views that economic and social rights are indispensable to women's equality and empowerment, and that explicit conceptualization and creative interpretation are necessary for their realization. As discussion moved from general debate to the detail of the wording of the Agreed Conclusions, it became clear that Swaziland's hostility to women's human rights was shared by several other vocal states, including Egypt, Pakistan, the Sudan, Cuba, and China. Thus the negotiation of the Agreed Conclusions was often tortuously semantic and highly politicized. The final text was the result of compromise and struggle between often vastly different narratives of gender, rights, equality, citizenship, and humanity.

Those states that were antagonistic to the idea of women's human rights contested all of the wording that would have supported an indivisibility approach in the agreed conclusions, leaving only two indivisibility references near the end of the final text, both of which addressed actions to be taken within the UN system. One of these, involving indivisibility in the sense of contesting hierarchies, was proposed by JUSCANZ.[74] After several deletions (in italics) and the inclusion of some new language (in bold), the paragraph finally read as follows:

Given the importance of general comments in clarifying **the provisions** [replacing *the content of States' obligations and the articles*] of human rights treaties the Committee on the Elimination of Discrimination Against Women **is invited to** [replacing *should*] draw up joint general comments with other treaty bodies, **within their respective mandates**, on the **universality**, indivisibility, **interdependence and interrelatedness** of human rights and should discuss these and other collaborative activities at the annual chairpersons meeting.[75]

Clearly, the altered language is designed to limit linkages in the work of the different treaty bodies and restrict the creative potential of general comments developed collaboratively. The new wording attempts to confine the cooperative endeavors of CEDAW to a narrow reading of the mandate of each separate treaty regime. These changes run counter to the expert group's calls for increased interconnection, innovation, and creativity.

There were two other instances involving the rejection of indivisibility in the first sense of rejecting hierarchies and forging linkages between different categories of human rights. One was the response to the draft wording suggesting that treaty bodies develop a better understanding of the rights contained in other human rights instruments "such that their interpretation and application of human rights norms promotes the full and equal enjoyment [of] all human rights."[76] This wording elicited the comment from Pakistan that surely human rights treaty bodies "monitor" human rights (as opposed to "interpreting" and "promoting" them). Canada defended the proposed wording by arguing that it was an effort to give more detail to what is meant by "mainstreaming" human rights, but the end result was that the wording above was deleted, and the remaining text imagines a less expansive role for treaty bodies.[77] The other instance was the distinction drawn between "human rights treaties" and "human rights *standards*," the latter wording being unacceptable to states like China, Egypt, Cuba, and Pakistan because it was understood to import a range of other documents, including ILO conventions, into the Agreed Conclusions, thus promoting unwarranted linkages.[78]

The core group of states that were implacably unsupportive of women's human rights also resisted any wording that might open possibilities for gender-inclusive indivisibility. They rejected any references that could be construed as supporting the "creative interpretation" of existing human rights norms, and firmly eliminated any avenues that might lead to the recognition of new human rights. I will give two examples, but there were many others. The first was that every reference to the "work of treaty bodies," not just the one I have already mentioned, was debated until it was agreed that it be followed by the limiting phrase "within their mandates." The second example was the debate about whether work on gender issues by treaty bodies and by human rights "*scholars*" should be "widely disseminated."[79] The reference to the work of scholars was deleted after China and Cuba objected to its inclusion, presumably because it too was a means of promoting innovative interpretations of human rights norms. The effect of changes like these was to ensure that treaty bodies restrict the scope of their activities and work in relative isolation from each other and from scholarly debate. This was a clear rejection of the inventive, connecting strategies suggested by the expert group and a major set-back for the struggle to realize the indivisibility, in the sense of inclusion, of women's human rights.

One reference to structural indivisibility remained in the final document, in the last paragraph:

Specialised agencies and other bodies of the United Nations system, as well as other international financial and national trade organisations, should develop innovative ways of integrating the promotion of women's enjoyment of their human rights in all their policies and programmes.[80]

This wording is almost identical to that originally proposed, but its retention in the final text was due more to the chair's adept response to Pakistan's objection that "these issues" had no place in this document, than to the efforts of those who wanted to forge links between human rights concerns and trade policies. The chair's response was that the wording was "nothing new," that these organizations had been called on before to take account of human rights considerations, and that if there was concern about the text itself there was no shortage of agreed text from elsewhere that could be used in its place.[81]

Perhaps the most illuminating discussion, with respect to indivisibility in the third sense of linking human rights with economic and social structures, was in connection with a paragraph in the draft conclusions that recommended actions to be taken by governments with respect to their legal and regulatory frameworks. The wording had been proposed by Canada and read as follows:

Consider the creation of independent mechanisms to review and modify economic and social policies in light of human rights commitments.[82]

The discussion of this paragraph began with a state, hostile to women's human rights, questioning the idea that human rights could affect economic and social policies. The EU joined Canada in strongly supporting the wording, explaining that the concern was that they had been delinked in the past and that it was necessary to develop a linkage. Egypt suggested that the implication was "rather offensive" and that economic and social policies could not just be based on human rights considerations, and Syria and Mexico agreed.

Surprisingly, given the vehemence of those who rejected any linkages between human rights and socioeconomic policies, a rewording was eventually adopted and, instead of deletion, the original paragraph was replaced with the following:

Mainstream a gender perspective into all economic and social policies in order to promote the human rights of women and girls, including their right to development.[83]

However, the final wording omits the important reference to "independent" mechanisms and, with the introduction of the notion of mainstreaming, neatly circumvents mention of "review and modification" and thus avoids the inference that fundamental change to the status quo may be necessary. The concept of gender mainstreaming was used several other times at CSW42 to answer concerns about human rights treaty bodies taking a more innovative role. This suggests an equal treatment approach to mainstreaming that directly repudiates the expert group's recognition that fundamental and transformative restructuring will, in many instances, be necessary. It would seem that the notion of mainstreaming a gender perspective has come to mean different things to different people and, as Mary Robinson had observed in her remarks, was little more than "fashionable terminology."[84]

When these outcomes are measured against the expert group's call for a new standard of equality, and my suggestion that an "indivisibility approach" might contribute to this end, there is very little that matches. First, there is no evidence of the expert group's integrated typology that counters the Cold

War hierarchies of human rights standards. In fact, the reverse was evidenced in the perception by many Southern states of an *opposition* between social and economic rights and the right to development. The same states also resisted any acknowledgment that economic and social rights have a particular significance for women and are essential to women's empowerment. Indivisibility in the sense of gender inclusivity was also firmly cast aside. Any reference that could be construed as promoting the creative or expansive interpretation of human rights treaty norms was actively opposed. The possibility of recognizing the need for newly formulated rights taking account of women's gendered experience was not even contemplated. Finally, the expert group's emphasis on the interdependence of women's human rights with other structures of international concern such as peace, democracy, and sustainable development was also clearly rejected. In particular, there was concerted resistance to any attempt to link human rights and economic and social policies, which were seen as different and divisible, rather than indivisible, categories.

The lack of accord between the expert group's report and the agreed conclusions is of great concern. With respect to the strategies suggested by the expert group, it must be said that, outside a core group of predominantly Northern states, it seemed to have little resonance. Therefore, women's human rights advocates need to confront the apparent rejection of the report's advice and ask, in particular, why it is that Southern states appear to be wedded to the human rights hierarchies of the Cold War years and less committed to recognizing their obligations with respect to economic and social rights. Further, why are many Southern states so strenuously resisting the re-visioning that is necessary to ensure that women's human rights are included in the human rights heartland and that links are forged between human rights and economic development?

The Future of an Indivisibility Approach

Recognizing the interdependencies between different categories of human rights, and between human rights and macroeconomic and security arrangements, raises complex foundational issues about the dignity that human rights law sets out to protect and whether the present shape of human rights discourse is capable of providing that protection.[85] It is apparent that the hierarchical categories of the first fifty years of developments since the UDHR are failing to assist us to a deeper understanding of the world's post-Cold War diversities and fragmentations. This failure leaves certain parts of the international human rights regime to flounder in the face of the imperatives of the liberalized global marketplace. New ways to work across the divisions and oppositions of the past must be found, as evidenced by the experience of CSW42.

It is perhaps not coincidental that such a stark example of the failure of states to move from the rhetoric of indivisibility to its practice occurs in the context of women's human rights, which demand that human rights law apply in the domestic realm of the household itself. As Martin Scheinin pointed out in his background paper for the expert group, social and economic rights and women's rights were simultaneously accepted as human rights for the first time in the UDHR.[86] So, it was not until women were specifically recognized as subjects of human rights law that the importance of the indivisibility of social and economic rights became fully apparent, and the silences of gender in the Enlightenment tradition were revealed. Further, it was not until the former colonies of Europe became active participants in the shaping of international law that the issues of race discrimination and the third generation of human rights, especially the right to development, were recognized.

But despite these advances, the human rights regime must be pushed further from its Enlightenment roots, toward an integration of its many parts, in order to fully embrace its multiplicitous philosophical foundations. A new paradigm of indivisibility could potentially redraw the entire human rights heartland. Instead of working with lists and hierarchies of mutually exclusive and competing rights, it could equip us with new ways to imagine and practice networks of interconnections and interdependencies. It could, further, bring transparency to gendered relations of power. An indivisibility approach could provide a starting point for the new standard of equality that the expert group called for and become a model for the "fundamental restructuring" and "transformation" of institutions and systems that is required before women's human rights will be realized in practice. Finally, a framework of indivisibility could make the human rights paradigm truly effective as an umbrella for the PFA and enable the interlinking of all twelve of its critical areas to move from rhetoric to theory and practice.

The question then becomes one of how to develop such a conceptual framework. The CSW42 experience indicates that there is not much hope that it will emerge from multilateral forums emanating from the FWCW and the UN more generally, at least not at this point in time. This is so partly because many developing states are unwilling to cede further aspects of their sovereignty, and are distrustful of what appear to be Northern agendas, in a world of still growing disparities in wealth and power. Until there are equitable solutions to the extremes of wealth and poverty on which to base solidarity between North and South, the emergence of the embryonic global "community interest" that Bruno Simma identifies remains a distant ideal.[87] Until there is such solidarity, tensions between the North and the South will continue to haunt and distort discussions of human rights indivisibility.

So the hope for an indivisibility paradigm and a new standard of equality lies with grassroots women's movements in coalition with other local movements for social and economic justice. From such disparate starting points, built on the everyday lived realities of the indivisibility of human rights, the hope and the vision that are a necessary foundation for the development of transnational conversations about indivisibility can be found. It is from such conversations that a conceptual framework and indivisibility practices will emerge. The very idea of modern human rights began with grassroots movements, and the further development of our understanding of human rights relies on the very same sources. This realization poses very real challenges to the human rights and women's NGOs that participate in the multilateral forums of the UN. The point, made by many before me, is that the major human rights NGOs reflect the interests of the North, in their prioritization of civil and political rights.[88] Further, the major networks of women's organizations have neglected many economic and social rights, as well as the right to development, in their prioritization of violence against women.[89] This is reflected in the paradox of the PFA's embrace of the language of human rights, while it also neglects social and economic rights and does not engage adequately with issues of structural indivisibility. Without the clear, broad-based, and practical promotion of indivisibility by international NGOs, the multilateral forums of states will continue to understand human rights and free trade as separate categories, refuse to condone creative and connecting interpretations of human rights, and still deny the legitimacy of women's human rights.

Realizing the indivisibility of all human rights has already been a protracted struggle, commencing with the adoption of the UDHR in 1948. This struggle continues in the lessons we can draw from CSW42. But without a conceptual framework for mapping the interconnections that flow from recognizing the indivisibility of human rights, we lack the political and juridical means to demand that social and economic rights be given a permanent position on the global agenda together with other human rights, and to insist that women's rights are indeed human rights.

Conclusions

The principle of indivisibility provides a language for contesting the hierarchies and exclusions of human rights discourse, so it is hardly surprising that it has increasing rhetorical appeal in the post-Cold War environment. The revival of "indivisibility talk" by human rights advocates is one response to the global disruption of macroeconomic boundaries and public-private spheres that has resulted in a downsizing of the human rights obligations of states. This rhetoric is also a response to the gendered hierarchies and exclusions of human rights law itself. The appeal of the idea of indivisibility is that it suggests an organizing principle that highlights interconnections, interdependencies, and holism in the increasingly fragmented global paradigm of human rights.

The experience of CSW42 illustrates that the traditional hierarchies of human rights law continue to be brought into service, as states battle over economic and social priorities and refuse to substantially alter the male boundaries of the human rights regime. Yet economic globalization is not necessarily inconsistent with women's economic and social rights if it is based on respect for all human rights and the pursuit of economic and social justice. But it is necessary for grassroots women's and peoples' movements to build a human rights discourse based on this realization, and for human rights NGOs to promote practices of indivisibility, before it has any chance of emerging as a commitment from the multilateral forums of states.

The concept of the indivisibility of human rights is an idea that can assist in the urgent task of resisting the downsizing of the human rights regime, if we are able to give it conceptual content and make it a conscious practice. The idea of indivisibility could also help to envisage a new standard of gender equality that is not based on models of protection or comparison with men. The visionary human rights contributions that have so far emerged from women's diverse local experiences must continue to be developed. Realizing the indivisibility of human rights in all its senses is a huge conceptual and practical task that is essential to fully realizing women's equality.

Part II. Current Themes:
Applying Cross-Cutting Analysis

Human Rights Mean Business: Broadening the Canadian Approach to Business and Human Rights

CRAIG FORCESE

At the turn of the new century, as at the beginning of the last, the world's nations are a disparate series of economies varying enormously in their characteristics. Speaking generally, in the north, countries have passed through an industrial revolution, through a period of progressive and incremental improvements in standards of living and through several centuries of gradual, if imperfect, diffusion of wealth through the ranks of society. In the south, for various reasons, nations evidence fewer of these transformations. In the developed nations, fundamental human rights, including labor rights, have been advanced, codified, and, for the most part, observed. In developing countries, even where these standards have been codified, many are often ignored, sometimes egregiously.

At the same time, by reason of a complex mix of developments in information and communication technology, and an incremental codification of liberalized trade and, increasingly, investment rules, the international economy has become "globalized." Economic integration and globalization are relatively nonproblematic where globalization links developed nations with broadly homogeneous views on fundamental human rights standards. They become more controversial where they integrate developed and developing countries with different records on human rights. In the latter circumstances, trade and investment have the potential to straddle a range of human rights environments, prompting two critical questions. First, to what extent should northern businesses be expected to apply the international human rights standards by which they abide in their home jurisdiction in countries where they are not compelled to observe these rights? Second, to what extent should businesses evaluate, and respond to, the broader human rights impact of their trading or investment operations in countries with repressive, human rights-abusing regimes?

Notably, businesses have been grappling with similar questions for some time. For example, in 1850, Belgian textile manufacturers and mine operators decided among themselves to ban child labor in their facilities. Dissenters from the compact found it advantageous to continue hiring children, thereby undercutting the prices of the competitors abiding by the rules. In the absence of laws of general application forcing defectors to conform to the minimum age requirements of the agreements, the ethical operators found it impossible to maintain their standards and returned to employing children.[1]

Meanwhile, in apartheid era South Africa, foreign multinationals bolstered, both directly and indirectly, the regime's capacity to stave off political liberalization. In this regard, two U.S. car companies were accused of supplying South African security forces with vehicles,[2] and at least one Canadian bank was a regular lender throughout the apartheid period to the country's military-industrial and nuclear industries.[3] Similarly, South Africa received vital assistance from key U.S. bankers and investors.[4] Further, U.S. firms in South Africa were concentrated in strategic sectors and provided key technological and infrastructure support in these areas.[5] In fact, U.S. companies played a critical role in bolstering South Africa's capacity for refining imported oil and provided capital and engineering skills for the country's coal liquification projects,[6] projects that were designed to make South Africa less vulnerable to external pressures.

Despite the significant consequences of their presence, these foreign firms demonstrated a great reluctance to intervene and influence South African government policy. For example, U.S. corporate executives argued that they were in South Africa "as guests of the South African government. To antagonize the Government [was] to jeopardize the companies' ability to function."[7] The U.S. business community's recalcitrance was eventually overcome by demonstrating that the consequences of inaction on human rights issues dwarfed those associated with action. The very real prospect that the U.S. Congress would impose sanctions in 1985 drove the U.S. Chamber of Commerce in South Africa, for the first time, to apply pressure on the Botha regime by imploring it "to . . . extend voting rights to Blacks, and open a dialogue with all races and political movements."[8] In 1985 President Reagan signed an executive order disallowing government export assistance to U.S. companies in South Africa that failed to abide by the Sullivan Principles, a code of conduct on business operations in the apartheid state.[9] Appeals for reforms to apartheid were made in South African newspapers by U.S. firms just before the president signed his order.[10]

Lessons can be drawn from both these examples. Implicit in the Belgian scenario are three themes of contemporary relevance. First, as with any other factor of production, economizing on labor in a fashion inconsistent with ethical norms may produce a competitive advantage to a firm and, taken on a national scale, a comparative advantage for a nation-state. Second, competitors disadvantaged by these practices are likely to seek similar advantages for themselves. Last, to be effective, any check on the market impetus to compete by debasing labor standards must be enforceable universally, lest defectors undermine the viability of the compact. Additional, pertinent lessons flow from the South African example. First, business operations in a country with a repressive, human rights-abusing regime are capable of bolstering that regime and increasing its staying power. Second, businesses will generally respond to human rights concerns where the consequences of inaction on human rights-related issues outweigh the consequences of action.

This chapter examines these contentions. First, it analyzes the phenomenon of "globalization" and the relationship between economic integration and human rights. It pays particular attention to the concept of "constructive engagement" and proposes that the simple maximization of integration is not the most effective way of prompting human rights-sensitive development. Next, it proposes two logical "prerequisites" to constructive engagement and illustrates the extent to which these requirements are ignored in the global marketplace. Finally, it draws on the findings of the chapter to critique the Canadian government's present approach to economic integration and human rights. The chapter concludes that present Canadian policies on business and human rights are inadequate and recommends a series of reforms to these strategies.

Globalization and Public Policy

Globalization, broadly put, is the dismantling of barriers between countries. Clearly, part of what is termed "globalization" reflects new advances in technology and communications, developments that are diffuse in origin and not easily attributable to the policy agenda of governments. On the other hand, the other dimensions of globalization — those associated with increased trade and investment — reflect a progressive codification of liberalized international trade and investment laws. These developments have at their origin concrete policy decisions by governments.

GLOBALIZATION AND HUMAN DEVELOPMENT

The underlying economic justification for liberalized trade stems in large part from the concept of comparative advantage.[11] Under the classical comparative advantage model, countries engaged in trade can specialize in those endeavors that represent the most efficient allocation of their factors of production. Such a division of labor will prompt a net increase in the amount of product in circulation and lower prices than would exist if the countries were to produce the whole range of products in a closed economy. The net result will be universal gains from trade. Thus, the economic justification for liberalized trade is improvements in net economic well being.[12]

In many instances, however, trade and economic integration have been justified, not simply as a method for maximizing prosperity, but ultimately as a means of serving laudable political ends. The lynchpin of the modern trade regime, the General Agreement on Tariffs and Trade, was the brainchild of policymakers persuaded that the prolonged Depression of the 1930s and the Second World War were, in part, the product of beggar-thy-neighbor trade policies.[13] These policies were in turn the result of an anarchic international law trade regime.[14] Similarly, the European Coal and Steel Community, the precursor of the European Economic Community, and now European Union, was explicitly an effort to internationalize control over those smokestack industries most closely associated with armament production.[15]

In more recent times, proponents of economic integration between northern nations and those with poor records on human rights have urged that economic integration, or "constructive engagement," in the form of trade and investment, will meet important human development and human rights goals by sparking political liberalization — defined as including observance of human rights — in countries governed by repressive regimes. In Canada, the Business Council on National Issues (BCNI), the country's foremost business lobby group, has enunciated a constructive engagement position, arguing that companies should engage in more business with nondemocratic countries because "trade will act as a positive catalyst for change."[16] Similarly, the most recent Canadian government foreign policy statement notes that "human rights tend to be best protected by those societies that are open — to trade, financial flows, population movements, information and ideas about freedom and human dignity."[17] In a November 1998 statement, Canadian Foreign Minister Lloyd Axworthy repeated these assertions:

The issue [of the relationship between trade and human rights] has never been a crude tradeoff between promoting commerce or human rights. They are not mutually exclusive but mutually reinforcing. The promotion of good governance, democracy and human rights are essential to the creation of a climate for sustainable economic development which benefits everyone. Economic prosperity in turn enhances the prospects for stable societies that allow human rights to flourish.[18]

Supporters of constructive engagement argue that the multinational business presence in repressive countries may promote political liberalization and greater respect for human rights by exposing populations to liberal, human rights-supporting values.[19] Contact with transnational businesses is also viewed as "promot[ing] greater integration of the host country in the international community, thereby enlarging its exposure to the shared values of civilized nations."[20]

The positive spin-offs of this so-called "demonstration effect" will be reinforced by the economic growth prompted by trade and investment. This economic expansion will bring new wealth to the society and, through "trickle-down," permit the development of a middle class. The demands of this burgeoning middle class — particularly its aspirations for political participation — will, in turn, fuel the political liberalization process. Thus, economic liberalization, investment, and the operations of the free market will, through their own inexorable logic, subvert repressive governments. In the words of USA*Engage, the anti-sanctions U.S. business lobby group, market-oriented economic development causes social changes that impede authoritarian rule. These include widespread education, the opening of society to the outside world, and the development of an independent middle class. . . . This growing middle class has profound long-term political implications. . . . A well-educated independent middle class does not depend on the state for economic advancement, and thus is far more free to challenge political control. A government faced with this change must seek the support of the middle class and must respond to middle class demands for greater political freedoms, the rule of law and the elimination of corruption.[21]

To justify its position, the business group points to a strong empirical correlation between per capita income and freedom.[22]

EVALUATING GLOBALIZATION AS PUBLIC POLICY

By the logic outlined above, a principal public policy justification for economic integration has been, and remains, tied to human development. Thus, globalization is not a public policy end in itself, but merely a means to an end. It is a tool of prosperity and development whose worth and effectiveness deserves to be measured, not in terms of how closely the tool approximates the ideal of free trade per se, but with reference to how well the policy contributes to the human objectives for which it is developed. Thus, economic integration is only successful where it increases wealth, security and human rights-sensitive development.

The Organization for Economic Cooperation and Development (OECD) argued in a 1998 study that "Trade and foreign direct investment are major engines of growth in developed and developing countries alike. . . . In the last decade, countries that have been more open have achieved double the annual average growth of others."[23] However, critics urge that this economic integration and economic growth will not automatically induce respect for human rights. The widely respected political scientist Samuel Huntington, while generally supportive of the constructive engagement model, would disagree with its single-minded economic determinism.[24] Huntington points to a loose correlation between wealth as measured by gross national product/capita and democratization to hypothesize that countries in the middle-income brackets are most prone to make the transition to democracy. He uses case studies to argue that "economic development appears to have prompted changes in social structure and values that, in turn, encouraged democratization."[25] Yet, while "An overall correlation exists between the level of economic development and democracy . . . no level or pattern of economic development is in itself either necessary or sufficient to bring about democratization."[26] Other scholars have gone even further, concluding that "democracy and respect of human rights are not linked to economic development."[27]

In fact, the empirical evidence relating to constructive engagement is unconvincing.[28] A simple statistical exercise run in 1999 for the purpose of this chapter confirms the views of critics. Data on foreign direct investment as a percentage of GDP in 1980 and 1996 were drawn from the 1998 World Bank Development Indicators. As a measure of human rights, data from the 1997 Freedom House civil rights report were collected.[29] Several Pearson product moment coefficient tests were run to test for any correlation between good human rights records, as measured by Freedom House, and foreign direct investment (FDI) as a percentage of gross domestic product GDP.[30] In no instance was there any statistically significant correlation between foreign direct investment and human rights.[31] In other words, the analysis produced no evidence that those nations with high rates of foreign direct investment, as a percentage of their GDP, were more respectful of human rights than nations with lower rates.

Taken together, these findings support the view that economic liberalization alone is not a sufficient prerequisite for political liberalization. As one observer puts it, "economic growth and prosperity, if upheld in a politically restrictive context, are unlikely to pave the way for a sustainable drive toward democracy. . . . A reform strategy that focuses on both economic liberalization and the expansion of civil society will be the most viable."[32] Notably, complaints can be made that no such balanced approach is evident in many of the countries that have been "constructively engaged."[33] Similarly, even if one were to accept the constructive engagement model's validity, what follows suggests that foreign businesses often fail to live up to the theory's expectations.

The Prerequisites of Constructive Engagement

Logically, a finding that raw economic liberalization does not automatically lead to improved respect for human rights suggests, at the very best, that certain prerequisites of constructive engagement must be met if improvements in the human rights environment are to flow from economic integration. It is submitted that there are two, logical prerequisites for the effective operation of constructive engagement: adhering to workplace labor rights and avoiding complicity with human rights abuses.

Labor Rights

The liberalizing influence of business activities will likely be felt only if businesses abide by human rights standards in their own workplaces — or in the workplaces of their sourcing partners — that, at a minimum, exceed local standards. Clearly, there can be no "demonstration effect" if there is no demonstration by the firm itself. Similarly, it seems unlikely that there can be a demonstration of human rights-reinforcing "liberal democratic values" if firms turn a blind eye to abuses by their suppliers. Nor is it likely that there can be expedited growth of a middle class via economic trickle-down if the firm or its suppliers pay local wage rates in an environment where wages are actively and coercively repressed.

There remains a fair measure of debate as to what baseline standards companies should employ in their overseas operations where local standards are poor or simply not enforced. Concern has been expressed in the south that labor standards not be inconsistent with the level of economic development characteristic of the country. A government whose country's comparative advantage is said to rest on inexpensive labor costs is reluctant to see its competitiveness eroded by artificially rigid labor standards. Some northern firms pledge to apply home country standards in their overseas operations. The Confederation of Danish Industries, for example, reportedly has a set of guidelines requiring companies to pursue the same level of "social responsibility in their new host country as in their home country."[34] However, the simple importation of northern standards seems the approach most likely to give rise to excessive standards. The better approach is to apply baseline international norms.

In recent years, much attention has focused on a subset of international labor rights viewed by an increasing number of observers as fundamental and, arguably, universal. In the mid-1990s, the OECD identified four "core" labor standards found in ILO and UN conventions as human rights. These are freedom of association;[35] nondiscrimination in the workplace;[36] a ban on exploitative child labor;[37] and, a ban on forced labor.[38] According to the OECD, violation of these norms is a matter of particular humanitarian concern.[39] Labeled "fundamental principles" by the ILO, these four standards were invoked in the June 1998 ILO Declaration on Fundamental Principles and Rights at Work, a call for all ILO members to ratify the conventions containing these rights. In fact, the International Labor Organization and UN conventions in question are widely, though not universally, ratified by the states of the world.[40] It is these broadly affirmed rights that increasingly are being viewed as the minimum labor rights baseline.

Yet, while these norms are widely recognized by the world's nations, they are often honored in the breach.[41] Clearly, observing these rights increases the short-term cost of labor. As a consequence, as labor represents an important, if declining, cost of production, there may be strong incentives for companies and countries to compete by debasing even these minimal international labor standards.[42] The OECD, in a 1996 study, found "evidence that some governments felt that restricting certain core labor standards would help attract inward FDI."[43] In addition, the OECD has conceded that some firms may in fact respond to the cost advantages of repression. The OECD notes that "in a number of . . . countries which are among the primary destination for OECD investment, the record of compliance with core labor standards is tarnished, particularly with respect to freedom-of-association rights, although to different degrees." According to the OECD, "there is no definitive evidence on the extent to which FDI responds to the level of core labor standards." In fact, "low or non-existent labor standards may have a detrimental effect on FDI decisions. They indicate a risk of future social discontent and unrest, and include the risk of consumer boycotts." However, "it is readily admitted that expectations of high profitability due to the economic environment provided in host countries may be able to outweigh some of the concerns foreign investors [have] about low levels of observance of core labor standards by host government[s]."[44] Further, while the OECD was not able to identify what impacts multinationals have on core labor rights, it did note that multinationals employ most of the workers in the world's export processing zones (EPZs). As such, "the radically lower degree of unionization in EPZs in comparison with the domestic economy as a whole could suggest that [multinational businesses] do not contribute to the improvement of the practical situation of unions"[45] and, one might infer from other practices in these zones,[46] of labor rights generally. This conclusion, coupled with the rash of recent controversies related to poor labor practices by suppliers for major northern firms operating overseas,[47] suggests that the common approach of many businesses to core labor standards is strongly inconsistent with the first prerequisite of constructive engagement.

AVOIDING COMPLICITY

Logically, the improvements in human rights predicted by the constructive engagement model will occur only if the presence of the firm does not result in increased repressive activity by the regime that counters any positive human rights impacts the firm's presence might have. Further, the firm's presence must not reinforce the capacity of an abusive regime to stave off the demands for political liberalization predicted by the constructive engagement model.

In this regard, it is wrong to assume that business will invariably act in a fashion detrimental to repressive regimes. Increasingly, there are examples of "complicity" by businesses that increase the human rights-abusing *activity* of a repressive regime or augment the human rights-abusing *capacity* of that government.

With respect to *repressive activity*, the mere presence of a firm may induce a regime to increase its repressive activities and engage in human rights-abusing behavior. Thus, a regime may use repressive means to supply resources to a company by, for example, clearing people off oil-rich lands, something that is occurring in Sudan (see discussion below). In Colombia, meanwhile, Human Rights Watch has criticized two major multinational oil consortiums for retaining the services of the Colombian military to protect their pipelines. These security forces have been implicated in massive human rights abuses, including killings, beatings, and arrests.[48] In Indonesia, government army officials hired as security at a mining site on Irian Jaya have been accused of torturing and extrajudicially executing local people opposed to the mine.[49] In Nigeria, oil companies have been implicated in "the systematic suppression by Nigerian security forces of protesting local communities."[50] In Burma (Myanmar), Burmese forces providing security for the massive Yadana pipeline are said to have committed "violations against villagers along the pipeline route, including killings, torture, rape, displacement of entire villages, and forced labor."[51] In Chad and Cameroon, a coalition of European and African environmental groups and German parliamentarians have pointed to a "noticeable increase in human rights violations" in the region surrounding another multinational corporation pipeline project.[52] More recently, in India, Human Rights Watch has accused a U.S. multinational firm of being complicit in efforts by security forces to quash protest against its power project.[53]

With respect to *repressive capacity*, there are several ways in which companies augment a regime's ability to engage in human rights-abusing behavior. First, the firm may produce products used by the regime that increase its repressive capacity. For example, as noted above, two U.S. car companies were accused of supplying apartheid era South African security forces with vehicles.

Second, the firm may be a major source of revenue that increases a regime's repressive capacity. For example, the Yadana pipeline project in Burma backed by U.S., French, and Thai companies will provide the Burmese junta with its largest source of foreign capital.[54] In 1993 Petro-Canada International abandoned its Burmese operations, but not before facing intense criticism for having paid the Burmese regime a nonrefundable $6 million cash "signing bonus" for permission to conduct oil explorations.[55] More recently, Vancouver-based Indochina Goldfields announced in November 1998 the start-up of a U.S.$300 million copper mine in Burma, one that is jointly owned by the regime's mining company.[56] Edmonton-based Mindoro Resources, meanwhile, has partnered directly with the regime in a Burma gold exploration project.[57] At present, Canadian oil company Talisman's operations in Sudan are providing significant revenue to the repressive Sudanese government (see discussion below).

Third, as with apartheid era South Africa, the firm may provide infrastructure in the form of roads, railways, power stations, oil refineries, or the like, that increases a regime's repressive capacity. For example, in Burma, a country where telephones and faxes are closely controlled by the government, several international telecommunications companies — including at least one Canadian firm — have supplied, directly or indirectly, telephone equipment to the military government. Human rights groups say that this technology has been monopolized by the military regime to conduct its affairs.[58] In Sudan the government is using an airstrip and other infrastructure built or operated by Talisman and its partners for its own purposes, including to mount attacks on civilians (see discussion below).

Finally, the presence of the firm in the country may provide international credibility to an otherwise discredited regime. For example, multinational firms in South Africa provided moral support to the apartheid regime[59] and augmented the ranks of the pro-South Africa lobby abroad preaching tolerance for apartheid. More recently, opponents of foreign investment in Burma argue that

Each new foreign enterprise that sets up shop in Burma only serves to validate the regime's belief that it can get away with resorting to slave-like practices to build the infrastructure these companies need. And above all, it is political legitimacy that [the regime] is after. It's the reason why, every time another Western business executive signs an investment deal with the Burmese military power, he or she is feted in the state-run media with a laudatory story and pictures with top army officials, everyone smiling in the camera.[60]

In Nigeria "Royal Dutch/Shell provided both increased financial investment and a diplomatic public relations shield for the Nigerian [military] government."[61] In Afghanistan, a major U.S. oil company concluded a pipeline agreement with the Taliban de facto regime and reportedly actively lobbied the U.S. State Department to extend formal diplomatic recognition to the Taliban, despite the group's poor record on human rights.[62]

In each of these examples, the contribution made by the firm augments the capacity of the firm to resist the changes supposedly induced by the firm's presence.

CONCLUSION

Taken together, the analysis in this section suggests that, if the stated human rights benefits of economic integration are to emerge, businesses operating overseas should be expected to apply international core labor rights in countries where these standards are not observed. Further, steps must be taken to mitigate the negative human rights impact of business trading or investment operations in countries with repressive, human rights-abusing regimes. In other words, as noted in a 1998 report on the Asia crisis by the Canadian Senate Standing Committee on Foreign Affairs, business "has an important role to play, both in human-rights promotion and in ensuring that it itself does not contribute to abuses."[63]

Yet, as will be argued below, there is reason to query whether, to date, the Canadian government's policies have been effective in encouraging businesses to meet the "prerequisites" of constructive engagement.

Strategies for Responsible Economic Integration

In 1997, in an open acknowledgment of the weaknesses of economic determinism as foreign policy, Foreign Affairs Minister Axworthy noted that "Trade on its own does not promote democratization or greater respect for human rights. . . . The key issue here is not a crude choice between trade or human rights, but rather a need for *responsible trade.*"[64] The present Canadian approach to "responsible trade," as described by Axworthy, appears to have three prongs of relevance to this chapter: first, working to define core labor standards at the ILO; second, taking a "leadership role" at the World Trade Organization (WTO) on core labor standards; and third, supporting voluntary business codes of conduct, particularly the 1997 International Code of Ethics for Canadian Business.[65] The development of core labor standards at the ILO is discussed above. The section that follows urges that while the government's efforts in the other two areas are laudable in principle, much remains to be done to ensure that the first prerequisite of constructive engagement — adherence to labor rights — is met. Further, the Canadian government to date has done virtually nothing to grapple with the second prerequisite of engagement — curtailing business complicity with repressive regimes.

RESPONSIBLE TRADE AND UNIVERSALIZING LABOR REGULATION

Labor rights were originally considered a legitimate part of the international trading regime.[66] After the Second World War, the negotiators of the International Trade Organization (ITO) charter proposed linking trade to important labor standards.[67] While the final version of the charter diluted these and similar provisions into a mere call for members to eliminate "unfair labor conditions, particularly in production for export,"[68] the proposed ITO would likely have gone much further in legitimating consideration of labor issues in the trade context than did the General Agreement on Tariffs and Trade, the key instrument in the international trade regime following the refusal of the U.S. Senate to ratify the ITO.[69]

Since the late 1980s, U.S. legislators, galvanized by the sense that foreigners are competing "unfairly," have been reasonably persistent in arguing that the future rounds of trade talks will be dominated by the "blue and green" agenda: labor and environment.[70] Little progress to that end was made during the 1986–94 Uruguay round of trade talks themselves and the issue proved extremely divisive at the failed Seattle round in 1999. With the collapse of the talks in Seattle, the most cogent statement of the WTO's position on labor rights remains that found in the December 1996 WTO Singapore Ministerial Statement. The statement indicated that WTO members "renew our commitment to the observance of internationally recognized core labor standards." However, it concluded that the "International Labor Organization (ILO) is the competent body to set and deal with these standards, and we affirm our support for its work in promoting them." It further opined, in keeping with the constructive engagement model, "that economic growth and development fostered by increased trade and further trade liberalization contribute to the promotion of these standards. We reject the use of labor standards for protectionist purposes, and agree that the comparative advantage of countries, particularly low-wage developing countries, must in no way be put into question."[71]

Given these assertions, the WTO clearly sees the principal actor in the labor rights area as being the ILO. Yet, the ILO is hamstrung by the absence of any enforcement powers. The ILO may not compel conduct by its members and has no capacity to impose sanctions for labor rights violations.[72] While the ILO has since January 1997 promoted such initiatives as "social labeling" certifying that all goods produced in a state's territory are the product of good working standards and has moved on developing international consensus on core labor rights, its reliance on suasion rather than sanctions remains problematic.[73] As one commentator has put it, the 1996 WTO Statement, coupled with the ILO's status, "leaves the protectors of labor standards in a troublesome position: as the sole agreed-upon authority on the issue, the ILO does not have the necessary means to achieve its goals, but instead has to rely on the commitment and action of the individual countries for progress in the labor context."[74]

For its part, the Canadian government does not support linkage between trade law and labor rights. In its November 1999 position paper on the Seattle round of WTO negotiations, the government urged that "attempts in recent years by the United States and other proponents to establish a link between labour issues and the WTO have stiffened the resistance of certain developing countries to any new initiatives in this area." Instead of adopting the U.S. approach, "Canada is working with like-minded trading partners to secure official observer status for the ILO at the WTO [and] supports the establishment of a working group at Seattle that would address labour and other social policy issues within the context of globalization and trade liberalization."[75] It remains to be seen what, if anything, will come of these initiatives.

Meanwhile, at the hemispheric level, Canada is a keen proponent of regional trade blocks. A supporter and member of the North American Free Trade Agreement (NAFTA), Canada is now promoting the Free Trade Area of the Americas (FTAA). This issue of labor rights has also been raised in this venue. In October 1999, the House of Commons Standing Committee on Foreign Affairs and International Trade indicated that "Though the Committee does not support the use of trade sanctions as a means of ensuring that FTAA members comply with ILO core labour conventions, it does believe that the ILO's role in protecting the fundamental rights of workers in the Americas, and even elsewhere in the world, must be enhanced under an FTAA." To this end, it recommended that "an FTAA supplementary accord on core labour standards should protect these rights to the extent that they are protected under national legislation."[76] In its response to the report, the government indicated that Canada supports a greater role for the ILO in the Americas and that "Canada will press for the adoption of a declaration of labour principles based on principles in the North American Agreement on Labour Cooperation and the Canada-Chile Agreement on Labour Cooperation."[77]

Unfortunately, expanding existing regional labor "side agreements" is likely to do little to promote prompt observance of labor rights. One recent study of the NAFTA labor side agreement concluded that, despite some meaningful contributions to institution and norm building,

After five years there has been measurable, or even visible, progress on only two of the objectives set forth in Part One of the Agreement: encouraging cooperation to promote innovation and encouraging publication and exchange of information. On the stated objectives to "improve working conditions and living standards, . . . promote . . . the labor principles, . . . promote compliance with, and effective enforcement by each Party of, its labor law, [and] foster transparency in the administration of labor law," there has been little, if any, visible progress.[78]

As a final observation, even if the Canadian government's vision of responsible trade does not extend to a formal linkage between trade and labor at the trade agreements, there is clearly room for the government to apply its vision of "core" labor rights unilaterally to Canadian companies. The Senate Standing Committee on Foreign Affairs has noted, for example, that the government "provides extensive trade and overseas investment promotion services, including the granting of invitations on Team Canada trade missions, without first assessing the company's human rights record."[79] The Standing Committee has recommended that "In order to ensure that Canadian public funds are being spent in a manner that complements Canadian values, the provision of federal assistance to support commercial activity should be made conditional on adherence to the minimum international standard for human rights."[80] In this regard, the Standing Committee cited with approval a recommendation that

Laws should be promulgated (a) conditioning government procurement on adherence by firms to . . . core labor rights in their overseas operations; (b) conditioning financial and investment support contributions by government agencies, including the Export Development Corporation and CIDA [Canadian International Development Agency], on adherence by firms to . . . core labor rights in their overseas operations; and (c) requiring that adherence to these [standards] be assessed with reference to independently audited reports.[81]

The government has thus far rejected any efforts to impose a formal human rights screen on financial support extended to companies by the government-owned Export Development Corporation (EDC)[82] and has not moved on any of the other proposals noted by the Senate, even though doing so would, in the words of the committee, "mesh well" with the government's endorsement of voluntary codes of conduct.

RESPONSIBLE TRADE AND VOLUNTARY CODES OF CONDUCT

Much discussion in recent years has focused on business codes of conduct, the most detailed of which commit businesses to adhere voluntarily to key labor and human rights. Governments have been active in promoting these codes. In the United States, the Clinton Administration has sought to defuse criticism of its failure to consider human rights concerns during its renewal of China's most favored nation trading status by promoting, albeit softly, a model voluntary code of conduct for U.S. businesses overseas and has played an active role in the development of the Apparel Industry Partnership, a code on overseas sweatshop labor. More recently, the European Parliament has adopted a resolution urging European enterprises operating in developing countries to develop a European code of conduct that would be fairly inclusive in content and robust in terms of implementation and monitoring.[83]

Codes of conduct are becoming increasingly commonplace, with some estimates suggesting that upward of 85 percent of large U.S. companies have codes of some sort.[84] Fewer companies have codes dealing with the human rights implications of their overseas operations. In a 1996 survey of 150 U.S. multinational corporations in sectors deemed likely to have supplier codes, San Francisco-based Business for Social Responsibility found that twenty-five firms had human rights codes.[85] Another survey by Boston-based Franklin Research and Development found that roughly 10 percent of U.S. multinationals had overseas human rights guidelines.[86] A more comprehensive survey on the child labor practices of U.S. retailers and textile manufacturers by the U.S. Department of Labor in 1996 revealed that of forty-two major textile retailers and manufacturers surveyed and willing to make public their responses, thirty-six had adopted some form of policy specifically prohibiting the use of child labor in overseas production facilities. Two of the respondents also had country human rights guidelines that they used to determine in which countries they would invest.[87] Finally, a content analysis of a 1998 international sourcing report from the New York-based Council on Economic Priorities surveying prominent U.S. corporations, suggests that 80 of the 145 responding businesses had codes of conduct containing labor rights standards.[88]

The proportion of corporations in Canada that have some sort of corporate code of conduct is also high. Accounting firm KPMG, in a survey published in 2000, found that 86.4 percent of respondents in a survey of Canada's largest 1,000 companies "have a document that outlines their values and principles."[89] However, a 1996 survey of the 98 largest Canadian businesses operating internationally suggested that relatively few Canadian companies have codes of conduct dealing with the human rights impacts of their overseas operations. While 49 percent of the respondent companies reported possessing international codes of conduct, only 32 percent had codes containing some of the core labor rights, and only 14 percent had codes containing all the core labor rights. Similarly, only 14 percent had any sort of provision touching on business relations with repressive regimes.[90] The more recent KPMG survey contained broadly similar results.[91]

EFFECTIVENESS OF CODES OF CONDUCT

Given these figures, it comes as no surprise that there is a sharp debate regarding the effectiveness of codes. The dilemma implicit in the use of corporate codes of conduct as means of promoting human rights is illustrated by the example of South Africa. In 1977, the Reverend Leon Sullivan, a member of the General Motors Board of Directors, proposed the Sullivan Principles dealing with the behavior of U.S. corporations in South Africa. The principles outlined a code of conduct designed to allow U.S. corporations to operate in South Africa without partaking in the systematic human rights abuses characteristic of the apartheid regime. Many observers feel that firms generally did a good job abiding by the principles.[92] However, the success of the codes stemmed not so much from the altruism or social responsibility of the corporations as from the realization that the alternative to the code was full scale economic sanctions. Corporations were also motivated by potent shareholder pressure from large public pension funds and constraints imposed by U.S. state and municipal governments on procurement from businesses operating in South Africa.[93] In the absence of these "big sticks," adherence to the Sullivan Principles may well have been less marked.[94]

Critics contend that most modern human rights codes have been introduced by corporations, not so much in response to a management commitment to corporate social responsibility, but largely in reaction to external pressures.[95] These pressures include developments in trade law, including the introduction by the United States of a series of unilateral measures protecting workers' rights.[96] Other developments in this area include the labor rights regime under the NAFTA side agreement and the (now diminished) prospect of linkages between trade and labor rights at the WTO.[97] Litigation in U.S. courts stemming from violations of human rights abroad has also served as an incentive to adopt codes.[98] Further, pressure for corporate social responsibility from consumers, whether private or institutional, has become more marked, particularly in the retail sector,[99] as have demands from shareholders and investors.[100]

These observations regarding the importance of external pressures in inducing appropriate corporate behavior are echoed in a March 1998 report from Canada's Department of Industry. Discussing conditions conducive to successful code development, the report notes that

While codes are voluntary — firms are not legislatively required to develop or adhere to them — the term "voluntary" is something of a misnomer. Voluntary codes are usually a response to the real or perceived threat of a new law, regulation or trade sanctions, competitive pressures or opportunities, or consumer and other market or public pressures. . . . [O]nce the code is in place, the initial pressure that led to its creation may dissipate, which could cause compliance among adherents to taper off.[101]

The study urges that "voluntary codes that are well designed and properly implemented can help achieve public-interest goals. . . . However, a code that is poorly designed, improperly implemented, or used in inappropriate circumstances, can actually harm both its proponents and the public."[102] As noted by other observers, a code of conduct "is not a corporate compliance program — it is only part of it, and maybe not even the more important part of a corporate compliance program."[103] As a consequence, "the existence of a formal written corporate code of conduct is evidence that a company has begun a process of instituting a self-regulation program, but it is not conclusive evidence that the process has been completed or that it is effective."[104]

Clearly, monitoring of a code is required to ensure compliance. In 1996, in its study of corporate codes dealing with child labor, the U.S. Department of Labor noted that "a credible system of monitoring — to verify that a code is indeed being followed in practice — is essential."[105] However, relatively few corporations have codes that provide for reliable monitoring, let alone the independent audits widely viewed by human rights groups as a key aspect of long-term code effectiveness.[106] As the Department of Labor put it, "most of the codes of the respondents do not contain detailed provisions for monitoring and implementation, and many of these companies do not have a reliable monitoring system in place."[107] Overseas investigation by the department revealed that "While monitoring for product quality, and even for health and safety conditions, is customary in the garment industry, the field visits by Department of Labor officials suggest that monitoring for compliance with provisions of the codes of conduct of U.S. garment importers dealing with other labor standards — and child labor in particular — is not."[108] Where there is monitoring "there seems to be relatively little interaction between, on the one hand, monitors, and on the other hand, workers and the local community. It also appears that monitors have a technical background in production and quality control and are relatively untrained with regard to implementation of labor standards."[109]

More recently, the 1998 Council on Economic Priorities report noted above suggests that only one-third of the companies with sourcing codes included language in their codes concerning monitoring. If past patterns are any indication, even fewer of these companies rely on independent monitoring. In Canada, meanwhile, only 14 percent of the respondent firms in the 1996 survey reported use of independent monitors, while the 2000 KPMG survey suggests that even where companies include labor rights in their codes, few actively monitor these rights.[110]

"RESPONSIBLE TRADE" AND THE GOVERNMENT POLICY CONCERNING CODES OF ETHICS

Despite repeated endorsement of codes of conduct as a component of "responsible trade," Canadian government success in this area has been muted. As noted above, the Canadian government endorsed a very general international code of ethics in 1997.[111] The code takes the form of a statement of vision, beliefs, values, and principles, but contains no specific guidelines on application. On the positive side, the code pledges companies to support and promote the protection of international human rights within businesses' "spheres of influence" and not to be "complicit" in human rights abuses. The companies also vow to promote freedom of association and expression in the workplace and ensure consistency of firm practices with universally accepted labor standards, such as child labor. On the negative side, the code does not articulate exactly which human rights standards will be met, other than freedom of association and exploitation of child labor, nor precisely what each firm will do to guarantee these rights. More critically, the code includes no real provisions relating to implementation, let alone independent monitoring. Further, almost three years after its introduction, the code only has some fourteen signatories. After reviewing this code, the Senate Standing Committee on Foreign Affairs recommended that "the federal government work together with business organizations to establish a Canadian business ethics code, the coverage of which would be considerably greater than the one currently in place."[112]

More recently, the minister of foreign affairs appointed a former Liberal member of Parliament to "facilitate exploratory discussions among interested business, labor and nongovernmental organizations on the issue of voluntary codes of conduct to guide Canadian businesses when choosing foreign suppliers."[113] At the time of this writing, those discussions, principally between the Retail Council of Canada and a coalition of nongovernmental organizations known as the Ethical Trading Action Group (ETAG), have stalled, principally over the issue of free association rights.[114]

Finally, in the wake of controversy over Talisman Energy in Sudan in early 2000, the government formed a new "task force" on corporate social responsibility and indicated that it was beginning "a major discussion and consultation with Canadian companies to further strengthen codes of conduct and other means that can be established, standards for behaviour of companies overseas."[115] It remains to be seen what will come of these initiatives.

While voluntary codes of conduct represent one popular approach to overseas human rights concerns, a poorly drafted and implemented code of conduct is, at best, useless and, at worst, counterproductive insofar as it gives the appearance of action where none has been taken. Notably, in part because of the pressure/response mode of code development and because of the expense and technical difficulty in developing the independent monitoring necessary to render these codes credible, "claims about the transformative potential of private initiatives may be overstated."[116] If, as the research cited above suggests, codes are successful to the extent that the external pressures are strong, then the development and effective implementation of codes will continue to be dependent on the glare of publicity and will disproportionately affect companies with an image and a reputation to protect, particularly those in the consumer goods sector. Maintaining and broadening the spotlight on the multitude of companies, and ensuring adherence to codes, will tax the limited resources of human rights and labor groups, effectively rendering many companies immune from scrutiny.

Further, given the present preoccupation with corporate codes of conduct, some concern may be expressed that a focus on such voluntary measures will take pressure off governments to work toward more systematic means of encouraging respect for international human rights, such as linkages between trade and human rights. Relying on the existence of codes to justify a failure to take more binding action would be problematic for two reasons. First, any view on the part of policymakers that codes represent a replacement for mandatory measures ignores the fact that codes are generally developed as a response to external pressures. Second, as was noted recently by a European Parliament rapporteur on codes of conduct, "Voluntary regulation can do a great deal to promote better practice, but the worst offences will only ever be prevented through national and international laws and binding rules. Such systems can operate in parallel: binding rules to ensure minimum standards and voluntary initiatives to promote higher standards."[117] Thus, at best, voluntary codes represent a partial solution.

In this context, any endorsement by the Canadian government of voluntary codes must, first, be of well-drafted codes containing a series of prerequisite guarantees. The most reasonable standards required of the code would be core labor rights. Second, given past experience with poorly implemented codes, only codes that contain some measure of independent and credible monitoring are worthy of endorsement. Third, any code endorsement undertaken by the government should be complemented by measures creating what the federal industry department calls "conditions conducive to successful code development"; namely, "pressures for code development." Taking the steps recommended by the Senate Standing Committee in the section above would undoubtedly constitute important pressures for code development, as would liberalizing the restrictions on ethical shareholder activism extant in the present federal corporate law.[118] Finally, given the shortcomings of voluntary measures as an overarching regulatory tool, the present government fondness for codes should in no way detract from a more aggressive Canadian policy favoring a multilateral linkage between trade and labor.

RESPONSIBLE TRADE AND REPRESSIVE REGIMES: THE MISSING AGENDA

As with labor rights violations, many of the examples of business complicity with repressive regimes outlined above might be addressed, at least in part, by the adoption of detailed and effectively implemented codes and guidelines by companies. Like the Sullivan Principles, these codes would outline how firms will relate to regimes that engage in human rights abuses. A number of U.S. firms have adopted such measures on either a formal or an ad hoc basis.[119] Further, as noted above, the 1997 code of ethics endorsed by the Canadian government does indicate that companies will "not be complicit in human rights abuses." Yet the missing agenda in Canada relates to how the government will respond where Canadian companies do not act responsibly and are insulating acknowledged and seemingly incorrigible pariah regimes from the anticipated liberalizing effects of constructive engagement. The situations in Burma and Sudan provide cases in point.

BURMA

Burma is one of the most egregious human rights abusers in the world. In 1997 many Western nations concluded that engagement with Burma was ineffectual. The United States imposed unilateral economic sanctions against Burma, while Europe and Canada imposed limited trade sanctions.[120] In justifying its action, the Canadian government noted that "Canada's promotion of international human rights is founded on our longstanding principle of effective influence. . . . Dialogue and engagement generally offer the best vehicle to effect change. . . . Dialogue is, however, impossible without a willing partner. Burma's ruling State Law and Order Restoration Council (SLORC) has consistently rebuffed efforts by Canada and other countries to engage in dialogue."[121]

Foreign Minister Axworthy observed that "The actions we have taken . . . are intended to convey the seriousness of our concerns over the suppression of political freedoms and our frustration with Burma's failure to curb the production and trafficking of illegal drugs."[122] However, unlike the U.S. measures, the Canadian sanctions do not apply to investment in Burma, and the government has expressed strong reluctance to introduce more expansive sanctions, despite calls for such action from Burmese democratic leaders and the 1998 announcements of several joint ventures between Canadian firms and the repressive Burmese regime.[123]

The recognition by the Canadian government that diplomatic and trade engagement is not a workable policy vis-à-vis Burma and its failure to curtail the presence of Canadian companies in joint ventures with that country must be regarded as a clear human rights policy failure. Burma is a country in which it is virtually impossible to do business without supporting the regime at some level. As former U.S. ambassador to Burma Burton Levin puts it: "Foreign investment in most countries acts as a catalyst to promote change, but the Burmese regime is so single-minded that whatever [income] they might obtain from foreign sources they pour straight into the army while the rest of the country is collapsing."[124]

SUDAN

The Sudanese government is in the midst of a brutal civil war with ethnic groups in the country's south. In 1998 a senior member of Canada's oil patch, Talisman Energy of Calgary, acquired a 25 percent stake in what is known as the Greater Nile Petroleum Operating Company (GNPOC), an initiative located in south-central Sudan. Talisman's partners in the project are the national petroleum company of China (40 percent), the national oil company of Malaysia (30 percent), and the national petroleum company of Sudan (5 percent).

This relationship has enraged rebel leaders, who accuse Talisman of complicity with the dictatorship.[125] In North America, Talisman's presence in Sudan has prompted concerted criticism of the company. At the heart of the controversy are concerns that Talisman's presence is, in net, detrimental to human rights and human security. Specifically, Talisman's operations are said to be prolonging the civil war, both by contributing to conflict over oil fields and by generating, for the Sudanese regime, revenue used to bankroll the war.

In this regard, a November 1999 report from the UN rapporteur on Sudan suggests that the Sudanese government has used its military to "clear a 100-kilometre area around the oilfields" operated by Talisman.[126] More recently, the Canadian government-sponsored "Harker mission" to Sudan concluded that "there has been, and probably still is, major displacement of civilian populations related to oil extraction. . . . Sudan is a place of extraordinary suffering and continuing human rights violations, even though some forward progress can be recorded, and the oil operations in which a Canadian company is involved add more suffering."[127] Among other things, the Harker mission found that airfields and roads built, used and sometimes operated by the oil company have been employed by the Sudanese military in attacks against civilian populations.[128] These findings were confirmed very graphically by Amnesty International in May 2000. In its report, Amnesty noted that Sudanese forces "have used ground attacks, helicopter gun ships and indiscriminate high altitude bombardment to clear the local population from oil-rich areas." In the Talisman concession area, Amnesty speaks of government troops clearing the area around the town of Bentiu using helicopter gunships and high altitude bombardment by Antonov planes. Government troops, notes Amnesty, have reportedly committed mass executions of male villagers. Women and children are said to have been nailed to trees with iron spikes. There are reports from villages north and south of Bentiu that soldiers slit the throats of children and killed male prisoners who had been interrogated by having had nails hammered into their foreheads.[129]

In defending its presence in Sudan, the chief executive officer of Talisman has repeatedly assured shareholders that government revenues generated by the project will "be used for the benefit of the country's population, including building roads, schools and health facilities."[130] However, Sudanese government officials have been reported "as saying that the development of the oil fields is key to stepping up its program of forced Islamization of Christian and animist regions of Southern Sudan."[131] In particular, it is feared that oil will generate revenues used in the purchase of weapons. The Harker mission concluded, in fact, that "It is difficult to imagine a cease-fire while oil extraction continues, and almost impossible to do so if revenues keep flowing to the GNPOC [Greater Nile Petroleum Operating Company] partners and the [government of Sudan] as currently arranged."[132]

For its part, the Canadian Department of Foreign Affairs and International Trade indicated in October 1999 that "If it becomes evident that oil extraction is exacerbating the conflict in Sudan, or resulting in violations of human rights or humanitarian law, the Government of Canada may consider, if required, economic and trade restrictions such as are authorized by the Export and Import Permits Act, the Special Economic Measures Act, or other instruments."[133] However, upon the release of the Harker report, the Government announced a series of measures that do little or nothing to address problems caused by Talisman's presence in Sudan. On the latter issue, Minister Axworthy merely indicated that "Canada does not encourage private sector activity in Sudan. I expect Talisman, which has chosen to operate in this difficult environment, to nonetheless live up to the fundamental values of Canadians in conducting its business activities . . . Talisman must . . . ensure that their operations do not lead to an increase in tensions or otherwise contribute to the conflict."[134] Unfortunately, it is unclear what, if any steps, the Government of Canada will take should Talisman fail to respond to the minister's urgings.

Given these case studies, there is clearly a pressing need for the government of Canada to articulate a strong policy on how it will deal with Canadian corporate involvement with repressive regimes. For the last several years, confronted by calls for government action in the face of problematic Canadian corporate relations with human rights-abusing despots in several countries, the government has pleaded legal incapacity.

In this regard, some policymakers are apparently of the view that unilateral investment sanctions are impermissible under Canadian law.[135] However, the legislation in question, the Special Economic Measures Act, is clear that the cabinet may choose to impose sanctions where it is of the opinion that a grave breach of international peace and security has occurred that has resulted, or is likely to result, in a serious international crisis.[136] Clearly, this is a discretionary power, albeit one that is fettered. In the author's experience, the debate at present in policy circles focuses on what is meant by "grave breach of international peace and security." The Department of Foreign Affairs apparently takes the position that "grave breach of international peace and security" must accord with, or impose a more onerous standard than, the ill-defined international construction of this language. Thus, in its opinion, a breach would require a trans-border conflict and cabinet would be acting improperly to impose sanctions in the absence of such a conflict.

The department's position is very conservative and is largely inconsistent with the more flexible view of the act contained in the law's legislative history.[137] Critically, it has the effect of making it nearly impossible for the government to impose investment sanctions in most of the countries where Canadian business involvement with repressive regimes must be a cause of concern, including Burma and Sudan. The absence of a credible Canadian sanctions law undermines the leverage the Canadian government might have over business. As was the case with U.S. companies in South Africa, the possibility of sanctions should be viewed as a means of prompting companies to act responsibly in their investment decisions. The prospect of facing investment sanctions, should that complicity be with a serious, human rights-violating regime, might act as a real incentive to act ethically. As a consequence, reform of the Special Economic Measures Act to clarify its scope is urgently required if the Government is to respond to the second prerequisite of constructive engagement.

It should be noted that the threat of sanctions is not the only incentive mechanism available to the government to reduce the prospect of Canadian business complicity with pariah regimes. As discussed in the context of labor rights, other tools conditioning extension of certain government benefits on human rights performance are possible. In the particular case of pariah regimes, there is also a tax policy aspect. Canadian tax law allows Canadian companies to deduct a portion of their foreign business income tax from their Canadian taxes, even in the absence of a formal tax treaty between Canada and the foreign jurisdiction.[138] Even where Canada has annulled double taxation treaties on human rights grounds in the past, this unilateral tax relief has remained. Thus, when Canada annulled the Canada-South

Africa Double Taxation Agreement in 1985, critics argued that this move was largely symbolic, as companies were able to continue deducting taxes paid in South Africa and Namibia under the foreign tax credit provisions of the Income Tax Act.[139]

In 1998 the Senate Standing Committee on Foreign Affairs cited with approval a recommendation that the "government should publicly establish thresholds of systematic human rights abuses beyond which the government . . . [inter alia] will not provide tax credits for taxes paid to the regime."[140] This approach is a reasonable and logical way of reducing the incentive Canadian businesses might have to operate in countries where their operations contribute to human rights problems.

Conclusion

At present, the world community faces what Sir Leon Brittan calls "moral implications of globalization."[141] If governments do not address these issues, globalization risks fueling an antiliberalization backlash[142] and social anomie, leading some commentators to wonder if the world "may be moving inexorably toward one of those tragic moments that will lead historians to ask, why was nothing done in time."[143] As the OECD notes, "Much of the disquiet of policy-makers and broad segments of the population about liberalization owes to the fact that adjustment to a liberalized environment is . . . borne before the wider and larger tangible benefits can begin to be felt."[144] As a consequence, governments must "implement a set of policies whose central aim must be to shorten the time it takes for societies to adjust to changed economic circumstances."[145] In the context of international human rights, an assumption that economic development abroad will automatically induce improvements in human rights is not supported by the empirical record. Concrete policies on human rights are required.

The Canadian government, at present, seems to favor strongly a policy of constructive engagement, but one nuanced by a three-pronged approach to "responsible trade." As this chapter has argued, this three-pronged approach leaves much to be desired. The present emphasis on voluntary business codes of conduct is particularly problematic. First, the single code that has been endorsed by the government is inadequate in both its scope and in terms of its provisions relating to implementation. Second, the government has done nothing to maximize corporate incentives to introduce, and abide by, codes of conduct. Third, there is some concern that the government will come to view voluntary codes as a replacement rather than a supplement for more binding measures, such as a more robust linkage between the international trade and labor regimes. In this last regard, its attitude toward the linkage issue has been, at best, lukewarm. If Canada has been playing a leadership role at the WTO, as urged by Minister Axworthy, then it has led, to date, to the maintenance of the status quo. Finally, the government has failed to deal adequately with circumstances where Canadian companies are lending support to repressive regimes.

Unfortunately, multinational corporations continue to justify poor human rights practices by appealing to global competition. As in the Belgium of 1850, "If they held to higher standards, they claim, their rivals would instantly overwhelm them."[146] Meanwhile, as in the South Africa of the 1970s and 1980s, other firms have justified inaction on state abuses of human rights — sometimes committed in response to the firm's presence — by arguing that "it would be wrong to affront" the sovereignty of the countries in which they have invested.[147] Given these views, limited progress will be made until recalcitrant companies see a business incentive in acting responsibly. As one observer has put it, companies will "see the light" when they "feel the heat."[148]

If Canada is to forestall objections to liberalization by adopting policies that, in the OECD's words, "shorten the time it takes for societies to adjust to changed economic circumstances," then it should take the steps outlined in this chapter. These measures would help ensure that when Canadian businesses go abroad, they are part of the solution, not part of the problem. Otherwise, the much-touted promise of economic integration may be delayed, if not stalled, and the policy of "constructive engagement" risks becoming, to use the words of one critic, "two weasel words used in succession."[149]

5
Feminism After the State: The Rise of the Market and the Future of Women's Rights

KERRY RITTICH

The rise of the market and eclipse of the state has become one of the defining conditions of contemporary social change. The settled expectation that the state could be prevailed upon to secure greater equality and welfare for its citizens is eroding, swept away by new desire to promote the efficiency and productivity of markets. The result has been a fundamental alteration to the language and terms in which political reform must now be pursued, accompanied by new constraints on the horizon of possibilities for social justice.

The crucial idea animating the current framework is by now almost too familiar: it is that the market is the best if not the sole institution for furthering a host of social goods and objectives. So important is the market as a vehicle of growth and prosperity, in the view of its most fervent adherents, that objectives which are incompatible with its demands must be abandoned or held in abeyance, even if this means that goals such as equality and redistribution must be sidelined in the process. The softer version of the argument leads to the same place: international forces and the logic of "globalization" compel the path of the market whether we like its effects or not.

In tandem with the rise and dominance of the market is the eclipse and demotion of the state. Pundits, analysts, politicians, and even many progressive social reformers intone that the era of the state, the brief Golden Age which lasted from the end of World War II until about the mid-1970s, is now decisively over. In this widely circulating narrative, the unprecedented growth that fueled and enabled the interventionist and redistributive welfare state is gone with no prospect of return.[1] Instead we must look to the market to fulfill our individual and collective desires.

There is hardly a country that has failed to experience a new sense of retrenchment and constraint about the use of the state as a vehicle of social and economic engineering. The state, it is said, is no longer capable of fulfilling the limitless list of demands that societies at large are capable of generating. Nor can it stand behind citizens as the guarantor of even the most basic standard of living. Instead, individuals must seek their fortunes and take their chances with the market. So, too, must nation-states, which are advised that they pursue paths independent of the imperatives of global markets at their peril.[2]

Yet at the same time as the market is rising and the role of state is being cut back, human rights are still firmly fixed on the public agenda. Moreover, human rights are now often mentioned in the same breath as market reform and development.[3] Market reformers, too, are talking the language of rights.

The transformation in the relationship between the state and the market is relevant to human rights projects of every kind. However, these developments represent a particularly significant turn of events for anyone involved in antisexist work. While some of the interests of market reformers and feminists may overlap, the market poses new challenges to how human rights are conceived. However uncertain the outcome is, it seems naive to imagine that current arguments and strategies will suffice. Conflicting claims all posed in the name of furthering rights may be deeply destabilizing, requiring women's rights activists not simply to lobby on behalf of women but to justify anew why their conception of human rights should prevail over another.

The following questions emerge from this encounter. What does it mean to be in favor of human rights for women when market reformers also claim to be in favor of human rights? What happens to the old strategies for reform once the state has been demoted? How are feminists to argue with the defense that resources are at a premium or simply no longer there? How are arguments concerning the regulatory limitations thrown up by globalization to be met? What should the response be to the argument that many cherished transformative goals, including greater equity and redistribution, are simply no longer proper public goals? In such a world, how do we, *can* we, sell women's rights on the market?

Although no final or "global" assessment of its effects is possible, the rise of the market generates a number of concerns. First, a relatively effective and well-endowed state has been one of the major background conditions of nearly every project to improve the status of women. Against and with culture, society, and tradition, the state has classically been the entity called upon to effect and implement transformative gender change. When rights become the vehicle for change, a powerful state becomes yet more central. Legally, the state is the entity responsible for ensuring that human rights obligations, however defined, are met. Any failure of the state or constraints on its ability to act thus poses an inescapable challenge to all rights-based claims. Second, global economic integration itself appears to be generating greater vulnerability and insecurity on the part of workers, a disproportionate number of whom are women.[4] However, regulatory and policy responses are so far largely absent, precluded or discouraged by the idea that they run counter to the demands of the market. The risk of structural disadvantage for women in the markets in which we are to now have faith appears high.

One of the most urgent priorities is to rethink the possible projects and trajectories for the empowerment of women in light of this turn to the market. We need to consider how this shift from the state to the market has affected the agenda for social transformation. Only if we do this, can we figure out if, how, and in what ways we need to either join or resist the hegemony of the market. It seems unlikely, given the varied ways in which the turn to the market manifests itself, that a single analysis will prove persuasive or definitive. However, the following observations are intended to provoke a sense of urgency in thinking about this problem in concrete contexts.

The prospects for women become more visible if these developments are placed in relief against the history of social reforms in the West. It has long been observed by feminists, antiracists, and antipoverty activists that reliance on the state carries a number of risks. State programs ostensibly designed to assist the disadvantaged have historically been accompanied by paternalist interventions which work to undercut the autonomy and authority of those who are the object of attention. Assistance by the state is a mixed blessing and offers of state aid and intervention are to be approached warily.

Gender and racial bias in the crafting of social assistance has often meant that women are cast as welfare or charity recipients who, moreover, may be compelled to defend their moral worth in order to receive aid.[5] By contrast, state programs instituted to assist men, such as pensions and unemployment insurance, are typically characterized as the earned entitlements of deserving citizens. Welfare benefits accordingly are continually at risk of being cut back while social security benefits are something that governments tamper with at great peril.

Finally, various parts of the state apparatus work at cross purposes and are subject to capture by special interests; the result is that initiatives in the public good may be derailed or defeated both directly and indirectly. As long as most women lack significant economic and political power, they are likely to be the "special interests" who can be ignored rather than those who will be heard and prevail in the contest over resources.

Notwithstanding those limitations, the state has always been the privileged locus and agent of reform in both the domestic and international women's rights movement. Although there have always been grassroots strategies for social change, almost every objective which has been identified and adopted within the women's human *rights* community has required some action on the part of the state. The programs of action which have been developed at the international level to address gender issues, from the Nairobi Forward-Looking Strategies[6] to the Beijing Platform,[7] are pervaded with calls on the state to assist, underwrite, support, finance and facilitate in myriad ways improvements in the status of women.

While these documents contain basic demands for reforms to ensure that laws are nondiscriminatory, they also contain countless exhortations to states to either channel new resources to women or to reallocate existing resources in a more equitable manner. No objective escapes this need for either more resources or more regulatory "intervention." For example, the eradication of violence against women and increased reproductive health and freedom both require greater public resources, whether in the form of more police resources, greater health expenditures, or new public education projects.

The turn to the market appears to place enormous constraints on these efforts: both more money and more intervention on the part of the state are precisely what are now said to be ruled out. Fears about (de)regulatory competition and calls to increase national competitiveness and productivity in global markets all tend to operate in the service of the idea that a good market is one which leaves capital relatively unencumbered and unfettered by national, local, or "particular" concerns.

Marketing Women's Rights

In the wake of the battles that beset the drafting of the Beijing Platform, it is no secret that the language of equality and the nature of human rights are contested territory, both among different women's groups and between women's rights activists and those furthering quite different agendas. By now, feminists are wearily experienced in the ways in which family values, freedom of religion, and cultural autonomy, all values which shelter under the capacious reach of the international human rights regime, are regularly contra posed to initiatives to improve the status of women.

The debate over the virtues and limitations of market-centered policies represent one of the most important new fronts in the social justice wars. The deployment of rights claims by promarket reformers promises to raise the stakes in this debate. All human rights activists have to confront the fact that the discourse of human rights can be and is being used to support varied agendas, some of which may run directly counter to transformative goals. Feminists in particular need to engage in a critical analysis of the uses of human rights discourse in proposals for economic reform.

The focus on human rights on the part of market reformers seems to have a number of different sources. Institutions such as the World Bank have come to recognize the value of women to the general project of development. As a result, development strategies now frequently include references to the importance of special measures to assist women as well as the institution of nondiscrimination policies and the enhancement of women's rights.[8] Second, market reformers are deeply preoccupied with the issue of good economic governance[9] and the implementation of market-friendly legal institutions and rules.[10] Human rights now sometimes appear in this context too. Third, human rights may form part of the general political and economic case for market reform.

What is evident is that, on a rhetorical level, market reform has become increasingly allied with the pursuit of human rights. Through claims such as that markets are the natural and necessary arena for the exercise of human freedom, or that markets further democracy and human rights while nonmarket-based societies or incompletely market-based societies are incapable of or deficient at furthering human rights, market reformers suggest that respect for markets is necessary to, if not coextensive with, respect for human rights.

At the same time, the state is represented as the principal threat to democracy and freedom. Limits on state power and "arbitrary" state interventions through rights are therefore crucial. Moreover, markets are precisely the instrument needed to perform this task, because the ability of capital to invest or depart exerts a disciplinary power over states while market actors create a demand for law.[11] Private property rights have pride of place in this market-friendly conception of rights: not only do they promote work, encourage investment, and reward individual effort and good judgment, they also counteract totalitarian political tendencies and contribute to social stability.[12] Thus, protecting property rights becomes not simply foundational to markets but integral to human rights.

Because of the normative power of human rights discourse, market reforms gain credibility and stature by the degree to which they can be associated with the furtherance of human rights. More important, through the language of rights which is common to both market regimes and human rights, specific regulatory, policy, and institutional structures become linked to the defense of human rights and associated with the presence or absence of the rule of law. For example, the respect for property rights and the enforcement of contracts, key legal and institutional concerns among market reformers, are often described simply as "respect for rights" and increasingly, respect for "human rights." This linkage permits reformers to argue from the inviolability of property rights to the respect for the rule of law, thus forging an apparently necessary and inevitable link between markets and human rights.

While market reformers have so far proved adept at establishing potential links between markets and human rights, this relationship remains highly contingent. As the recent debates at the highest levels of the international financial institutions disclose,[13] there is no stable consensus about the requirements of good economic governance or the desirability of different forms of regulation. Market-based societies take many institutional forms, and there is no single set of rules and regulations that is unequivocally associated with economic growth over time.

Stability and certainty are also lacking in the field of human rights. The new prominence of human rights discourse among activists and social reformers has resulted in a rapidly expanding corpus of human rights. The human rights community frequently speaks about respect for human rights in ways that suggest that human rights are reenforcing and conflict-free; indeed, the equality, indivisibility, and interdependence of all human rights are now enshrined in the Vienna Declaration of Human Rights.[14] Notwithstanding, many human claims remain contested and aspirational; others remain unrecognized for all practical purposes. In any event, rights claims may conflict with each other in particular circumstances if not as a general rule.

One of the unavoidable implications of this state of affairs is that there is enormous potential for contestation and conflict in the mutual pursuit of markets and human rights. Arguments about the automatic harmonization and convergence of markets and human rights or the natural congruence of all human rights are unlikely to provide closure to this debate. Rather, the fact that parties on all sides can, and frequently do, frame their claims in terms of rights should invite a rethinking of any assumption on the part of women's rights or human rights advocates that rights claims will provide a trump even at the normative level in such debates[15] or that in sheltering under the umbrella of human rights, progressive reformers have found a place of refuge. However, it also suggests that market reformers do not have the last word on human rights.

In order to assess the claim that reforms make it better or worse for any particular group, we need to know both what sort of market is envisioned and what idea of human rights is at stake. We need to know the specific regulatory structure that is proposed and the background conditions against which market reforms are to be implemented. We also need to know how different groups are positioned in the market and how the division of labor functions, both within particular sectors of the economy and within households. In short, there are myriad contingencies that might affect the outcomes of market reforms. Nonetheless, there are reasons to interrogate the links between markets and human rights.

Human rights have always been projects in the diffusion and normalization of particular cultural values and political institutions. For this reason, the discourse of human rights retains an imperial impulse cached within its universalist frame. This is the source of the endless debate around universalism and cultural relativism that is part of the organizing structure of the field. It also lies at the heart of the persistent critiques that have been levied by Third World international scholars and activists about the uses of human rights by activists from the West. However, human rights have been used against dominant practices for liberatory, transformative purposes as well. Women's rights activists have used the normative power of human rights to relentlessly challenge dominant conceptions of the normal, the everyday, in particular, normal practices in the family and the market. It is the critical valence of human rights that activists have hitched to the pursuit of social and political change that is now at risk.

Current market reforms can also be understood as a project to normalize and standardize certain practices, rules, and institutions in an attempt to both reflect and construct the normal or optimal relationship between the state and the market. In the words of Suzanne Berger, "The case for convergence or harmonization of national structures . . . rests on the notion of a unique, natural, hence legitimate, set of institutions and market rules for capitalism."[16] To the extent that human rights form part of this venture, it is likely that some normalized and standardized version of human rights will come to prevail as well. While this might appear to be a beneficial development, it carries a number of risks; as the project of market reform becomes conjoined with human rights rhetoric, the effect may be to flatten its critical or transformative edge.

First, the perceived demands of markets can be expected to feed back into the way that human rights are conceptualized and reshape the definition of a human rights-respecting society. The attempt to construct a version of human rights that is consistent with the project of market reform seems destined to set limits on the use of the discourse; at minimum, it is likely to reestablish a hierarchy within the corpus of human rights. This process of recognition, prioritization, and exclusion of rights in turn might be expected to place limits on the social and economic policies, as well as the resources, that can be legitimately marshaled to further transformative political objectives. Second, the discourse of human rights may lose much if not all of its critical bite against the "normal" institutions and practices of liberal market societies. Third, as the concepts of markets and human rights become more closely interwoven, human rights complaints are likely to be leveled at those practices that are perceived to be "market deviant." Indeed, practices that might otherwise be defended as congruent with if not necessary to human rights may themselves come to be characterized as violations of rights. Instances of this trend are already discernible, for example in the area of pay equity, which will be discussed below. Finally, to the extent that the arguments about the convergence and harmonization of markets and human rights succeed, crucial investigations of the links between market reforms and adverse effects for certain individuals, groups, regions, communities, and states may be foreclosed or simply seem unnecessary.

It is worth thinking through the extent to which these tendencies might place constraints on transformative gender projects. Marginalized groups classically attempt to engage the power of human rights discourse by shifting the focus away from civil and political rights, the traditional human rights priorities, to the relatively more neglected economic, social, and cultural rights and "third generation" rights to development. Alternatively, they attempt to attract both attention and legitimacy by reconceptualizing new and old issues as questions of human rights.

Both of these techniques have been used by women's rights groups. Feminists have argued that the use of human rights as a vehicle to empower women and redress sex disadvantage compels heightened attention to economic, social, and cultural entitlements.[17] In addition, using both internal and external modes of critique, they have extended the conception of human rights to cover harms typically experienced by women.[18]

It is significant for women, then, that to the extent that human rights form part of the agenda for market reform, what is incorporated is a relatively restricted vision of rights. Respect for human rights in a market-centered society appears to have little if anything to do with the expansive list of concerns reflected in CEDAW;[19] instead, "market friendly" approaches to human rights remain decidedly minimalist. Market reformers typically make no mention of social and economic rights or, for that matter, the right to development; indeed, they emphatically reject most notions of social entitlements and resist the redistribution of resources in more than trivial ways. As large parts of the total corpus of human rights are sacrificed to fit the market, so often are aspirations to greater equality and concrete commitments to improving access to resources.

The constraints that a commitment to unfettered markets place on substantive entitlements and progressive social agendas is already evident in current discussions around the development of international labor rights in the global economy. Endorsing a distinction between "core rights" and other labor standards, the ILO Declaration on Fundamental Principles and Rights at Work identifies as fundamental rights: freedom of association, the elimination of forced labor, the abolition of child labor, and the elimination of employment discrimination.[20] However, the declaration makes no attempt to incorporate as worker entitlements such traditional labor concerns as minimum wages, maximum hours, and health and safety standards. Nor does it address what are arguably central problems for workers in the global economy, the growing insecurity and continuous wage competition that global production engenders. Instead, it makes clear that the declaration should not be used for protectionist purposes or to call into question the comparative advantage of any country.[21]

The commitment to procedural and associational rights rather than substantive improvements in the position of workers reconceives important parts of the traditional workers' rights agenda and largely accommodates rather than challenges the strength of capital in global markets. It also reflects the concerns of developing nations who fear that the motivation of higher labor standards is to undercut their single most important comparative advantage in global production, low cost (often female) labor. However legitimate such concerns may be, in the encounter with the market, the space to pursue workers' rights has been simultaneously remodeled and reduced.

The dangers of the linkage between markets and human rights for a host of disadvantaged groups, including women, seem clear. Every sign on the horizon suggests that many of the projects and policies that have been advanced in the name of women's human rights may be placed to the side or defined out of the canon. Because of the limitations on state action which are perceived to flow from economic integration and capital mobility, women's rights are at risk of being categorized as: the claims of a "special interest" group which can and should be ignored; undesirable state intervention; burdensome social costs which can no longer be afforded; or impediments to the productive operation of the market.

However seductive and even encouraging it may seem that market reformers have now taken up the banner of human rights, those who think of human rights as vehicles for the empowerment of the disadvantaged need to examine closely the way that the rhetoric of human rights is now being deployed. At minimum, the mass of conflicts over the concept of human rights and the very different ideas about social justice and how to obtain it which lie barely submerged below the surface need to be confronted and exposed.

Gender Equity in the New Market Regime

What form do "market-friendly" approaches to equality take? In particular, how is gender equity promoted in market-centered regimes?

The starting point is gender blindness and gender neutrality. In the view of most market reformers, women are entitled to participate in the market and to sell their services on the same terms as men. For this reason, market reformers typically support anti-discrimination measures with respect to access to education and participation in labor markets. However, it is not clear that concerns about discrimination will extend beyond overt, intentional barriers to market entry based on sex.[22] While "adverse effect" or "adverse impact" discrimination and systemic discrimination are recognized in varying forms in the domestic civil and human rights laws of Canada and the United States,[23] as discussed below, measures to redress systemic discrimination which require an assessment of the impact of facially neutral laws and practices on specific groups are often rejected as incompatible with markets and targeted for repeal.

To the extent that any special consideration for women is thought necessary, "market-friendly" solutions that make virtually no demands on state resources and do not require regulation of market activity tend to be encouraged. Variants of these approaches are now avidly promoted by the international financial institutions as the preferred way to advance women's economic prospects. A classic example is the micro-enterprise credit program announced at the Fourth World Conference on Women in Beijing in 1995 by the World Bank. The Consultative Group to Assist the Poorest (CGAP), a multiparty effort modeled after the successful Grameen Bank of Bangladesh, lends small amounts of capital to women who would otherwise have no access to resources; the loan recipients then collectively guarantee the repayment of each other's debts. This solution is so popular with the bank that it now invariably appears at the top of the list of solutions to women's labor market problems. The Self-Employed Women's Association (SEWA), a trade network assisting women engaged in low-wage labor, home-based work, and the marketing of homemade goods in India,[24] is also repeatedly invoked as a model for women.

Institutions such as the World Bank also encourage an expanding role for NGOs and the "community" or "civil society" in program development and service delivery for the poor or disadvantaged.[25] This is a trend which is consonant with the move toward decentralized and privatized welfare and service provision; it can be expected to increase in tandem with the diminished role for the state.

The very same strategies are also enthusiastically endorsed by the international human rights community and reflected in documents such as the Beijing Platform.[26] At least part of the reason is the following: human rights activists are naturally interested in empowering people at the local level and avoiding the well-documented defects and drawbacks of top-down social reform. The result is at least a partial convergence between "grassroots" strategies and the market-based strategies for combating poverty among women.

The prominence given to solutions such as micro-enterprise credit should give us pause. Projects such as these are sure to form part of the transformative agenda for women in the future. However, these strategies cannot be regarded as anything close to an adequate response to the labor market problems facing women, nor can they substitute for other solutions. The enthusiasm of institutions such as the World Bank for such innovations is not difficult to comprehend; they are seen as "win-win" solutions. In general, such programs displace responsibility to the "private" realm, often without equivalent shifts in resources. Although some seed money may be involved, in general, they require little in the way of dedicated resources. Moreover, they interfere not at all with the general trajectory toward devolution of services, deregulated markets, and minimal states.

These projects should be identified as the valiant self help strategies they are. Yet communities and NGOs frequently face funding constraints equal to or greater than those of the state and often cannot hope to fill the gap created by the elimination or absence of state subsidies. Moreover, there is ample evidence that the withdrawal of state funding and services which is characteristic of market-driven development itself may directly exacerbate the disadvantage of women. Women routinely experienced measurable deterioration in well being and status relative to men upon the implementation of structural adjustment programs in Latin America and sub-Saharan Africa during the debt crises in the 1980s and 1990s. Marked by extreme fiscal austerity and reductions of funding in the social sector, they imposed new burdens on women and undermined a range of investments and activities which were crucial to redressing gender disadvantage.[27] Similarly disadvantage was visible in Central and Eastern Europe where, in general, women suffered disproportionately high levels of unemployment when labor market supports such as subsidized child care were reduced or eliminated.[28]

However desirable these market-friendly strategies are, it is important to see them as a very partial and limited solution to the economic disadvantage of women. Moreover, the enthusiasm of market reformers for these projects should be identified as part of a larger strategy in which other solutions which do entail state action or regulatory reform, solutions that will undoubtedly be essential to redress gender inequity in many cases, are barred from consideration because they conflict with the current ideology about the proper role of the state in a market economy.

Pursuing Labor Market Equity

Women typically face a raft of complex barriers to labor market participation. Among the most significant are caregiving and reproductive obligations that, unless shared or compensated in some way, tend to position women at a disadvantage to men in paid employment.[29] As a consequence of the retrenchment of the state and the privatization of many social services, many women now labor in the market in conjunction with increasingly onerous "private" obligations. Countless women simply bear the burden of combining paid and unpaid work, with little prospect or expectation that it could be otherwise. The women who will fare worst in this scenario are not the middle class and professional women in the industrialized economies, some of whom have achieved the market success that is imagined by reformers and are consequently able to purchase services in the market. Instead, it is abundantly clear that among the most exploited and disadvantaged women are those in developing countries, as well as the immigrants, ethnic minorities, and nonwhite women who almost invariably constitute the peripheral economy in the industrialized economies.

Although they offer no alternatives, market reformers are categorically *not* enthusiastic about many of the strategies that have been identified as crucial to securing labor market access for such women on more favorable terms, such as regulations mandating extensive maternity and parental leave, state-subsidized day care,[30] and pay or employment equity initiatives. Instead, these options are now ostensibly beyond consideration because of the imperative to reduce the tax and regulatory burdens on capital. The general skepticism toward labor market regulation also works to impair the extension of labor and employment standards and benefits to those engaged in the burgeoning forms of "flexible," nonstandard work in the economy. Many of the poorest and most vulnerable of these workers, both in industrialized and developing nations, are women.[31] The following brief examples illustrate the direction of current market-based reforms and their implications for women.

Pay Equity

One of the most basic and least contentious demands of the women's human rights movement has been labor market access and wage parity for women. In some states, attempts to advance this goal have taken the form of pay equity or comparable worth legislation. Such legislation is designed, within a limited sphere, to redress the persistent undervaluation of women's work that flows from occupational segregation by gender. It ensures that equivalent work between men and women, typically evaluated in terms of skill, effort, responsibility, and working conditions, is compensated at equivalent rates.[32] How is this rather modest goal faring in the era of the market?

A recent ruling on pay equity in the Canadian federal public service sparked a flurry of protest,[33] including calls on the editorial pages of a national newspaper for repeal of the legislation.[34] Although cloaked in an argument over whether the tribunal had adopted the appropriate methodology for calculating the disparity in wages, at base, the dispute is over the desirability of comparing the value of work done by men and women.

Opponents of pay equity argue that there is no "objective" way of comparing the value of the work that men and women do, they object to the cost of pay equity adjustments, and they contest the entire enterprise of interfering with the market valuation of women's labor. This, despite the fact that it is unfettered market forces that have produced the continued undervaluation of women's work in a gender-segregated labor market.

Part of what is going on is a realization that the implementation of the most basic of anti-sexist goals, equal pay for work of equal value, may cost a considerable sum of money. Because the sum has accumulated over time, a result of the lengthy passage of the case through the adjudicative process and the resistance encountered to the implementation of the legislation at every stage, it is now visible as a cost to the taxpayer in ways that other expenditures are not. Although it could be argued that years of underpayment relative to men has effectively required female employees to subsidize the services provided, quick on the heels of this financial calculation are admonishments to call off the whole enterprise. Many adherents of market solutions, including some who would no doubt imagine themselves to be liberal and egalitarian, want no part of such remedies.

Developments such as these might be taken as a harbinger of the future. To the extent that the eradication of gender disadvantage involves the redistribution of resources, in an era of market dominance, such efforts are likely to be increasingly resisted on both normative and economic grounds.

DEALING WITH REPRODUCTIVE LABOR

It has by now long been observed among feminists and many development economists,[35] even if it is often ignored or resisted in the mainstream development community, that productive economic activity comprises both market and nonmarket work. Notwithstanding this resistance, it is uncontentious that nonmarket labor contributes enormously to national economies.[36] What is less obvious is that market activity is also heavily reliant on uncompensated, so-called "unproductive" labor.

In all societies, women perform the bulk of unpaid work. Apart from the disadvantage that arises because women are not directly compensated for a large part of their labor, this unpaid work constrains women's labor market options. Because of the disparity in reproductive obligations between men and women, disadvantage in the labor market cannot be redressed without considering the organization of the private sphere and the resources that cross the boundary between households and markets.

Remedying the ongoing disadvantage for women in the market thus appears to require compensating or cross-subsidizing this unpaid work in some way. This is an old problem, one that predates the dominance of market-centered policies. However, it has taken on a new urgency as reductions in state support for caregiving work and the decline of dependence on male providers compel more women to enter the labor market. Current market reform proposals do not begin to contemplate redressing the disparities in work and leisure between men and women or transforming the manner in which work is organized across the boundaries of the market and the household. Instead, market reform projects are designed to protect markets from such distributive and social considerations.

LABOR MARKET (DE)REGULATION

Given the gendered division of labor, there is no obvious way to deal with the persistent devaluation of women's paid work or the disadvantage in the labor market engendered by women's reproductive obligations short of regulating the market for labor. However, market-centered reforms appear to place formidable barriers to the strategies to redress such economic disadvantage. Market reformers exhibit a marked antipathy to regulatory interventions except to the extent that they enhance the efficiency of transactions. Labor market regulations as a class do not pass this test; instead, they are routinely characterized as impediments to efficiency and growth[37] and, frequently, as undesirable or illegitimate exercises in redistribution as well.[38]

Current market reforms are marked by attempts to institute a sharp separation between public and private concerns and underpinned by claims that there are distinct and appropriate functions for different institutions and actors in market societies. Under market-centered logic, distributional concerns are be dealt with through taxation and income transfers rather than regulatory responses, as interventions to alter the allocation of resources and power in the market "distort" the operation of efficient markets. They are thought to be increasingly unavailable in any event because of the regulatory competition inherent in integrated markets. Yet at the same time there are a host of reasons why "excessive" taxation and redistribution are also unwise or impossible. In short, market reformers provide no clear way out of this structural disadvantage experienced by women.

How a direct collision between the demands for ever more efficient markets and equity for women is to be avoided is unclear, for it is the boundaries of the market and the appropriate regulatory structure governing market activity that are both central to market ideology and the place where the transformation must occur if the prospects for women are to be improved.

While there are likely to be a range of responses and solutions to this dilemma, the following elements have to be pieces of the puzzle. It has long been established that the market is a constructed institution formed through countless decisions on the part of the state about how and when to intervene or abstain from intervening. As a result, the market is inevitably both subject to and the product of various forms of regulation.[39] When the primacy of "private" rights over regulation is invoked, the inescapable hand of the state in structuring private transactions and enabling the exercise of power and coercion by private actors is often shielded and obscured in the process. It is clear that these insights need to be publicly revived and rearticulated as part of the case for reexamining the way that markets function. This is a task that should become easier, however, as market reformers themselves make the case not simply for "deregulation" but also for specific forms of protection and regulatory interventions to enhance efficiency. Such demands should stimulate a closer look at the way that different forms of regulations create incentives for certain types of behavior, shift costs and burdens, and allocate income to different groups. It should also lead to a greater appreciation of the extent to which choice is involved in the design of markets.

As this exercise takes place, it will be crucial to argue *against* the trend toward cordoning off the market from the state and other social spheres such as the household and the community. Such barriers prevent an appreciation of the functional interdependence of market and nonmarket activity and the position of particular groups within it. Instead, we need to trace the links and chart the real flow of labor, resources, entitlements, and power between the market and the state on one hand, and the market and the family and community on the other. Only then can we appreciate the way in which the economy operates as a whole; only then are we in a position to consider how the regulatory and policy options that are available might affect the prospects of different groups.

6
Advancing Safe Motherhood Through Human Rights

REBECCA J. COOK

The Challenge

Every year worldwide, an estimated 585,000 women die of complications of pregnancy and childbirth,[1] a rate of 1,600 maternal deaths each day. At least seven million women who survive childbirth suffer serious health problems, and a further fifty million women suffer adverse health consequences after childbirth.[2] The overwhelming majority of these deaths and complications occur in developing countries, and most could be prevented by cost-effective health interventions.[3] Countrywide maternal mortality rates present the largest discrepancy in any public health statistics between developed and developing countries.[4]

The causes of maternal deaths and disabilities are multiple and complex.[5] They range from the most immediate medical causes to the more extenuated health system and sociolegal conditions. They include

medical causes, consisting of direct medical problems, such as excessive bleeding during pregnancy or delivery, or infection, and of indirect preexistent or coexistent medical problems that are aggravated by pregnancy, such as anemia or malaria;

health systems laws and policies that affect availability, accessibility, acceptability, and quality of reproductive health services; and

underlying sociolegal conditions, such as lack of enforcement of minimum age of marriage laws and of alternatives to early marriage and childbearing for teenage girls.[6]

Local assessment and examination through public health, legal, and social science research may show that the immediate and extenuated causes may vary according to community.

The failure adequately to reduce maternal mortality represents one of the greatest social injustices of our times. It highlights the failure and even the refusal of political, religious, health, and legal institutions to address the most fundamental way in which women are different from men. These hundreds of thousands of avoidable deaths each year are continuing evidence and condemnation of the unstated presumption on which many societies are organized, namely that the lives of mothers are expendable and that women do not matter.

My thesis is that the preventable rate of maternal mortality is but a symptom, a tragic symptom, of a larger social injustice of discrimination against women and violation of women's human rights that societies are unwilling to prevent, remedy, and punish. The impressive work of the health professions in recent decades to devise effective health interventions[7] and monitor their availability and use[8] is a necessary, but not sufficient condition, for the reduction of maternal mortality. The reduction of avoidable maternal death is a matter not only of effective health interventions, but also of social justice.

The overarching challenge in applying human rights to advance safe motherhood is to characterize women's multiple disempowerments, not just during pregnancy and childbirth, but from their own births, as a cumulative injustice that governments are obligated to remedy. The task ahead is to show how the reproductive health risks that women face are not mere misfortunes and unavoidable natural disadvantages of pregnancy, but rather injustices that societies are obligated to prevent and remedy through their political, health, and legal systems. The recharacterization of avoidable maternal mortality from a health disadvantage to a social injustice places governments under a legal obligation to remedy the injustice.

There are two related conditions for the advancement of safe motherhood through human rights.

First, it must be recognized that simply describing a claim as a human right does not in itself give it the legal force that human rights possess. Claims gather legitimacy through the growing recognition that they are not simply concessions that individuals want for themselves, and that their denial is an injustice within the standards of fairness societies take pride in protecting. The first condition is therefore that avoidable maternal mortality be recognized as a denial of human dignity constituting an injustice which states are obligated to remedy.

Second, countries must be able to recognize that claims to human rights arise from within their own cultures, traditions, and constitutions, and that their duties are not an imposition that other countries want to place on them. Countries' standards of fairness are frequently found within their own constitutions, legal orders, and ethical codes. When the treatment of women is considered unjust, it is not only because countries are violating international treaties, but also because they are failing to satisfy the standards of their own constitutions and laws through which they profess to govern themselves. The second condition is therefore that countries recognize that they are violating their own values by neglecting to address the preventable causes of maternal mortality.

The historic confrontation mounted against racism has much in common with the confrontation now being mounted against the sexism that conditions maternal mortality. The right of racial nondiscrimination was not achieved simply by naming it a human right. Countries like the United

States and more recently South Africa had to come to terms with the fact and injustice of their own racism before advancement was possible toward its elimination. Similarly, describing safe motherhood as a human right will not advance women's interests in safe maternity before the institutions of political, religious, professional, social, and other power within countries come to terms with the fact and injustice of their own sexism. Discrimination against women that leaves their survival in maternity of insufficient importance to compel the allocation of protective resources must be tackled in order for safe motherhood to be advanced.

Human Rights Relevant to Safe Motherhood

Many of the human rights that currently exist in national laws and regional and international human rights treaties can be applied to advance safe motherhood. The fact that human rights have been applied so infrequently to governmental neglect of avoidable maternal mortality shows that human rights are still tied to their gendered origins. However, the enforcement of human rights in recent decades to advance women's access to reproductive health services and information provides promise of their capacity for development to advance safe motherhood.[9] Significantly, documents developed through the 1994 United Nations Conference on Population and Development,[10] held in Cairo, its five-year review, popularly called Cairo Plus Five,[11] the 1995 UN Fourth World Conference on Women,[12] held in Beijing, and its five-year review, Beijing Plus Five,[13] set standards for holding governments accountable.

Sources

Sources of human rights are found in all national legal systems and in international and regional human rights treaties based on the Universal Declaration of Human Rights, adopted by the UN General Assembly in 1948.[14] The Universal Declaration itself was not proposed as a legally enforceable instrument, but it has gained legal acceptance and legal enforceability through a series of international human rights conventions. The primary modern human rights treaty concerning women's rights is the Convention on the Elimination of All Forms of Discrimination Against Women ("Women's Convention").[15] This gives expression to the values implicit in the Universal Declaration of Human Rights and reinforces the declaration's two initial, legally binding, implementing covenants, the International Covenant on Civil and Political Rights ("Political Covenant")[16] and the International Covenant on Economic, Social and Cultural Rights ("Economic Covenant").[17]

Similarly derived from the Universal Declaration are the Convention on the Rights of the Child ("Children's Convention")[18] and the regional human rights conventions of legal force, including the European Convention for the Protection of Human Rights and Fundamental Freedoms ("European Convention"),[19] the American Convention on Human Rights ("American Convention"),[20] the American Declaration of the Rights and Duties of Man,[21] and the African Charter on Human and Peoples' Rights ("African Charter").[22]

Human rights treaties have committees that monitor state compliance with their obligations to bring their laws, policies, and practices into compliance with treaty provisions. For example, the Women's Convention established the Committee on the Elimination of Discrimination Against Women (CEDAW), the Political Covenant established the Human Rights Committee, and the Economic Covenant established the Committee on Economic, Social, and Cultural Rights to monitor state compliance with these respective treaties. These committees make concluding observations on reports submitted by governments on what they have done to bring their laws, policies, and practices into compliance with the respective treaties.

These committees also issue general comments or recommendations that give guidance on the content and meaning of the different rights. For example, CEDAW issued General Recommendation 24 on women and health,[23] explaining states' legal duties to respect rights by not obstructing their exercise, to protect rights by taking positive action against third party violators, and to fulfill rights by employing governmental means to afford individuals the full benefit of their human rights. This recommendation applies human rights to women's health in the following ways: "The obligation to *respect rights* requires States Parties to refrain from obstructing action taken by women in pursuit of their health goals. States Parties should report on how public and private health care providers meet their duties to respect women's rights to have access to health care."[24]

The recommendation explains that states are obliged to change laws or policies that, for instance, require women to seek the authorization of their husbands, parents, or health authorities to obtain health services, because such laws or policies obstruct women's pursuit of their health goals. This recommendation also explains that "laws that criminalize medical procedures only needed by women and that punish women who undergo those procedures" may violate the Women's Convention.[25]

The general recommendation further explains that: "The obligation to *protect rights* relating to women's health requires States Parties, their agents and officials to take action to prevent and impose sanctions for violations of rights by private persons and organizations."[26] The recommendation emphasizes that the duty to protect requires the "enactment and effective enforcement of laws that prohibit . . . marriage of girl children,"[27] which would reduce the risks of premature pregnancy and hazardous maternity.

General Recommendation 24 goes on to make clear that "The obligation to *fulfil rights* places an obligation on States Parties to take appropriate legislative, judicial, administrative and budgetary, economic and other measures to the maximum extent of their available resources to ensure that women realize their rights to health care."[28]

The general recommendation explains that studies showing high rates of maternal mortality and morbidity within particular countries suggest that states parties might be in breach of their duties to fulfill women's rights of access to health care.

HUMAN RIGHTS

Human rights to advance safe motherhood can be clustered into three categories: rights relating to life, liberty, and security of the person; rights relating to maternity and health; and rights relating to equality and non-discrimination on grounds such as sex, marital status, race, age, and class.

RIGHTS RELATING TO LIFE, LIBERTY, AND SECURITY OF THE PERSON

The right to life is emerging from its historical origins of ensuring only the right to fair legal proceedings before imposition of capital punishment. The European Commission of Human Rights considered a complaint that a maternal death violated a woman's right to life under article 2 of the European Convention on Human Rights, which states that "everyone's right to life shall be protected by law." The Commission held the case inadmissible on technical grounds, but took the opportunity to emphasize that the right to life has to be interpreted to require states not only to take steps to prevent intentional killing, but also to take measures necessary to protect life against unintentional loss.[29]

The UN Human Rights Committee has explained that "the expression 'inherent right to life' cannot be properly understood in a restrictive manner, and the protection of this right requires that States adopt positive measures."[30] In explaining what positive measures might be adopted, the Committee gave as an example measures necessary to reduce infant mortality and to increase life expectancy.[31] The effective protection of the right to life of women requires that positive measures be taken that are necessary to ensure "access to appropriate health-care services that will enable women to go safely through pregnancy and childbirth and provide couples with the best chance of having a healthy infant."[32] Data on persistently high levels of maternal mortality put states on notice that they may be in breach of their obligations to take effective measures to protect women's right to life.

Some national courts are beginning to give an expanded meaning to the right to life in ways that could be applied to require ministries of health to address the causes of preventable maternal deaths. For example, the Supreme Court of India decided that the right to life was breached when various government hospitals denied a complainant emergency treatment for serious head injuries.[33] The Court explained that the state cannot ignore its constitutional obligation to provide adequate medical services to preserve human life on account of financial constraints and even detailed which measures the state might take to comply. The Venezuelan Supreme Court recognized the interrelationship between the right to life and the right to health in articles 58 and 76 respectively of the 1961 Venezuelan Constitution, when ruling in favor of a claim for HIV and related treatment.[34] While the successful claim was brought on behalf of 172 individuals living with HIV, the Court applied the decision to all people who are HIV positive in Venezuela.

It is timely to explore how a claim might be brought on behalf of women whose lives and health are at risk because of lack of life saving obstetric care. Such a claim would be feasible in Venezuela, and in light of the Supreme Court of India's judgment it might be credible in India and other countries, especially Commonwealth countries. Governmental health administrations might be wise to plan their resource allocations and programs in anticipation of this level of judicial sympathy with claimants.

Courts are beginning to import notions of health into the meaning of the right to security of the person and of the right to be free from inhuman and degrading treatment. The Inter-American Commission on Human Rights envisions a right to the satisfaction of basic health needs as part of a right to personal security. The Commission stated that the "essence of the legal obligation incurred by any government . . . is to strive to attain the economic and social aspirations of its people by following an order that assigns priority to the basic needs of health, nutrition and education. The priority of the 'right to survival' and 'basic needs' is a natural consequence of the right to personal security."[35]

In the concluding observations on the report on Peru, the Human Rights Committee observed that "clandestine abortions are the main cause of maternal mortality" in Peru.[36] It found that the restrictive abortion law of Peru that denied women abortion, even in cases of rape, subjected women to inhuman treatment contrary to article 7 of the Political Covenant. The Committee recommended "that the necessary legal measures should be taken to ensure compliance with the obligations to respect and guarantee the rights recognized in the Covenant,"[37] including rights to found a family and to protection of family life. This requirement of legal reform provides the promise that governments can be held to account for the duties they have assumed to protect women's interests not only to found families, but also to survive to enjoy life within those families.

Decisions of human rights tribunals have required states to ensure that health services are provided when their denial would constitute inhuman treatment. The European Court of Human Rights held that a governmental deportation of a person at an advanced stage of terminal AIDS to his own country, where he would have no hope of receiving appropriate care, would constitute inhuman treatment, contrary to article 3 of the European Convention.[38] Similarly, the Human Rights Committee concluded that denying a prison inmate any adequate medical treatment for his mental condition, even when he was liable to capital punishment, constitutes inhuman treatment, contrary to article 7, and denial of respect for the inherent dignity of his person, contrary to article 10(1) of the Political Covenant.[39] Accordingly, a state might be held bound to ensure provision of obstetric care, because lack of such provision could constitute inhuman treatment and denial of respect for the inherent dignity of women.

In challenging justice systems to apply human rights to advance safe motherhood, one might open by arguing that those factors, whether they be health or social factors, that put a woman at an increased risk of maternal mortality, deny her rights to life, liberty, and security of the person and her right to be free from inhuman and degrading treatment. If governments neglect to provide the conditions necessary for women to make free choices of maternity and to provide the services necessary for safe pregnancy and childbirth, they are accountable for violations of women's human rights.

RIGHTS RELATING TO MATERNITY AND HEALTH

The special contribution women make to society through maternity and motherhood is recognized in many national constitutions and human rights treaties through what might be called the right to maternity protection. The right to maternity protection is established through an amalgamation of rights requiring the protection of motherhood, family life, the highest attainable standard of health, and, for instance, rights with respect to maternity protection during employment.

Although many national constitutions and human rights conventions state that the family enjoys special protection from the state, they have yet to be effectively applied to require governments to provide the services necessary to maximize the chances of women surviving pregnancy and childbirth in good health. Necessary though these provisions are, their focus tends to link protection of women's health to motherhood and care of infants and children, reinforcing a perception that protection of women's health is an instrumental means of serving children, rather than a right for women to enjoy for themselves. Whatever the motivation is for such provisions, they obligate states to ensure that motherhood is safe. However, they require enforcement to improve the provision of necessary care and conditions for this purpose. The right to maternity protection could be applied to prevent and remedy the occurrence of vesico-vaginal fistula (VVF) and its variants, a maternal disability arising from obstructed labor that has been reported particularly in Africa and Asia.[40] It has been explained that:

an obstetric fistula is a hole which forms in the vaginal wall communicating into the bladder (vesico-vaginal fistula — VVF) or the rectum (recto-vaginal fistula — RVF) or both (recto-vesico-vaginal fistula — RVVF), as a result of prolonged and obstructed labour. . . . The immediate consequences of such damage are urinary incontinence, faecal incontinence if the rectum is affected, and excoriation of the vulva from the constantly leaking urine and faeces. . . . Women who have survived prolonged obstructed labour may also suffer from local nerve damage which results in difficulty in walking, including foot drop.[41]

VVF, RVF, and RVVF are serious health dysfunctions of early marriage and childbearing, but they also carry a social stigma that can be devastating to those who cannot obtain prompt surgical repair. It has been explained that:

Most victims of obstructed labour in which the fistula subsequently occurred will also have given birth to a stillborn baby. In some areas, a high percentage of fistulae occur during the first pregnancy. Women who live in cultures where childlessness is unacceptable will therefore suffer from this fact alone. As long as they are incontinent of urine they are also likely to be abandoned by their husbands on whom they are financially dependent, and will probably be ostracised by society.[42]

Moreover, in many situations the "social isolation compounds the woman's own belief that she is a disgrace and has brought shame on her family. Women with VVF often work alone, eat alone, use their own plates and utensils to eat and are not allowed to cook for anyone else. In some cases they must live on the streets and beg."[43]

The right to health is protected by regional and international human rights instruments as well as by different national constitutions.[44] For example, the Inter-American Commission on Human Rights found that the Brazilian government had failed to take timely and effective measures to preserve the health of the Yanomami Indians,[45] and had thereby violated article 11 of the American Declaration of the Rights and Duties of Man, which provides that "every person has the right to preservation of his health through sanitary and social measures relating to . . . medical care."

International human rights legal tribunals have made some progress in protecting women's rights relating to their reproductive health. In examining whether an injunction prohibiting provision of information regarding the availability of abortion services violates the right to freedom of expression, the European Court of Human Rights explained that the injunction

has created a risk to the health of those women who are now seeking abortions at a later stage in their pregnancy, due to lack of proper counseling, and who are not availing of customary medical supervision after the abortion has taken place. Moreover, the injunction may have had more adverse effects on women who were not sufficiently resourceful or had not the necessary level of education to have access to alternative sources of information.[46]

It would seem, therefore, that human rights tribunals will be especially vigilant in reviewing cases concerning infringements on giving or receiving information that is necessary to protect women's health, and where such infringements disproportionately impact women who lack resources or education.

General Comment 14 of the Committee on Economic, Social, and Cultural Rights, addressing article 12 of the Economic Covenant, which protects the right to the highest attainable standard of health, explains that the right requires the following interrelated features:

availability (health care services have to be of sufficient quantity);
accessibility (services, including information, have to be physically and economically accessible to everyone without discrimination);
acceptability (services have to be culturally appropriate, that is, respectful of the cultures of individuals, minorities and communities, and sensitive to gender and life-cycle requirements); and
adequate quality (services have to be scientifically appropriate and of adequate quality).[47]

Laws and policies that unreasonably restrict health services according to these criteria would not comply with this performance standard. For instance, a law or policy requiring unnecessarily high qualifications for health service providers will limit the availability of services that contribute to safe motherhood. Examples are policies that require excessive qualifications for health service providers to perform cesarean deliveries. Such policies may be proposed in good faith in order to ensure excellence in health care. However, it is poor policy, and may be a human rights violation where health care is jeopardized, to allow the excellent to be the enemy of the good, or the good the enemy of the adequate.

National courts are beginning to address the availability of health services. For example, the Constitutional Court of South Africa has considered whether a public hospital is required under Section 27 of the South African Constitution to provide long-term dialysis treatment for a claimant's chronic renal failure.[48] The Court found that a government is not required to do so, because constitutional obligations regarding the right of access to health care services can be limited by lack of resources. The Court explained, however, that emergency services cannot be denied when a person suffers a sudden catastrophe which calls for immediate medical attention. Thus, it would seem that under the South African Constitution, and possibly under similar provisions of other national constitutions, women seeking emergency obstetric care have a right of reasonable access to such treatment.

A state's willingness in principle to give effect to women's rights to health and safe motherhood may be deterred by the fear that full implementation will have indeterminate economic consequences for the national health budget. However, a World Bank study "estimated that providing a standard 'package' of maternal and new-born health services would cost approximately $3 [U.S.] per person per year in a developing country; maternal health services alone could cost as little as $2 per person."[49]

While much work is still required to apply the right to health care effectively so as to ensure the availability, accessibility, acceptability, and quality of maternity services, treaty bodies have made some significant beginnings through their concluding observations on country reports. For example, the Committee on Economic, Social, and Cultural Rights, in its concluding observation on the report by The Gambia, explained that "Regarding the right to health in Article 12 of the [Economic] Covenant, the Committee expresses its deep concern over the extremely high maternal mortality rate of 1,050 per 100,000 live births. UNICEF identifies the main causes to be haemorrhage and infection related to the lack of access to [appropriate services] and poor services."[50]

In its concluding comments on the report of Morocco, CEDAW "noted with concern the high rates of maternal mortality in Morocco, the high number of unattended births, the unavailability of safe abortion and the need to develop further reproductive and sexual health services, including family planning."[51]

RIGHTS RELATING TO EQUALITY AND NONDISCRIMINATION ON GROUNDS
SUCH AS SEX, MARITAL STATUS, RACE, AGE, AND CLASS

The greatest threat to women's reproductive health is their inability to exercise their rights to equality. The transcending human rights violation that explains the unduly high prevalence of maternal mortality, including such risk factors as malnutrition of girl children resulting in anemia, premature marriage leading to premature pregnancy, lack of means for child spacing, and, for instance, lack of emergency obstetric care, is that women do not enjoy the status and significance in their communities that men enjoy.

Often sex discrimination is aggravated by discrimination on grounds of women's marital status, race, and age, usually leaving young women of a minority racial group and of lower socioeconomic status the most vulnerable to the risk of maternal death. Statistics on disparity in the risk of maternal death between minority and majority populations show up to ten times greater risk between, for instance, the aboriginal population and the non-aboriginal population in Australia.[52] Differences exist even where populations live in the same cities, such as in the United States, where the black population has a relative risk of maternal death 4.3 times higher than that of the nonblack population.[53]

Equality requires that we treat the *same* interests without discrimination, for example, in access of people of both sexes to education, but that we also treat *different* interests in ways that adequately respect those differences, particularly in women's distinct interests in safety in pregnancy and childbirth. Rights to equal protection of different interests are violated when governments fail to address the fundamental biological difference between men and women through which, year after year worldwide, many hundreds of thousands of women die, unnecessarily. Men and women are equal, co-dependent partners in human societies, and the biological difference between them should not be invoked as immutably destining women for maternal mortality or morbidity.

The devastating paradox of many societies in their observance of human rights is that they discriminate against women where differences between the sexes should not matter, such as in access to educational, political, spiritual, economic, and other opportunities, and ignore the distinction where it is critical, namely in women's need for maternal health care. If political, professional, religious, and other influential institutions in every society would put the effort into serving women's particular needs for maternal health care that they have put into discriminating against women in areas where sexual differences should not matter, considerable advancement would be achieved toward safe motherhood.

The contribution of discrimination against women on grounds of their sex and, for instance, age to high rates of avoidable maternal mortality can be reduced through determined applications of human rights well recognized in national laws and constitutions and in national endorsements of international human rights conventions. Governments are in violation of their obligations to bring their laws into compliance with the human right to sexual nondiscrimination when they fail to reform clinic policies that discriminate against women, such as clinic policies or laws that: require women requesting health services to obtain the authorization of their husbands,[54] have a differential impact on girls, such as parental authorization requirements for adolescents to obtain reproductive health services,[55] fail to provide reproductive health services to adolescent girls according to their evolving capacities to understand and make choices, consistent with the Children's Convention,[56] fail to ensure the protection of confidentiality of women presenting with sex-specific conditions that might be stigmatizing, for example, treatment of women with an out-of-wedlock pregnancy or who are pregnant as a result of sexual violence, and criminalize medical procedures that only women need, such as abortion. When governments fail effectively to apply existing laws that protect women and girls, such as laws that set a minimum legal age of marriage or prohibit child marriages, and require the allocation of health resources proportionate to women's specific needs to go safely through pregnancy and childbirth,[57] they are in violation of their obligations to apply their legal and administrative authority to protect all their citizens equally.

Performance Standards

Performance standards enable courts and treaty monitoring bodies to determine whether governments are meeting their obligations to respect, protect, and fulfill rights relating to safe motherhood. There are various standards that show whether governments are meeting their human rights obligations with regard to safe motherhood. Performance standards include but are not limited to:

standards in national legislation and developed by national courts, for example, that require access to certain kinds of care such as emergency care;[58]
standards in international documents, such as those developed by the Cairo and Beijing processes;[59] and
standards that have evolved through the treaty monitoring bodies, such as those requiring equality in access to health care.[60]

Some treaty bodies, such as CEDAW, use the agreed goals of the Cairo and Beijing process as performance standards to determine whether states are in compliance with or violation of their obligations under the Women's Convention.[61]

UN agencies have developed indicators that are used to give a general overview of the reproductive health situation in particular settings. They include but are not limited to:

health status indicators, such as measures of maternal mortality and morbidity;
health service indicators that show the availability and, for example, the accessibility of services, such as the percentage of births attended by skilled birth attendants; and
health policy indicators, such as laws and policies favorable to adolescent health, or the degree of enforcement of a legal age of marriage.

Some of these indicators are more developed than others, the health policy indicators being the least well developed. No single indicator can reflect the complete maternal health status of a community. Indicators can be used in different ways in the human rights context. Where they show, for instance, that certain groups of ethnic women in a country are in poor reproductive health, this might suggest that the government needs to do more to comply with its obligations to ensure the right to equality in access to obstetric services.

Indicators can show trends over time. When trends show improvement, this suggests that governments are progressing toward the realization of the right to the highest attainable standard of reproductive health. When the trends do not show improvement or when they indicate continuing poor reproductive health, the data could then shift the burden to governments to explain the situation. If the indicators show default in satisfying performance standards, a government could be said to be in violation of its people's right to the highest attainable standard of reproductive health.

World Health Organization (WHO) global indicators for monitoring reproductive health could be applied to determine the status of women's health in a community,[62] and whether the standards of availability, accessibility, acceptability, and quality of reproductive health services are being met. They include:

maternal mortality ratio;
percentage of births attended by skilled health personnel;
number of facilities with functioning basic essential obstetric care per 500,000 population;
number of facilities with functioning comprehensive essential obstetric care per 500,000 population; and
percentage of obstetric and gynecology admissions owing to abortion.[63]

WHO estimates that only 55 percent of women in the developing world are attended at delivery by a health worker who has received at least the minimum of necessary training.[64] A skilled birth attendant can ensure hygiene during labor and delivery, provide safe care, recognize and manage complications, and, if needed, refer the mother to a higher level of care. The Cairo Plus Five document offers a standard by which to measure the degree of compliance with the right to the highest attainable standard of health:

In order to monitor progress towards the achievement of the Conference's goals for maternal mortality, countries should use the proportion of births assisted by skilled attendants as a benchmark indicator. By 2005, where the maternal mortality rate is very high, at least 40 per cent of all births should be assisted by skilled attendants; by 2010 this figure should be at least 50 per cent and by 2015, at least 60 per cent. All countries should continue their efforts so that globally, by 2005, 80 per cent of all births should be assisted by skilled attendants, by 2010, 85 per cent, and by 2015, 90 per cent.[65]

Impressive work has suggested how to convert health service indicators on the availability and use of obstetric services into legal standards that treaty bodies could use to consider whether governmental measures taken are appropriate to fulfilling women's right to health in an equitable way.[66] This work recommends that governments address the following six questions:

1. Are there enough health facilities providing life saving care for women with obstetric complications?
2. Are these facilities equitably distributed across the population?
3. Are pregnant women using these facilities?
4. Are pregnant women with obstetric complications using these facilities?

5. Are these facilities providing enough life saving surgery to meet the needs of the population?
6. Is the quality of these services adequate?[67]

These six questions could be helpful to treaty bodies in assessing reports from countries with high rates of maternal mortality. An inadequate answer to any one of these questions suggests that a state is not complying with its positive obligations to provide maternity care and would at least shift the burden to its government to explain the steps that it is taking to protect women during pregnancy. Where answers show serious lack of provision of basic obstetric services, treaty monitoring bodies might want to go beyond expressing their "concern" or "serious concern," to show how and why states are violating women's rights to health in general, and to obstetric services in particular.

The Way Forward

Governmental neglect of preventable causes of maternal death and pregnancy-related ill health is an affront to women's dignity, but is only one aspect of a larger pattern of systemic unlawful discrimination against women. The work ahead is to emphasize not simply the fact but the injustice of preventable maternal mortality and that these avoidable tragedies require governmental accountability. Governments as such, individual members of governments, and supporters of unjust governmental policies that violate human rights can be held to political and perhaps legal account, or at least be publicly shamed for their indifference to maternal mortality, and compelled to devote resources at their command to address and reduce the enormity of the injustice.

The task of advancing safe motherhood through human rights is formidable. It must begin with a diagnosis of laws and policies affecting safe motherhood,[68] whether found in national constitutions and laws or in cultural and religious practices. The diagnosis must include an assessment of the legal literacy and community understanding and acceptability of rights and norms to advance safe motherhood. Finally, it must identify women's capacity to exercise rights to advance safe motherhood, including their ability to access legal services to enforce obligations to observe rights.[69]

The task of advancing safe motherhood through human rights is both intense and broad. Its intensity is related to inquiries into many of the close to 600,000 maternal deaths annually to determine points of failure in national health care, legal, and other systems. Its breadth is the challenge of translating human rights into the right of each person to the dignity of human status.[70]

Momentum for advancing safe motherhood exists in the political commitments made by governments in Cairo and Beijing. The challenge is to reinforce these commitments through recognition of legally enforceable duties. In the past, reproductive health organizations, both governmental and non-governmental, have not given sufficient priority to human rights strategies, in the same way that human rights agencies have not given priority to maternal health concerns. With inspiration and leadership, reproductive health professionals and human rights activists could intensify their efforts to work more effectively together to stem the tide of preventable maternal mortality and morbidity and achieve an advance toward safer motherhood.

7

Canada's New Child Support Guidelines: Do They Fulfill Canada's International Law Obligations to Children?

MARTHA SHAFFER

In May 1997, after years of study, Canada altered its method of calculating child support by adopting child support guidelines for claims brought under the Divorce Act, 1985.[1] The adoption of the guidelines was fueled in part by a concern that the existing method of calculating child support had been generating low awards that did not adequately provide for children's economic needs.[2] A 1981 discussion paper described this concern in the following terms:

In some cases the family's financial resources are simply insufficient to provide adequate child support. In these situations the problem of low child support awards is part of the larger problem of poverty in Canada, which is intensified by the onset of divorce. However, in other families the resources are available but they are simply not being shared in a manner that would allow all family members to benefit from similar standards of living following divorce. This is confirmed by the fact that such a larger proportion of women and children live in poverty following divorce. The fact that these resources are not being shared can be attributed to the method of determining support and the allocation of costs between the parents.[3]

By standardizing the amount of child support awarded at different income levels, the guidelines were touted as a measure that would reduce child poverty attributable to the economic upheaval that occurs at marriage breakdown.

Reducing child poverty is, obviously, a laudable goal. It is also consistent with Canada's international obligations and, in particular, with Canada's responsibilities as a ratifier to the Convention on the Rights of the Child ("Children's Convention"). Article 27 of that convention provides that states have responsibilities to ensure that children receive adequate financial support either from their parents (or others who are responsible for them) or from the state.[4] While the primary responsibility to provide for the child lies with parents, the state is responsible for adopting measures to assist them to provide support and to provide material assistance in the event that they are unable to adequately meet children's needs.

In this chapter, I seek to examine the extent to which Canada's child support laws, and in particular the child support guidelines, can be seen to accord with Canada's obligations under article 27 of the convention. I argue that the guidelines may well have a salutary effect on child support for those children whose fathers have the economic means to pay.[5] In this respect, the guidelines reflect the emphasis Canada has historically placed on ensuring that children receive support from "private" sources before turning to the state. I argue that the enactment of child support guidelines and the enforcement mechanisms that accompany them demonstrate that Canada has taken seriously some of its obligations under article 27, those ensuring that parents financially support their children. However, Canada has been far less diligent in meeting its other obligations under article 27, those ensuring that the children whose parents cannot provide adequate financial support receive the resources they need from the state. Finally, I will argue that the emphasis placed on the guidelines, as well as the public resources that go into monitoring and refining them, may actually be at odds with the agenda of eliminating child poverty by deflecting concern away from the broader issues of poverty in Canada.

The UN Convention on the Rights of the Child and Canada's International Obligations to Eradicate Child Poverty: Public Versus Private Support

One of the most innovative features of the UN Convention on the Rights of the Child is its recognition of the interdependence of civil and political rights on the one hand, and economic, social and cultural rights on the other.[6] In order to secure the recognition of children's inherent dignity and right to self-determination, the Convention on the Rights of the Child contains provisions for the protection of children from harmful acts and practices,[7] as well as provisions enabling children's participation in decisions affecting their lives.[8] In addition, the convention also includes a number of provisions concerned with the development and welfare of children. These provisions place states parties under an obligation to ensure that children enjoy a reasonable standard of living and access to basic services such as health care,[9] social security,[10] and education.[11] By integrating children's civil and political rights with their right to the provision of basic needs, the convention embraces the idea that overcoming the problem of child poverty is an essential condition of children's self-determination.

While several of the articles in the Convention on the Rights of the Child touch on poverty-related concerns, the most direct is article 27. That article provides:

States Parties recognize the right of every child to a standard of living adequate for the child's physical, mental, spiritual, moral and social development.
The parent(s) or others responsible for the child have the primary responsibility to secure within their abilities and financial capacities, the conditions of living necessary for the child's development.
States Parties, in accordance with national conditions and within their means, shall take appropriate measures to assist parents and others responsible for the child

to implement this right and shall in the case of need provide material assistance and support programs, particularly with regard to nutrition, clothing and housing.

States Parties shall take all appropriate measures to secure the recovery of maintenance for the child from the parents or other persons having financial responsibility for the child, both within the State Party and from abroad. In particular, where the person having financial responsibility for the child lives in a State different from that of the child, States Parties shall promote the accession to international agreements or the conclusion of such agreements, as well as the making of other appropriate arrangements.[12]

A number of important features emerge from this provision. First, there is an understanding that children have an international legal right to an adequate standard of living. Second, parents or other private individuals responsible for the child have the primary responsibility for ensuring that this right is respected. Third, the state also has a role to play in ensuring that children's right to an adequate standard of living is respected. This role includes assisting parents to provide financial and other types of support to their children and creating mechanisms to ensure that parents or other persons who have a duty to support children actually fulfill their obligation. In addition, the state is required to "provide material assistance and support programs, particularly with regard to nutrition, clothing and housing" where parents or others are unable to provide the standard of living to which children are entitled.

The Convention on the Rights of the Child thus sees responsibility for the support of children as being shared between parents and state, with the primary obligation falling to parents. Nonetheless, it is clear that the state has an important role in the support of children where parents are unable to meet this obligation and in ensuring that those parents who can meet their support obligation do so. Determining whether Canada meets its obligations under article 27 of the Children's Convention requires an assessment of the dual aspects of the state's role in providing support to children. To assess whether Canada has fulfilled its obligations to ensure that parents bear the responsibility of supporting their children, I will examine the provisions in Canadian family law governing child support and support enforcement. To assess whether Canada has fulfilled its obligations to provide for children whose parents do not have the means to provide adequate support, I will discuss the state of social assistance programs in Canada.

Private Support Obligations: Child Support Obligations in Canadian Family Law

In Canada family law is an area in which both the federal and provincial governments have some degree of jurisdiction. The federal government has jurisdiction over the family by virtue of the Divorce Act, 1985, which provides not only for the dissolution of marriage, but also for spousal support, child support, and child custody. For their part, the provinces have control over family law by virtue of various provincial statutes that govern property division at marriage breakdown, spousal support, child support, and child custody. As an example of provincial legislation, I will focus on Ontario where the statute governing child support is the Family Law Act.[13]

Both the Divorce Act and the Family Law Act contain provisions that impose obligations on parents to financially support their children. The relevant provision of the Divorce Act, sec. 15.1(1), provides that parents may be ordered to pay support for any "children of the marriage." A child of the marriage is defined in section 2(1) as any child under the age of majority who has not withdrawn from parental charge, or a child over the age of majority who, by reason of illness, disability or other cause, is unable to withdraw from parental charge or to provide the necessaries of life. While the language of the Divorce Act makes it sound as though the awarding of child support is highly discretionary (providing, as it does, that a court *may* make a child support order), in fact the obligation to pay child support is taken very seriously under the Act. The Divorce Act contains a number of statutory bars to granting a divorce, one of which is the failure on the part of the parents to ensure that adequate arrangements have been made for the support of the children of the marriage. Section 11(1)(b) specifically provides that "it is the duty of the court to satisfy itself that reasonable arrangements have been made for the support of any children of the marriage . . . and, if such arrangements have not been made, to stay the granting of the divorce until such arrangements have been made." In one recent case, the New Brunswick Court of Queen's Bench stayed a divorce petition twice because the parents' agreement did not contain adequate support for their children.[14]

Similar obligations for parents to provide financial support for their children are found in provincial legislation. For example, the Ontario Family Law Act provides in section 31(1) that "every parent has an obligation to provide support, for his or her unmarried child who is a minor or is enrolled in a full-time program of education, to the extent that the parent is capable of doing so." This obligation is subject to section 31(2), which provides that the obligation to pay child support does not extend to a child who is sixteen years of age or older and who has withdrawn from parental control. It is important to note that the child support obligation under the Family Law Act, and its counterparts in the other provinces, apply to parents regardless of their formal marital status. In other words, unlike the Divorce Act, which applies only to parents who are legally married, provincial family law statutes impose obligations to pay child support on parents who have cohabited in a common law relationship or who have conceived a child in a relationship of shorter duration. As a result of provincial legislation, parents have an obligation to support their children regardless of the nature of their relationship with the child's other parent.

The net effect of these provisions in the Divorce Act and provincial legislation such as the Family Law Act is that Canada has created legally enforceable obligations on parents to financially support their children under both
the federal and the provincial law. The presence of these statutory obligations is, of course, consistent with the requirement in article 27 of the Convention on the Rights of the Child that parents or other private parties have
primary responsibility for the support of children and that states enact
measures to implement the child's right to receive this support.[15] It is also
indicative of the view within Canadian law and Canadian society that child
support should be first and foremost a "private" responsibility, that is, a
responsibility to be shouldered by individuals with a sufficiently strong connection to the child rather than by the state.

The emphasis in Canadian law on private responsibility to support children extends beyond the simple creation of child support obligations in
federal and provincial legislation. The primacy of private support over support through public means is also illustrated by the definitions of who may
constitute a "parent" under both federal and provincial family law statutes.
Under both the Divorce Act and provincial family law statutes, the obligation to pay support extends beyond a child's biological or adoptive parents.
For example, under the Divorce Act a "child of the marriage" to whom
support may be owed is defined as including "any child for whom [the
spouses] both stand in the place of parents" and "any child for whom one is
the parent and the other stands in the place of a parent."[16] Similarly, the
Family Law Act defines parent in section 1 as including a person "who has
demonstrated a settled intention to treat a child as a child of his or her
family."[17] Both the provision in the Divorce Act and the corresponding
provisions in provincial legislation have produced a considerable amount of
case law holding that child support obligations can be imposed on stepparents who have taken an active role in the upbringing of a stepchild.
Furthermore, in the recent case of *Chartier v. Chartier*,[18] the Supreme Court
of Canada held that a person who has been found to have acted in the place
of a parent cannot unilaterally terminate that status after the relationship
with the child's parent breaks down. Finally, the obligation to pay child
support can be imposed on a stepparent even where the child's biological or
adoptive parents are still involved with the child, but lack sufficient financial
resources to adequately meet the child's needs. In fact, the child support
guidelines make explicit reference to the allocation of responsibility to support a child as between parents and stepparents in section 5. That section
provides that "where the spouse against whom an order for support of a
child is sought stands in the place of a parent for a child, the amount of the
order is, in respect of that parent or spouse, such amount as the court
considers appropriate, having regard to these Guidelines and any other
parent's legal duty to support the child."

The effect of these provisions and of the *Chartier* decision is to create another private source of financial support for the child. Thus, instead of looking to the state for financial assistance after a second relationship breaks down, the child is to look first to his or her biological or adoptive parents and stepparents. The obligation on stepparents ensures that there is another private pocket from which child support may be paid before turning to the public purse. In a society characterized by a fairly high rate of marriage/relationship breakdown, the ability to require stepparents to pay child support likely has a significant impact in terms of reducing the demand on public funds.[19]

Another measure designed to reduce demand on public funds arises from the requirement in provincial legislation that biological parents (usually fathers) pay child support even if they had nothing more than a brief sexual relationship with the child's other parent. As I have already noted, provincial family law statutes require parents to pay financial support for their children, regardless of whether the children were born or adopted into a formal marriage, a common law arrangement, or were the product of a casual sexual encounter between the parents. Provincial statutes also permit courts to make declarations of paternity which, although they may be relevant in other settings, are clearly crucial in cases involving casual encounters.[20] These provisions interact with social assistance regulations to ensure that children receive financial support from private sources before turning to the state. Under the various provincial social assistance schemes, women may be unable to receive benefits for their children unless they can show that they have attempted to obtain child support from the father of the child.[21] This requirement is enforced even where the child was conceived during a very brief relationship or through a casual encounter. It may also be enforced where the mother or the child has been a victim of violence at the father's hands. If a child support order is made, the amount of the award is deducted on a dollar for dollar basis from the woman's social assistance benefits. Again, the requirement that fathers pay support for their children regardless of their relationship with the children or with the mother reflects the primacy of private provision of child support as does the ability to deduct the amount of the support award from social assistance payments.

A final way in which family law reflects the emphasis on private provision of child support is through the creation of provincially funded enforcement agencies in most provinces. In Ontario, the relevant agency is the Family Responsibility Office. Once a child support order has been granted or an agreement regarding child support made, the order or agreement can be filed with the provincial enforcement agency, which will take enforcement steps, should the spouse paying child support fall into arrears. The effect of these agencies is to bolster the obligation to pay child support by ensuring that support orders are respected. Before the creation of these agencies, the collection of child support arrears was a private responsibility in the sense that it was up to the parent receiving child support payments to initiate enforcement proceedings in the event that the payor parent failed to live up to his obligations. Private enforcement is, however, costly, and where child support payments are not being made, the parent entitled to those payments may find it financially difficult if not impossible to bring enforcement proceedings. This, in turn, proves costly for the state if it means that children who are entitled to receive private child support end up receiving state benefits because the custodial parent cannot afford to enforce a support order. State funded enforcement agencies attempt to alleviate this problem by taking on the burden of collecting unpaid support instead of requiring custodial parents to go to court whenever default occurs. Again, the very existence of these agencies can be seen as a testament to the importance in Canadian law of private sources of child support.

It is also significant that enforcement mechanisms have been strengthened in recent years at both the federal and provincial levels. At the federal level, stricter enforcement mechanisms were enacted as part of a package of reforms to child support law which included the enactment of the guidelines.[22] The reforms included amendments to the Family Orders and Agreements Enforcement Assistance Act that add income tax data banks kept by Revenue Canada to the information banks that can be searched to locate persons who have defaulted on their support obligations,[23] and amendments that permit federal licenses to be denied to support defaulters. In Ontario, enforcement mechanisms were strengthened in 1996 with the creation of the Family Responsibility Office, which was given more stringent powers than the Family Support Plan, the enforcement agency it replaced. These new powers include permitting support orders to be registered as security interests under the Personal Property Security Act, making payments under the Worker's Compensation Act (for workplace-related injuries) subject to garnishment proceedings and, perhaps most significantly, permitting the registrar of motor vehicles to suspend a payor's driver's license if the payor is in arrears.[24]

The recently enacted child support guidelines are further manifestations of this emphasis on private child support obligations. Essentially, child support guidelines are a way of structuring the child support obligation. They attempt to standardize child support awards based on the income of the noncustodial spouse and the number of children for whom he is required to pay support. Thus, the guidelines consist of a series of tables that provide the amount of child support a noncustodial spouse has to pay based on his income and his province of residence.

These guidelines were enacted as a result of widespread dissatisfaction with the previous method of calculating child support. Prior to the guidelines, child support was determined according to the *Paras* rule,[25] which required the court to determine the amount required to support the particular child and to apportion that amount between the parents in proportion to their income. Although this method of calculation sounds fine in principle, there was considerable concern, particularly among women's groups, that the amounts generated by the *Paras* formula were insufficient.[26] This concern was compounded by the fact that child support payments were taxable in the hands of the parent receiving them, which meant that the already inadequate amounts awarded were further reduced after taxation.[27] The *Paras* method was also criticized for yielding inconsistent awards in similar cases, making it unfair for children and their parents and difficult for lawyers to advise clients as to the amount of support appropriate in their case.

That the guidelines were enacted in response to these concerns is clear from the objectives of the guidelines, set out in section 1. That section provides that the objective of the guidelines are fourfold:

(a) to establish a fair standard of support for children that ensures that they continue to benefit from the financial means of both spouses after separation;
(b) to reduce conflict and tensions between the spouses by making the calculation of child support orders more objective;
(c) to improve the efficiency of the legal process by giving courts and spouses guidance in setting the levels of child support orders and encouraging settlement; and
(d) to ensure consistent treatment of spouses and children who are in similar circumstances.

A final claim made of the child support guidelines, as noted at the beginning of the chapter, is that they would help reduce child poverty by ensuring that adequate amounts of child support would be awarded.

Although it is still too early to assess the impact of the guidelines, two observations can be made. First, if the guidelines succeed in accomplishing their objectives, they will be a positive development for children who receive private support from their parents.[28] Children will benefit from both the strengthening and structuring of the child support obligation that the guidelines and the stringent enforcement measures that have accompanied them bring about. However, it is also clear that the guidelines will only have a modest effect on child poverty. Many poor children will not benefit from these guidelines, for reasons I will discuss in greater detail below.

All the child support provisions described thus far — the creation of child support obligations for children born within and outside of marriage, the expansive definition of parent, the creation of state-funded enforcement mechanisms and the child support guidelines — show how Canada takes its obligation in the first part of article 27 of the Children's Convention seriously, at least to a point. These provisions imposing support obligations on parents (and on persons who stand in the place of parents) attempt to ensure that parents have "the primary responsibility to secure, within their abilities and financial capacities, the conditions of living necessary for the child's development." The provisions concerning enforcement attempt to fulfill the obligation article 27 imposes on states to "take appropriate measures to assist parents . . . to implement this right" and to "take all appropriate measures to secure the recovery of maintenance for the child from the parents." In other words, the emphasis that Canadian law has placed on securing support from private persons before turning to the state dovetails with the view expressed in article 27 that parents or other persons responsible for children bear the primary responsibility of ensuring that children's needs are met.

Although, as I have argued, the emphasis Canada places on private support demonstrates that Canada takes some of its obligations under article 27 seriously, it is possible to argue that even in this regard, Canada has not done enough. Article 27(3) speaks of a requirement to "take appropriate measures to assist parents and others responsible for the child" to implement the child's right to an adequate living standard. Arguably such measures go beyond simply establishing statutory child support obligations and state-supported mechanisms of enforcement. A state that is truly committed to assisting parents to fulfill economic obligations toward their children would do more to ensure that parents have the means to provide a decent standard of living for their children. Measures of this sort would include access to education and training programs, the existence of affordable child care programs, and the creation of jobs paying an adequate wage. The fact that Canada has not embraced these more radical antipoverty measures demonstrates that Canada has done significantly more to ensure that it has fulfilled its obligation to require parents to support their children than it has in fulfilling the second obligation under article 27, that of providing material assistance to children whose parents cannot provide adequate support.

Canada's Social Programs: The Perpetuation of Child Poverty

Canada's success (or lack thereof) in making material provision for poor children requires an examination of the measures Canada has adopted to tackle the problem of poverty generally. Put briefly, Canada's record on this score has been nothing short of dismal, particularly in light of Canada's enviable economic position relative to most countries. For the last several years, Canadian public policy has been in the grips of an aggressive tax cutting and deficit reduction agenda, which has lead to the erosion of Canada's social programs. As a result, over the last several years the situation of poor children has been getting worse, rather than better. In fact, according to antipoverty groups, the number of children living in poverty increased by 49 percent between 1989 and 1999.[29]

One of the most significant developments in the dismantling of the welfare state was the creation in 1995 of the Canada Health and Social Transfer (CHST).[30] The CHST replaced the Canada Assistance Plan (CAP), which had been the cornerstone of Canada's social programs since the 1960s.[31] In the Canadian federal system, the provinces are primarily responsible for the provision of social programs, but the cost of these programs is shared with the federal government. CAP was the mechanism that structured the cost sharing relationship between the federal and provincial governments for a wide range of social welfare programs. As Martha Jackman explains, CAP imposed a number of important conditions on provincial programs in order to be eligible for federal funding:

CAP requires that assistance be available to any person in need, regardless of the reasons of the need for assistance; that levels of provincial assistance take into account the basic requirements of recipients, in terms of food, shelter, clothing, fuel, utilities, household supplies and personal requirements; that welfare services in the provinces continue to be developed and extended; that provincial residency requirements and waiting periods not be imposed, and that appeal procedures from decisions relating to assistance be made available.[32]

By imposing these conditions CAP created "a degree of national uniformity in the design and delivery of provincial welfare programs and services that would not otherwise have been possible."[33]

The repeal of CAP and its replacement with the CHST restructured the funding relationship between the federal and provincial governments, effectively giving the provinces greater control over social programs. Under CHST, the federal government provides a predetermined amount of funding to the provinces to allocate among three areas: health, postsecondary education, and welfare. The federal government no longer matches provincial funding for welfare programs as it did under CAP. In addition, most of the eligibility requirements that existed under CAP were abolished under the CHST such that the only condition now required to receive federal funding for social assistance programs is the prohibition on provincial residency requirements. This has meant that provinces, such as Ontario, have been able to drastically restructure their social programs and to introduce controversial measures such as workfare,[34] measures that would not have been possible under CAP. Finally, in addition to giving the provinces greater control over the design of social programs, the federal government also slashed its transfer payments to provinces for education, health, and social programs by $7 billion between 1995 and 1998.[35]

The federal government was not alone in cutting its expenditures on social programs during this period. Cost cutting in the name of deficit reduction was also occurring at the provincial level as well. Between 1995 and 1998, Ontario, for example, slashed its funding of social programs by $4 billion.[36] These cuts included substantial cuts to the level of benefits paid to people in receipt of social assistance. In 1995 alone, Ontario cut social assistance benefits by a full 21.6 percent.[37]

Drastic reforms to the unemployment insurance system (now renamed "Employment Insurance") were also taking place over this same period. As a result of these reforms, eligibility for employment insurance was significantly curtailed and the level of benefits paid to those who passed the eligibility threshold was reduced. According to LIFT, an Ontario-based, antipoverty organization, the proportion of unemployed persons eligible for "employment" benefits has dropped from over 80 percent in 1990 to just under 30 percent in 1998.[38]

The effect of all these changes has been dramatic. Specifically in terms of children, statistics compiled by Campaign 2000, a coalition of "over 70 national, provincial and community partner organizations,"[39] paint a deeply disturbing picture. In its 1999 Federal Report Card, Campaign 2000 found that between 1989 and 1999 the number of poor children had increased 49 percent and the number of children in very poor families (families with incomes less than $20,000 in constant 1997 dollars) increased by 48 percent. Campaign 2000 also found that the number of children in working poor families increased by 44 percent and that between 1989 and 1999 the number of children in families requiring social assistance increased by 51 percent. Further, between 1989 and 1999 the number of children in unaffordable rental housing almost doubled and since 1989 twice as many families rely on food banks to feed their children. The Ontario figures are worse than the national average.[40] In Ontario, the number of poor children had more than doubled between 1989 and 1999, increasing by 118 percent. The number of children in families earning less than $20,000 had increased by 137 percent and the number of children in working poor families was up by 142 percent. The number of children requiring social assistance in Ontario was not available. The number of Ontario children living in unaffordable housing increased by 130 percent. All of these figures attest to the fact that child poverty is becoming an increasingly serious problem.

These developments have not gone unnoticed at the international level. As a ratifier of the Covenant on Economic, Social, and Cultural Rights, Canada is required to present periodic reports to the Committee on Economic, Social, and Cultural Rights which monitors compliance on the realization of rights covered by articles 1 to 15 of the Covenant. In December of 1998, the committee released its most recent report on the status of the Covenant rights in Canada. Although the committee made some positive remarks, its observations on Canada's performance were overwhelmingly negative. For example, the committee noted that, while for the previous five years Canada has ranked at the top of the United Nations Development Program's (UNDP) Human Development Index for overall quality of life, Canada ranks tenth on the list for industrialized nations on the UNDP's Human Poverty Index.[41] The committee concluded from this that Canada "has the capacity to achieve a high level of respect for all Covenant rights" but has not done so.[42] The committee also noted that in adopting a deficit reduction economic agenda involving cuts to social expenditure, Canada had not "paid sufficient attention to the adverse consequences for the enjoyment of economic, social and cultural rights by the Canadian population as a whole, and by vulnerable groups in particular."[43] The committee cited a number of "principal subjects of concern" including the replacement of CAP with the

CHST,[44] the "successive restrictions to unemployment insurance benefits" which have resulted in "fewer low-income families [being] eligible to receive any benefits at all," the provincial cuts to social assistance rates, the lack of affordable housing and levels of homelessness that are so high that "the mayors of Canada's ten largest cities have now declared homelessness a national disaster,"[45] and the increased need for food banks. The committee noted that Canada's social and economic policies have disproportionately affected aboriginal persons, who live in conditions of extreme social and economic deprivation, and women, particularly single mothers, the vast majority of whom live in poverty.

Most recently, the United Nations Human Rights Committee, which monitors Canada's compliance with the International Covenant on Civil and Political Rights, has pointed to the inadequacy of Canada's antipoverty measures. In particular, the committee expressed concern that women, especially single mothers, had been disproportionately affected by poverty and by recent cuts in social programs. The committee also observed that poverty has left children in Canada without the protection "to which they are entitled under the Covenant."[46]

The statistics on child poverty indicate that Canada's deficit reduction agenda and the deep cuts to social welfare programs it has entailed are not compatible with realizing Canada's obligation under article 27 of the Convention on the Rights of the Child. Rather than "in the case of need" providing "material assistance and support programs, particularly with regard to nutrition, clothing and housing," the cutbacks and reforms that have occurred both at the provincial and federal levels have exacerbated the problems of child poverty, homelessness and hunger. The policies leave no question that Canada has failed to take its obligation to poor children (and to the poor more generally) seriously. The latest federal/provincial child poverty initiative, the Child Tax Benefit (CTB), is yet another case in point. Launched in 1998 amid a fanfare of claims concerning the governments' commitment to fighting child poverty,[47] the CTB is "a 'system' of benefits for low and moderate income families with children" which includes "income support, as well as programs designed to assist low-income families."[48] The CTB does not, however, benefit children whose parents receive social assistance because provinces are entitled to "claw back" the supplement from welfare recipients. The hypocrisy of claiming to be addressing child poverty through an income supplement while at the same time clawing back the supplement from those children who arguably need it the most was not lost on the UN Committee on Economic, Social, and Cultural Rights. The committee expressed concern that, in all but two provinces,[49] the CTB "is meant to be given to all children of low-income families, [but] is in fact only given to children of working poor parents."[50] The committee recommended that the scheme be "amended so as to prohibit provinces from deducting the benefit from social assistance entitlements."[51] A government committed to fulfilling its obligation to provide for children in need would neither have permitted a claw-back of the CTB, nor have allowed child poverty to worsen in the interests of tax cuts and deficit reduction.

Conclusion

By examining child support obligations that exist within Canadian family law and the current state of social assistance programs, I have attempted to show that Canada does a relatively good job of meeting some of its international legal obligations toward children but a poor job of others. Canada has gone to great lengths to ensure that children receive financial support from their parents by creating legal obligations on parents to support their children and state-funded enforcement mechanisms in the event of parental noncompliance. Canada has not, however, taken any serious steps toward fulfilling its international legal obligation to provide support to children whose parents are incapable of supporting them. On the contrary, the recent steps Canada has adopted to address poverty have made the situation for poor children worse rather than better.

This analysis should make it clear why the recent child support guidelines cannot be seen as measures that fulfill Canada's international legal obligations to children. First and foremost, the child support guidelines are not measures that address child poverty in any comprehensive way. Instead, the guidelines fall squarely within one set of obligations that exist at international law — those requiring states to ensure that parents provide financial support to their children. While the guidelines may turn out to have a salutary impact in respect of these obligations by adding structure and consistency to the child support obligation, the guidelines do nothing to address child poverty more generally. For one thing, the majority of poor children live in two-parent homes,[52] so child support obligations that kick in when relationships break down are irrelevant. For another, strengthening the private obligation to pay child support will not benefit children whose fathers cannot be located or who do not have the financial means to pay. The only way to provide these children with an adequate living standard is through antipoverty policies, the very policies that Canada has been dismantling.

Finally, while child support guidelines stand to benefit children whose parents can pay child support, they may have the insidious effect of undermining efforts to put child poverty on the political agenda. The creation of the guidelines, and the significant efforts that are being made to monitor and hone them, allow the government to claim that it is taking action against child poverty. The efforts made on the child support front may thus make it increasingly difficult to force the government to acknowledge that poverty is a growing problem. The unfortunate result of the child support guidelines may be that measures that will help some children will unwittingly harm others.

Part III. Giving Meaning: Protection and Justiciability of Economic, Social, and Cultural Rights

Implementing Economic, Social, and Cultural Rights: The Role of National Human Rights Institutions

BARBARA VON TIGERSTROM

The implementation of economic, social, and cultural rights has been historically a problematic area in international human rights law theory and practice. Among other problems, the history of neglect of these rights has meant that the means to prevent and remedy violations remain underdeveloped. Equally frustrating is the fact that institutions and programs that should be expected to contribute to the realization of economic, social, and cultural rights often fail in this role and in some cases are even counterproductive, causing further harm where they should be providing assistance.

Given this situation, the development of effective measures for the realization of economic, social, and cultural rights is an endeavor of the utmost urgency and importance. These measures are traditionally understood to include legislative and constitutional reforms; they may also include a range of other measures. Among these is the use of nonjudicial institutions which have a role in protecting human rights and which may, in particular, be well placed to monitor, protect, and promote economic, social, and cultural rights. It has been suggested that specialized commissions be established to assume responsibility for the protection of these rights at a national level. They would carry out a variety of functions ranging from reporting to the Committee on Economic, Social, and Cultural Rights to public education.[1] Such an institution would undoubtedly be a great asset, but in its absence existing institutions may be able to carry out some functions that would contribute to the protection of economic, social, and cultural rights.

Within the broader category of nonjudicial institutions, the focus of this chapter is the institution of the ombudsman[2] and, to a lesser extent, human rights institutions (sometimes referred to as "national human rights institutions") and similar complaint resolution mechanisms in international institutions. The valuable role of ombudsman and similar institutions in human rights protection is receiving increased attention and recognition. In particular, these institutions may play a significant role in protecting economic, social, and cultural rights. Their jurisdiction often includes relevant areas, and their institutional characteristics allow them to work effectively in these areas that are typically marked by weak legal protection at the national and international levels.

The purpose of this chapter is to show how these institutions may assist in the promotion and protection of economic, social, and cultural rights, such that they should form an important and even necessary—though not sufficient—part of an effective effort to realize these rights. The first part provides an overview of the functions and characteristics of these institutions; the second part reviews some of their functions of particular relevance to economic, social, and cultural rights, illustrated by examples from several countries and an international institution. The chapter concludes with an analysis of some of the advantages and disadvantages of using these institutions to protect and promote economic, social, and cultural rights and factors that may determine their effectiveness.

National Human Rights Institutions

FUNCTIONS AND CHARACTERISTICS

As noted above, the term "national human rights institutions" denotes a broad category of institutions that may exercise a variety of functions for the protection of human rights at a national or local level. This category includes ombudsman offices and human rights commissions. Although each of these traditionally has its own particular characteristics, the boundaries between them are increasingly blurred, especially in the more recently established institutions, many of which are hybrid forms.

The classical ombudsman model is derived from the Swedish institution of that name which was established in 1809.[3] Generally speaking, an ombudsman is an official who receives and investigates complaints from the public against the government. The classical ombudsman has been described as having four essential characteristics,[4] although exceptions to each are commonly found. First, the institution is independent of government. Usually it is established by a constitutional or legislative provision, although in some countries the institution has been created and the ombudsman appointed by the executive, an arrangement that has been criticized as compromising the independence of the ombudsman.[5] Independence may also be guaranteed by other means, such as provisions in the legislation or constitution controlling the appointment and dismissal of the ombudsman, providing for the institution's budget, and preventing conflicts of interest, for example. The second characteristic is that the classical ombudsman generally acts in response to complaints from members of the public, although it is also common for the ombudsman to have the power to initiate investigations on her or his own motion. Third, the ombudsman typically will only respond to a complaint if other available avenues have been exhausted, for example, if the individual has already complained directly to the body concerned and remains dissatisfied with the result. The ombudsman may be expressly prohibited from investigating a matter that is the subject of an ongoing judicial proceeding. Finally, the fourth characteristic is that the remedies provided by the ombudsman are generally not legally enforceable but rather take the form of recommendations and reports. The ombudsman relies chiefly on the powers of persuasion and public pressure to obtain compliance.

Ombudsman institutions also share certain other characteristics. They generally act quickly, there may be a time limit on responses to complaints, and the informal procedures allow for more expeditious investigations. The simplicity and informality of the procedures, as well as the fact that they are provided without cost, render the institution widely accessible. The ombudsman and her or his staff generally have broad powers of investigation, including the power to require the production of documents, require responses in writing or in the form of oral testimony from persons involved, and inspect premises. These powers may or may not be subject to potential restrictions on the grounds of secrecy or national security.

The modern ombudsman institution has spread from western Europe around the world; a recent survey found over 320 ombudsman institutions in 89 countries.[6] The institution, known variously as, for example, ombudsman, parliamentary commissioner, citizen's advocate or aide, public protector, inspector general, médiateur, protecteur du citoyen, defensor del pueblo, or procurador de los derechos humanos, has adapted to each new environment, so that there is now considerable variation in structure and function between the institutions. Most notably, some offices, including many of those more recently established, have broader mandates and powers than the traditional model. Some are entrusted with general responsibility for the protection of human rights and may have some powers of enforcement and the power to initiate court actions. These "hybrid" offices fulfill the functions of an ombudsman and of a human rights commission with broad powers concerning human rights. In addition to receiving and investigating complaints, ombudsman and especially hybrid offices may have the power to undertake investigations on their own initiative, to supervise or propose legislative reforms, and to take other measures to protect human rights.

NATIONAL NONJUDICIAL INSTITUTIONS AND HUMAN RIGHTS

A role in the protection of human rights comes naturally to the ombudsman, placed as it is between the people and their government, and its purpose devoted to fairness, human dignity, and protecting members of society from abuses of power. The functions of the ombudsman with respect to human rights are most obvious in the case of offices with broad express mandates for the protection of human rights, but even the traditional and more narrowly defined institutions have a role to play in this respect. Increasing attention is being paid to the potential use of ombudsman institutions to assist in the protection and promotion of human rights,[7] including economic, social, and cultural rights.[8] For example, the Committee on Economic, Social, and Cultural Rights adopted a general comment on "the role of national human rights institutions in the protection of economic, social, and cultural rights," in which it recognized that the work of national human rights institutions including ombudsman offices, human rights advocates and "people's defenders" (défenseurs du peuple and defensores del pueblo) is an important means by which steps may be taken in the progressive realization of the International Covenant on Economic, Social, and Cultural Rights (ICESCR).[9] The general comment urges national human rights institutions and states parties to ensure that appropriate attention be given to economic, social, and cultural rights in their work and suggests a list of activities that could be undertaken in that regard.[10]

The extent to which the ombudsman may play an active and direct role in protecting human rights, and in particular economic, social, and cultural rights, will depend on a number of factors, including the ombudsman's powers and jurisdiction, her or his terms of reference, and the extent of legal implementation of these rights in the relevant jurisdiction.[11] For example, the functions of the ombudsman may or may not expressly include the protection of human rights. In cases where express jurisdiction to protect a certain right or category of rights is not conferred on the institution, it may nevertheless indirectly protect those rights. Human rights norms may inform the ombudsman's analysis in determining whether the conduct of public authorities has been improper, unfair, or unlawful.[12]

Nonjudicial Institutions and the Protection of Economic, Social, and Cultural Rights

A number of different kinds of activities commonly undertaken by ombudsman offices and other complaint mechanisms may contribute to the protection of economic, social, and cultural rights.[13] The following discussion of some of these activities will be illustrated by examples from several different countries.

INVESTIGATION OF COMPLAINTS AND SYSTEMIC PROBLEMS

THE TRADITIONAL OMBUDSMAN

Actions to "remedy deficient administrative performance" have been identified as one of the ways in which rights such as the right to food may be protected and provided with effective remedies for violations.[14] Administrative action or inaction in any area related to economic, social, and cultural rights may result in depriving individuals of their rights. As the key institution responsible for addressing "deficient administrative performance," the ombudsman clearly has a role to play. As the Honorable Justice Florence Mumba has noted, for example, "In Africa, most essential services are provided by the State. . . . The services are delivered through public institutions manned by public officials who exercise a lot of discretion," and complaints often arise with respect to this exercise of discretion.[15] As one report notes, "Ombudsman offices in jurisdictions such as the United Kingdom, Canada and Australia examine the denial or reduction of benefits for members of the public who rely on income support."[16] Recently the New Zealand ombudsman noted that "many cases each year brought [to the Ombudsman] . . . by social welfare beneficiaries can be said to have, as a backdrop" the right to an adequate standard of living recognized in the Universal Declaration of Human Rights.[17] Administrative actions may have significant impact on individuals' economic and social rights, including rights to work, social security, an adequate standard of living including food and housing, health and education. Cultural rights, including the right to participate in cultural life, the right to benefit from scientific progress, and the right to scientific and creative freedom, although they have traditionally received even less attention than economic and social rights, may also be affected by administrative decisions or actions within an ombudsman's jurisdiction.

The complaints in these areas show the substantial hardship that can follow from an administrative decision, action, inaction, or delay. Individuals may be deprived of their sole source of income, unable to work, denied health care, or evicted from their homes. Such deprivations, when they are the result of unfairness or unlawfulness on the part of government officials, are both instances of maladministration within the scope of the ombudsman's mandate and, potentially, violations of the state's obligation to respect economic, social, or cultural rights contrary to the norms and legal obligations of international human rights law.

The ombudsman, in attempting to resolve these types of complaints, may be able to avoid or rectify problems affecting individual complainants. The ombudsman's work may also be of benefit to many people who would otherwise have faced similar situations, through the impact of remedial action taken in response to the ombudsman's recommendations. It may also have indirect effects, such as broader changes to administrative practice, policy, or legislation following an investigation, or the general deterrent effect of the ombudsman's scrutiny.[18] These indirect effects are important since they considerably expand the office's influence. Ombudsman offices also commonly have the power to undertake investigations on their own motion, and this provides an even greater scope for addressing social and economic problems arising from maladministration, especially those of a systemic nature. Stephen Owen writes that "As skills and experience accumulate in an ombudsman's office, there evolves both the capacity and the responsibility to identify and remedy systemic causes of recurring unfairness." This "systems approach" is a "supplement to the more traditional role of reacting to individual complaints."[19] An office that uses a broad, systemic approach may also "serve as a resource for government institutions in identifying and preventing recurring unfairness" and may be asked "to review or even take part in the development of administrative policies."[20] An increasing willingness to take on this preventive role is one of the most important developments in the work of classical legislative ombudsmen, and enhances the effectiveness of the ombudsman in promoting human rights.[21]

HYBRID OMBUDSMAN/HUMAN RIGHTS INSTITUTIONS

The possibilities are even greater for institutions that combine a traditional ombudsman role with an explicit jurisdiction to protect human rights. An increasing number of ombudsman offices, especially among those more recently established, although they retain many of the features of the classical ombudsman, have broader mandates and more extensive powers than the typical classical office. For example, some "human rights ombudsmen" have a general mandate to protect the human rights of the nation's (or locality's) population. In carrying out their mandate, these offices may be permitted to take actions beyond the powers of the traditional ombudsman, such as initiating legal actions, making binding decisions, or taking other necessary interim measures to protect individuals at risk for human rights violations. Because of the greater breadth of their activity, these ombudsmen may be expected to take a more direct and active role in protecting all human rights, including economic, social, and cultural rights. The particular rights that a human rights ombudsman is empowered to protect may depend on the legal acceptance and implementation of the rights by the national government. The ombudsman's jurisdiction will typically include those rights that are contained in the national constitution and legislation and/or in international agreements ratified by the state.[22] In some cases this will include economic, social, and cultural rights.[23]

Some of the newer, hybrid offices have directed action specifically toward economic, social, and cultural rights, for example, in Eastern Europe, the Polish Commissioner for Civil Rights Protection (CCRP), and in Latin America, the human rights ombudsman of El Salvador. The establishment and functioning of these offices must be understood in their particular historical contexts. In Poland the "extremely painful process of introducing a market economy resulted in the unemployment and pauperization of large segments of society,"[24] and the CCRP thus was faced with many complaints related to poverty and social conditions. In El Salvador socioeconomic polarization and widespread poverty both helped to cause, and were exacerbated by, the civil war.[25] Economic and social issues are seen as "vital to the nation's reconciliation and reconstruction."[26]

The Polish CCRP in fact predates the nation's political and economic transition, having been one of the last efforts at reform of the communist regime.[27] The office was established in 1987, by the Act of 15 July 1987 on the Commissioner for Civil Rights Protection.[28] The first Commissioner was appointed later that year, and activities began in 1988.[29] Provisions on the CCRP were incorporated into the Constitution in 1989,[30] and have been included in chapter 9 of the new Constitution.[31] The Constitution (article 208) and the Act (article 1) state that the CCRP is to safeguard the rights and freedoms of citizens as set out in the constitution and other legal instruments. The Act further says that "In cases involving protection of the civic rights and liberties, the Commissioner shall investigate whether, due to any action or default on the part of agencies, organizations, or institutions responsible for compliance and implementation of such rights and liberties, the law and/or principle of community life and social justice have been breached" (article 1[3]). Thus the CCRP is concerned with the legality of acts, unlike offices such as the British ombudsmen who investigate complaints of "maladministration" rather than illegality.[32]

Initially, confusion and frustration resulted from popular misconceptions about the role of the office: "the mass media expected that the Commissioner, acting like a Robin Hood, would, for example, allocate housing to those in need and substitute for the administration in other similar situations."[33] Economic transition "Coupled with the drastic deterioration of the social safety net . . . led to numerous complaints 'against poverty' with which the Commissioner [was] obviously powerless to cope."[34] However, within its limits the office of the CCRP has nevertheless taken an active role with respect to economic and social issues.[35] Indeed, even taking a strict legal approach there is plenty of scope for such activity, given that the Constitution (both the old Stalinist constitution and the new text adopted in 1997) includes a broad range of economic, social, and cultural rights.[36] Furthermore, the CCRP has promoted the use of international law in the area of human rights.[37] Given this legal background, the CCRP has a fairly broad and stable basis upon which to address the legality of measures affecting economic, social, and cultural rights. "These rights are increasingly being denied because of budget problems but, as CCRP, Professor Tadeusz Zielinski felt obliged to warn repeatedly that people cannot be denied benefits to which they have a constitutional right simply because of a shortage of money: 'I solved the dilemma I found — the law or the inviolability of the budget — in favour of the law.' "[38]

Where an infringement of rights has been found, the CCRP has the power to demand that civil proceedings, prosecutions, or administrative proceedings be instituted or to appeal decisions.[39] The Commissioner may also file motions before the constitutional tribunal or request from the tribunal a binding interpretation of a statute.[40]

It is significant that the Commissioner apparently relies explicitly on international as well as constitutional norms in the area of economic, social, and cultural rights in his investigations, analyses, and decisions. The Commissioner has referred both to the Constitution and to articles in the ICESCR in his assessment of employment, housing, health protection, standards of living, social insurance, and education,[41] concluding that "the basic international standards of the individual's social and cultural rights set forth in the International Convention on Economic, Social, and Cultural Rights (ratified by Poland) and whose counterparts are the rights of Polish citizens described in [the Constitution] . . . are not being met satisfactorily."[42]

The Procuraduría para la Defensa de los Derechos Humanos (the PDDH, or Office of the Human Rights Ombudsman) in El Salvador has also devoted considerable attention to economic and social issues. The establishment of the office came about as part of the reconciliation and reconstruction process following years of civil war in El Salvador.[43] This process was designed to be a comprehensive one, "aim[ing] at nothing less than eliminating the cause of the conflict: a militarized society, riven by profound economic and social inequalities and a closed political system" and devoting particular attention to human rights and institutional reforms.[44] The Mexico Agreement contains an agreement to create the position of the national ombudsman for the defense of human rights, as one of the constitutional and judicial reforms.[45] Chapter 3 of the Chapultepec Agreement outlines the reform of the judicial system, including an article providing for the appointment of the National Ombudsman for Human Rights and the drafting of the organic law of the Office of the National Ombudsman.[46]

Following the signature of the peace agreements, constitutional reforms were adopted, including an article on the functions of the PDDH.[47] The organic law governing the office was promulgated in February of 1992.[48] The first ombudsman was appointed at that time and the office began its activities in July of that year. Upon its establishment, the PDDH assumed responsibility with respect to all human rights violations since the signature of the peace agreements, although ONUSAL (the UN verification mission) continued to play a significant role for the first few years of the PDDH's existence.[49]

The organic law provides for a broad range of functions and powers for the Human Rights Ombudsman. The basic functions of the office include investigating human rights violations, assisting victims, monitoring detention of prisoners and other government actions, commenting on proposed laws affecting human rights, formulating proposals and recommendations, and generally ensuring respect for human rights.[50]

During investigations the ombudsman has the power to carry out inspections, interview relevant persons, and demand the production of documents or other evidence.[51] If an investigation reveals a violation of human rights, the office must issue a report of the facts and its conclusions, and take

whatever actions are appropriate to bring about the cessation of the violation, including initiation of legal action. The report may contain recommendations, including recommendations for the compensation of victims or for
the reform of policies or laws.[52] Recommendations must be complied with by
law,[53] although in practice many authorities have ignored the recommendations of the PDDH.[54] In the case of noncompliance, or in cases of grave and
systematic violations, the ombudsman may publish a public report or criticism on the matter.[55] Special investigations and reports, and the establishment of mechanisms to oversee compliance with recommendations, are
permitted in cases of "systematic practice of violation of human rights or
situations of special gravity or national significance."[56]

The human rights protected by the PDDH include "civil and political
rights, economic, social, and cultural rights, and the Third Generation rights
contemplated in the constitution, valid laws and treaties, as well as those
contained in declarations and principles approved by the United Nations or
the Organization of American States."[57] Given the context in which the
office was established and the persistence of political violence in El Salvador,
it was natural that considerable emphasis would be placed on the investigation of serious violations of physical integrity and security. This emphasis is
reflected in the organic law, for example in special provisions relating to the
inspection of detention centers and the maintenance of a registry of prisoners.[58]

The other major problem to be addressed in the postconflict measures is
the persistence of economic and social inequalities in the country.

As long as there are sectors of the population who live below all standards of human
decency in a state of extreme poverty, the conditions will be there for the situation to
degenerate into a new conflict. . . . Decent housing, jobs, education and health must
be the fundamental objective of the Government's policies and the effort is one in
which all sectors of the population, without exception, must be engaged.[59]

Economic and social rights are equally within the jurisdiction of the PDDH,
since they are specifically referred to in the organic law and included in the
Constitution,[60] and El Salvador is a signatory to the ICESCR and the Protocol of San Salvador.[61] The office has increased its activity in this area. Since
a major restructuring with the assistance of the United Nations Development Program (UNDP),[62] the office has contained a Department of Economic, Social, and Cultural Rights.[63] The investigation unit of the department is responsible for investigating all complaints relating to violations of
economic, social, and cultural rights received by the office.

Unfortunately, the general problems that have hampered the effectiveness of the PDDH likely will continue to affect its work in this area. The
office has suffered from a chronic shortage of resources, and state officials
have been resistant to its activities and recommendations.[64] Furthermore,

some of the root causes of economic and social rights violations are beyond the effective scope of the PDDH's action: for example, in its report it places some responsibility for the deterioration of social and economic conditions on the structural adjustment program imposed on El Salvador,[65] and the task of rebuilding a strong economy in the postconflict period is an extremely difficult one.[66] Thus the situation in El Salvador shows both the potential and the limits of the ombudsman's activity in the area of economic, social, and cultural rights.

CORRUPTION CONTROL

One serious form of maladministration that has a profound effect on economic and social rights is government corruption. "Corruption in public office is another factor that negatively affects economic, social, and cultural rights. . . . Resources which would normally be applied to programmes for the protection of rights are waylaid to benefit private individuals."[67] United Nations agencies such as the UNDP have made note of the "development implications of corruption."[68] It is not difficult to imagine the potential benefits from redirecting resources to social services and other government functions and the impact this could have on the population's enjoyment of economic, social, and cultural rights.

An independent institution such as the ombudsman may be useful in combating government corruption.[69] Although in many instances the corrupt actions of government officials may be beyond the legal and practical scope of an ombudsman's investigations, the classical ombudsman's jurisdiction does sometimes include actions that are unlawful,[70] which could include misappropriation of public funds, acceptance of bribes, and other forms of corrupt dealing. Even if there is, as seems often to be the case, a provision that the ombudsman may or must refer such cases to an appropriate authority,[71] the referral and any investigation done by the ombudsman will help to bring such misconduct to light.

Some ombudsman offices also have special functions and powers to address the problem of corruption in government. For example, the Ombudsman Commission in Papua New Guinea has been very active in investigating corruption in government institutions.[72] The Commission operates under a dual legislative mandate: the Organic Law on the Ombudsman Commission and the Organic Law on the Duties and Responsibilities of Leadership. The Constitution also gives the commission the authority to enforce the Leadership Code of Papua New Guinea, a constitutionally entrenched code of conduct that applies to all senior government officials (with the exception of the Governor General).[73] In essence, the Commission plays two roles, the "traditional ombudsman role" and the "extra dimension" of investigating allegations of misconduct contrary to the Leadership Code.[74] The powers of the Commission under the Organic Law on the Duties and Responsibilities of Leadership are more extensive than under the Organic Law on the Ombudsman Commission, including the power to issue directions, make declarations, and initiate prosecutions.[75]

Further examples can be found in other parts of the world. Two of the relatively new offices in Africa, the Inspector General of Government (IGG) in Uganda and the Office of the Ombudsman in Namibia, combine broad jurisdiction over human rights with a mandate to eliminate corruption in public office. Established in 1986 and 1990, respectively, by constitutional provisions as well as by statute, these two offices have been described as examples of a "second-generation" model of the ombudsman in Africa.[76] In Uganda, the new constitution's provisions relating to the powers of the IGG state that the "Inspectorate of Government shall have power to investigate, cause investigation, arrest, cause arrest, prosecute or cause prosecution in respect of cases involving corruption, abuse of authority or of public office" and the IGG "may, during the course of his or her duties or as a consequence of his or her findings, make such orders and give such directions as are necessary and appropriate in the circumstances"[77] — broad and, for an ombudsman, unusual powers presumably intended to make the IGG more effective in combating corruption and serious human rights abuses. It has been noted in the Ugandan context that some instances of corruption directly implicate economic and social rights such as the right to housing, for example, since a significant number of corruption investigations have involved housing and land issues:

The DAPCB [Departed Asians Property Custodian Board, a government agency], described by one writer as a huge "Pork Barrel," into which the politician of the day can reach to distribute fat to his circle of supporters, is the principle [sic] means utilized by successive governments to distribute political patronage, and in the quest of private accumulation. Consequently, forcible evictions occur on spurious grounds and in direct violation of the terms and conditions of tenancies entered into between the parties. . . . Many of these cases have involved widows and orphans, who are usually in an economically weak position and in most instances do not have easy access to alternative forms of accommodation.[78]

Such cases clearly show the interconnection between corruption and the violation of economic and social rights, here in a direct and individualized manner. In other instances the connection may be not quite so direct, but still significant.

The Namibian Ombudsman is also empowered to investigate corruption in public office as well as human rights violations.[79] In recent years, several other countries have established specialized offices to deal with matters of corruption. For example, Tanzania has established the Enforcement of Leadership Code Commission.[80] There seems to be increasing awareness of the potential role of ombudsman institutions in combating corruption, both among ombudsmen and in the larger international community.[81]

OTHER ACTIVITIES

Through their primary sphere of activity, which is investigating complaints and other matters that come to their attention, ombudsmen and other nonjudicial human rights institutions identify, analyze, and attempt to resolve problems, including violations of human rights by government actors. In doing so they contribute to the protection of human rights, including specifically economic, social, and cultural rights, either directly by addressing violations, or indirectly by increasing government accountability and influencing government administration and policy. A number of other types of activities, often within the jurisdiction of these institutions, may also have a role to play.

PUBLIC EDUCATION

It is quite common for national human rights institutions of all types to include public education as part of their mandate. These activities attempt to increase awareness about the office itself and what it does, in order to make the institution more accessible and encourage people to use it if they have a complaint. The public education programs also disseminate information about human rights and promote dialogue in the community about human rights issues. These initiatives may be valuable in raising awareness about economic, social, and cultural rights and relevant activities by the institution.

LEGISLATIVE AND CONSTITUTIONAL REFORM

An ombudsman or human rights commissioner may be formally or informally responsible for helping to evaluate and develop law and policy in relevant areas. Sometimes this role is specifically provided for in the mandate of the institution. For example, the Polish CCRP has reviewed and commented on new legislation to avoid infringements of human rights.[82] Under the Act, he is permitted to propose legislative initiatives or amendments (article 16[2][1]). Analyses of health, labor, social insurance, and housing issues, including critiques of legislative and regulatory initiatives, have been carried out by the CCRP, with specific reference both to constitutional standards and Poland's obligations under the ICESCR.[83]

The functions of the Human Rights Ombudsman in El Salvador also include proposing reforms for the protection of human rights and issuing opinions on laws that affect human rights.[84] The Latvian National Human

Rights Office is authorized to "carry out an analysis of Latvian legal norms in order to determine their compliance with international human rights treaties which are binding to Latvia";[85] the Ukrainian Human Rights Representative is responsible for "facilitating the process of bringing legislation of Ukraine on human rights and citizens' rights and freedoms in accordance with the Constitution of Ukraine and international standards in this area."[86]

MONITORING AND REPORTING

Ombudsman offices receive complaints from the public and may conduct their own investigations into systemic problems. They commonly produce detailed reports and statistical analyses of complaints and their activities. This information is made public in the form of annual reports and may also be contained in reports or recommendations to the relevant parts of government. Given this role in collecting and disseminating information about government performance, it would seem obvious that these offices can make a meaningful contribution to monitoring a state's progress in implementing its obligations under the ICESCR, both in terms of noting general trends and in identifying specific problem areas. The patterns of complaints received may, for example, indicate that the government is failing to meet its obligations to respect or protect a particular right and may help in identifying the sources or causes of violations. Furthermore, cooperation between national institutions may provide an important opportunity for comparative analyses.

National human rights institutions may also have a role to play in the international reporting procedure. It has been suggested that an ombudsman office should not be responsible for preparing reports required under a treaty, since this would compromise the independence of the office, which requires it to maintain some distance from the government and not to speak on its behalf. However, it can contribute in other ways, for example by providing information to those preparing the report or submitting its own independent report to the Committee on Economics, Social and Cultural Rights.[87]

ACCESS TO INFORMATION

Given the importance of access to information for the exercise of many economic and social rights, ombudsman institutions with jurisdiction over information (as well as attention to complaints involving access to information by general ombudsmen) may offer indirect protection of such rights. Specialized institutions with a mandate in this area may also be found in some instances. For example, information commissioners, who receive complaints regarding problems in accessing government information, have been operating for many years in Canada (both at the federal level and in several provinces, either as a separate office or within the general legislative ombuds-man's office). Many jurisdictions around the world now have commissioners or offices responsible for data protection and access to information.[88]

INTERNATIONAL INSTITUTIONS

As the popularity of the ombudsman model has spread, recent years have seen initiatives to establish ombudsmen or ombudsman-like institutions at the international level as well as within individual states. For example, the European Ombudsman, named by the European Parliament in 1995, is responsible for dealing with complaints about maladministration or denial of legal rights by European Community institutions or bodies. Another important development is the establishment of nonjudicial complaint reso-lution mechanisms similar to an ombudsman office within international financial institutions. The best known of these is the Inspection Panel of the World Bank, which was established in 1993. Similar bodies have been estab-lished in other international financial institutions, for example the Inter-American Development Bank (Independent Investigation Mechanism) and the Asian Development Bank (Inspection Committee).

The Inspection Panel receives requests for inspection from affected par-ties in the territory of a borrower country, claiming that "an actual or threatened material adverse effect on the affected party's rights or interests arises directly out of an action or omission of the Bank to follow its own operational policies and procedures during the design, appraisal and/or implementation of a Bank-financed project."[89] As of October 2000, the In-spection Panel had registered eighteen requests for inspection.[90] Requests for inspection have complained of adverse effects on health, standards of living, economic well being and food production, and alleged violation of policies on resettlement, indigenous peoples, environmental assessment and poverty reduction.[91]

The Inspection Panel's potential influence is limited by a number of fac-tors: for example, its findings are not binding, and its terms of reference limit it to a consideration of whether existing policies were complied with, not whether those policies are adequate to protect the rights and interests of affected persons. It has also been subjected to criticism, for example, by those who argue it is not sufficiently independent.[92] Extensive reforms would be required to achieve a meaningful integration of human rights norms into development finance. However, the importance of this institu-tional development should not be minimized. The Inspection Panel has been called the "most notable example" of "introducing some human rights standards into [international financial institutions'] work."[93] It is, therefore, of interest both for its own potential impact and as a possible model for other institutions to establish mechanisms for preventing, monitoring, and reme-dying violations of human rights by internationally organized activities — the work of international financial institutions being of particular interest in the area of economic and social rights.

Nonjudicial Institutions for the Protection of Human Rights: Possibilities and Limits

STRENGTHS AND ADVANTAGES

One of the most important characteristics of the ombudsman and similar institutions is accessibility, both in terms of ease of access to the office itself and of making complaints, and the lack of barriers to access such as cost and complexity of procedures. This is a significant advantage because it means the office is more likely to be used by members of low income and marginalized groups who may be particularly at risk for violations of their economic, social, and cultural rights. A survey indicated that "the vast majority [of ombudsmen] believed they served at least as many poor as affluent people" and "two-fifths of the total ombudsmen believed they served mainly poor clients."[94]

The flexible approach and broad jurisdiction of ombudsman-type institutions are also important to their potential effectiveness in this area. In scrutinizing administrative actions or decisions, the ombudsman asks whether they are fair, not just whether they conform to the letter of the law. "Unfairness includes improper discrimination, arbitrary or oppressive behaviour, arrogance, delay, and unreasonableness by public officials, all of which may be impractical, inappropriate, or impossible to challenge at law."[95] In making this assessment of fairness, the ombudsman may be guided by standards in international human rights law.[96] Thus it would be open to an ombudsman to criticize a decision partly on the basis that it deprived an individual of an internationally recognized economic, social, or cultural right, even if the decision was legal according to the applicable national or local laws.

This is particularly important in the context of economic, social, and cultural rights for two reasons. First, these rights are less likely than civil and political rights to be implemented in domestic law, where such implementation is necessary for the rights to be enforceable at the national level. The ombudsman's ability to appeal to broader standards of fairness and equity thus allow the ombudsman to consider these rights on an equal basis despite their lack of formal legal implementation. Second, one of the most common problems cited with respect to protecting economic, social, and cultural rights is the difficulty of their justiciability. Although this is a problem that must be dealt with in a variety of ways, including the development of judicial expertise in the area and the encouragement of continued legal and academic interpretation of the rights and obligations, the current situation is such that the courts are particularly weak mechanisms for enforcing these rights. Generally, this means that additional mechanisms are all the more important in this area. In particular, the ombudsman, because of the flexible criteria the office is entitled to use in evaluating actions, is less hampered by a lack of precise justiciable standards for determining violations of economic, social, and cultural rights. Given his or her experience in many of the relevant areas of government activity, an ombudsman may also be well placed to contribute to the development of such standards.

LIMITS

Recognizing the limits of a nonjudicial institution's jurisdiction and activity is essential in order to have realistic expectations of the institution's capacity, to identify the need for other mechanisms, and to avoid undermining the credibility of the institution by attempting to act beyond its jurisdiction. The limits on an institution's activity and effectiveness will vary considerably depending on the type of institution, its powers and functions, and the political and economic climate in which it works, therefore the discussion that follows will necessarily be merely a general overview.

First, the institution must realistically assess its own and the government's capacity to protect and ensure rights given the prevailing socioeconomic situation. The ICESCR, in article 2(1), explicitly acknowledges such limits when it states that states parties have an obligation to take measures to implement the covenant "to the maximum of its available resources." National human rights institutions that have been active in the area of economic and social rights have found that the socioeconomic situation of the people and the actions of the government must be considered within this context. For example, Hungary's Parliamentary Commissioner for Civil Rights and her Deputy reported that "We perceived *social security and the basic needs of living* as representing the most serious concern for our complainants."[97] They investigated many complaints relating to social and economic matters, but stated, "In the majority of the problems related to social support (welfare) we were unable to help. We had to accept that funds available to the local governments for providing aid were too small compared to the number of those in need."[98]

However, even in such cases, the institution's role, though constrained, may be of considerable importance. The Hungarian Parliamentary Commissioner noted that "in such cases we tried to explore possible latent discriminations. We studied the regulations on equitableness in the decrees of the local governments, and we called the attention of the mayors" to particularly grave cases.[99] This kind of investigation can be helpful in promoting implementation of the ICESCR and other legal commitments, since these contain obligations to eliminate discrimination as well as to ensure rights in general terms.[100] Furthermore, the scrutiny of an ombudsman is of value even when the economic conditions are such that the government's resources are limited. The obligations of a state are qualified, not erased, by a situation of economic hardship. The relevant provision of the Covenant has been interpreted to mean that in the case of scarcity, a state must allocate resources on a priority basis to the satisfaction of at least essential economic and social needs.[101] Recall that the Polish CCRP "has felt obliged to warn repeatedly that people cannot be denied benefits to which they have a constitutional right simply because of a shortage of money."[102]

Other limits, specific to the ombudsman as an institution, stem from the nature of the institution, its jurisdiction, and its powers. With the great diversity among contemporary ombudsman offices, it is difficult to generalize with respect to these characteristics. The traditional ombudsman has authority to make recommendations as to the administration and application of government laws and policies, not as to the substantive content of those laws and policies. There are exceptions to this general rule, even among general legislative ombudsmen that more or less conform to the traditional model: for instance the Ontario Ombudsman can take action with respect to a decision or act that "was in accordance with a rule of law or a provision of any Act or a practice that is or may be unreasonable, unjust, oppressive, or improperly discriminatory."[103] However, the traditional conception of the ombudsman's role is that he should direct his attention to "administrative policy," the "translation and application of broad legislative policy to individual situations," rather than the content of the legislative policy itself.[104] The international development bank inspection mechanisms such as the World Bank Inspection Panel are similarly limited to examining compliance with bank policy, not the content of the policy itself. This may preclude institutions from addressing some infringements that result from legislative policy, rather than administrative policy or implementation.

Another limitation, the individualistic, complaint-driven approach to investigations, has been attenuated in many cases, since ombudsmen and hybrid institutions often have the authority to conduct own-motion investigations and are increasingly using this power to undertake systemic inquiries that go beyond the circumstances of individual complaints. To the extent that an institution's activity is restricted, by law or otherwise, to investigating individual complaints, its effectiveness in protecting and promoting economic, social, and cultural rights will be limited, since many of these problems will likely be of a systemic nature.

Finally, a shortage of financial and human resources will have a significant negative impact on an institution's ability to be effective in this area. Some offices, for example the Human Rights Ombudsman's office in El Salvador,[105] have been chronically underfunded and this will obviously limit the extent of their activities. While all areas will likely be affected, economic, social, and cultural rights may suffer disproportionately, for a number of reasons. First, as already noted, the problems associated with infringements of these rights may often be of a systemic nature, which means their investigation is likely to consume a great deal of time and resources. Furthermore, especially in countries where there is a history, and perhaps an ongoing occurrence, of serious violations of physical security and integrity, these matters will likely be given priority, diverting resources and attention from economic, social, and cultural rights. Finally, given the historical neglect of economic, social, and cultural rights, institutions in any country may be expected to lack expertise in this area, at least relatively speaking. Therefore, an office may need to make a concerted effort to gain the expertise, documentation and other resources it needs to deal effectively with economic, social, and cultural rights issues. This is one area where international cooperation can be of great assistance.

Enhancing the Effectiveness of the Ombudsman's Work in Economic, Social, and Cultural Rights

The United Nations Centre for Human Rights (now the Office of the High Commissioner for Human Rights), in its handbook on national human rights institutions, identifies six "effectiveness factors," elements "which may be considered essential to the effective functioning of national institutions," and which are generally applicable to different kinds of institutions in different contexts:

independence;
defined jurisdiction and adequate powers;
accessibility;
cooperation;
operational efficiency; and
accountability.[106]

This section will comment on some of these factors as they relate specifically to effectiveness in the protection and promotion of economic, social, and cultural rights. Of course, maximizing the strengths and addressing the limits discussed in the previous section, where possible, will also enhance the institution's effectiveness.

The jurisdiction and powers of the ombudsman provided for in the relevant statute or constitutional provisions will be determinative, to a large extent, of the ombudsman's ability to deal with infringements of economic, social, and cultural rights in various ways. There are several different aspects to the ombudsman's jurisdiction that may be relevant. The first aspect concerns the bodies with respect to which the ombudsman may take complaints or otherwise initiate investigations, and whether these include the government departments or agencies, or other parties most involved in economic, social, and cultural matters. A subissue here which is increasingly important is the extent to which privatization may take service providers outside the jurisdiction of the ombudsman.[107]

Next, the constitutive provisions may define the substance of complaints that the ombudsman is permitted to investigate, for example, unlawful behavior, unfairness, other forms of maladministration, or any combination of these. The breadth with which this is defined may be important in determining whether an ombudsman can investigate a complaint about violations of economic, social, and cultural rights. The broadest are those that allow the ombudsman to investigate any complaints of alleged violations of human rights. However, other factors may be significant, such as whether the ombudsman is expected to investigate alleged acts that are unfair, or only those that are unlawful. The effect of these provisions will also be determined by their interaction with external factors, since in a state in which economic, social, and cultural rights are fully implemented in the national laws, the investigation of unlawful acts will have a broader scope in this area than in a jurisdiction where such implementation has not yet been accomplished.

The governing law normally also specifies the persons from whom the ombudsman may receive complaints. The likelihood of effectively addressing violations of economic, social, and cultural rights is increased if the ombudsman may receive complaints from groups as well as individuals. The nature of these rights is such that they sometimes can only be addressed with reference to groups.[108] The ombudsman will also be able to offer more comprehensive protection if he or she can take complaints from or on behalf of persons likely to be in a vulnerable position, such as children, noncitizens, or nonresidents of the country, and persons in institutions. Some statutes make specific provision for such cases.[109]

The powers granted to the ombudsman usually include the power to initiate own-motion investigations, in at least some situations. The existence of this power and its breadth will often be crucial to the ombudsman's effectiveness, again because of the systemic nature of many economic, social, and cultural rights violations, which means that they may not be the subject of an individual complaint or properly dealt with in an individually focused investigation. In addition, the power to investigate on the ombudsman's own motion is important in reaching vulnerable populations, according to the UN Handbook:

The power to conduct investigations suo moto can be an extremely important and far-reaching one. Children, women, the poor, the homeless, the mentally or physically incapacitated, prisoners, and members of religious, ethnic and linguistic minorities are all, due to their unequal status, especially vulnerable to human rights abuses. It is ironic but generally true that these same vulnerable groups are also most likely to be unaware of their rights and of the mechanisms which exist to protect those rights. Even where knowledge does exist, victims of human rights violations do not often have advocates to act on their behalf and may be extremely reluctant to approach an official agency in order to lodge a formal complaint.[110]

In this emerging area of human rights protection, cooperation will also be very important. Cooperation with nongovernmental organizations, inter-governmental organizations and other ombudsmen or human rights commissions can help an office to develop its capacity for protecting rights through the sharing of resources and expertise and learning from the successes and problems of each organization.[111]

Finally, the independence of the office cannot be sufficiently emphasized. Economic and social matters are often likely to be controversial, so the ombudsman will not be able to take effective action unless the ombudsman's independence is adequately protected by constitutional and legislative provisions. The importance of independence has been noted, particularly in the context of corruption investigations.[112] Commentators have recognized the need for independence of the judiciary in cases relating to economic, social, and cultural rights,[113] and many of the same factors apply to ombudsmen investigating violations. There are a number of different elements contributing to the independence of an institution, including legal and operational autonomy, financial autonomy, appointment and dismissal procedures, and a composition reflecting sociological and political pluralism.[114] Particular attention should be paid to each element to ensure the greatest possible degree of independence.

Concluding Remarks

The foregoing has been an attempt to show some of the ways in which the ombudsman institution, in its many forms, may be — and in many cases already is — of assistance in the protection and promotion of economic, social, and cultural rights. While it is important for an office not to overextend itself or overstep the boundaries of its jurisdiction, within limits the ombudsman can be effective in providing protection and raising awareness of these rights and their violations. The ombudsman may have an important role to play in monitoring and encouraging a state's compliance with its international obligations under the ICESCR and other sources of international law, including the progressive realization of rights and the elimination of discrimination in their enjoyment. To a significant extent, the protection of economic, social, and cultural rights is already part of the activities of many ombudsmen, and it is simply a matter of increasing awareness of this role and considering its potential.

Obviously, the ombudsman or similar institutions will not be the only answer in the continuing quest for effective implementation measures. The activities discussed above cannot on their own provide sufficient protection to fulfill a state's obligations to respect, protect, and ensure rights or to provide effective remedies for rights violations. However, the potential impact of a well-designed and adequately funded office should not be underestimated either, and this means that support for developing institutions should be included in programs for international assistance and technical cooperation. Ideally, an independent ombudsman-type institution with sufficient powers and resources, and a staff committed to the protection of human rights, will form one part of a comprehensive implementation plan for the realization of economic, social, and cultural rights.

Bringing Economic, Social, and Cultural Rights Home: Palestinians in Occupied East Jerusalem and Israel

LEILANI FARHA

Within the practice of human rights, historically, civil and political rights have been privileged over economic, social, and cultural rights,[1] with the Cold War capitalist, liberal states having promoted the former and socialist states having promoted the latter. Paradoxically, the end of the Cold War and the dismantling of socialist structures, policies and ideologies has coincided with a new emphasis on economic, social, and cultural rights at the international level, an emphasis which appears to be gaining strength as we enter the new millennium. While this new emphasis can be expected to encourage initiatives seeking to protect and promote those rights at international, regional, national, and local levels, it is important to realize that this new emphasis is in many ways simply a recognition of the various local initiatives that have been taking place for many years. This realization is important because it is only through learning from local activities and experiences that the new emphasis at the international level can produce concrete results at the local level.

Consequently, this chapter examines the activities and experiences of Palestinians living in occupied East Jerusalem and those living in Israel in using international human rights law and mechanisms in their struggle for equality, autonomy, and statehood. In particular it highlights the collaboration between an international nongovernmental organization and two local organizations to this end. The primary purpose of this essay is to document the activities and experiences that have resulted from this collaboration and to assess their benefits. In doing so, it should serve to guide similar efforts in other places, as well as to inform the new emphasis on economic, social, and cultural rights at the international level.

The examination undertaken here is divided into three parts. The first part provides an overview of the housing situation of Palestinians living in East Jerusalem and inside Israel. This overview exposes the central and defining role that housing, land and property play in Israel's laws, policies, and practices that define Palestinians' everyday struggles. The second part provides an outline of a housing rights framework and the right to adequate housing under international human rights law and then chronicles how international law and legal mechanisms have been used by Palestinian groups.

The third part offers an assessment of the economic, social, and cultural rights activities undertaken by Palestinian groups from the perspective of those working in the field. The chapter concludes with a brief comment on the broader implications of the Palestinian experience for the practice of economic, social, and cultural rights.

Palestinian Housing

As a result of the 1948 and 1967 wars between Palestine and Israel, Palestinians now live in two groups: those within the territory that is now Israel and those within the territory that Israel occupied in 1967, namely East Jerusalem, the West Bank and Gaza. Approximately 150,000 Palestinians currently reside in occupied East Jerusalem, comprising just under 50 percent of the population;[2] 850,000 Palestinians live in Israel, comprising 19 percent of the total population of Israel. Since the establishment of the State of Israel in 1948, and the annexation of East Jerusalem in 1967, successive Israeli governments have sought to "Judaize" both areas by systematically discriminating against Palestinians with respect to housing and land. In the next two sections the most pressing land and housing issues facing each of these groups of Palestinians are reviewed.

Housing in Occupied East Jerusalem

The housing conditions of Palestinians living in occupied East Jerusalem are principally informed by Israel's goal to "Judaize" Jerusalem,[3] that is, to change the demographic makeup of the city by increasing the Jewish presence and severely limiting the Palestinian presence to no more than 24 percent of the population.[4] This has been a government policy of both the Labour and the Likud parties since Israel occupied East Jerusalem in 1967, realized through a number of bureaucratic restrictions on construction in the West Bank and through the replacement of the planning regime and the Jordanian Planning and Construction Law in 1967 with Israeli planning and housing.[5] De-Arabizing the population in East Jerusalem is a policy that has been reinvigorated by successive state governments and mayors of Jerusalem since the signing of the Oslo Accords in 1993, which left the final status of Jerusalem to be negotiated at a later date. Consolidating the annexation of East Jerusalem by turning Jerusalem into a Jewish dominated city is a means of ensuring that Jerusalem is the unified capital of Israel and the Jewish people (wherever they live), a core objective of Zionist ideology and its expression through the State of Israel.

The principal methods used to carry out the Judaization of Jerusalem include house demolitions and discriminatory zoning laws used in conjunction with rapid settlement expansion.[6] These are briefly described below.

HOUSE DEMOLITIONS

According to the Palestine Human Rights Information Centre (PHRIC), between January 1994 and March 1997 at least 252 families or over 2,000 people in the Occupied Territories including East Jerusalem were forcibly evicted from their homes as a result of house demolitions or sealings.[7] In occupied East Jerusalem itself, on average, fifty Palestinian homes are demolished each year by Israeli officials,[8] though recently this average has increased as the Israeli government pushes to Judaize Jerusalem before engaging in "final status" talks.

Regardless when they occur, house demolitions almost always follow the same pattern.

The operation is usually carried out at night to ensure least disturbance [resistance], or if during the day, a curfew is imposed or a closed military area declared. The first formal notification the family receives of an impending demolition or sealing order is when the soldiers arrive at the house and inform the family that they have a period, typically between half an hour and two hours, to remove their belongings from the house. Sometimes there is no opportunity to remove belongings or the soldiers may do it themselves, often breaking or damaging household possessions in the process. The length of time given and the curfew ensure that the family has no opportunity to contact their lawyer or other assistance.[9]

Demolitions are executed suddenly, in an atmosphere of a major military operation with an accompaniment sometimes of several hundred armed soldiers. Bulldozers are most commonly used to carry out demolitions.[10] House demolition often results in serious damage to neighboring houses. Once the house is demolished, families are not provided with alternate accommodation. Not surprisingly, rather than being rendered homeless or living in a tent, many of the evicted families return to the original site of their homes to rebuild and, as a result, risk being forcibly evicted again.

Building or renovating a house without an Israeli government-issued permit is the primary reason Palestinian houses are demolished in East Jerusalem. These building permits (required for dwellers living on the southern outskirts of Ramallah to the northern edge of Bethlehem) are impossible for Palestinians to obtain.[11] Beyond bribery or acting as an informant or land seller for the Israelis, the only way a Palestinian can receive a building permit is if the applicant can prove sole ownership of or title to the plot of land on which he or she wishes to build or renovate.[12] As the Israeli government knows, this is practically impossible because when Israel occupied what is now East Jerusalem, 80 percent of the land was privately owned by Arabs but only one-third had been formally surveyed and registered by the Jordanian government (which had control over East Jerusalem prior to 1967). Since 1967 no land registration for Palestinians has been permitted,[13] and the Israelis do not recognize ownership rights to unregistered land. In turn, approximately 80 percent of applications for permits are rejected and, for those granted, "bribes" can range from U.S.$2,500 to U.S.$10,000.[14]

As a result, Palestinians living in overcrowded and poorly serviced housing in occupied East Jerusalem have few choices: they can continue to live in deplorable conditions, they can build or renovate without a permit and risk house demolition and then homelessness,[15] or they can move out of East Jerusalem to the West Bank or outside Palestine altogether. As such, the threat of house demolition is an effective means of controlling and altering demographics in the region.

DISCRIMINATORY ZONING LAWS AND SETTLEMENT EXPANSION

Since 1967, Israeli settlement policy in Jerusalem has been directed toward a single overriding goal: the consolidation of Israeli control over Palestinian East Jerusalem in order to prevent any future division of the city. In political and functional terms, this has involved declarations of a "united" Jerusalem as the "eternal" capital of the Israeli state, combined with the transfer of government offices and the extension of municipal authority and services to East Jerusalem. Demographically, it has meant strenuous efforts to construct housing for Israelis — not Palestinians — and to encourage settlement of Israelis and Jews from other countries in the Palestinian parts of the city.[16] Despite the fact that it is generally agreed that the Oslo Accords imply a "good faith" freeze on settlement expansion until the matter is resolved at final status talks,[17] settlement expansion continues to be used to alter the demographics of Jerusalem. This was witnessed in 1996–97 when then Prime Minister Benjamin Netanyahu authorized the construction of a 6,500-unit Jewish settlement, Har Homa, in East Jerusalem.[18]

To create and expand settlements in East Jerusalem, Israel has built neighborhoods and roads for Jewish settlers on land owned by Palestinians, which it has confiscated.[19] The Palestine Human Rights Information Centre reports that, between January 1994 and March 1997, 36,711 dunums (approximately 9,000 acres) of Arab land in the Occupied Territories, including East Jerusalem, have been confiscated by Israeli authorities for settlement expansion.[20] The Israeli government has further increased the Jewish presence in Jerusalem by confiscating Palestinian-owned land in the West Bank, building Israeli settlements upon the land and then officially designating the newly settled areas as part of what the government refers to as "Greater Jerusalem."[21]

Beyond demolishing houses and seizing land, the Israeli government has expropriated Palestinian land through the use of zoning policies that discriminate against Palestinian landowners and benefit Jewish citizens of Israel. For example, the municipal government of Jerusalem has zoned much of the available land (much of which is Palestinian owned) in East Jerusalem as "green," ostensibly prohibiting construction on the land. In many cases, however, the building of Jewish housing stock on this land has been permitted even though Palestinians wishing to build on the same parcel of land have been prohibited from doing so.[22] The Har Homa settlement is an example of a converted "green" area.

To ensure a cap on the Palestinian population in East Jerusalem, the Israeli government has also developed specific regulations for building heights and densities in Arab and Jewish neighborhoods. The "sparse" zones are reserved for Palestinian neighborhoods where it is permissible to build on 150 square meters per dunum (-¼ acre) of land. This stands in contrast with Jewish neighborhoods where it is permissible to build on 2000 square meters per dunum of land. Moreover, Palestinians are only allowed to build houses that are two stories high while in the same zone — sometimes just across the street — Israelis can build up to seven stories high.[23]

HOUSING FOR PALESTINIANS LIVING INSIDE ISRAEL

The second class status of Palestinian citizens of Israel manifests most clearly in issues around land ownership and housing conditions. As in East Jerusalem, Israeli government policy in respect of its Palestinian citizens is one of population transfer, founded on a desire to control the demographic makeup of Israel to ensure the Judaization of all regions by removing the Palestinian population and exerting absolute control and sovereignty over as much land as possible, even if that land is Arab owned. A number of strategies have been used to dispossess the Palestinian minority in Israel, including those reviewed below.

LAND ADMINISTRATION AND PLANNING REGULATION

A public body, the Israel Lands Administration (ILA), controls 93 percent of the land supply in Israel. The ILA is regulated in law through covenanted contracts between the Government of Israel and the World Zionist Organization (WZO), the Jewish Agency (JA), and the Jewish National Fund (JNF), bodies which, according to their charters, offer national lands (and housing) exclusively to *Jewish* nationals.[24] In effect, therefore, Palestinian citizens of Israel are excluded from settlement and development in 93 percent of the total area of the State of Israel.[25]

UNRECOGNIZED VILLAGES

Approximately 60,000 Palestinian Arabs — most of whom are Bedouins[26] — live in the "unrecognized villages" which constitute hundreds of communities varying in size and population scattered throughout Israel, north (Galilee) and south (Negev).[27] These villages all predate the State of Israel, some going back hundreds of years to the Ottoman Empire era. To the Bedouin, land represents their ability to maintain economic self-sufficiency and reflects their identity. This territorial link is crucial for the survival of the Bedouin heritage as an indigenous people.[28] Many of the Bedouin villages are referred to as "unrecognized" because "officially" they do not exist, having been excluded by Israeli governments from plans and maps of Israel. To minimize the number of Palestinian towns and villages, and to put as much land as possible at the disposal of the Jewish community, the Israeli planning authorities refuse to incorporate the villages into official planning schemes.[29] Instead, the government's current position is that it will accept land ownership claims only if the Arab Bedouin agree to give up 80 percent of their traditional lands. At the same time, state policy continues to forcibly evict these people and destroy their villages to compel them to leave their traditional lands and relocate into one of seven government-planned townships. These townships are completely incompatible with Bedouin culture and customs. Not only are the Bedouin forced to abandon their agricultural activities but the townships in which they are settled lack such adequate infrastructures as a working sewage system and alternate job opportunities.[30]

Since it is illegal for unrecognized villages to be connected to national infrastructure networks, all these villages suffer from a lack of basic services including water, electricity, and telephone lines. In most villages there are no schools and children are required to travel long distances for their education. This, coupled with the fact that there is a distinct lack of paved and connecting roads between villages, means that many children are simply denied an education.[31]

The Israeli planning and building law classifies all of the lands on which the unrecognized Arab villages are situated as "agricultural." This classification prohibits the construction of any type of structure, including houses, mosques, roads, and other infrastructure and prohibits repairs to existing structures. In turn, all of the existing buildings or houses in the unrecognized villages are threatened with demolition. Between 1988 and 1996 approximately 2,100 houses were demolished in the Arab villages under the pretext that they were unlicensed.[32] House demolitions are particularly demoralizing in the unrecognized villages. Villagers are often required by the state to destroy their own homes. If they do not oblige, demolition is carried out without notice by Israeli authorities, leaving the residents suddenly homeless. After the forced eviction is carried out, the authorities commit the homeowners to trial and, regardless of the trial outcome, fine them for the costs associated with the demolition, creating situations of double or triple jeopardy.[33]

HOUSING CONDITIONS AND HEALTH

Of particular concern in many Arab communities in Israel are the health conditions of housing, in particular sewage systems and deterioration of water networks. In 1997 the Galilee Society of Health and Community Services carried out a survey that indicated that of the nine largest Arab communities (those which would most likely have the best developed infrastructures) one-third were without sewage systems at all and in only one case were the houses actually connected to the sewage system.[34] Lack of sewage collection combined with the fact that many Arab communities are losing close to 20 percent of their water due to poorly maintained water networks leads to a contamination of the drinking water supply which, in turn, can cause outbreaks of typhoid and dysentery.[35]

Embracing Economic, Social, and Cultural Rights

Both groups of Palestinians — those in Israel and those in the Occupied Territories — have long felt the pain of the government of Israel's attack on their economic, social, and cultural rights. For many years Palestinians resisted such attacks by claiming and enforcing their civil and political rights on the understanding that once they achieved these rights, economic, social, and cultural rights would follow. More recently, however, Palestinian human rights advocates in both regions have recognized that neglect of their economic, social, and cultural rights plays into the hands of Israel's policy of Judaization which is being implemented through economic, social, and cultural structures that are the cornerstone of the State of Israel. This has resulted in the understanding that the right to housing is a useful human rights norm. It provides a window onto the land issues, which are at the heart of the Palestinian struggle. This recognition owes much to the involvement of Habitat International Coalition (HIC).[36] HIC was instrumental in introducing Palestinians to international economic, social, and cultural human rights laws and mechanisms as a means of addressing their immediate concerns over housing and hence their broader concerns over autonomy, equality, and statehood. HIC has worked collaboratively with two local organizations in particular — the Palestinian Human Rights Information Centre (PHRIC) and the Arab Association for Human Rights (HRA) — to develop local initiatives to address the housing and land issues confronting Palestinians in both regions and to bring the housing and living conditions of Palestinians to the attention of the international community. This collaborative work is manifested in the establishment of two coalitions: the Palestine Housing Rights Movement (PHRM), centered in East Jerusalem, and the Arab Co-ordinating Committee on Housing Rights (ACCHR) in Israel.

After outlining the housing rights framework adopted by these campaigns, I will draw on interviews with representatives from HIC, PHRM, and ACCHR to describe the activities undertaken by these coalitions both at home and at the United Nations.

HOUSING RIGHTS FRAMEWORK

A "housing rights framework" uses the human right to housing, as defined in international human rights law, to understand and address civil, cultural, economic, political, and social issues and experiences of disadvantaged groups and individuals. This framework lends itself to the utilization of international mechanisms, such as those within treaty monitoring bodies, to enforce human rights.

The right to housing is found in a number of international human rights instruments, the most important of which is the International Covenant on Economic, Social, and Cultural Rights (ICESCR), which Israel ratified in 1992. Article 11(1) of the ICESCR states, "The States Parties to the present Covenant recognize the right of everyone to an adequate standard of living for himself and his family including adequate food, clothing and housing and to the continuous improvement of living conditions."[37] The single most authoritative legal interpretation of the right to housing is found in General Comment 4,[38] adopted by the United Nations Committee on Economic, Social, and Cultural Rights (CESCR), the body responsible for monitoring state compliance with the ICESCR. General Comment 4 stipulates that the right to housing means more than merely having a roof over one's head and should be seen as the "right to live somewhere in security, peace and dignity."[39] The general comment also identifies seven aspects that go to the "adequacy" of housing: (1) legal security of tenure including legal protections against forced eviction, harassment, or other threats; (2) availability of services, materials, and infrastructure such as potable water, sanitation and washing facilities, refuge disposal, and site drainage; (3) affordability; (4) habitability such that inhabitants are protected against the elements, structural hazards and disease; (5) accessibility to all; (6) suitability of location, allowing access to employment options, health care facilities, schools, and other social facilities; and (7) cultural adequacy and appropriateness.[40]

As a state party to the ICESCR, Israel is legally obliged to respect, protect, promote, and fulfill the right to housing.[41] Adopting a housing rights framework, therefore, has enabled the Palestinians to use international human rights monitoring bodies, in particular the CESCR, in their struggle to protect their rights. The basis of CESCR's monitoring is periodic reports regarding the measures adopted and progress made in implementing and achieving the observance of the rights contained in the covenant, which the state parties are required to submit under ICESCR.[42] Once this report is received, the committee reviews it in two stages. A working group reviews the report in a preliminary manner and forwards a list of issues for written response to the state party. Subsequently, the CESCR holds a two-day oral review of government compliance. NGOs are invited to make oral and written submissions during both stages of the review. After considering all of the information it has received, the CESCR concludes its consideration of states parties' reports by issuing "concluding observations." Concluding observations constitute the comments of the committee regarding the implementation of the covenant obligations by a given state party.

Bringing the International Right to Housing Back Home

Prior to and in concert with activities at the UN, Palestinians in both regions have undertaken a variety of local activities to promote, protect, and enforce the right to housing at the community level. This is because international human rights law and activities at the international level will have little resonance locally and will achieve few of the desired results if these activities are not rooted in local initiatives to effect change.[43] Central to building and sustaining housing rights campaigns in East Jerusalem and inside Israel has been the development of relationships, built on trust over time, between local and international organizations.[44] The HIC's long-term commitment to the PHRM and the ACCHR has allowed for genuine interaction and commingling of international and local efforts, ensuring a flow of information between the local and international levels. This ensures a bottom-up cycle whereby on-the-ground realities directly inform international developments pertaining to the Palestinian struggle and these developments are then fed back into the local movement to be used to support their struggles and initiatives.

Many of the local housing rights activities in East Jerusalem occurred between 1994 and 1995, just after the Oslo Accords were reached. Yasser Arafat had just returned from exile. Palestinians in the Occupied Territories were feeling cautiously optimistic and had access to new resources from foreign aid. At that time, activities included: protests against settlement expansion; a conference on women's housing rights; a public registration for those in East Jerusalem and environs whose houses either had been demolished or were under the threat of demolition; a ten-day consultation with the then UN Special Rapporteur, accompanied by a representative from HIC, on the right to adequate housing; and, after the establishment of the PHRM, the drafting of the Jerusalem Declaration, Draft Charter on the Palestine Housing Rights Movement. All of these activities were organized by and for Palestinians and were planned as a means of promoting awareness about housing rights as well as to create some momentum around these issues.

Unfortunately, it has been difficult to maintain the momentum necessary to sustain the housing rights movement in East Jerusalem in light of the unabated expansion of Israeli settlements, confiscation of Palestinian land

and demolition of Palestinian houses, worsening economic conditions, and corruption within the Palestine National Authority (PNA), which keeps it from protecting Palestinian interests.[45] Despite these adverse circumstances and the need to focus on day-to-day survival, the PHRM continues to undertake various activities including the documentation of human rights abuses and training sessions with organizations from abroad.[46]

The ACCHR commenced their activities in the area of economic, social, and cultural rights after Israel ratified the ICESCR in 1992. Working with the assistance of HIC, the ACCHR's initiatives on housing rights have focused on educational events targeted at school children, women, and social service workers. Members of the ACCHR have also directly lobbied the Israeli government to change its policies and laws that have adverse consequences for Palestinian citizens of Israel.

Alongside these various initiatives, litigation strategies have also been employed in both regions. In occupied East Jerusalem, litigation has centered on challenging house demolition orders. Inside Israel, a few cases have challenged land expropriation and house demolition, however, these have been framed using civil and political rights rather than economic, social, and cultural rights. The ACCHR has identified this as one of the weaknesses within the movement and expects to work with legal centers in the future to encourage lawyers to incorporate an economic, social, and cultural rights perspective or framework in their casework.[47]

EDUCATION

In order to claim housing rights, for international advocates to assist in this effort, for UN human rights mechanisms to be used effectively, and for the media to properly cover the relevant issues, education must occur at all levels: locally, internationally, within the NGO sector and beyond. In the Palestinian context, local and international NGOs, international human rights advocates, various United Nations officials, and members of the local and international press have all been involved in housing rights education.

This education has come in a variety of forms. HIC's education on the housing and living conditions of Palestinians commenced in 1991, when Joseph Schechla approached HIC and asked them to consider becoming involved in the region.[48] HIC's first official activity was to educate itself by conducting an in-depth and intense fact-finding mission that introduced the organization to the housing and living conditions of Palestinians in Gaza, the Occupied Territories including East Jerusalem, and inside Israel. HIC visits the region regularly to continue this information-gathering process and has encouraged the housing rights movement in Palestine to educate other members of the international community about their housing and living conditions. In 1994, upon the invitation of the PHRM, the then United Nations Special Rapporteur on the Right to Housing, Justice Rajindar Sachar, visited the region to learn more about the housing and living conditions of Palestinians. In late 1997, a member of the UN Committee on Economic, Social, and Cultural Rights responsible for coordinating the review of Israel under the ICESCR, also undertook an unofficial visit to learn firsthand about the status of economic, social, and cultural rights for Palestinians.[49]

To educate a wider international audience, the housing rights campaigns in both regions, the Occupied Territories and inside Israel, have produced short but powerful videos explaining some of the land and housing problems that each group faces. The video that emerged from the Occupied Territories has received widespread exposure, having been aired by public television stations across the world as well as at the opening ceremony of a United Nations Committee on Trade and Development meeting in Paris, France.[50] Both videos were also widely viewed in 1996 at the UN World Conference, Habitat II, in Istanbul, Turkey.

While educating members of the international community about the housing and living conditions of Palestinians, the Palestinian housing rights campaigns are simultaneously educating other Palestinian organizations, professionals, and local populations about their rights under the ICESCR and the various mechanisms available to help enforce those rights. For example, with the assistance of HIC, the ACCHR has developed a solid understanding of the UN human rights mechanisms and is currently conducting seminars with other local organizations such as the Galilee Society and the Working Group on the Status of Palestinian Women in Israel so that they too can learn to use the UN mechanisms to promote the mandates of their respective organizations and to encourage Israel to comply with its legal obligations under the ICESCR.[51] Similarly, in occupied East Jerusalem education and training seminars and workshops on housing and other economic, social, and cultural rights are being held with grassroots organizations and Palestinians living in refugee camps who are threatened with forced eviction.[52]

As the work of the housing rights campaigns evolves, so too do the educational needs of local organizations. Once the fundamentals about the right to housing and the UN system reached grassroots organizations and NGOs in different sectors, the need for further education and training was identified to ensure that the work to promote, protect and enforce housing and other rights takes firm hold in civil society. In turn, HIC, Youth for Unity and Voluntary Action (YUVA),[53] and the two Palestinian housing rights movements have commenced educational seminars on social mobilization and alternative planning, to introduce local organizations and coalitions to proven strategies for mobilizing and coordinating communities to participate in programs which seek to meet local needs and protect, promote and enforce individual rights.[54]

PALESTINIAN HOUSING CAMPAIGNS AT THE UN

The United Nations human rights system has been used quite extensively in both regions to draw international attention to the housing and living conditions of Palestinians, issues of crucial importance in the region but which have eluded the attention of most UN bodies. The UN human rights system has also been seen as a strategy to effect change and as a catalyst to initiate and encourage local activities to protect, promote, and enforce housing rights for Palestinians.[55] The PHRM and the ACCHR have undertaken these activities in consultation and collaboration with HIC. The two housing rights movements have adopted different strategies at the UN in keeping with the distinct social, economic, and political characteristics of each region.

Because of difficulties in sustaining the housing rights movement in occupied East Jerusalem, the PHRM has primarily focused on two UN bodies, the UN Subcommission on the Prevention of Discrimination and Protection of Minorities and the CESCR.[56] The ACCHR, on the other hand, has virtually "blitzed" the UN human rights system. This is because, until recently, the international community seemed unaware that there are close to a million Palestinian citizens of Israel and that they are targets of discrimination by its government. To break this silence, the ACCHR has used a multitude of UN human rights mechanisms including those at the Subcommission on the Prevention of Discrimination, the UN Commission on Human Rights, the Minority Rights Working Group,[57] the Committee on the Elimination of Racial Discrimination, the Committee on the Elimination of All Forms of Discrimination Against Women, and the CESCR. Most of the time and energy of the PHRM and the ACCHR has been spent working with the CESCR. This section highlights these activities.

Since 1995 both groups, with the assistance of HIC, have taken full advantage of the opportunities available to NGOs to better inform CESCR about the economic and social conditions for Palestinians in occupied East Jerusalem and in Israel. In the lead up to the committee's review of Israel, the PHRM, the ACCHR, and HIC have made oral submissions and presented videos to the committee at several sessions to assist the committee in informing itself as fully as possible with respect to the status of economic, social, and cultural rights for Palestinians in Israel and occupied East Jerusalem.[58] The ACCHR and PHRM also prepared and submitted extensive written reports as well as briefing notes and fact sheets to complement and substantiate their oral statements. When representatives from the ACCHR and the PHRM were unable to travel to Geneva, HIC made oral statements at the committee on their behalf to keep the issues alive and to put situations requiring urgent attention on the committee's agenda. During committee sessions, the ACCHR, the PHRM, and HIC met with a number of committee members to clarify points raised in their submissions. They also invited a committee member to visit the region to see firsthand the actuality of the contents of their submissions to the committee.

The cumulative effect of these efforts was to both fast-track and transform the two-stage review of Israel by the committee. In April 1996 the ACCHR and the PHRM attended the UN to inform the committee of the housing and living conditions of Palestinians in Occupied East Jerusalem and Israel and to draw to their attention the urgency of the housing situation for Palestinians in East Jerusalem.[59] After hearing compelling submissions from the ACCHR and the PHRM, the committee issued a letter to the government of Israel questioning Israel's compliance with its obligations under the ICESCR and, in light of the urgency of the situation, requesting that the government of Israel submit its overdue initial report to the committee "as soon as possible" and in advance of the committee's fifteenth session in November 1996.[60] At that time, Israel's report was two years overdue. Though the report on Israel's compliance with the ICESCR was not received by the committee until November 1997, the committee's letter was at least one of the factors that influenced the government of Israel to submit its report to the committee in a fairly expeditious manner.[61]

Using the NGO procedures available at the committee's presessional working group, the ACCHR and PHRM provided the committee with oral and written submissions regarding inadequacies and omissions in the government of Israel's report. These submissions, along with their other activities at the committee, appear to have had an impact. Of the forty-four questions contained in the list of issues, almost one-third are related to housing and land use, and of these most of the questions reflect a detailed and thorough understanding of the issues.[62]

After providing its written responses to the list of issues, the government of Israel was orally reviewed by the committee at its nineteenth session in November 1998. The intensity and quality of the committee's review of Israel can be attributed, at least in part, to the work of the ACCHR and the PHRM. The questions posed by many of the committee members demonstrated a sophisticated and thorough understanding of many of the issues of concern to both the ACCHR and the PHRM. For example, on its second day of review, Virginia Dandan outlined some of the key issues about which the committee wanted to hear more from the Israeli government delegation, including the issue of disproportionate homelessness of Palestinians. When the government queried the figure quoted by Dandan for the numbers of homeless in Jerusalem, and implied that homelessness was not an issue in Jerusalem,[63] Dandan replied that in May 1998 she had met with a number of homeless families in Jerusalem who were living in tents with services provided by international agencies.[64] That reply would not have been possible had Dandan not been invited to the region by the ACCHR and the PHRM to bear witness to the housing and living conditions of Palestinians.

The ACCHR's and PHRM's efforts to have their housing rights recognized and protected are also clearly reflected in the committee's concluding observations on Israel. Almost all of the housing and land related concerns presented to the committee by the Palestinian housing movements are touched upon in the "Principal Subjects of Concern" section of the concluding observations. For example, at paragraph 21 the committee expresses concern "over the continued Israeli policies of building settlements to expand the boundaries of East Jerusalem and of transferring Jewish residents into East Jerusalem with the result that they now outnumber Palestinian residents";[65] in the following paragraph the committee expresses its extreme concern over the continued practice of house demolition, land confiscation, and adoption of policies resulting in substandard housing and living conditions, including overcrowding and lack of services for Palestinians in East Jerusalem.[66] The committee also devotes three full paragraphs to the "Unrecognized Villages," expressing extreme concern for the fact that these villages lack water, electricity, sanitation, and roads, which in turn affects access to health care, education, and employment opportunities.[67]

One of the strongest recommendations issued to the government of Israel by the committee relates to housing rights. The committee calls upon the government of Israel

To cease the practices of facilitating the building of illegal settlements and constructing bypass roads, expropriating land, water and resources, demolishing houses and arbitrary evictions. The committee urges the state party immediately to take steps to respect and implement the right to an adequate standard of living, including housing, of Palestinian residents of East Jerusalem and the Palestinian Arabs in the mixed cities.[68]

The concluding observations are remarkable for refocusing the question of Palestine on the core structural and systemic issues related to land, which are at the heart of the Palestinian struggle in both regions. The committee's concluding observations are equally remarkable for exposing Israel's strategy of using the denial of Palestinian's economic, social, and cultural rights to determine their political fate. The committee does this for example by linking the expansion of settlements — an issue that is considered "political" in nature and stands at the heart of the Palestinian-Israeli conflict — with the right to an adequate standard of living for Palestinians and then by directing the government of Israel to cease its expansion of Jewish settlements.[69]

Results and Assessment

Assessing the achievements or progress by the two groups of Palestinians in adopting a housing rights approach in occupied East Jerusalem and inside Israel is not a straightforward task. Activists in the region are clear that if "achievement" were measured by determining whether, in the wake of the UN activities, the actual number of housing rights violations and land expropriations had declined or if the government of Israel had taken political and legal steps toward acknowledging and recognizing Palestinian statehood, then the housing rights approach might be regarded as a failure. Activists in this region agree, however, that a better measure of progress or achievement is one which is forward-looking, which recognizes that change occurs incrementally and which focuses on the impact of the housing rights campaigns on local populations and the political agenda. The results flowing from the UN activities at CESCR and those flowing from the local activities supportive thereof are reviewed below.

Results of UN Activities: Shaming the Government

The ICESCR does not have an individual complaints procedure such as an optional protocol, which means that the committee's concluding observations and other jurisprudence have limited enforcement. In turn, the right to housing, and jurisprudence pertaining to this right, generated at the international level, can best be used to shame or embarrass governments into upholding their international legal obligations.[70] Though shaming a government seems a weak tool, the Palestinians have been able to maximize its effectiveness by drawing on the fact that Israel presents itself to the international community as a Western democracy amid a sea of Arab totalitarianism. Palestinians have been quick to present the UN with information regarding the laws, policies, and practices of the Israeli government that cast doubt on Israel's status as a free and democratic state.

The most tangible outcomes as a result of this strategy have been in response to the pressure being applied by the ACCHR with respect to the rights of Palestinians living inside Israel, particularly in the "unrecognized villages." Largely as a result of the ACCHR's housing rights campaign and its work at the UN to internationalize this issue, the Rabin government agreed to recognize seven of the "unrecognized villages" and despite the fact that the Netanyahu government suspended this decision, the ACCHR and HIC are quite confident that this issue will be resolved under the current government.[71]

The coordinator of ACCHR has also reported that the ACCHR's pressure tactics have altered the interaction between the government of Israel and NGOs with respect to the government's reporting responsibilities to the UN. Broadly speaking, the ACCHR's efforts have resulted in Israel acknowledging the existence of and the position of the Palestinian citizens of Israel for the first time.[72] As an example, he noted the differences between the CERD report submitted by the Israeli government in the 1980s and the report submitted in the late 1990s.[73] The changes in the report over a decade are due to the fact that NGOs (including Palestinian NGOs) are now included in the government's reporting process.

The ACCHR's focus on housing rights influenced the Association for Civil

Rights in Israel to challenge a law forbidding non-Jews from purchasing state land controlled by the Jewish Agency. In a recent landmark decision, the Israeli Supreme Court ruled that it is illegal to prevent Palestinian citizens of Israel from acquiring state-owned land in Israel.[74]

Israel has also been embarrassed into action as a result of the efforts of the PHRM and the ACCHR at the committee. As noted above, after receiving detailed and reliable NGO reports on the housing and living conditions of Palestinians in East Jerusalem and inside Israel, the committee strongly urged Israel to submit its overdue report to the committee in a timely fashion, which it did, facilitating the review of Israel in late 1998.

To ensure that Israel continues to feel this pressure from the committee, the concluding observations stipulate that the government of Israel was to submit to the CESCR, in time for the twenty-third session in November 2000, detailed information on the realization of economic, social, and cultural rights in the occupied territories including East Jerusalem.[75] The committee also requested updated information from the government on target dates for recognizing the "unrecognized villages" and a plan for delivery of basic services to villagers.[76] It remains to be seen whether the committee's concluding observations on Israel can be used effectively by NGOs to embarrass or pressure the government of Israel into complying with the committee's suggestions and recommendations.

The committee's concluding observations also put pressure on and shame the government of Israel by shifting the focus of the Palestinian struggle back to fundamentals, that is, land issues and the structural instruments and institutions which the State of Israel has employed to dispossess Palestinians of their land. At paragraph 11, the committee notes with "grave concern" that the Status Law of 1952 authorizes the World Zionist Organization/Jewish Agency and its subsidiaries, including the Jewish National Fund, to control most of the land in Israel, since these institutions are chartered to benefit Jews exclusively. Despite the fact that the institutions are chartered under private law, the State of Israel nevertheless has a decisive influence on their policies and thus remains responsible for their activities. A state party cannot divest itself of its obligations under the covenant by privatizing governmental functions. The committee takes the view that large-scale and systematic confiscation of Palestinian land and property by the state and the transfer of that property to these institutions constitutes an institutionalized form of discrimination because these agencies by definition would deny the use of these properties to non-Jews. Thus, these practices constitute a breach of Israel's obligations under the covenant.[77] The committee then recommends that the government of Israel review the status of its relationship with the WZO/JA and its subsidiaries, including the JNF, with a view to remedying the problems identified by the committee in paragraph 11, cited above.

Schechla notes that the very facts on the ground created by the State of Israel have "come home to roost" by way of the committee's concluding observations. In his estimation, the committee's observations address structural issues which other UN bodies have overlooked for the past fifty years and reinforce the cardinal points in the Palestinian struggle: that the discrimination against Palestinians is institutionalized, that housing is linked to land as a principal focus of victimization, and that the human rights violations against Palestinians are systematic.[78] Israel's angry written rebuttal to the committee's concluding observations — which avoids a discussion of the structural issues raised by the committee — if nothing else, is indicative that the committee's pressure is being felt by the government.

RESULTS OF LOCAL ACTIVITIES: EMPOWERING PALESTINIANS

While the results obtained from shaming the government are worthwhile advances in the housing rights struggle of Palestinians, local activists argue that the most significant achievements identified or anticipated as a result of the housing rights campaigns are those flowing from the activities that are prerequisites to and integral components of effective participation in UN international human rights mechanisms, in particular, community education and community mobilization. These achievements are discussed below.

SKILLS AND EDUCATION

Participation in housing rights campaigns has resulted in the development of a wide variety of skills in the NGO sector. For example, the UN activities have required NGOs to learn how to prepare and present reports, how to mobilize and campaign, how to work collaboratively, how to use the UN system and how to lobby at both international and local levels. These skills are now being transferred to other activists and leaders in the NGO sector through workshops and training courses. As a result, a growing number of Palestinian activists are beginning to use economic, social, and cultural rights discourse as well as the UN human rights system to fulfill their organizational mandates and to improve the everyday lives of Palestinians.

The education process also seems to have reached the PNA which is now beginning to cooperate with civil society in the development of the Palestinian National Plan of Action for Human Rights, which will involve the technical assistance and support of the UN Office of the High Commissioner for Human Rights and will probably focus specifically on the right to housing as one of its sectors.[79]

Moreover, to ensure that future generations of Palestinians understand economic, social, and cultural issues as human rights, the ACCHR has initiated a series of human rights workshops in secondary schools. Having targeted schools in the North and South Negev, the ACCHR has reached approximately 11,000 students and intends to further extend this program over the next few years.[80]

MONITORING AND DOCUMENTATION

Mobilizing around various activities at the UN has required the PHRM and the ACCHR to ensure that housing rights violations are monitored and systematically documented. The importance of documentation cannot be overestimated. It provides the evidence or proof required to make solid, supportable human rights claims and, in the relatively new field of economic, social, and cultural rights, documentation is a vital component of establishing the legitimacy of these rights.[81] According to participants in the PHRM, the need to constantly monitor and document housing rights violations sustained the housing rights movement in East Jerusalem, for without this focus the energies of the PHRM would have been spent solely on coping with housing and other rights violations, obscuring the need for documentation.[82]

INTERNATIONALIZING THE ISSUES

In the belief that international support can assist the Palestinians in achieving equality, autonomy, and statehood, an aim of both the ACCHR and the PHRM has been to ensure that, beyond informing local organizations and communities about their rights, the international community (e.g., the United Nations, regional bodies, and individual states) is made aware of the housing and living conditions of Palestinians. There is now some evidence that indicates that the housing rights campaigns are reaching the international community. The PHRM has generated interest in the housing issues of Palestinians living in the Occupied Territories in countries throughout the world, as indicated by the release of the video which has been translated into several languages, distributed to every region of the world, and aired in many countries. The ACCHR coordinator stated that the plight of the Palestinian citizens of Israel is also gaining international attention. Government representatives from external affairs in Holland and the United Kingdom recently traveled to the region to visit the "unrecognized villages" and Bedouin communities that they had read about in UN reports and news clippings. The ACCHR is hopeful that these visits will translate into the application of greater international political pressure on the government of Israel to respect, protect, and fulfill the rights of *all* citizens of Israel, Jews and non-Jews alike.

EMPOWERMENT

Ultimately, there is little doubt that the empowerment of the NGO sector, as well as local populations, has been a central achievement in both housing rights campaigns. Palestinians can now attach a legal claim, and one with moral persuasion, directly to their experiences of unfairness and injustice within the housing sector. This affirms what Palestinian victims of housing rights violations know and experience on a visceral level: housing is fundamental to their survival as a people, and to their humanity, and that acts such as housing demolition, land confiscation, and the eradication of villages are an affront to human dignity and are at the root of their struggle. In turn, empowered by this knowledge and legal framework, the PHRM and the ACCHR are now assisting Palestinians to translate what were once regarded as housing needs into specific legal claims backed by the force of law.

This empowerment has been augmented by the results of the work at the United Nations. One activist with whom I spoke noted that the interest shown by the UN with respect to everyday housing issues faced by Palestinians in both regions makes Palestinians feel less alone in their struggle.[83] This is particularly so for Palestinian citizens of Israel who, until recently, were an invisible minority not only within Israel but also within Palestinian circles and the international community, for these groups have focused their attention primarily on the plight of the Palestinians living in the Occupied Territories and Gaza. During the review of Israel by the committee, a number of Palestinian NGO representatives commented that it was difficult to listen to the government of Israel give false answers to or evade the committee's questions. At the same time, it was fortifying to hear the government of Israel being asked hard-hitting questions by independent economic, social, and cultural rights experts, in an international human rights forum. The questions put to the Israeli government delegation were regarded by Palestinian onlookers as validation of their suffering and any wrongs imposed with respect to economic, social, and cultural matters.

These achievements may seem small, but their value lies in what they mean for the past and for the future. By returning to the basic, core elements of the struggle, Palestinian activists have ensured that the work of their activist predecessors for Palestinian sovereignty based on Palestinian land carries on into the future.[84] Moreover, activists in the region believe that these activities and their "results" are foundational steps on the way to creating a sustained human rights culture. They will have lasting implications for the economic, social, and cultural conditions of Palestinians in occupied East Jerusalem and Israel and, as such, will contribute to the realization of the broader Palestinian struggle for equality, autonomy, and statehood.

Concluding Comment

The Palestinian experience of incorporating economic, social, and cultural rights into their existing struggle for equality, autonomy, and statehood demonstrates how issues that have been traditionally defined using civil and political human rights can also be understood and articulated from an economic, social, and cultural rights perspective. At the same time, it demonstrates both the practical and political significance of economic, social, and cultural rights at the domestic level.

The Palestinian case study also demonstrates that for the new emphasis on economic, social, and cultural rights at the international level to be of benefit to local struggles, it must operate through collaborative activities. Local groups will have to continue to work together because, as the Palestinians learned, this allows for the consolidation of work, ensures diversity of experience and expertise, and assists in the pooling of resources. At the same time, for local groups to understand, access, and effectively use international human rights law and mechanisms, collaborative work with international organizations will be necessary. These collaborations ensure that the appropriate information reaches the appropriate UN bodies and therefore that the legal standards and decisions generated at the international level are both informed by and relevant to local situations.

At the same time, the Palestinian housing rights campaigns expose that while the development of new international legal standards and decisions is useful to their struggle, the real gains are those generated and experienced at home. In other words, the housing rights framework is a catalyst for producing a number of activities and results at the local level which will likely have a longer-term impact on the Palestinian situation than will the generation of new international standards and decisions. At its most fundamental, the housing rights framework provides Palestinians with a new opportunity to collaborate locally. In fact, HIC found that it has actually assisted in resolving or at least ameliorating conflicts between organizations:

We have found that having an external focus, such as the need for the preparation of alternative reports and testimony for [UN] human rights bodies, brings together previously incompatible organizations. Combined with the mediating role that HIC has played at the local levels, this has led to the groups staying together and developing further work[85]

The adoption of the housing rights framework has thus established results at both the international and local level — results that Palestinians recognize as beneficial to their struggle for equality, autonomy, and statehood. The Palestinian experience is important for the new emphasis on economic, social, and cultural rights at the international level because it highlights the role which these rights can play in local organizations' activities and in achieving results of local significance, and demonstrates the possibility of meaningful interaction between local and international work.

The Maya Petition to the Inter-American Commission on Human Rights: Indigenous Land and Resource Rights and the Conflict over Logging and Oil in Southern Belize

S. JAMES ANAYA

In many parts of the world, lands that are rich in natural resources continue to be inhabited by peoples whose origins in the lands predate those of the states that engulf them. In such areas, efforts on the part of states and transnational corporations to develop the natural resources frequently come into conflict with the indigenous inhabitants and their claims to the lands and resources in question. This genre of conflict has implications not just for the physical well-being of indigenous people who subsist from fragile ecosystems, but also for the integrity of their cultural and social patterns, which are often dependent on land resources, and for their own economic development potential. Given the frequency and magnitude of conflicts over lands claimed by indigenous peoples, such conflicts increasingly are a matter of concern for policy and decision makers at the international level. The international system for the protection of human rights, in particular, is being tested in its capacity to address indigenous peoples' concerns over lands and natural resources in the face of development efforts by outsiders. The international human rights regime is being pressed to move beyond its traditional concern for the autonomy of the individual and to address claims that are being made by entire groups and that extend into the economic and cultural domains.

A case in point concerns that of the Maya people of southern Belize. In the last several years, the government of Belize, through its Ministry of Natural Resources, has granted at least seventeen concessions for logging on lands totaling approximately 480,000 acres in the Toledo District, the country's most southern political subdivision. The two largest of these concessions, which together cover some 185,000 acres of previously pristine tropical forest, were granted to two apparently related Malaysian companies that operate in Belize as Atlantic Industries Ltd. and Toledo Atlantic International Ltd. Added to the logging interests is a concession for oil exploration, which the Belize Ministry of Energy, Science, Technology, and Transportation granted several years ago to AB Energy, Inc., a company based in the United States. The oil exploration concession, which will automatically convert to a concession for oil extraction if commercially viable quantities of petroleum are found, is for 749,222 acres of the lowland portion of the Toledo District.

The rural parts of the Toledo District that are affected by the logging and oil concessions are inhabited primarily by Maya people, descendants of the Maya civilization that flourished throughout substantial parts of Mexico and Central America hundreds of years prior to European colonization in the Western Hemisphere. The Maya live in some thirty-seven villages throughout the Toledo District, and number over ten thousand. Through a campaign of several years, Maya leaders and organizations protested to government officials against the concessions and the failure of Belize's law and public administration to adequately recognize and protect Maya rights in lands and natural resources. In late 1997, Maya organizations filed a lawsuit in the Supreme Court of Belize to have the logging concessions enjoined and declared in violation of Maya rights. Government officials never responded with anything more than statements of general and unfulfilled commitments to address Maya concerns, and the lawsuit stalled with no action on the part of the courts.

After having failed in their efforts before Belize authorities at the domestic level, the Maya petitioned the Inter-American Commission on Human Rights, an agency of the Organization of American States. The petition was filed by the Toledo Maya Cultural Council (TMCC) on behalf of the Maya villages of the Toledo District and their members. The TMCC is a Maya nongovernmental organization that was formed to advocate for the varied interests of the Maya people in Toledo. It is governed by an executive committee that is elected by delegates of the Maya villages and is comprised of both Mopan- and Ke'kchi-speaking Maya individuals. In filing the petition the TMCC was assisted by attorneys from the Indian Law Resource Center, a U.S.-based advocacy organization dedicated to promoting the rights of indigenous peoples.

On the basis of arguments constructed from relevant international human rights instruments, the TMCC petition to the Inter-American Commission on Human Rights asserts that the Maya people have rights to the land and natural resources within much of the area affected by the logging and oil concessions, and that those rights have been violated by the government's actions and inaction. The petition seeks to have the commission call upon the government of Belize to suspend or cancel the logging and oil concessions until suitable agreements can be negotiated with the Maya people. It also urges the commission to call for reforms in the legal and regulatory system of Belize in order to provide state recognition and effective protection for Maya rights over lands and resources. The Maya petition to the Inter-American Commission represents the first time Belize finds itself accused of specific violations of human rights before an international human rights body. Substantial portions of the petition are reproduced below.

The Threat of Environmental Degradation in Southern Belize

Belize is a relatively young country with a diverse population. It gained its independence from Great Britain in 1981 and adopted a constitution that includes principles of democracy and human rights as foundational precepts. It has a small, predominantly English-speaking population of about 200,000, of which somewhat more than 10,000 are Maya. The non-Maya population is comprised of a variety of groups marked by diverse ethnic characteristics that reflect complex immigration and settlement patterns dating back to at least the early period of British rule in the nineteenth century. Although it has become a retirement destination for an increasing number of North Americans and Europeans, Belize shares many of the economic and social difficulties of its Central American and Caribbean neighbors. Unlike many other less developed countries, however, Belize has a well-structured system of conservation programs that has earned it a reputation as an environmentally friendly place where natural wonders abound. Tourists from around the world are attracted to Belize's barrier reef—the second largest in the world and one of the healthiest coral habitats anywhere—and to inland resorts that provide access to lush tropical forests and animal sanctuaries.[1]

Most of the environmentally protected areas that draw substantial earnings from tourism, however, are in the northern part of the country, well insulated by distance from the roar of bulldozers and the whir of chainsaws that are felling trees, or from the tremor of seismic blasts and drilling that search for oil, in the southern Toledo District. Environmentalists and forestry experts have identified the logging in Toledo as a major threat to the ecology of the area, which includes a broad diversity of plant and wildlife species.[2] Particular concern has been raised about siltation of the streams that feed into lagoons and seawaters surrounding the delicate reef at its southern extension. The problem, according to close observers of the situation, is not that forestry is inherently bad, but that the government of Belize is unwilling or unable to enforce elementary principles of sustainable forestry that would minimize environmental impacts and avert substantial long-term or permanent damage. The environmental harm that might result from oil development is itself staggering. Oil exploration under the concession to AB Energy is still in its early stage and has not yet had a major impact on the environment. But if oil development proceeds to the production stage, the ensuing consequences may be devastating for the natural environment and the people who live within it. In other less developed countries in which the oil industry has operated, toxins have been released in the process of oil extraction that have caused severe illness and death among human inhabitants; such pollutants, furthermore, have caused degradation in wildlife and plant species. Widespread social ills also have been associated with the penetration of the oil industry and its work force into the habitats of previously insular communities. The Inter-American Commission on Human Rights itself documented such negative effects of the oil industry in its examination of the human rights situation in Ecuador.[3]

While the environmental threat presented by the logging and oil concessions has raised concerns among urban elites in Belize and elsewhere, the Maya people of the Toledo District are the ones most affected by the concessions. The thirty-seven villages throughout the district in which the Maya of Toledo live are all either within or in close proximity to the lands over which logging and oil development concessions have been granted. Lands around the villages that are used by the Maya for agricultural and other subsistence purposes, including hunting and fishing, are included in the concession areas. From the standpoint of the Maya people who live in the affected areas, the actual and potential further environmental degradation constitutes a threat to their physical well-being and subsistence, which are dependent on the territorial space in which the Maya and their ancestors traditionally have lived.

THE ASSERTION OF MAYA INTERESTS IN LANDS AND NATURAL RESOURCES

But the issue at hand for the Maya is not just one of concern over the natural environment; it is also, and perhaps more fundamentally, one of ownership and control over the lands and resources at stake. The logging and oil development concessions represent a model of development that succumbs to the profit-motivated interests of forces from outside the target locality that are eager to see the remaining natural resources of less developed countries converted into financial bounty. This model can be witnessed throughout parts of the developing world, particularly in areas inhabited by indigenous peoples, where much of the world's remaining commercially viable stands of tropical timber exist. Governments claim for themselves the prerogative of disposing of natural resources, and they exercise this claimed prerogative in favor of commercial enterprises with, at best, secondary consideration of the legitimate interests of the people who may be affected by the resource development projects. In their petition to the Inter-American Commission on Human Rights, the Maya are directly challenging this model by asserting property rights over lands and forest resources that the government of Belize has encumbered and by attempting to alter the government's course of conduct to accommodate those rights.

The Maya petition asserts land and resource rights on the basis of historical occupancy and ongoing customary land tenure. Early in the twentieth century, the British colonial administration established "reservations" for the benefit of several of the Maya villages within lands considered to be "Crown lands." These reservations, now on presumed national lands, continue to exist and include roughly half the Maya villages. In any event, the customary land tenure patterns of even those villages that were granted reservations extend well beyond the reservation boundaries. The petition to the Inter-American Commission asserts rights over the aggregate territory of their customary land tenure independently of any government grant or specific act of recognition.

The Inter-American Commission on Human Rights and Its Capacity to Address Indigenous Peoples' Claims to Lands and Natural Resources

In filing its petition on behalf of Maya villages, the TMCC is testing the capacity of the international system for the protection of human rights, in particular at the regional level, to function as a vehicle for the effective implementation of existing and emergent norms relevant to indigenous peoples. The Inter-American Commission on Human Rights is empowered to promote the observance of human rights among the members of the Organization of American States and to act on complaints or petitions that allege particular violations of human rights. The TMCC petition represents one of the first cases brought to the commission in which the central issue is that of control over lands inhabited by indigenous peoples.[4]

The primary terms of reference for the Inter-American Commission are the American Convention on Human Rights, in relation to states that are parties to that convention, and the American Declaration of the Rights and Duties of Man, in relation to states (like Belize) that are OAS members but not parties to the American Convention. Neither of these instruments specifically mentions indigenous peoples, indigenous land and resource rights, or rights related to the natural environment. However, the TMCC petition constructs arguments for such rights on the basis of the rights to life, property, and equality under the law, and other human rights affirmed in the American Declaration on the Rights and Duties of Man. The petition builds these arguments in part by linking these generally applicable human rights to developments that have occurred over the last several years at the international level regarding indigenous peoples. International intergovernmental institutions and their relevant agencies, including the InterAmerican Commission itself, increasingly have supported rights of indigenous people in relation to ancestral lands and the natural environment. Issues of indigenous lands and environmental concern are now generally viewed, in the international arena, as matters of human rights.[5]

While it is too early to fully gauge the utility of invoking the jurisdiction of the Inter-American Commission in this ongoing case, it is evident that the petition by the TMCC has been a factor in prodding the government of Belize to address Maya concerns. Not long after the petition was filed, the government agreed to enter negotiations with the TMCC over the issues raised in the petition, and to do so within a procedure that is being monitored by the Inter-American Commission. The commission will refrain from adjudicating the case as long as negotiations proceed toward a settlement.

As of late September 1999, however, negotiations had stalled, as new concessions were granted for logging within Maya traditional lands, and the government refrained from providing any clear indication that it was willing to alter its course of development activity and recognize Maya rights over the lands in question on the basis of customary land tenure patterns. Maya leaders were pressing the Inter-American Commission to help get negotiations on a fruitful track or, failing that, to proceed to adjudicate the case, determine that Belize is responsible for violations of human rights, and make appropriate recommendations.

The Maya appear to be aware that the logging and oil development controversy, as well as the larger issue of their land rights, are complex matters that are best worked out through negotiated solutions that seek to accommodate the legitimate interests of all concerned. But, typically of indigenous peoples, they are relatively powerless in the domestic political sphere to move the government toward a framework of negotiation based on recognition and understanding of the Maya people and their relationship with ancestral lands and resources. The Maya are now attempting to use the sphere of international human rights law to invoke scrutiny by an international human rights body to shift the balance of power and terms of debate in their favor. Indigenous peoples throughout the world are confronted by similar problems of state-sponsored industrial encroachment onto their ancestral lands, and many likewise are framing and asserting their interests in terms of international legal entitlement. Whether or not the strategy adopted by the Maya will succeed for them is yet to be seen. In principle, the international system for the protection of human rights, and the Inter-American Commission on Human Rights in particular, should be capable of assisting the Maya.

Portions of the Petition to the Inter-American Commission are presented below verbatim. Most original notes have been omitted; those remaining follow the original numbering and appear in square brackets in the text and the Notes section of this volume.

PETITION

TO THE
INTER-AMERICAN COMMISSION ON HUMAN RIGHTS
SUBMITTED BY
THE TOLEDO MAYA CULTURAL COUNCIL ON BEHALF OF
MAYA INDIGENOUS COMMUNITIES OF THE TOLEDO DISTRICT
AGAINST
BELIZE

Attorneys for Petitioner:

S. James Anaya

Deborah Schaaf

Steven Tullberg

INDIAN LAW RESOURCE CENTER

602 North Ewing Street

Helena, MT 59601

United States of America

Telephone: (406) 449–2006

Facsimile: (406) 449–2031

August 7, 1998

I. Introduction

1. The TOLEDO MAYA CULTURAL COUNCIL ("TMCC") hereby submits this petition to the Inter-American Commission on Human Rights (the "Commission") against the State of Belize (the "State" or "Belize" or the "State of Belize"). TMCC, a non-governmental organization that represents the Mopan and Ke'kchi Maya people of the Toledo District of southern Belize, seeks redress for the violation of the rights of the Toledo Maya indigenous communities over lands and natural resources.

2. Disregarding Maya property, cultural, and other rights, the State of Belize has granted numerous concessions for logging and oil development on lands traditionally used and occupied by Maya communities in the Toledo District. Parts of these Maya traditional lands that are affected by the concessions are within areas designated as reservations for Maya communities. The State granted the logging and oil concessions without consulting the Maya people and without duly considering their rights or interests in lands and resources both within and outside of the reservations. Logging operations have proceeded with negative impacts on the natural environment upon which the Maya depend for subsistence, and planned large-scale oil development activities threaten further environmental damage.

3. The logging and oil concessions are part of a pattern of government neglect that generally threatens the Maya people, their culture, and their relation with the lands and natural resources upon which they depend. Communications of protest to the responsible government officials about the concessions and the failure of State agents to recognize Maya land and resource rights have gone unanswered.

4. Furthermore, a lawsuit filed in the Supreme Court of Belize to stop the logging and gain judicial affirmation of Maya land and resource rights has not produced any results. Over a year and a half has passed since the lawsuit was filed, and the judicial system of Belize has failed to render any substantive decision on the case.

5. The acts and omissions of Belize described in this petition constitute violations of the right to property, the right to cultural integrity, rights related to a safe and healthy environment, the right to consultation, and the right to judicial protection. These rights are affirmed and protected by the American Declaration of the Rights and Duties of Man (the "American Declaration") and other provisions of international human rights law. TMCC seeks the Commission's assistance in reversing the acts and omissions of Belize that violate Maya rights and in safeguarding those rights in the future. The Commission's involvement is particularly important since, as set forth below, domestic remedies are ineffective or unavailable.

II. Jurisdiction

6. The Inter-American Commission on Human Rights has competence to receive and act on this petition in accordance with Articles 1.2(b), 18, 20(b), and 24 of the Commission's Statute.

III. The Victims and the Petitioner

7. The victims in this case are the Mopan- and Ke'kchi-speaking communities of the Toledo District of Belize and their members, whose property, cultural life and physical well-being are being adversely affected by the acts and omissions complained of in this petition. . . .

8. These communities are part of the larger indigenous Maya people. Detailed information on the named Maya villages and their demographics is in the 150-page *Maya Atlas*, [1] which was produced by TMCC and the Toledo Alcaldes Association, the organization of the *alcaldes*, or principal leaders, of the Maya villages. Professional geographers from the University of California at Berkeley assisted in the production of this atlas.

9. This petition is submitted on behalf of the victims by the TOLEDO MAYA CULTURAL COUNCIL, a non-governmental organization that is registered and recognized under the laws of Belize. . . .

10. TMCC is governed by a General Assembly which meets every two years and is open to all Maya in the Toledo District. The General Assembly elects an Executive Committee, which is comprised of an equal number of Ke'kchi and Mopan Maya individuals. As members of Maya communities of Toledo, these individuals who sit on the Executive Committee are themselves among the victims in this case. . . .

IV. Facts

A. The Maya and Their Lands

12. People who are identified as Maya have, for centuries, formed organized societies that have inhabited a vast territory—which includes the Toledo District of southern Belize—long before the arrival of Europeans and the colonial institutions that gave way to the modern State of Belize. Among the historical and contemporary Maya people of the Middle American region encompassing Belize, distinct linguistic subgroups and communities have existed and evolved within a system of interrelationships and cultural affiliations. The contemporary Mopan- and Ke'kchi-speaking people of the Toledo District are the descendants or relatives of the Maya subgroups that inhabited the territory at least as far back as the time of European exploration and incursions into Toledo in the seventeenth and eighteenth centuries. . . .

14. The life and continuity of the Maya communities of Toledo are dependent upon a matrix of subsistence and cultural practices that are carried out within the lands that the Maya have used and occupied for centuries. These practices include swidden agriculture, hunting, fishing, gathering, and religious uses of specific sites. . . .

20. Maya land use patterns are governed by a system of customary rules that form part of the social and political organization of Maya communities. Within this traditional land tenure system, Maya villages hold land collectively, while individuals and families enjoy subsidiary rights of use and occupancy. . . .

22. The traditional land use and occupancy of each of the Maya villages of Toledo are illustrated by maps that are included in the *Maya Atlas*. The illustrated village land areas adjoin with each other and with other areas that are used in common by two or more Maya villages and form a larger territorial unit. This composite territory of traditional Maya land use and occupancy is also illustrated in the *Maya Atlas*.

B. THE GRANTING OF LOGGING CONCESSIONS ON MAYA LANDS

23. Since 1993, the Ministry of Natural Resources of Belize has granted numerous concessions for logging on a total of over half a million acres of land in the Toledo District. Logging under these concessions is ongoing or imminent. The areas of ten of the concessions include reservation and non-reservation lands that are traditionally used and occupied by the Maya. A single logging concession for 159,018 acres was granted to a Malaysian timber company, Toledo Atlantic International, Ltd. The area of this one concession includes a third of the Maya villages of the Toledo District and endangers roughly half of the Maya population of the District. Another Malaysian logging company, Atlantic Industries, Ltd., began operations in September 1995 in the Columbia River Forest Reserve, an area used by the Maya for hunting and gathering, and finished construction of one of Central America's largest sawmills in February 1996.

24. None of the Maya villages ever agreed to any of the logging concessions. Nor was the granting of the concessions preceded by meaningful consultations with the Maya. There is no indication that government officials otherwise considered Maya land use patterns or cultural practices in the affected areas when they granted the concessions, and no accommodations for Maya interests or rights have been made as the logging has proceeded. . . .

C. THE NEGATIVE ENVIRONMENTAL IMPACT OF THE LOGGING ON MAYA LANDS

26. The concessions granted by the Ministry of Natural Resources in the Toledo District are for logging . . . cover areas of land that include vulner-

able soils, primary forest growth and important watersheds that are critical parts of the natural environment upon which the Maya depend for subsistence. In various parts of the Toledo District, logging activities are damaging essential water supplies, threatening access to and use of Maya sacred sites, and straining plant and wildlife populations. Noise from the logging and the disruption of plant and animal life is affecting Maya hunting, fishing, and gathering practices, which are essential to Maya cultural and physical survival. . . .

32. The nature of the logging presently ongoing in the Toledo District threatens long-term and irreversible damage to the natural environment upon which the Maya depend. The permeability of the soil and the drainage patterns of the Toledo region allow the characteristics of the soil to change very rapidly if substantial land areas are stripped of forest cover. If the soil is altered in this way, the capacity of the forest to regenerate will be severely impaired, with devastating consequences for Maya subsistence patterns. A loss of topsoil and impaired forest regeneration would be devastating to the rotational system of farming used by the Maya. A stunted forest would further, and possibly permanently, diminish the availability of wildlife and plant resources, and soil erosion could permanently damage stream flows that are vital to water supplies. Damage to stream flows, in turn, could result in siltation threatening to coastal areas, including mangroves and coral reefs.

33. The threat of future and greater environmental damage is intensified by the inability or unwillingness of the State of Belize to adequately monitor the logging and enforce its environmental standards. The Forest Department of the Ministry of Natural Resources has proved itself incapable of or unwilling to monitor the logging concessions that have been granted to date. "Much of the logging illustrates poor management practices, and scant control from the Forest Department." Furthermore, evidence exists of substantial illegal logging by concession holders that goes unchecked by the Forest Department. Loggers have repeatedly been observed forging government certifications for felled timber. . . .

D. Concessions for Oil Development in the Toledo District

36. The environmental damage caused by the logging stands to be compounded by oil development activities. In late 1997, TMCC learned that the Ministry of Energy, Science, Technology and Transportation of Belize had approved the application of AB Energy, Inc. to engage in oil exploration activities in the Toledo District. The permit is for exploration within Block 12, one of several areas in Belize that is designated by the government as open to oil development. Block 12 covers 749,222 acres in the lowland portion of Toledo, much of it land that is used and occupied by the Maya. It

encompasses most if not all of the many Maya villages in Toledo District. AB Energy plans to have exploration wells in areas that will affect the villages of Crique Sarco and Sunday Wood especially.

37. Industry practice and the laws of Belize dictate that a contract for petroleum operations guarantees oil extraction rights if commercially viable oil deposits are located. [49] In that event, oil extraction activities may continue for a period of up to twenty-five years. [50] Thus, Belize, in granting oil exploration rights to AB Energy, has handed over a substantial portion of Maya traditional territory to potential long-term oil development and production activities. This concession, like the multiple logging concessions, was granted without any consultation with the Maya and apparently without any regard for Maya traditional land tenure. Moreover, the concession was granted in virtual secrecy, without public awareness about it until after it was approved.

38. Details about the concession to AB Energy and about that company remain sketchy. Citing confidentiality requirements, the government refused to release detailed information about the concession in responding to a request made by TMCC through its attorneys. That the concession exists as a threat to the Maya, however, is not a matter of doubt.

39. In the absence of detailed information on the concession, the Maya can only fear the worst from the planned oil development. In other areas where oil development has occurred on lands inhabited by indigenous peoples, the effects of the oil activities have been devastating. Indigenous communities have suffered illness from toxins released in the oil development process and pollutants have caused degradation in the wildlife and plant resources that are critical to indigenous subsistence. Indigenous peoples have also suffered adverse social impacts as the result of an influx of non-indigenous workers and settlers who move onto their lands in connection with the oil development activities. The Commission observed and documented such negative impacts from oil development in its recent study on the situation of human rights in Ecuador. [52] Without specific guarantees for their land tenure patterns and for measures to mitigate against the effects of oil development, the Maya are threatened with the same fate suffered by indigenous people elsewhere. . . .

E. Lack of Recognition and Adequate Protection of Indigenous Lands

41. The granting of concessions for logging and oil development in the Toledo District, with no regard for Maya customary land tenure and without adequate consultation, is part of a larger pattern of neglect on the part of the State. Government officials have uniformly refused to recognize Maya rights or interests in lands on the basis of Maya customary land use and

occupancy. The government position has been to narrowly interpret interests in lands and resources within the State's formal system of land titling, leasing, and permitting. Because Maya customary land tenure is not reflected in that formal system, it is simply ignored.

42. Earlier in this century the British colonial government established a system of reservations for several Maya villages. That system remains part of the formal land administration system of Belize. However, in both its geographic extent and qualitative attributes, the reservation system falls short of providing recognition or adequate protection of Maya customary land tenure. Only about half of the Maya villages are included in reservations, and the boundaries of those reservations remain ill defined. Further, to the extent the boundaries can be discerned, it is apparent that the reservation areas encompass only a fraction of the land areas used by the reservation villages for cultivation and for other subsistence and cultural activities. Qualitatively, the reservation regime provides inadequate security for Maya land tenure. Under the relevant legislation, lands within the reservations are deemed national lands and given up to the discretionary authority of the government with no specific guarantees for Maya interests. [57] . . .

F. Failed Efforts to Petition Government Officials

46. The Maya people have repeatedly attempted, without success, to have the government address and resolve their concerns about Maya land tenure and natural resource concessions in the Toledo District. . . .

G. The Ineffectiveness of Judicial Procedures Invoked by the Maya

64. Having failed to halt the logging and achieve official recognition of their land rights through direct appeals to the government, lobbying efforts and peaceful demonstrations, Maya leaders initiated judicial proceedings. This avenue, however has been equally fruitless because the proceedings have been unduly prolonged. . . .

V. Exception to Exhaustion of Domestic Remedies

78. Article 37.1 of the Commission's regulations specifies: "For a petition to be admitted by the Commission, the remedies under domestic jurisdiction must have been invoked and exhausted in accordance with the general principles of international law." However, article 37.2(c) establishes that the requirement of exhaustion of domestic remedies of article 37.1 shall not apply when, *inter alia*, "there has been unwarranted delay in rendering a final judgment under the aforementioned remedies." Thus, because of the unwarranted delay in the domestic judicial proceedings that were initiated

to seek vindication of Maya rights, the requirement that domestic remedies be exhausted is inapplicable in this case.

79. Diligent efforts have been made through the domestic judicial system to achieve redress that would obviate this petition, but to no avail. Over a year and a half has passed since TMCC and the Toledo Alcaldes Association filed their motion for constitutional redress with the Supreme Court of Belize. But that action, which remains *sub judice*, has failed to produce a single substantive judicial decision. Article 37.2(c) of the Commission's regulation reflects the general principle of international law that domestic remedies need not be exhausted where the remedy would be inadequate or ineffective. [87] The inordinate delay by the Supreme Court of Belize in adjudicating the lawsuit filed by the Maya people of the Toledo District renders that remedy both ineffective and inadequate.

80. "Formal" access to domestic remedies does not necessarily lead to "real and effective" remedies. [88] The Maya people of Toledo have formal access to domestic remedies, and they have utilized this access by initiating the lawsuit before the Supreme Court of Belize. But where a delay in reaching a judgment on the merits has made the relevant judicial proceedings "functionally inoperative," those proceedings need not be exhausted. [89] The mere fact that the result of a particular remedy is unfavorable to those who petition the Commission does not by itself demonstrate the nonexistence or exhaustion of all effective domestic remedies. [90] However, the lack of any result at all, as is the case here, leads to a "sufficient showing of the ineffectiveness and inadequacy of those remedies." [91]

81. There can hardly be any question of undue delay in the proceedings that were initiated by the Maya before the Supreme Court of Belize. Affidavits and other documentary evidence have been before the court for over a year. Yet the court has not rendered any decision on the merits of the case, despite its order that the case would be decided on the basis of such documentary evidence. [92] Nor has the court held a hearing or otherwise responded to the motion for interlocutory relief, which was filed several months ago. [93] Government officials have aided in the delay, by failing to respond to the request for the production of documents and by successfully pressing the Court for an indefinite continuance of the hearing on the motion for interlocutory relief. [94] Furthermore, government officials have failed to respond to the proposal for a settlement of the lawsuit that was submitted by TMCC and Toledo Alcaldes Association.

82. The Maya continue their efforts before the Supreme Court of Belize, but such efforts increasingly are demonstrated to be an exercise in futility because of the delay. The domestic lawsuit focuses on the logging as a violation of Maya rights, and does not mention the oil concessions. This is because the government had kept the oil concessions secret until almost a year after the lawsuit was filed. In any case, the futility of the lawsuit as to the

logging also establishes the ineffectiveness of any domestic judicial remedy in regard to the oil concessions. It is hard to imagine how the Belize judicial system could effectively function to bring scrutiny to bear on the oil concessions on the basis of an assertion of Maya land rights, where it has failed to do so in regard to the logging concessions. Hence, under the principle of effectiveness in domestic remedies, the exception to the exhaustion requirement extends to the claim against the oil concessions, as well as to the claim against the logging, which is presently before the Belize Supreme Court.

83. The Commission has stated that "[t]he mere fact that the pursuit of domestic remedies continues does not mean that the Commission is not authorized to analyze the case, for this would allow the State to conduct investigations and domestic judicial processes, prolonging them unreasonably without the Inter-American system being able to intervene." [95] In this same vein, the Inter-American Court of Human Rights has admonished: "The rule of prior exhaustion must never lead to a halt or delay that would render international action in support of the defenseless victim ineffective." [96] Substantial likelihood exists that international action will become futile if natural resource extraction and Maya land issues are left to languish any further in the Belize judicial systems. With each passing day, the logging being challenged encroaches more onto the lands upon which the Maya depend for their economic and cultural survival. To avoid such futility the Commission should proceed immediately to admit and act upon this petition, in accordance with Article 37.2(c) of its regulations, even though domestic remedies are formally still pending.

VI. Timeliness

84. Ordinarily, under Article 38.1 of the Commission's regulations, a petition to the Commission should be lodged within six months of notification of the final ruling that comprises the exhaustion of domestic remedies. However, Article 38.2 provides that in cases such as the present in which the requirement of exhaustion does not apply, "presentation of a petition to the Commission shall be within a reasonable period of time, in the Commission's judgment, as from the date on which the alleged violation of rights has occurred, considering the circumstances of each specific case."

85. The circumstances of this case are such that this petition is being presented within a reasonable period of time. The acts and omissions being complained of—that is, the failure of the State to adequately take account of Maya interests in its administration of lands and natural resources—are ongoing. TMCC and the Maya people have been diligent in trying to resolve the matter at the domestic level. Their efforts include a lawsuit to stop the logging and a motion for interlocutory relief as part of that lawsuit. The motion for interlocutory relief was scheduled for hearing on May 19, 1998, but was continued indefinitely. TMCC is now bringing the matter to the

Commission as it is becoming increasingly apparent that domestic remedies will not be effective.

VII. Absence of Parallel International Proceedings

86. The subject of this Petition is not pending in any other international proceeding for settlement.

VIII. State Responsibility for the Violation of Maya Human Rights

87. By virtue of the facts described above, Belize is internationally responsible for violating rights that are affirmed in the American Declaration of the Rights and Duties of Man and in other provisions of international human rights law. As a member of the Organization of American States and a party to the OAS Charter, Belize is legally bound to promote the observance of human rights. The Inter-American Court on Human Rights has declared that the rights affirmed in the American Declaration are, at a minimum, the human rights that OAS member states are bound to uphold. [97] Thus, Belize incurs international responsibility for any violation of rights articulated in the American Declaration, as well as for the violation of rights affirmed in any treaty to which Belize is a party.

88. By permitting environmentally damaging logging, and potentially damaging oil development, on lands used and occupied by the Maya of the Toledo District, Belize is acting in violation of the right to property, the right to cultural integrity, the right to a safe and healthy environment (which is derivative of other rights), and the right to consultation. Belize has further incurred international responsibility because its competent officials have failed to recognize and guarantee, by appropriate legislation or otherwise, the customary land tenure of the Maya. Such international responsibility arises by virtue of the principle of equality under the law and the duty of states to adopt effective measures to secure indigenous property and other rights that are related to land and resource use. Finally, Belize is in violation of the right of judicial protection as a result of the failure of its judicial system to proceed expeditiously to provide redress for the violation of Maya land and resource rights.

A. STATE RESPONSIBILITY FOR THE CONCESSIONS

89. Acting through its Ministry of Natural Resources, Belize has granted numerous concessions for logging and at least one for oil development on lands used and occupied by the Maya in the Toledo District. The granting of these concessions and the activities that Belize has permitted under them constitute violations of rights affirmed in the American Declaration and in other relevant international instruments.

THE RIGHT TO PROPERTY

90. Article XXIII of the American Declaration of the Rights and Duties of Man affirms the "right to own such private property as meets the essential needs of decent living and helps to maintain the dignity of the individual and of the home." This right includes the right to be free from unreasonable state interference with the enjoyment of property and from uncompensated takings thereof. [98] The right to property affirmed in Article XXIII, especially when considered in light of the fundamental principle of non-discrimination, embraces those forms of individual and collective landholding and resource use that derive from the customary land tenure system of the Maya of the Toledo District.

91. Traditional Maya patterns of use and occupancy of lands and natural resources are discussed above and detailed in several supporting documents. [99] These patterns correspond with a system of customary rules that determine individual and collective entitlements to lands and natural resources. For the Maya, this customary land tenure system and the usages it sanctions give rise to forms of property that are no less essential to a decent living and dignity of the home than formal State-granted property rights are for others.

92. The common law, which is shared among the diverse domestic legal systems—such as that of Belize—that derive from the British legal tradition, upholds property rights of indigenous peoples on the basis of traditional land tenure. Within this body of common law doctrine, "aboriginal rights" to lands exist by virtue of historical patterns of use or occupancy and may give rise to a level of legal entitlement in the nature of full ownership, referred to as "native" or "aboriginal title." [100] Apart from such native or aboriginal title in its fullest sense, aboriginal property rights may exist in the form of free-standing rights to fish, hunt, gather, or otherwise use resources or have access to lands. [101] In rendering the leading judgment of the High Court of Australia in the case of *Mabo [No. 2] v. Queensland*, [102] Justice Brennan explained the basis for aboriginal property rights, particularly native title, as follows:

Native title has its origin in and is given its content by the traditional laws acknowledged by and the traditional customs observed by the Indigenous inhabitants of a territory. The nature and incidents of native title must be ascertained as a matter of fact by reference to those laws and customs. [N]ative title . . . may be protected by such legal or equitable remedies as are appropriate to the particular rights and interests established by the evidence . . . whether possessed by a community, a group or an individual. . . . Of course in time the laws and customs of any people will change and the rights and interests of the members of the people among themselves will change too. But so long as the people remain as an identifiable community, the members of whom are identified by one another as members of that community living under its laws and customs, the communal native title survives to be enjoyed by the members according to the rights and interests to which they are respectively entitled under the traditionally based laws and customs, as currently acknowledged and observed. [103]

93. As a former British colony, Belize is a common law jurisdiction. [104] In the absence of any domestic judicial authority to the contrary, the common law of Belize should be deemed to incorporate the common law doctrine that upholds the property rights of indigenous peoples on the basis of customary land tenure. This proposition follows from the practice of the courts in Belize, which is to look to precedents of other common law countries especially in the absence of controlling local judicial authority. [105] Under the common law doctrine of aboriginal rights, the Maya of Toledo have property rights to lands and resources on the basis of their traditional patterns of use and occupancy. [106]

94. Independently of the common law of domestic legal systems, indigenous systems of land tenure give rise to property interests that, along with other forms of property, are embraced and affirmed by Article XXIII of the American Declaration. The fundamental principle of nondiscrimination, which is itself enshrined in the Declaration and is part of general international law, leads to this interpretation of the reach of the right to property articulated in Article XXIII. A contrary interpretation of Article XXIII would allow discrimination to persist against indigenous peoples with regard to their own modalities and forms of landholding and resource use. [107]

95. Within the framework of the overriding principle of nondiscrimination, the Commission has recognized the existence of property rights that derive from indigenous peoples' own traditional forms of land use and occupancy. The Commission's proposed American Declaration on the Rights of Indigenous Peoples, in its Article XVIII, refers to the right to property in the following way:

1. Indigenous peoples have the right to the legal recognition of their varied and specific forms and modalities of their control, ownership, use and enjoyment of territories and property.

2. Indigenous peoples have the right to the recognition of their property and ownership rights with respect to lands, territories and resources they have historically occupied, as well as to the use of those to which they have historically had access for their traditional activities and livelihood. [108]

96. In this same vein, the Draft United Nations Declaration on the Rights of Indigenous Peoples states:

Indigenous peoples have the right to own, develop, control and use the lands and territories, including the total environment of the lands, air, waters, coastal seas, sea-ice, flora, fauna and other resources which they have traditionally owned or otherwise occupied or used. This includes the right to the full recognition of their laws, traditions and customs, land-tenure systems and institutions for the development and management of resources, and the right to effective measures by States to prevent any interference with, alienation of, or encroachment upon these rights. [109]

97. These statements of indigenous land and resource rights are consistent with the relevant provision of the International Labour Organisation's Convention (No. 169) on Indigenous and Tribal Peoples. That Convention requires:

The rights of ownership and possession of the peoples concerned over the lands which they traditionally occupy shall be recognized. In addition, measures shall be taken in appropriate cases to safeguard the right of the peoples concerned to use lands not exclusively occupied by them, but to which they have traditionally had access for their subsistence and traditional activities. [110]

Belize is not among the several American states that have ratified ILO Convention No. 169. However, this article of the Convention, like the land rights provisions of the Proposed American Declaration and the Draft U.N. Declaration, are appropriately considered as articulating the implications of the right to property, which is found in Article XXIII of the American Declaration.

98. In sum, the Maya of the Toledo District have rights of property over the lands and resources that they traditionally have used and occupied, and the character of these rights is a function of Maya customary patterns. These property rights are embraced and affirmed by Article XXIII of the American Declaration.

99. Maya property rights include rights of occupancy as well as rights of access to, and use or ownership of, natural resources, in accordance with Maya traditional patterns which are described above and in the supporting documents. [111] Whatever the precise character of these rights, or of the limitations that may reasonably be placed upon them, their existence cannot simply be ignored by public officials, otherwise they are not rights at all.

100. The Ministry of Natural Resources has granted numerous concessions to log on vast portions of the lands used and occupied by the Maya, and it has further encumbered Maya traditional lands with an oil development concession, without any consideration of Maya rights within those lands. Furthermore, acts and omissions attributable to the State have allowed the logging to proceed on Maya traditional lands without Maya consent and without any compensation or mitigation for the adverse impacts caused by the logging. [112] These conditions make for a flagrant violation of the right to property, for which Belize is responsible.

THE RIGHT TO CULTURAL INTEGRITY

101. The international responsibility of Belize in this case is also a function of its obligation to protect the integrity of the Maya culture, of which

Maya land use patterns are an essential part. Maya agricultural and other land use patterns are linked with familial and social relations, religious practices, and the very existence of Maya communities. [113] Several rights articulated in the American Declaration support the enjoyment of such critical aspects of Maya culture, including the right to property (Article XXIII) just discussed in relation to lands and resources, as well as the right to religious freedom (Article III), the right to family and protection thereof (Article VI), and the right to take part in the cultural life of the community (Article XIV). The Commission has observed that, "[f]or indigenous peoples, the free exercise of such rights is essential to the enjoyment and perpetuation of their culture." [114]

102. Notably, the Charter of Civil Society for the Caribbean Community, adopted by heads of government of the State members of the Caribbean Community on February 19, 1997, stipulates:

The States recognise the contribution of the indigenous peoples to the development process and undertake to continue to protect their historical rights and respect the culture and way of life of these peoples.

103. The obligation of Belize to protect the Maya culture arises particularly by virtue of its status as a party to the International Covenant on Civil and Political Rights. The Commission has on several occasions affirmed its competence to determine state responsibility by reference to international instruments other than the American Declaration and the American Convention on Human Rights, when such other instruments are relevant to a case that is properly before the Commission. [115]

104. Article 27 of the Covenant on Civil and Political Rights states:

In those States in which ethnic, religious or linguistic minorities exist, persons belonging to such minorities shall not be denied the right, in community with the other members of their group, to enjoy their own culture, to profess and practise their own religion, or to use their own language.

105. Relying especially on Article 27, the Commission repeatedly has affirmed that international law protects minority groups, including indigenous peoples, in the enjoyment of all aspects of their diverse cultures and group identities. [116] The Commission has held that, for indigenous peoples in particular, the right to the integrity of culture covers "the aspects linked to productive organization, which includes, among other things, the issue of ancestral and communal lands." [117]

106. In its Proposed Declaration on the Rights of Indigenous Peoples, the Commission once again articulated the obligation of states to respect the cultural integrity of indigenous peoples, expressly linking property rights and customs to the survival of indigenous cultures. Article VII of the Proposed Declaration, entitled "Right to Cultural Integrity" states:

1. Indigenous peoples have the right to their cultural integrity, and their historical and archeological heritage, which are important both for their survival as well as for the identity of their members.

2. Indigenous peoples are entitled to restitution in respect of the property of which they have been dispossessed, and where that is not possible, compensation on the basis not less favorable than the standard of international law.

3. The states shall recognize and respect indigenous ways of life, customs, traditions, forms of social, economic and political organization, institutions, practices, beliefs and values, use of dress, and languages. [118]

107. The United Nations Human Rights Committee has confirmed the Commission's interpretation of the reach of the cultural integrity norm, in its General Comment on Article 27 of the Covenant:

[C]ulture manifests itself in many forms, including a particular way of life associated with the use of land resources, especially in the case of indigenous peoples. That right may include such traditional activities as fishing or hunting and the right to live in reserves protected by law. The enjoyment of these rights may require positive measures of protection and measures to ensure the effective participation of members of minority communities in decisions which affect them. [119]

The Committee has made clear that indigenous peoples' traditional land use patterns are elements of culture that states are to take affirmative measures to protect under Article 27, apart from whether or not states recognize indigenous ownership rights over the lands and resources that are subject to traditional uses. [120]

108. Accordingly, the Human Rights Committee found Article 27 to be violated in circumstances similar to those confronting the Maya of the Toledo District. In *Ominayak, Chief of the Lubicon Lake Band of Cree v. Canada*, [121] the Committee determined that Canada had violated Article 27 by allowing the provincial government of Alberta to grant leases for oil and gas exploration and for timber development within the ancestral territory of the Lubicon Lake Band. The Committee found that the natural resource development activity compounded historical inequities to "threaten the way of life and culture of the Lubicon Lake Band, and constitute a violation of Article 27 so long as they continue." [122]

109. It is no less the case here that indigenous cultural integrity is being denied. Maya land and resource uses, which are at the core of Maya culture, are imperiled by ongoing and planned natural resource extraction activities in the Toledo District. By permitting these activities through logging and oil development concessions, without any apparent consideration much less protection of Maya cultural patterns, Belize has denied the right of the Maya to enjoy their culture and maintain its integrity, in violation of Article 27 of the International Covenant on Civil and Political Rights and related provisions of the American Declaration.

THE RIGHT TO A HEALTHY ENVIRONMENT

110. The logging being permitted by Belize is causing substantial environmental harm. That harm, and the further environmental degradation that is likely to result from the oil concessions, threatens not only Maya culture, but also Maya physical well-being. The environmental damage undermines Maya food sources and threatens contamination of soils and waters, which would have adverse direct health consequences for the Maya.

111. The American Declaration affirms the right to life (Article I) and the right to the preservation of health and well-being (Article XI). These and the other provisions of the American Declaration highlighted above, along with Article 27 of the International Covenant on Civil and Political Rights, as a whole broadly protect both the physical well-being and cultural integrity of the Maya of the Toledo District. The Commission has acknowledged that "[c]ertain indigenous peoples maintain special ties with their traditional lands, and a close dependence upon the natural resources provided therein — respect for which is essential to their physical and cultural survival." [125] This connection between indigenous territory and survival is demonstrated by the situation of the Maya. [126] Given the bond between the Maya and their natural environment, the enjoyment of the above rights for the Maya is dependent on a habitat that is secure from environmental degradation. The obligation of Belize to uphold the physical well-being and cultural integrity of the Maya, therefore, necessarily entails an obligation to provide for a safe and healthy environment.

112. The need for states to protect the natural environments upon which indigenous peoples depend was expressly recognized by the United Nations Conference on Environment and Development, held in Rio de Janeiro in 1992. The principal resolution adopted by the Conference, the "Rio Declaration," affirms that human beings "are entitled to a healthy and productive life in harmony with nature." [127] Within this conceptual framework, the Rio Declaration states:

Indigenous people and their communities, and other local communities, have a vital role in environmental management and development because of their knowledge and traditional practices. States should recognize and duly support their identity, culture and interests and enable their effective participation in the achievement of sustainable development. [128]

113. Additionally, in chapter 26 of its detailed program of action, known as "Agenda 21," the Rio conference recognized that "Indigenous people and their communities have an historical relationship with their lands and are generally descendants of the original inhabitants of such lands." [129]

114. In accordance with the Rio documents, the Commission's proposed American Declaration on the Rights of Indigenous Peoples provides that "Indigenous peoples have a right to a safe and healthy environment, which

is an essential condition for the enjoyment of the right to life and collective well-being." [130] In this same vein, the United Nations Declaration on the Rights of Indigenous Peoples states that "Indigenous peoples have the right to the conservation, restoration and protection of the total environment and the productive capacity of their lands, territories, and resources." [131] These norms are implicit in the provisions of the American Declaration and the Covenant on Civil and Political rights cited above, when those provisions are applied in the context of the indigenous peoples whose individual and collective well-being are dependent upon continued utilization of traditional collective systems for the control and use of territory.

115. Belize has utterly failed to meet its obligation to guard against the degradation of the natural environment upon which Maya physical and cultural survival depend. Government officials have been unwilling or unable to enforce environmental norms against logging practices that have caused extensive damage and that threaten further, long-term damage. [132] The Commission has recognized that the "absence of regulation, inappropriate regulation, or lack of supervision in the application of extant norms may create serious problems with respect to the environment which translate into violations of human rights." [133] Not only has Belize failed to protect the environment, it has actively facilitated the environmental threat to the Maya by permitting logging and oil development under terms that do not account for Maya customary land tenure and resource use. [134] Belize is thus internationally responsible in regard to those human rights that, considered as a whole in the present context, translate into a right to a safe and healthy environment.

THE RIGHT TO CONSULTATION

116. Also implicit in the human rights provisions that protect Maya interests in lands and natural resources is the right to be consulted in a meaningful way about any decision that may affect those interests. Within the framework of Article 27 of the International Covenant on Civil and Political Rights, the United Nations Human Rights Committee has recognized the imperative of ensuring indigenous peoples' effective participation in decisions that may affect their traditional land and resource use. [135] This right of consultation relates to the right to participate in government, which is found in Article XX of the American Declaration, and it derives, moreover, from the fundamental principle of self-determination. [136] Self-determination is a principle of general international law, which is affirmed in multiple international instruments, including the Covenant on Civil and Political Rights. At its core, self-determination means that human beings, individually and collectively, have a right to be in control of their own destinies under conditions of equality. For indigenous peoples, the principle of

self-determination establishes, at a minimum, the right to be genuinely involved in all decision making that affects them. [137]

117. The Commission's Proposed Declaration on the Rights of Indigenous Peoples states: "Indigenous peoples have the right to participate without discrimination, if they so decide, in all decision making, at all levels with regard to matters that might affect their rights, lives and destiny." [138] The Proposed Declaration, in addition, affirms their right "to be informed of measures which will affect their environment, including information that ensures their effective participation in actions and policies that might affect it."

118. ILO Convention No. 169 clarifies that indigenous peoples' right to consultation extends even to decisions about resources that remain under state ownership:

In cases in which the State retains the ownership of mineral or sub-surface resources or rights to other resources pertaining to lands, governments shall establish or maintain procedures through which they shall consult these peoples, with a view to ascertaining whether and to what degree their interests would be prejudiced, before undertaking or permitting any programmes for the exploration or exploitation of such resources pertaining to their lands. [140]

Further, Convention No. 169 establishes that indigenous peoples "have the right to decide their own priorities for the process of development as it affects their lives . . . [and hence] they shall participate in the formulation, implementation and evaluation of plans and programmes for national and regional development which may affect them directly." [141]

119. The required consultations with indigenous peoples must be more than formalities or simply processes by which they are given information about development projects. Clear, complete, and accurate information is necessary. But while necessary, such information alone is not sufficient for effective participation in decision making. Rather, in order to be truly effective, the consultations should also provide indigenous peoples a full and fair opportunity to be heard and to genuinely influence the decisions before them. ILO Convention No. 169 stipulates that consultations "shall be undertaken in good faith and in a form appropriate to the circumstances, with the objective of achieving agreement or consent to the proposed measures." [142]

120. Nothing even remotely approaching such consultations has been provided for the Maya of the Toledo District in relation to the logging and oil concessions. [143] Most of the logging concessions were granted without public knowledge, much less in direct consultation with the affected Maya communities. The Belize Forest Department held public meetings about the management plan for the concession to Atlantic Industries Ltd. for logging in the Columbia River Forest Reserve, but those meetings provided

only vague and incomplete information. [144] The granting of the oil exploration concession to AG Energy was no less than secretive. [145] The Maya themselves have attempted to initiate a process of dialogue with the government by which they could influence decision making about the natural resource development projects that engulf them. But these attempts have been consistently rebuffed. [146] Belize has denied the Maya meaningful consultation, and this denial is a violation of Maya human rights.

B. State Responsibility for the Failure to Recognize and Secure Territorial Rights

121. As established above, the Maya have rights in relation to lands and natural resources, and Belize has granted logging and oil development concessions in violation of those rights. The conduct of Belize in this regard is substantially due to the failure of the State to recognize and secure Maya territorial rights in the first place. [147] The legal system of Belize and its governing officials do not recognize Maya customary land tenure as a source of property rights, and the State does not otherwise provide adequate protection for the matrix of Maya cultural and subsistence practices related to lands and resources. This absence of recognition and protection is itself a source of international responsibility on the part of Belize.

THE RIGHT TO EQUALITY UNDER THE LAW

122. The failure to recognize as legally valid indigenous peoples' own systems of landholding and resource use is a form of discrimination that violates the fundamental right to equality under the law, a right upheld by Article II of the American Declaration on the Rights and Duties of Man. Various studies of the United Nations and the Organization of American States have concluded that indigenous peoples historically have suffered racial discrimination, and that one of the greatest manifestations of this discrimination has been the failure of state authorities to recognize indigenous customary forms of possession and use of lands. The U.N. Committee on the Elimination of Racial Discrimination has observed:

In many regions of the world indigenous peoples have been, and are still being, discriminated against, deprived of their human rights and fundamental freedoms and . . . have lost their land and resources to colonists, commercial companies and State enterprises. Consequently the preservation of their culture and their historical identity has been and still is jeopardized. [148]

123. This situation of discrimination and its historical origins were examined during a seminar of experts convened by the United Nations to study the effects of racial discrimination on indigenous-state relations. The seminar concluded that "[i]ndigenous peoples have been, and still are, the

victims of racism and racial discrimination." [149] The seminar's report elaborates:

Racial discrimination against indigenous peoples is the outcome of a long historical process of conquest, penetration and marginalization, accompanied by attitudes of superiority and by a projection of what is indigenous as "primitive" and "inferior." The discrimination is of a dual nature: on the one hand, gradual destruction of the material and spiritual conditions [needed] for the maintenance of their [way of life], on the other hand, attitudes and behaviour signifying exclusion or negative discrimination when indigenous peoples seek to participate in the dominant society. [150]

124. The Maya of the Toledo District are among the segments of humanity that have suffered this history of discrimination. Government officials not only acknowledge the history of discrimination and colonization against the Maya, but also overtly seek to perpetuate it by invoking it as a basis for continuing refusal to recognize Maya customary land tenure. [151]

125. Patterns of discrimination against indigenous peoples cannot be allowed to persist in the modern world. Hence the U.N. Committee on the Elimination of Racial Discrimination, in elaborating upon the nondiscrimination norm in the context of indigenous peoples, admonished states to "recognize and protect the rights of indigenous peoples to own, develop, control and use their communal lands, territories and resources." [152]

126. Eradication of the legacies of historical discrimination requires adherence to the principle of equality of the kind exemplified by the Australian High Court in *Mabo v. Queensland [No. 2]*. [153] In that case the High Court, reversing over a century of Australian jurisprudence and official policy, recognized "native title," that is, a right of property on the basis of customary indigenous land tenure. Justice Brennan represented the view of the majority of the Court in characterizing as "unjust and discriminatory" the past failure of the Australian legal system to embrace and protect native title. Earlier, in *Mabo v. Queensland [No. 1]*, [154] Justices Brennan, Toohey, and Gaudron, in a joint judgment, had expressed the Court's majority view that a legislative measure targeting native title for legal extinguishment was racially discriminatory and hence invalid. In regard to the indigenous Miriam people of the Murray Islands, the justices viewed the negative differential treatment of their claim to native title as "impair[ing] their human rights while leaving unimpaired the human rights of those whose rights in and over the Murray Islands did not take their origins in the laws and customs of the Miriam people." [155]

127. Belize similarly accords negative differential treatment of indigenous customary land tenure, in violation of the principle of equality under the law. The entire administrative and formal legal apparatus of Belize fails to recognize Maya rights to lands and resources on the basis of customary land tenure. This failure impairs the human rights of the Maya, while leaving

unimpaired the human rights of those whose rights in and over the Toledo District did not take their origins in Maya laws and customs.

THE OBLIGATION TO EFFECTIVELY SECURE RIGHTS

128. The obligation of Belize to uphold, on a nondiscriminatory basis, Maya property, cultural and other rights in relation to lands and natural resources includes the obligation to take the measures necessary to make those rights effective. International law generally requires states to adopt the legislative and administrative measures necessary to ensure the full enjoyment of the human rights they are obligated to uphold. [156] This includes the obligation to adjust the state governing apparatus to bring it in conformity with applicable human rights norms. [157] Belize, therefore, cannot escape international responsibility by reference to its domestic laws or administrative practices that fail to include recognition of Maya human rights in relation to lands and resources. [158] Rather, Belize has the obligation to change its internal practices to recognize those rights and, moreover, to take affirmative steps to protect them.

129. The Commission has stated that, because of their vulnerable conditions vis-à-vis majority populations, indigenous groups may require certain additional protections beyond those granted to all citizens, in order to bring about true equality among the nationals of a state. [159] The "prevention of discrimination, on the one hand, and the implementation of special measures to protect minorities, on the other, are merely two aspects of the same problem: that of fully ensuring equal rights of all persons." [160] Referring specifically to indigenous peoples' rights to maintain customary land and resource uses, the United Nations Human Rights Committee has affirmed that "[t]he enjoyment of those rights may require positive measures of protection." [161]

130. Given the typical centrality of lands and natural resources to the cultural and physical survival of indigenous peoples, and to their enjoyment of human rights in general, [162] the obligation of states to take affirmative measures of protection in this regard is *sui generis*. ILO Convention No. 169 articulates the nature and scope of this *sui generis* obligation as follows:

Governments shall take steps as necessary to identify the lands which [indigenous] peoples concerned traditionally occupy, and to guarantee effective protection of their rights of ownership and possession. . . . Adequate procedures shall be established within the national legal system to resolve land claims by the peoples concerned. [163]

131. Similarly, the Commission's Proposed American Declaration on the Rights of Indigenous Peoples affirms that they "have the right to an effective legal framework for the protection of their rights with respect to the natural resources on their lands." [164] Additionally, the Proposed Declaration

enjoins states to "give maximum priority to the demarcation and recognition of properties and areas of indigenous use." [165]

132. Agenda 21, the detailed program of action adopted by the U.N. Conference on Environment and Development further manifests the *sui generis* obligation of states to take affirmative measures to protect indigenous peoples' rights in lands and natural resources. Within the context of recognizing indigenous peoples' "historical relation with their lands," Chapter 26 of Agenda 21 calls on states to adopt and give effect to the following measures, among others:

(i) Adoption or strengthening of appropriate policies and/or legal instruments at the national level;

(ii) Recognition that the lands of indigenous people and their communities should be protected from activities that are environmentally unsound or that the indigenous people concerned consider to be socially and culturally inappropriate;

(iii) Recognition of their values, traditional knowledge and resource management practices with a view to promoting environmentally sound and sustainable development. [166]

133. At a minimum, Belize is obligated to adopt legislation or other appropriate measures to identify the geographic extent of Maya traditional lands and specifically define the legal attributes of Maya land tenure and resource use, in accordance with Maya custom. Without such measures, the Maya will not be secure in the enjoyment of their property, cultural, and other human rights, which are dependent on traditional patterns of land and resource use. Rather than adopt such measures, however, Belize has left the Maya vulnerable to incursions by outsiders onto their lands and to official land and resource management practices that altogether deny Maya rights.

C. State Responsibility for Lack of Judicial Protection

134. The Maya have attempted, without success, to obtain redress through domestic avenues for the foregoing violations of rights regarding lands and resources. [167] Maya efforts at the domestic level include a lawsuit filed with the Supreme Court of Belize, but this method of obtaining relief has been ineffective. [168]

135. In itself, this failure of Belize to provide effective judicial protection for Maya rights constitutes a violation of the American Declaration, particularly in regard to its Article XVIII. This article affirms the right to "resort to the courts to ensure respect for . . . legal rights" and, furthermore, provides that there should be available "a simple, brief procedure whereby the courts will protect" against acts of authority that "violate any fundamental constitutional rights. [169]

136. The right to judicial protection, upheld by Article XVIII of the American Declaration, is affirmed in similar terms by the American Convention

on Human Rights. In regard to the obligations of states under the American Convention, the Inter-American Court of Human Rights has stated:

States Parties have an obligation to provide effective judicial remedies to victims of human rights violations (Article 25), remedies that must be substantiated in accordance with the rules of due process of law (Article 8(1)), . . . According to this principle, the absence of an effective remedy to violations of the rights recognized by the Convention is itself a violation of the Convention by the State Party in which the remedy is lacking. [170]

Accordingly, the Commission has found that the lack of an effective judicial remedy implies, not just an exception to the exhaustion of domestic remedies, but also a violation of the substantive right to judicial protection, which is upheld by the Inter-American human rights system. [171]

137. TMCC and the Toledo Alcaldes Association, as the major Maya representative organizations in the Toledo District, filed an action for constitutional redress with the Supreme Court of Belize, pursuant to a procedure provided for in Article 20 of the Constitution of Belize. [172] By their lawsuit, TMCC and the Alcaldes Association sought relief against the logging on Maya traditional lands and against the failure of government officials to recognize Maya land rights on the basis of customary land tenure. They alleged violations of rights to property and equality under the law, which are rights protected by the Belize Constitution. The Maya applicants for constitutional redress submitted substantial documentation to support their assertion of constitutionally protected property rights over the lands in question, including expert reports by an archeologist, a geographer, and two anthropologists, as well as a detailed legal analysis of the relevant facts and legal precedents. The lawsuit also includes a motion for emergency interlocutory relief against the logging, a motion that was supported by additional documentation demonstrating the environmental damage being done and further threatened by the logging.

138. Over a year and a half has passed since the lawsuit was initiated, and four months have gone by since the motion for emergency interlocutory relief was plead. The Belize Supreme Court has yet to reach a decision on the merits or on the motion for interlocutory relief. The efforts of the Maya in the Belize judicial system have only been met by dilatory tactics on the part of the government, tactics in which the Belize Supreme Court has acquiesced. Most notably, at the government's urging, the court continued the hearing date for the motion for interlocutory relief and has failed to set another hearing date or otherwise take action on the motion — a motion that by its very character requires prompt judicial action. It is evident that the Maya are being denied the right of judicial protection of Article XVIII of the American Declaration, which requires access to the courts and a simple, brief procedure for the protection of fundamental rights.

139. Although the Constitution of Belize provides for a judicial procedure

to protect constitutional rights, that procedure has been ineffective as a means of protecting Maya rights. A state's obligation to provide effective judicial remedies is not fulfilled simply by the existence of courts or formal procedures, or even by the ability to resort to the courts. Rather, a state must take affirmative steps to ensure that the remedies provided by the state through its courts are "truly effective in establishing whether there has been a violation of human rights and in providing redress." [178] Despite the amount of time that has passed and the voluminous evidence that has been submitted to the Belize Supreme Court, the court has not progressed toward a determination of the rights or violations alleged by the Maya, much less toward any redress for those violations. It appears that the court is entirely nonfunctional in regard to the lawsuit brought by the Maya, who have been left defenseless within the domestic legal system as their human rights continue to be trampled upon.

140. An essential element of effectiveness is timeliness. The right to judicial protection requires that courts adjudicate and decide cases expeditiously. [179] The Commission has stated emphatically: "There is no question but that the duty to conduct a proceeding expeditiously and swiftly is a duty of the organs entrusted with the administration of justice." [180] The need for swift judicial action is enhanced when, in cases like the present, the alleged violations are ongoing and threaten to be irreparable. Even if they are forthcoming, judicial remedies are ineffective if they come too late.

141. As established above in the argument for an exception to the exhaustion of domestic remedies, the proceedings initiated by the Maya in the Supreme Court of Belize suffer from undue delay. That delay renders those proceedings ineffective to protect the Maya from acts of authority that violate their rights. [181] Because of its international obligation to provide effective judicial remedies, Belize is internationally responsible for this shortcoming of its judicial system. This international responsibility is in addition to that incurred as a result of the primary acts and omissions of government officials that infringe on Maya rights over lands and resources.

IX. Request for Relief

142. By reason of the foregoing, TMCC, on the behalf of the Maya indigenous communities of the Toledo District, named above, respectfully requests that the Commission place itself at the disposal of the parties to mediate a friendly settlement of the disputes described herein, pursuant to the Commission's role of promoting respect for and defending human rights as set forth in the Charter of the Organization of American States and in the Statute of the Commission.

143. Alternatively, if no friendly settlement is reached, TMCC respectfully requests that the Commission prepare a report setting forth all the facts and applicable law, declaring that Belize is internationally responsible for viola-

tions of rights affirmed in the American Declaration of the Rights and Duties of Man and in other instruments of international law, and recommending that Belize:

(a) suspend all permits, licenses, and concessions for logging, oil exploration or extraction, and any other natural resource development within lands traditionally used and occupied by Maya people in the Toledo District, and ensure that such natural resource development activity does not occur, until a suitable arrangement is negotiated between the Government of Belize and the indigenous communities concerned;

(b) engage in dialogue with the Maya communities of the Toledo District, through their freely chosen leaders and representatives, to determine whether and under what circumstances natural resource development activity may go forward on lands used and occupied by the Maya;

(c) establish and institute a legal mechanism under domestic law, acceptable to the indigenous communities concerned and in conformity with the legal standards stated in this petition, that will result in the official recognition of Maya customary land tenure and resource use, provide specific guarantees therefore, and lead to the prompt demarcation of Maya traditional lands;

(d) suspend consideration of all future permits, licenses, or concessions for timber, oil, or other natural resource development within the Toledo District, until the land tenure issues affecting the Maya communities of the District have been resolved, or unless a specific written agreement has been reached between the government and the Maya community or communities affected by the proposed concession;

(e) establish and implement, in coordination with the affected Maya communities, a plan to mitigate and repair the environmental harm caused by the logging and oil exploration activities on lands used and occupied by the Maya;

(f) pay moral and pecuniary damages incurred by the Maya communities as a result of the logging and oil development activities on their traditional lands, and pay all costs the communities and TMCC have incurred in defending the communities' rights;

(g) provide any other relief that the Commission considers appropriate and just.

X. Request for Precautionary Measures

144. TMCC further requests that the Commission, pending a friendly settlement or its final recommendations in this case, and in accordance with

Article 29 of its regulations, call upon Belize to adopt precautionary measures to avoid irreparable harm to the Maya communities and their members. Such precautionary measures should consist of the immediate suspension of all permits, licenses, and concessions for logging, oil exploration, and other natural resource development activity on lands used and occupied by the Maya in the Toledo District, and specific measures to ensure that the logging and such other natural resource development activity in fact ceases and does not start again unless pursuant to a suitable arrangement negotiated with the affected Maya communities under the auspices of the Commission's good offices.

145. On at least one previous occasion the Commission has acted under Article 29 of its regulations to urge precautionary measures of the kind requested here. On October 30, 1997, the Commission called upon the State of Nicaragua to adopt precautionary measures for the purpose of suspending the concession granted to a foreign timber company for logging on the traditional lands of the Awas Tingni indigenous community. [182] The need for precautionary measures to guard against irreparable and potentially devastating and widespread harm to indigenous communal existence is no less urgent for the Maya of the Toledo District. . . .

Notes

Introduction

1. General Assembly Resolution 421 (V), 4 December 1950.
2. International Covenant on Economic, Social, and Cultural Rights and International Covenant on Civil and Political Rights, adopted 16 December 1966, GA Res. 2200A (XXI).
3. General Recommendation 24 on Women and Health, UN Doc. A/54/38/ Rev.1, chapter 1 (1999).
4. Craig Scott, "Toward the Institutional Integration of the Core Human Rights Treaties," this volume.

Chapter 1. Toward the Institutional Integration of the Core Human Rights Treaties

The author would like to thank the Social Sciences and Humanities Research Council of Canada for its generous financial support.
1. The six treaties and committees are (1) the Convention on the Elimination of Discrimination Against Women ("the Women's Discrimination Convention") and Committee (CEDAW); (2) the Convention on the Rights of the Child ("Children's Convention") and Committee (CRC); (3) the Convention on the Elimination of All Forms of Racial Discrimination ("Racial Discrimination Convention") and Committee (CERD); (4) the Convention Against Torture and Other Cruel, Inhuman, or Degrading Treatment or Punishment ("Torture Convention") and Committee (CAT); (5) the International Covenant on Economic, Social, and Cultural Rights (ICESCR) and Committee (CESCR); and (6) the International Covenant on Civil and Political Rights (ICCPR) and the Human Rights Committee (HRC).
2. See Craig Scott, "Reaching Beyond (Without Abandoning) the Category of 'Economic, Social and Cultural Rights'," *Human Rights Quarterly* 21 (1999): 633–700; and Craig Scott, "Bodies of Knowledge: A Diversity Promotion Role for the UN High Commissioner for Human Rights" in *The Future of UN Human Rights Treaty Monitoring*, ed. Philip Alston and James Crawford (Cambridge: Cambridge University Press, 2000), 403.
3. See the illustration used of migrant workers' housing under the European Social Charter where it is argued that the holistic jurisprudence of the Committee of Independent Experts (now the European Committee of Social Rights) would be far

from assured within the UN treaty order due to the categorical separation of the treaties, Scott, "Reaching Beyond," 658–59.

4. Scott, "Bodies of Knowledge," Section B, "Valuing Diversity of Knowledge," 406–11. It is important to acknowledge that expertise and experience are overlapping forms of knowledge. This point will not be developed in the present chapter other than simply to note that informal experience can be said to generate a type of expertise while formal expertise is often incomplete or underdeveloped without experience of the world or issues being studied.

5. Ibid., 406.

6. The reference to each treaty "having" a partial picture refers not to a limited, category-bound focus that is *inherent* in the treaty's terms, but to a focus that is a *contingent* (albeit inevitable) buildup of a body of doctrinal knowledge and associated community of understandings within each treaty order.

7. It will be noted that the term "human rights committees" is used interchangeably with reference to human rights "treaty bodies."

8. See, for example, Report of the Secretary-General, *Follow-Up Action on the Conclusions and Recommendations of the Sixth Meeting of Persons Chairing the Human Rights Treaty Bodies*, UN Doc. HRI/MC/1996/2 (15 August 1996), para. 69, reporting CEDAW's request for a formal analysis by the human rights secretariat of how other treaty bodies get information from NGOs. [hereinafter 1996 Follow-up Report].

9. For a leading study on this theme, see Michael C. Dorf and Charles F. Sabel, "A Constitution of Democratic Experimentalism," *Columbia Law Review* 98 (1998): 267–473.

10. Mara Bustelo, "The Committee on the Elimination of Discrimination Against Women at the Crossroads" in Alston and Crawford, *Future of Human Rights Treaty Monitoring*, 99. CEDAW is serviced by a different secretariat from the other five committees, the Division for the Advancement of Women, which operates out of the UN's New York location. The Office of the UN High Commissioner for Human Rights (Office of the UNHCHR) services the rest of the five committees and operates out of the UN's Geneva location. This state of affairs has meant that CEDAW's interaction with the other committees, both formal and informal, has been impeded. Since 1992 CEDAW has requested that it be located in Geneva with the other committees and serviced thereby by the Centre. Ibid., 83. In 1996 the UN Secretary General informed the committee that the 1996–97 program budget did not accommodate the request. In their 1996 meeting, the chairpersons reaffirmed their support for CEDAW's request and expressed regret that the request had not been respected, adding that "They share the Committee's view that the Committee cannot function properly if its secretariat is physically separated from the secretariat of all the other human rights treaty bodies." *Report of the Seventh Meeting of Persons Chairing the Human Rights Treaty Bodies*, UN Doc. A/51/482 (11 October 1996), para. 46 [hereinafter Chairpersons' Report, 7th Meeting, 1996, and similarly for other such reports].

11. At the 1995 meeting the General Assembly authorized finances to fund the annual meetings. Chairpersons' Report, 6th Meeting, 1995, UN Doc. A/50/505 (4 October 1995), para. 3.

12. The High Commissioner for Human Rights, state delegations, representatives of a number of UN specialized agencies, the chairperson of the Commission on Human Rights rapporteurs, and so on.

13. On the first occasion when such oral interventions were permitted, 11 NGOs, including Amnesty International, Defense for Children International, Women's International League for Peace and Freedom, Anti-Racism Information Service (ARIS), and Lawyers Committee for Human Rights, are listed as having made presentations. Chairpersons' Report, 8th Meeting, 1997, UN Doc. A/52/507 (21 Octo-

ber 1997), para. 10. At the chairpersons' tenth meeting, the second of 1998, 55 states sent representatives. Chairpersons' Report, 10th Meeting, 1998, UN Doc. A/53/432 (25 September 1998), para. 11.

14. For example, the Chairpersons' Report, 6th Meeting, 1995, recommends that the committees "take increased cognizance of the related activities of regional human rights mechanisms" (para. 24) and "increase their cooperation and exchange with United Nations non-conventional human rights bodies and mechanisms" (para. 25). The Chairpersons' Report, 8th Meeting, 1997, recommended that committee members should refrain from participating in consideration of reports from their own states (para. 29), which should make requests for assistance from specialized agencies and other UN bodies more precise (para. 51).

15. Two of the more interesting ones were made at the seventh and eighth meetings. In 1996, the chairpersons "recommend that the Centre for Human Rights [now the Office of the UNHCHR] engage in an active dialogue with Bretton Woods institutions so that in reference to human rights standards by these institutions, the applicable United Nations human rights instruments will be given a preeminent role." Chairpersons' Report, 7th Meeting, 1996, para. 56. Because these institutions are normative outlaws in the sense that they are not subject to any direct review by the committees, despite their interstate membership, it would appear that the committees are interested in developing some kind of nascent accountability and see bureaucrat-to-bureaucrat engagement as a possible place to start. In 1997 the chairpersons sought a "report . . . from the Legal Counsel [of the UN] which would explore the feasibility of devising more innovative approaches in dealing with future and existing amendments to the human rights treaties." Chairpersons' Report, 8th Meeting, 1997.

16. In the most recent meetings, the chairpersons have begun to request the secretariat to play a coordinating role with respect to both the information-sharing and recommendation functions. For instance, in 1997 the chairpersons asked that a succinct "activities profile" be prepared on each committee which would cover the period preceding each future chairpersons' meeting and that, starting with the ninth meeting in 1998, the chairpersons be provided with a chart showing the follow-up action that had been taken (by the committees and other actors to whom recommendations may be addressed) "in response to each of the specific recommendations" contained in the chairpersons' report from the preceding meeting. Chairpersons' Report, 8th Meeting, 1997, paras. 72–74.

17. In 1995 the chairpersons "both welcome and endorse" General Comment 24." Chairpersons' Report, 6th Meeting, 1995, para. 17.

18. By 1998 the controversy over General Comment 24 had drawn the International Law Commission (ILC) into the fray. With Alain Pellet as commission special rapporteur, the ILC continues its study on reservations to treaties. In implicit response to the Human Rights Committee, the ILC produced a document called "Preliminary Conclusions of the International Law Commission on Reservations to Normative Multilateral Treaties Including Human Rights Treaties." *Official Records of the General Assembly, Fifty-Second Session Supplement No. 10* (A/52/10), paras. 125–27. In turn, the chairpersons in 1998 objected to certain features of the ILC's approach, saying, inter alia: "The chairpersons . . . considered, however, that the [ILC Preliminary Conclusions] draft was unduly restrictive in [some] respects and did not accord sufficient attention to the fact that human rights treaties, by virtue of their subject matter and the role they recognize to individuals, could not be placed on precisely the same footing as other treaties with different characteristics. . . . They requested their Chairperson [i.e., the chairperson of the chairpersons, who is elected annually by the chairpersons at the start of their meeting] to address a letter to the Interna-

tional Law Commission on their behalf to reiterate their support for the approach reflected in General Comment No. 24, and to urge that the conclusions proposed by the International Law Commission be adjusted accordingly." Chairpersons' Report, 9th Meeting, 1998, UN Doc. A/53/125 (14 May 1998), paras. 17 and 18. Later in 1998, at its second meeting that year, the chairpersons drew attention again to their position on the special nature of human rights treaties. Chairpersons' Report, 10th Meeting, 1998, para. 51.

19. The 1996 Follow-up Report, para.18 (reporting on the fifth meeting of the chairpersons).

20. Ibid., para. 20. And see Andrew Byrnes, "Uses and Abuses of the Treaty Reporting Procedure: Hong Kong Between Two Systems" in Alston and Crawford, *Future of Human Rights Treaty Monitoring*, 287, 296.

21. "[A] careful review of all the relevant materials provided no basis upon which to conclude that the States parties to the Covenant intended to permit its unilateral denunciation by a state party. Moreover, the right to make such a denunciation would not seem to be compatible with the nature of the Covenant. The chairpersons therefore called upon all members of the international community to do everything possible to uphold the integrity of the human rights treaty system in general, and that of the International Covenant on Civil and Political Rights in particular." Chairpersons' Report, 8th Meeting, 1997, para. 29.

22. General comment on issues relating to the continuity of obligations to the International Covenant on Civil and Political Rights, UN Doc. CCPR/C/21/Rev. 1/Add. 8 (29 October 1997).

23. Chairpersons' Report, 9th Meeting, 1998, para. 25.

24. Ibid.

25. "The chairpersons considered that there was *a very strong basis, in both law and policy*, to support the consideration of a situation in the absence of a report, once repeated requests had failed to persuade a state to honor its treaty obligation to report." Ibid. (emphasis added). While this passage may, to some, suggest something just short of a firm collective conclusion, the chairpersons conclude their analysis, three paragraphs later, with a consensus in favor of the approach, stated as follows: "As a final resort, . . . committees should be willing to consider proceeding with a consideration of the situation, on the basis of information provided by the State Party and taking account of all other relevant information." Ibid., para. 28.

26. Ibid., para. 27.

27. Chairpersons' Report, 6th Meeting, 1995, para. 34. See also paras. 31, 35. The expert group met in 1995 as a follow-up to the Vienna Declaration and Program of Action. Five other recommendations of the expert group were also endorsed by the Chairpersons (ibid., para. 34) and all six were reiterated verbatim in 1996. Chairpersons' Report, 7th Meeting, 1996, para. 58.

28. As canvassed in the 1996 Follow-up Report, paras. 100–108.

29. Ibid., para. 103 (CHR Resolution 1996/22).

30. Ibid., paras. 106–8.

31. Ibid., para. 105.

32. Ibid., para. 101. This followed from a recommendation of the Commission on the Status of Women and consultations between the division and the secretariat for the five other treaty bodies, at the time the Centre for Human Rights. Ibid. It seems that the division also consulted with members of one committee, the HRC, ibid. At the tenth meeting of the chairpersons a background paper on gender integration in the work of all six committees, prepared by the Division for the Advancement of Women, was circulated (UN Doc. HRI/MC/1998/16). Chairpersons' Report, 10th Meeting, 1998, para. 13.

33. Report of the Secretary-General, *Improving the Effectiveness of the Human Rights*

Treaty Bodies, UN Doc. HRI/MC/1997/2 (29 July 1997), para. 38 [hereinafter 1997 Follow-up Report].

34. Chairpersons' Report, 8th Meeting, 1997, para. 63. Whether simply one more (coincidental) sign of UN systemwide attention to gender equality or a partial response to the chairpersons' invitation, the UN Division for the Advancement of Women (the CEDAW secretariat) organized a workshop on human rights and gender equality in late 1998 that brought together members of the UN Inter-agency Committee on Women and Gender Equality and of the Organisation for Economic Co-operation and Development/Development Assistance Committee (OECD/DAC) Working Party on Gender Equality. For its Report of a Workshop held 5–7 October 1998, FAO Headquarters, Rome, Italy, see *A Rights-Based Approach to Women's Empowerment and Advancement and Gender Equality* (New York: UN Division for the Advancement of Women, 1998).

35. Chairpersons' Report, 8th Meeting, 1997, para. 64.

36. Not unrelated is another recommendation on a pan-treaty, cross-cutting issue found two paragraphs later: "The chairpersons recommended that each treaty body give careful attention to the measures which it might take in relation to the relevant human rights aspects of HIV/AIDS." Ibid., para. 66. One further example of the chairpersons identifying a common normative issue that all six committees should address is the recommendation in 1995 that "each treaty body, in its examination of state party reports, investigate compliance by states parties with the extensive obligations regarding education and the provision of public information on human rights in general." Chairpersons' Report, 6th Meeting, 1995, para. 20. Not only is this another example of a normative issue spanning the six-treaty order but also it is a good example of the interdependent nature of the various cross-cutting sectors so far addressed by the chairpersons, as education and information are key components of advancing gender equality, health, and HIV/AIDS prevention. The most recent initiative in this cluster of cross-cutting issues, again with gender integration a central aspect, is a recent "joint statement" on the indivisibility of human rights: see discussion below.

37. Chairpersons' Report, 6th Meeting, 1995, para. 36.

38. Chairpersons' Report, 8th Meeting, 1997, paras. 23, 24.

39. Later in the same report, the chairpersons said simply but quite emphatically: "The general view of the chairpersons was that it was neither practicable nor desirable to envisage joining the six human rights bodies into a single committee." Ibid., para. 38.

40. This suggestion grew out of dissatisfaction of the committees with not having been appropriately involved in either the preparation or the formal negotiations of the various recent world conferences in the human rights fields. Chairpersons' Report, 6th Meeting, 1995, para. 22. UN legal counsel issued a legal opinion that does little to help give the committees (each alone or as a group) some kind of internal UN personality that would allow a more active engagement with the rest of the UN. The legal counsel, with respect to committee representation at conferences, stated the standard position that it is up to states to decide who to invite to such conferences and that, once invited, nonstate entities can have observer status. 1996 Follow-up Report, paras. 59, 60. In response, the chairpersons reiterated their call for a more official "distinct status that would enable them [the committees] to participate in all relevant meetings." Chairpersons' Report, 7th Meeting, 1996, para. 34. They specifically requested the UN General Assembly to adopt a resolution that in effect would constitute the desired status at least in terms of creating presumptive rights for each treaty body to participate in meetings of interest to them.

41. Thus, for example, a treaty body council could seek to build on the participation of both the CESCR and the CRC in an expert group on the right to housing that

was preparatory to the Habitat II conference. Although not formally acting as a treaty-body mission, their joint presence at least ensured that the generalist perspective of the ICESCR and the specific focus of the CRC were brought to bear at that world conference. A consolidated treaty-body perspective could well have been enhanced if the other treaty bodies had also sent members.

42. See especially Robin Lakoff, *Language and Woman's Place* (1975; New York: HarperTorchbooks, 1989), and Robin Tolmach Lakoff, *Talking Power: The Politics of Language* (New York: Basic Books, 1990).

43. For example, insiders in the Council of Europe's human rights apparatus are convinced that the transfer of support services for the European Social Charter from the Social Affairs Directorate to the Human Rights Directorate had an important constitutive effect on both enhancing the status of the charter and pluralizing understandings of "human rights." See Craig Scott and Patrick Macklem, "Constitutional Ropes of Sand or Justiciable Guarantees? Social Rights in a Future South African Constitution" *University of Pennsylvania Law Review* 141 (1992): 40, n.117.

44. Parenthetically, there is also reason to be concerned about the institutional appropriations in human rights discourse outside the immediate realm of the treaty bodies. Most notably, it is very problematic if leading actors in the international NGO movement are identified in the popular mind with "human rights," but focus almost exclusively in their own mandates only on a limited spectrum of rights. For example, the exclusion of social and economic rights from most of the work of the Human Rights Watch group has been notorious in this respect. As for Amnesty International, it is perhaps the NGO most associated around the world with the human rights movement. AI at least does not seek to cover the field with its organization's name in the way the Human Rights Watch group has, but AI's active focus only on a subset of what we tend to categorize as "civil and political rights" does have a covering-the-field effect on what rights quickly come to the popular mind when they hear or see the term "human rights." It must be said that AI's educational campaigns do focus on the whole spectrum of rights within the UDHR.

45. Given the very general phrasing of many of the rights in the ICCPR, it is conceptually possible to imagine virtually all the other rights in the other treaties as also being protected within the ICCPR. The point may come when the Human Rights Committee acts sufficiently on the principle of the interdependence of human rights that it begins to earn its imperial title.

46. 1996 Follow-up Report, para.103 (emphasis added).

47. It is also not an encouraging sign that certain members of the Human Rights Committee have reacted with no small degree of pique and lack of grace to what they see as the evolving jurisdictional encroachment of the chairpersons. To substantiate the preceding sentence, some context must be set out in more detail than can be justified in the present context. See Craig Scott, "Turf: An Eye Witness Account of the Sovereign Sensitivities of the UN Human Rights Committee," (www.scottliterary .com/turf).

48. Philip Alston, *Final Report on Enhancing the Long-Term Effectiveness of the United Nations Human Rights Treaty System*, UN Doc. E/CN.4/1997/74 (7 March 1997), paras. 110, 14–35 (hereinafter 1997 Alston Report).

49. Philip Alston, *Interim Report on Study on Enhancing the Long-Term Effectiveness of the United Nations Human Rights Treaty Regime*, UN Doc. A/CONF.157/PC/ 62/ Add.11/Rev.1 (22 April 1993) (hereinafter 1993 Alston Report).

50. Chairpersons' Report, 10th Meeting, 1998, para. 26.

51. This brackets the parallel issue of a campaign for the removal of reservations. This is not the occasion to elaborate, but one price that will likely need to be paid for universal ratification will be a continuing tolerance for reservations. Thereafter the

current campaign to encourage states to remove their reservations could be taken up with full intensity.

52. Note that there would remain a denunciation problem. Only ICCPR, ICESCR, and CEDAW have no clauses permitting denunciation. To date, no states have reacted to the Chairpersons' and the Human Rights Committee's conclusions that withdrawal is prohibited from the ICCPR (and, by direct implication, ICESCR and CEDAW) by virtue of the absence of clauses specifically authorizing it: see discussion above on the denunciation issue. However, even if there is general acceptance of this no-denunciation interpretation for these three treaties, there would still remain three treaties that expressly allow states to withdraw from the treaty with requisite notice: CAT, CRC, and CERD.

53. Pooling diversity across six committees is one way to compensate for diversity deficits that result from ill-considered or random election results for any given committee. For both an empirical and normative account of recent and current disparities in different committees, see Scott, "Bodies of Knowledge," 411–22. Significantly, the chairpersons themselves have begun to cast a critical eye over problems of composition within some of the committees. In 1997, they said: "The chairpersons . . . urged that consideration be given to the importance of expertise related to the mandate of the treaty body, the need for balanced geographical composition . . . [and] . . . the desirability of an appropriate gender balance." Chairpersons' Report, 8th Meeting, 1997, para. 68. A year later they said (twice): "The chairpersons expressed strong concern at the geographical and gender imbalances reflected in the composition of certain of the treaty bodies. In particular, they noted that the number of African representatives within two of the committees was entirely unsatisfactory. They recognized that the election of members of the treaty bodies was entirely a matter for the States parties. Nevertheless they called upon States parties to make a concerted effort to remedy imbalances." Chairpersons' Report, 10th Meeting, 1998, para. 16 and, in a very unusual act of reiteration, again verbatim at para. 55. When, in the 1997 statement, the chairpersons used the phrase "appropriate . . . balance" in respect of gender, it is likely the modifier "appropriate" was carefully chosen in order not to prejudice the issue of whether the current composition of CEDAW (all twenty-three members are women) remains an appropriate state of affairs in light of the overall gender imbalance (in favor of men) across the other five committees and in light of the fact recent inroads in integrating a "women's rights" perspective into UN human rights discourse are just that recent and, as such, still tenuous in their hold. On a brief allusion to how CEDAW's composition fits within a theory of interactive diversity of knowledge, see the conclusion in Scott, "Bodies of Knowledge," 437. Broadly speaking, the argument for some judicious opening of CEDAW membership to the election of some men who are experts in women's rights issues will grow more powerful (1) the more integrated the institutional arrangements linking the six committees become, (2) the more gender perspectives become effectively integrated in the normative analysis of the six-committee order (in large part as a consequence of the institutional integration), and (3) the more the composition of the other five committees consistently includes a critical mass of women experts.

54. In his 1993 report, Alston recommended such a single consolidated report. 1993 Alston Report, 50.

55. 1997 Alston Report, paras. 91–93. The initial report of any state to a committee would have to be comprehensive. It would be thereafter that the committees would channel the focus.

56. Chairpersons' Report, 10th Meeting, 1998, paras. 30, 31; Chairpersons' Report, 9th Meeting, 1998, paras. 30; 34, 35.

57. Chairpersons' Report, 10th meeting, 1998, paras. 30, 31.

58. As already indicated, 1993 Alston Report, 55, Alston was a proponent of a consolidated report as early as his 1993 interim report, but he is aware of the concerns that consolidation can threaten diversity. On the parallel issue of the possible undesirable effects of institutional consolidation (into a single committee), he noted in his 1997 final report:

[M]any of the advantages [of consolidation] can equally well be portrayed as disadvantages, and vice versa, depending on the assumptions and perspectives of the observer. . . . It can be argued that the super-committee would, by virtue of its extensive purview and probably almost permanent sessions, develop enormous expertise. *The counter-argument is that the variety of expertise represented on the existing range of committees is greater than could ever be captured on a single committee.* . . . Or, it can be argued that a single committee would facilitate the effective integration of different concerns such as racial and sex-based discrimination, children's and migrant workers' rights, and economic, social and cultural rights. *The counter-argument is that some of those concerns might simply be glossed over and that the supervisory process would no longer serve to galvanize those sectors of the Government and of the community dealing with, or interested in, a specific issue.* (1997 Alston Final Report, 49, para. 182; emphasis added)

59. Of course the ongoing refusal of the Secretary-General to move CEDAW to Geneva means that any such coordination will be radically incomplete until such a move takes place.

60. 1997 Follow-up Report, para. 17.

61. The Centre for Human Rights in its 1997 follow-up report to the 1996 chairpersons' meeting has suggested that, in view of the fact that "the equal enjoyment of men and women of all human rights is an overarching principle of the six principal human rights treaties," the chairpersons may wish to "consider inviting an interested organization to convene a round-table or expert meeting to assist with the drafting of general comments on gender equality." Ibid., para. 38.

62. Chairpersons' Report, 10th Meeting,1998, paras. 34, 36.

63. Chairpersons' Report, 10th Meeting, 1998, para. 35.

64. Ibid.

65. See the suggestions of Committee members Wimer Zambrano, Jimenez Butragueño, and Texier in Committee on Economic, Social, and Cultural Rights, Summary Record of the 45th Meeting, 19th Session, 26 November 1998, UN Doc. E/C.12/1998/SR.45 (30 November 1998), paras. 1–11.

66. The consideration of the draft joint statement ended as follows:

10. The CHAIRPERSON said he took it that Committee members were in favour of adopting the draft joint statement in principle, on the understanding that their amendments and comments would be duly taken into account during consultations between representatives of the three different Committees with a view to drafting a final version.

11. It was so agreed.

CESCR, Summary Record, paras. 10–11. Note the term "representatives," which could be understood as allowing some members of each of the three committees to participate, with their three Chairpersons, in the final consultations.

67. Compare the draft as it appears in the Summary Record, para. 1, and the final joint statement that appears as a decision of the CESCR in the Committee's report in its eighteenth and nineteenth sessions: "Fiftieth Anniversary of the Universal Declaration on Human Rights: Joint Statement Adopted by the Committee on Economic, Social, and Cultural Rights, the Committee on the Elimination of Discrimination Against Women and the Human Rights Committee," in Committee on Economic, Social and Cultural Rights, *Report on the Eighteenth and Nineteenth Sessions (27 April– 15 May 1998, 16 November–4 December 1998)*, Economic and Social Council, Offi-

cial Records, 1999, Supplement No. 2, UN Doc. E/C.12/1998/26 (New York and Geneva: United Nations, 1999). The paragraph that was added as a result of the CESCR's input into the draft was paragraph 8, which reads as follows: "Unfortunately, the principle of the indivisibility of all human rights and the equality of all rights of men and women are still far from being reality: civil and political rights are too often given precedence over economic, social and cultural rights and real equality between men and women exists in no country." By the time of the CESCR's decision to adopt the joint statement, it had also been adopted by CEDAW. Bustelo, "At the Crossroads," 98. As of the end of May 2000, the Human Rights Committee had yet to adopt any version of the joint statement. It appears that the committee has discussed it officially only once. Human Rights Committee, Summary Record of the Second Part (Public) of the 1699th Meeting of 31 July 1998, in UN Doc. CCPR/C/SR.1699/Add.1. (Summary Record) (5 August 1999). Apart from the concerns expressed by some members in the cited summary record (e.g., that the joint statement was too focused on CEDAW, that other committees such as the CRC should have been included, that some revisions were desirable, and that the HRC may not have competence to sign onto joint statements), information from some committee members was that "members" of the committee "showed great skepticism" on two fronts: (1) "in relation to the quality" of the proposed joint statement; and, (2) more generally, with regard to the "usefulness of a joint statement approach."

68. Canada did in fact report in November 1998 to CESCR and in March 1999 to the HRC. There is a remarkable overlap of normative concern in each committee's concluding observations, due in significant part to Canadian NGOs submitting coordinated representations to both committees. For discussion of these two sets of concluding observations, including eight points of overlap, see Craig Scott, "Canada's International Human Rights Obligations and Disadvantaged Members of Society: Finally into the Spotlight?" *Constitutional Forum* 10 (1999): 97–111.

69. Common questions are not necessarily ideal. Diversity of perspective is perhaps more likely to emerge and to provoke mutual education among committee members across treaty boundaries if common questions are asked only where relatively easy consensus is achievable among all the committees on both the desirability and the formulation of a proposed question. Achieving an optimal balance would be the challenge. Commonality in areas of clear shared concern signals to states an authority based on solidarity of analysis, but it can also produce lowest-common-denominator phrasing that can fail to put the state on the spot to justify its conduct. The time available for intercommittee preparation and coordination will affect the balance. The more advance opportunity the committees have to collect and examine questions proposed by all the committees with respect to a particular state, the more likely it will be that each committee will be persuaded to sign on to a question proposed by other committees despite the question not having occurred to any of that committee's members or despite the question not being viewed as much of a priority by that committee.

70. For instance, where the first committee had inadequate opportunity to probe a given issue; where a state's representatives had pledged to provide a fuller response after returning to their state and consulting with counterparts in government; and where the state's representatives had prevaricated or otherwise given unsatisfactory answers to the first committee.

71. Whether states' consent to such procedural innovations would be required need not detain us here. As long as each committee exercises its own final judgment on its concluding observations (even if that includes an agreement on common conclusions with another committee), there would be no issue of inappropriate exercise of jurisdiction. However, if new approaches are to be tried experimentally, in advance of general adoption of the procedure for all similarly placed states, it may

well be prudent to secure an expression of willingness to participate in such experiments from the states in question.

72. See art. 17(2), CAT. Christine Chanet of France at one point served simultaneously on the Human Rights Committee and CAT.

73. The words "*All* that is required" should be read with a grain of salt, as the lack of a central coordinating mechanism for elections to the treaty bodies make cooperation very difficult to achieve, even if the will to cooperate were there. See Scott, "Bodies of Knowledge," 426–31, for a discussion of the collective action problems in the voting practice with respect to the committees. Recall also the current imbalances elections have produced on the (geographical and gender) diversity fronts to which the chairpersons have twice drawn attention.

74. See Georges Scelle, "Règles générales de la paix," *Collected Courses of the Hague Academy of International Law* 46, 1 (1933): 358–59, 421–27.

75. Probably the now classic statement of these kinds of structuring-the-entire-state positive obligations was made by the Inter-American Court of Human Rights when it said that the duty to ensure human rights "implies the duty of all the States Parties to organize the governmental apparatus and, in general, all the structures through which public power is exercised, so that they are capable of juridically ensuring the free and full enjoyment of human rights" *Velasquez Rodriguez v. Honduras*, 28 ILM 291 (1989), para. 166. The court went on to note: "The State has a legal duty to take reasonable steps to prevent human rights violations. . . . This duty to prevent includes all those means of a legal, political, administrative and cultural nature that promote the safeguard of human rights and ensure that any violations are considered and treated as illegal acts." Ibid., paras. 174, 175.

76. Notice the use of "should." It is not being assumed that the current CERD is positioned to offer the necessary insights that would be useful for CAT or that the current CAT would necessarily be receptive if those insights were available.

77. As can be seen, for example, from art. 13(1) of the ICESCR and art. 29(1) of the CRC.

78. Recall the chairpersons' recommendation on human rights education, Chairpersons' Report, 6th Meeting, 1995.

79. On health and nutrition (especially as relates to infant mortality), see Human Rights Committee, General Comment 6/16, *Right to Life (Article 6)*, reprinted in Manfred Nowak, *U.N. Covenant on Civil and Political Rights: CCPR Commentary* (Kehl am Rhein/Strasbourg/Arlington: N.P. Engel, 1993), 851. On homelessness, including its implications for health, see Human Rights Committee, Concluding Observations on Canada, UN Doc. CCPR/C/79/Add.105 (7 April 1999), para. 12.

80. *Airey v. Ireland*, 2 EHRR 305 (1979). For a discussion of the interpretive process involved in the implication in the *Airey* case, see Scott, "Reaching Beyond," 640–41.

81. *Johnston v. Ireland*, 8 EHRR 203 (1986).

82. See discussion of this approach to interpretation in Craig Scott and Philip Alston, "Adjudicating Constitutional Priorities in a Transnational Context: A Comment on *Soobramoney*'s Legacy and *Grootboom*'s Promise" *South African Journal of Human Rights* 16 (2000).

83. *Baker v. Canada (Minister of Citizenship and Immigration)* 2 SCR 817 (1999).

84. Art. 3(1) reads: "In all actions concerning children, whether undertaken by public or private social welfare institutions, courts of law, administrative authorities or legislative bodies, the best interests of the child shall be a primary consideration." It should be noted that the author acted as co-counsel for CCPI in *Baker*.

85. Factum, CCPI, in *Baker v. Canada*, accessible at ⟨www.web.net/ccpi/baker/factum.html⟩. As co-counsel for CCPI in the *Baker* case I was closely involved in drafting the factum.

86. Scott, "Reaching Beyond," 634–41.

87. This notion was first put forward in Craig Scott, "Social Rights: Towards A Principled, Pragmatic Judicial Role," *ESR Review* 1, 4 (March 1999): 5–6. *ESR Review* is a quarterly publication of the Community Law Centre (University of Western Cape) and the Centre for Human Rights (University of Pretoria).

88. For the leading book length study in English, see Andrew Clapham, *Human Rights in the Private Sphere* (Oxford: Oxford University Press, 1993). On German legal theory, see Oliver Gerstenberg, "Private Law, Constitutionalism and the Limits of the Judicial Role" in *Torture as Tort: Comparative Perspectives on the Development of Transnational Human Rights Litigation*, ed. Craig Scott (Oxford: Hart Publishing, 2001).

89. On indirect state responsibility, Craig Scott, "Multinational Enterprises and Emergent Jurisprudence on Violations of Economic, Social and Cultural Rights" in *Economic, Social and Cultural Rights: A Textbook*, 2nd ed., ed., Asbjørn Eide, Catarina Krause, Allan Rosas, and Martin Scheinin (The Hague: Nijhoff, 2000), chapter 32.

90. The CRC's guidelines for periodic reports are suggestive of just this synthesis. With respect to Art. 27(4), the CRC alerts states as follows:

F. Recovery of maintenance for the child Please indicate the measures adopted . . . and mechanisms of programmes developed to secure the recovery of maintenance for the child from the parents or other persons having financial responsibility for the child . . . including in cases of separation and divorce. Information should also be provided on:

Measures taken to ensure the maintenance of the child in cases where parents or other persons having financial responsibility for the child *evade the payment of such maintenance.*

Committee on the Rights of the Child, "General Guidelines Regarding the Form and Content of Periodic Reports to be Submitted by States Parties Under Article 44, Paragraph 1(b), of the Convention," adopted by the CRC at its 343rd meeting (thirteenth session) on 11 October 1996, as reproduced in Rachel Hodgkin and Peter Newell, *Implementation Handbook for the Convention on the Rights of the Child* (Geneva: UNICEF, 1998), 609 (emphasis added).

91. See, e.g., *Aguinda v. Texaco*, 850 F. Supp. 282 (South. Dist. N.Y., 1994); *Sequihua v. Texaco*, 847 F. Supp. 61 (South. Dist. Tex., 1994); *Doe I v. Unocal*, 963 F. Supp. 880 (Cent. Dist. Cal., 1997); *Doe I v. Unocal*, 27 F. Supp. 2d 1174 (Cent. Dist. Cal., 1998).

92. See the Human Rights Committee view on the extraterritorial application of the ICCPR in *De Casariego v. Uruguay*, Communication No. 56/1979 (1981), para. 10.1–10.3.

93. Muthu Sornarajah, "South East Asia and International Law — State Responsibility and Sex Tours in Asia," *Singapore Journal of International and Comparative Law* 1 (1997): 414 at 422.

94. For relevant general comments by the Human Rights Committee, see Human Rights Committee, General Comment 4/3, *Gender Equality*; General Comment No. 17/35, *Rights of the Child*; and General Comment 18/37, *Non-Discrimination*, reprinted in Nowak, *U.N. Covenant on Civil and Political Rights*, 850, 865, 868.

95. These facts are taken from a recent report. At this point in the narrative, some of the actors have been modified but none of the material facts. See "Mitsubishi's Apology for Sexist Advert," *ITF News* 3 (1999): 12. *ITF News* is the journal of the International Transport Workers' Federation. The reason for the modifications will be made apparent in the text.

96. Ibid.

97. Ibid.

98. On the human rights implications of states participating in unjustifiable sanctions regimes, see the recent rather oblique general comment on sanctions issued by

the CESCR, Committee on Economic, Social, and Cultural Rights, "The Relationship Between Economic Sanctions and Respect for Economic, Social and Cultural Rights," General Comment 8, UN Doc. E/C.12/1997/8 (5 December 1997).

As for the chairpersons, there has been some ineffectual grumbling along the following lines:

> 21. . . . it was once again regretted [by the chairpersons] that no . . . constructive relationship had yet been established between the treaty bodies and some key agencies, in particular the International Monetary Fund and the World Bank. The chairpersons welcomed the statement of UNDP that it intended to increase its cooperation with the Committee on Economic, Social and Cultural Rights, as a first step towards greater involvement in the work of the treaty bodies as a whole.

Chairpersons' Report, 10th Meeting, 1998, para. 21.

On the issue of the accountability of these institutions, recall the earlier-quoted passage in which the chairpersons requested the UN human rights bureaucracy to begin a "dialogue" with the Bretton Woods institutions and my suggestion as to the very embryonic form of accountability that this recommendation might represent. Chairpersons' Report, 7th Meeting, 1996.

On the issue of human rights in the global trading order, the Chairpersons have made a muted pitch for the UN human rights treaties and monitoring bodies to be taken seriously as the normative locus for human rights accountability of trade law:

> 49. The chairpersons note that one of the items on the agenda for the Ministerial Meeting of the World Trade Organization (WTO), to be held in Singapore in December 1996, concerns proposals to adopt a "social clause" which would link respect for human rights (notably freedom of association, non-discrimination in employment, and the elimination of exploitative child labour) to access to trade opportunities. They note that whatever the respective merits of such proposals, the system of treaty supervision in which the treaty bodies are engaged already provides an important avenue for monitoring compliance with States [sic] obligations in these and related areas and that a greater effort should be made to strengthen these existing opportunities.

Chairpersons' Report, 7th Meeting, 1996, para. 49.

99. For a leading statement that constitutional rights responsibilities cannot be avoided by devolution to nonstate actors, see J. La Forest in *Eldridge v. British Columbia (Attorney General)*, 3 SCR 624 (1997), para. 40: "Governments should not be permitted to evade their [Canadian] Charter [of Rights and Freedoms] responsibilities by implementing policy through the vehicle of private arrangements."

Chapter 2. From Division to Integration

1. This was also recognized in 1941 in U.S. President Franklin Roosevelt's "Four Freedoms Speech." Roosevelt called for four essential human freedoms: freedom of speech and expression, freedom of every person to worship God in his own way, freedom from want, and freedom from fear.

2. International Covenant on Economic, Social, and Cultural Rights, adopted 16 December 1966, entered into force 3 January 1976, GA Res. 2200 (XXI), 21 UN GAOR Supp. (No. 16) at 49, UN Doc. A/6316 (1966).

3. *Introduction to Economic, Social, and Cultural Rights: A Textbook*, ed. Asbjørn Eide, Caterina Krause, and Allan Rosas (Boston: Martinus Nijhoff, 1995), 29.

4. United Nations Charter, 26 June 1945, Can. T.S. 1945 no. 7, art. 55.

5. Matthew C. R. Craven, *The International Covenant on Economic, Social, and Cultural Rights: A Perspective on Its Development* (Oxford: Clarendon Press, 1995), 16–17.

6. GA Res. 217A (III) (1948), art. 22.

7. GA Res. 421 (V) (1950).

8. Ibid.

9. Craig Scott, "The Interdependence and Permeability of Human Rights Norms: Towards a Partial Fusion of the International Covenants on Human Rights," *Osgoode Hall Law Journal* 27 (1989): 792–93.

10. There were also four abstentions.

11. GA Res. 543 (VI) (1951).

12. GA Res. 2200A (XXI) (1966).

13. Kristin Nadasdy Wuerffel, "Discriminating Among Rights? A Nation's Legislating a Hierarchy of Human Rights in the Context of International Human Rights Customary Law," *Valparaiso University Law Review* 33 (1998): 376.

14. Statement to the World Conference, UN Doc. E/1993/22, para. 5.

15. Indeed, the differing approaches also reflected the human rights records of the countries involved: the Soviet Union was vulnerable to censure for its arbitrary imprisonment of dissidents, the United States for racial segregation, and France and Great Britain for their colonial policies.

16. Craven, *International Covenant on Economic, Social, and Cultural Rights*, 9.

17. Farrokh Jhabvala, "On Human Rights and the Socio-Economic Context," *Netherlands International Law Review* 31 (1984): 159.

18. Eide, *Introduction*, 22–23.

19. Ibid.

20. ICESCR, art. 2(1)

21. Craven, *International Covenant on Economic, Social, and Cultural rights*, 26.

22. Ibid., 108.

23. Jack Donnelly, *Universal Human Rights in Theory and Practice* (Ithaca, N.Y.: Cornell University Press, 1989), 33.

24. Craven, *International Covenant on Economic, Social, and Cultural Rights*, 110.

25. Eide, *Introduction*, 38.

26. Philip Alston and Bruno Simma, "Second Session of the UN Committee on Economic, Social, and Cultural Rights," *American Journal of International Law* 82 (1988): 605.

27. Craven, *International Covenant on Economic, Social, and Cultural Rights*, 25–26.

28. Philip Alston, "Out of the Abyss: The Challenges Confronting the New U.N. Committee on Economic, Social, and Cultural Rights," *Human Rights Quarterly* 9 (1987): 352.

29. Ibid., 351.

30. Ibid.

31. Robert E. Robertson, "Measuring State Compliance with the Obligations to Devote the 'Maximum Available Resources' to Realizing Economic, Social, and Cultural Rights," *Human Rights Quarterly* 16 (1994): 694.

32. Craven, *International Covenant on Economic, Social, and Cultural Rights*, 27.

33. Ibid., 28.

34. Ibid., 10.

35. Ibid., 33–34.

36. Alston and Simma, "Second Session," 604.

37. Craven, *International Covenant on Economic, Social, and Cultural Rights*, 31.

38. Ibid., 57.

39. Scott, "Interdependence and Permeability," 771.

40. Ibid., 801, 802, 802, n. 115.

41. Ibid., 771, 774.

42. Donnelly, *Human Rights in Theory and Practice*, 41.

43. Universal Declaration of Human Rights, arts. 23, 26, 25(1).

44. Abdullahi An-Na'im, "The Universal Declaration as a Living and Evolving

'Common Standard of Achievement,'" in *Reflections on the Universal Declaration of Human Rights: A 50th Anniversary Anthology*, ed. Barend Van Der Heijden and Bahia Tahzib-Lie (The Hague: Martinus Nijhoff, 1998), 48.

45. Pieter van Dijk, "The Universal Declaration Is Legally Non-Binding; So What," in Van Der Heijden and Tahzib-Lie, *Reflections*, 108.

46. Technically, the "creation" of the committee constituted a simple "renaming" of the Sessional Working Group.

47. Alston, "Out of the Abyss," 341.

48. Ibid., 347.

49. Scott Leckie, "An Overview and Appraisal of the Fifth Session of the UN Committee on Economic, Social, and Cultural Rights," *Human Rights Quarterly* 13 (1991): 546.

50. Ibid., 547.

51. Alston, "Out of the Abyss," 352–53.

52. Committee on Economic, Social, and Cultural Rights, General Comment 3 (14 December 1990), para. 10, UN Doc. E/C.12/1990/0 (1991).

53. Ibid., para. 2.

54. Ibid., para. 10.

55. Limburg Principles on the Implementation of the International Covenant on Economic, Social, and Cultural Rights (Maastricht, 2–6 June 1986), para. 16.

56. Ibid., para. 25.

57. Maastricht Guidelines on Violations of Economic, Social, and Cultural Rights (Maastricht, 22–26 January 1997), para. 6.

58. Limburg Principles, para. 9.

59. See ⟨www.oxfam.ca/about.international.htm⟩.

60. See ⟨www.oxfam.org.uk/campaign/basicr.htm⟩.

61. Ibid.

62. Leckie, "Overview and Appraisal," 566–67.

63. Committee on Economic, Social, and Cultural Rights, 8th Session, E/C.12/1993/WP.14.

64. Report of the Secretary-General, *Arrangements and Practices for the Interaction of Non-Governmental Organizations in All Activities of the United Nations System*, UN Doc. A/53/170 (10 July 1998), para. 48.

65. Vienna Plus-Five Global NGO Forum on Human Rights, *Final Document, Report of the Working Group on Effectiveness of and NGO Access to the UN System* (Ottawa, 1998). On 22–24 June 1998 representatives of several dozen NGOs met in Ottawa, Canada, to evaluate the status of human rights five years after the Vienna World Conference on Human Rights and fifty years after the adoption of the Universal Declaration of Human Rights.

Chapter 3. Defending Women's Economic and Social Rights

An earlier form of this essay was presented at the conference "Linking the Domestic and International: Human Rights into the 21st Century," University of Toronto Faculty of Law, 2–4 October 1998. Funding from the Australian Research Council helped me finish this project in 1999. Thanks to Leilani Farha and Lucie Lamarche for their helpful comments which went well beyond the limits of this piece and continue to help shape my thinking on equality and women's human rights.

1. Gordon Christenson, "The Federal Courts and World Civil Society," *Journal of Transnational Law and Policy* 6 (1997): 405, 413.

2. Committee on Economic, Social, and Cultural Rights, "Statement on Globalization and Human Rights," 1996, 18th session, para. 3: "if not complemented by

appropriate additional policies, globalisation risks downgrading the central place accorded to human rights by the United Nations Charter in general and the International Bill of Human Rights in particular. This is especially the case in relation to economic, social and cultural rights. Thus, for example, respect for the right to work and the right to just and favourable conditions of work are threatened where there is an excessive emphasis upon competitiveness to the detriment of respect for the labour rights contained in the Covenant."

3. Philip Alston, "The Myopia of the Handmaidens: International Lawyers and Globalisation," *European Journal of International Law* 8 (1997): 435, 438; Anne Orford, "Contesting Globalization: A Feminist Perspective on the Future of Human Rights," *Transnational Law & Contemporary Problems* 8 (1998): 171, 180.

4. Bruno Simma, "From Bilateralism to Community Interest in International Law," *Académie de droit international recueil des cours* 6 (1994): 221, 235–43, understands global "community interest" as corresponding with the "needs, hopes and fears of all human beings."

5. Brenda Cossman, "Reform, Revolution, or Retrenchment? International Human Rights in the Post Cold War Era," *Harvard International Law Journal* 32 (1991): 339, 345; Maria Luisa Bartolomei, "The Globalization Process of Human Rights in Latin America Versus Economic, Social and Cultural Diversity," *International Journal of Legal Information* 25 (1997): 156, 159; Alston, "Myopia," 442.

6. Peng Cheah, "Posit(ion)ing Human Rights in the Current Global Conjuncture," *Public Culture* 9 (1997): 233. Note that the claim that the right to development takes precedence over individual human rights is not consistent with the Declaration on the Right to Development, GA Res. 41/128 (16 December 1986), arts. 1, 6(3).

7. Krysti Guest, "Exploitation Under Erasure: Economic, Social, and Cultural Rights Engage Economic Globalizations," *Adelaide Law Review* 19 (1997): 73. Note, however, that economic and social rights have never been fully integrated into the international agenda. See Susan George, "The Structure of Dominance in the International Geo-Economic System and the Prospects for Human Rights Realization," in *Human Rights in Perspective: A Global Assessment*, ed., Asbjrn Eide and Berndt Hagtvet (Cambridge, Mass: Blackwell, 1988), 268.

8. Anne Orford and Jennifer Beard, "Making the State Safe for the Market: The World Bank's World Development Report, 1997," *Melbourne University Law Review* 22 (1998): 195; Susan Strange, *The Retreat of the State: The Diffusion of Power in the World Economy* (New York: Cambridge University Press, 1996).

9. Anne-Marie Slaughter, "The Real New World Order," *Foreign Affairs* 76 (1997): 183, 185.

10. Bharati Sadasivam, "The Impact of Structural Adjustment on Women: A Governance and Human Rights Agenda," *Human Rights Quarterly* 19 (1997): 630.

11. Johannes Morsink, *The Universal Declaration of Human Rights: Origins, Drafting and Intent* (Philadelphia: University of Pennsylvania Press, 1999), 232.

12. I would not go so far as Henry Shue, who argues that, because basic rights are mutually interdependent, the absence of even one of them means that none of the others can be enjoyed. See Henry Shue, *Basic Rights: Subsistence, Affluence, and U.S. Foreign Policy* (Princeton, N.J.: Princeton University Press, 1980), 60–78, 92–93.

13. Beijing Declaration and Platform for Action (PFA), United Nations, *Report of the Fourth World Conference on Women*, Beijing, 4–15 September 1995, UN Doc. A/CONF.177/20 (17 October 1995).

14. Craig Scott, "The Interdependence and Permeability of Human Rights Norms: Towards a Partial Fusion of the International Covenants on Human Rights," *Osgoode Hall Law Journal* 27 (1989): 769, 779.

15. The eighteenth-century French and American declarations of rights did not include social and economic rights: Virginia Declaration of Rights (1776); Declara-

tion of Independence (1776); Declaration of the Rights of Man and of Citizens (1789).

16. GA Res. 543(VI), 5 UN GAOR Supp. (No. 20) at 26, UN Doc. A/2119 (1952).

17. Proclamation of Teheran, International Conference on Human Rights, Teheran, 13 May 1968, art. 13.

18. See, generally, Barbara Stark, "The 'Other' Half of the International Bill of Rights as a Postmodern Feminist Text," in *Reconceiving Reality: Women and International Law*, ed. Dorinda Dallmeyer (Washington, D.C.: American Society of International Law, 1993), 20; Scott Leckie, "Another Step Towards Indivisibility: Identifying the Key Features of Violations of Economic, Social, and Cultural Rights," *Human Rights Quarterly* 20 (1998): 81.

19. Lisa A. Crooms, "Indivisible Rights and Intersectional Identities, or 'What Do Women's Rights Have to Do with the Race Convention?'," *Howard Law Journal* 40 (1997): 619; Berta Esperanza Hernández-Truyol, "Indivisible Identities: Culture Clashes, Confused Constructs, and Reality Checks," *Harvard Latino Law Review* 2 (1997): 199.

20. Philip Alston, "Development and the Rule of Law: Prevention Versus Cure as a Human Rights Strategy," in *Development, Human Rights and the Rule of Law*, report of a conference held in the Hague, 27 April–1 May 1981 (New York: Permagon, 1981), 31, 63.

21. Susana Fried, *The Indivisibility of Women's Human Rights: A Continuing Dialogue* (Rutgers, N.J.: Global Center for Women's Human Rights, 1994); Shelagh Day, "Making the Indivisibility of Women's Human Rights Real," Panel 1, Human Rights of Women, Commission on the Status of Women, 42nd session, New York, 2–13 March 1998.

22. Julie Dorf and Gloria Careaga Pérez, "Discrimination and the Tolerance of Difference: International Lesbian Human Rights," in *Women's Rights, Human Rights*, ed. Julie Peters and Andrea Wolper (New York: Routledge, 1995), 324; Amnesty International USA, *Breaking the Silence: Human Rights Violations Based on Sexual Orientation* (New York: Amnesty International, 1994).

23. Agenda 21, UN Conference on Environment and Development, Rio de Janeiro, June 1992, UN Doc. A/CONF.151/26/Rev.1 (1992), principle 25, "Peace, development and environmental protection are interdependent and indivisible"; Vienna Declaration and Program of Action, World Conference on Human Rights, Vienna, June 1993, UN Doc. A/CONF.157/24 (13 October 1993), para. 8, "Democracy, development and respect for human rights and fundamental freedoms are interdependent and mutually reinforcing"; Copenhagen Declaration and Program of Action, World Summit for Social Development, Copenhagen, 6–12 March 1995, UN Doc. A/CONF.166/9 (19 April 1995), para. 5, "social development and social justice cannot be attained in the absence of peace and security or in the absence of respect for human rights and fundamental freedoms."

24. PFA, Beijing (1995), paras. 138, 143(b).

25. Ibid., para. 246.

26. Ibid., paras. 47–48.

27. Convention on the Elimination of All Forms of Discrimination Against Women (CEDAW), UN Doc. A/Res.34/180 (1979), preamble.

28. There are some isolated examples of practices of indivisibility. For example, *F. H. Zwan-de Vries v. Netherlands*, Communication 182/1984 CCPR/A/42/40, 1160, and *S. W. M. Broeks v. Netherlands*, Communication 172/1984 CCPR/A.42/40, 139. In these decisions the Human Rights Committee recognized that art. 26 of the ICCPR also protects against discrimination in the enjoyment of the rights covered by the ICESCR.

29. Louis Henkin, *International Law, Politics, and Values* (Boston: Martinus Nijhof, 1995), 194.

30. See, for example, PFA, Beijing (1995), para. 213, reaffirming "that all human rights — civil, cultural, economic, political and social, including the right to development — are universal, indivisible, interdependent and interrelated."

31. Vienna Declaration (1993), para. 18.

32. PFA, Beijing (1995), paras. 213, 216.

33. Ibid., para. 14.

34. Anne Gallagher, "Ending the Marginalization: Strategies for Incorporating Women into the United Nations Human Rights System," *Human Rights Quarterly* 19 (1997): 283.

35. Dianne Otto, "Holding Up Half the Sky, But for Whose Benefit? A Critical Analysis of the Fourth World Conference on Women," *Australian Feminist Law Journal* 6 (1996): 7.

36. Orford, "Contesting Globalization"; Bartolomei, "Human Rights in Latin America."

37. Dorean Koenig and Kelly Askin, "International Criminal Law and the International Criminal Court Statute: Crimes Against Women," in *Women and International Human Rights Law*, vol. 2, ed. Kelly Askin and Dorean Koenig (New York: Transnational Publishers, 2000), 3.

38. Anne Orford, "The Politics of Collective Security," *Michigan Journal of International Law* 17 (1996): 373; Dianne Otto, "Whose Security? Reimagining Post-Cold War Peacekeeping from a Feminist Perspective," in *Security in a Post-Cold War World*, ed. Robert Patman (London: Macmillan, 1999), 65,

39. Commission on the Status of Women, 42nd Session, "Provisional Agenda," UN Doc. E/CN.6/1998/1.

40. Report of the Secretary-General, *Follow-Up to the Fourth World Conference on Women: Implementation of Strategic Objectives and Action in the Critical Areas of Concern," Thematic Issues Before the Commission on the Status of Women*, UN Doc. E/CN.6/1998/5 (23 January 1998), para. 3.

41. Commission on the Status of Women, "Agreed Conclusions on the Methods of Work for dealing with the Implementation of the Platform for Action," 1996/1.

42. PFA, Beijing (1995). Paragraph 96 is in the critical area of women's health. It was not under review at CSW42, but the question of sexuality was raised in the context of violence against women, where reference was made to violence on the basis of a woman's sexuality. In the face of strong resistance, Canada and the European Union both suggested alternative wording, including wording directly from para. 96. The reference to sexuality-related violence was eventually dropped entirely.

43. Caroline Lambert and Florence Martin, "Report on the 42nd Commission on the Status of Women," *Amnesty International: News from New York* 15 (April 1998): 1.

44. Reports from expert group meetings included "Adolescent Girls and Their Rights," UN DAW, EGM/AGR/1997/Rep.1; and "Gender-Based Persecution," UN DAW, EGM/GBH/1997/Rep.1.

45. Expert Group Report, "Promoting Women's Enjoyment of Their Economic and Social Rights," Abo/Turku, Finland, 1–4 December 1997, UN DAW, EGM/WESR/1997/Report.

46. Ibid., preface.

47. Secretary-General, *Follow-Up to the Fourth World Conference on Women*, para. 2.

48. Otto, "Holding Up Half the Sky."

49. PFA, Beijing (1995). Although the women's human rights chapter of the PFA reaffirms that "all human rights" include civil, cultural, economic, political and social rights, and the right to development (paras. 213, 231[a]), only one paragraph

in the chapter makes explicit reference to economic, social and cultural rights (para. 220).

50. CESCR, General Comment 3, para. 10, 1990, 5th session.

51. Expert Group Report, "Promoting Women's Enjoyment," para. 43.

52. Ibid., paras. 41, 42.

53. Ibid., preface, para. 6.

54. Otto, "Holding Up Half the Sky," 12–18. It is only in its approach to violence against women that the PFA develops an alternative equality narrative based on an analysis of the structural dimensions of gendered effects of power, rather than on a direct comparison with similarly situated men.

55. Expert Group Report, "Promoting Women's Enjoyment," preface, para. 6.

56. Ibid., para. 29. This approach was first suggested by Henry Shue, *Subsistence, Affluence.*

57. Limburg Principles on the Implementation of the International Covenant on Economic, Social, and Cultural Rights, UN Doc. E/CN.4/1987/17; "The Maastricht Guidelines on Violations of Economic, Social and Cultural Rights," *Human Rights Quarterly* 20 (1998): 691.

58. G. J. H Van Hoof, "The Legal Nature of Economic, Social and Cultural Rights: A Rebuttal of Some Traditional Views," in *The Right to Food*, ed. Philip Alston and Katarina Tomaevki (The Hague: Martinus Nijhoff, 1984), 97; Andrew Byrnes and Jane Connors, "Enforcing the Human Rights of Women: A Complaints Procedure for the Women's Convention," *Brooklyn Journal of International Law* 21 (1996): 679.

59. Expert Group Report, "Promoting Women's Enjoyment," paras 22, 40.

60. Ibid., para. 20.

61. Ibid., para. 32.

62. Some aspects of the right to an adequate standard of living are arguably covered in the PFA. For example, para. 256(k) refers to "women's equal access to housing infrastructure, safe water, and sustainable and affordable energy technologies." Further, the PFA does recognize that unilateral measures taken in response to armed conflict can "create obstacles to the full enjoyment of human rights, including the right of everyone to a standard of living adequate for their health and well-being and their right to food, medical care and the necessary social services," para. 145(h).

63. Expert Group Report, "Promoting Women's Enjoyment." Some of this work has since been undertaken. See ICCPR, General Comment 28, "Equality of Rights Between Men and Women (article 3)," CCPR/C/21/Rev.1/Add.10 (29 March 2000).

64. Expert Group Report, "Promoting Women's Enjoyment," para. 47.

65. Ibid., para. 48.

66. Ibid., para. 45.

67. On rights associated with reproductive choice, see *Report of the International Conference on Population and Development*, Cairo, September 1994, UN Doc. A/CONF.171/ 13 (1994), paras 4.1–4.23, 7.1–7.48, 8.19–8.35, 11.1–11.10; PFA, Beijing (1995), paras 89–130, 259–85; and Rebecca Cook, "International Protection of Women's Reproductive Rights," *Journal of International Law and Policy* 24 (1992): 643. On sexual orientation, see *Toonen v. Australia*, UN Doc. CCPR/C/50/D/488/1992 (31 March 1993), where the Human Rights Committee held that the reference to "sex" discrimination in the ICCPR included discrimination on the basis of sexual orientation. On home work, see "Convention Concerning Home Work," ILO Convention No.177 (1996), not yet entered into force. On housing, land, and property, see "Women's Equal Ownership of, Access to and Control over Land and the Equal Rights to Own Property and to Adequate Housing," resolution adopted by consensus, 56th session, UN Commission on Human Rights, 17 April 2000. On gendered

violence, see "Declaration on the Elimination of Violence Against Women," GA Res. 48/104 (20 December 1993); PFA, Beijing (1995), arts. 112–30. On the environment, see Agenda 21, chap. 24, which integrates gender equality and justice with environmental sustainability; and PFA, Beijing (1995), paras. 246–58. On disabilities, see "Declaration on the Rights of Disabled Persons," GA Res. 3447(XXX) (9 December 1975).

68. Expert Group Report, "Promoting Women's Enjoyment," para. 33.

69. Laura Reanda, "The Commission on the Status of Women," in *The United Nations and Human Rights: A Critical Appraisal,* ed. Philip Alston (New York: Oxford University Press, 1992), 265.

70. Expert Group Report, "Promoting Women's Enjoyment," paras. 49, 103–14.

71. Ibid.

72. Mary Robinson, UN High Commissioner for Human Rights, "Statement to CSW42," Tuesday, 3 March 1999 (author's notes).

73. The three panelists were Rose M. Migiro (United Republic of Tanzania) senior lecturer, Faculty of Law, Dar-Es-Salaam; Shanti Dairiam (Malaysia), director, International Women's Rights Action Watch Asia/Pacific; and Shelagh Day (Canada), special adviser on human rights, National Association of Women and the Law. The fourth panelist was Cecilia Medina (Chile), currently a member of the Human Rights Committee.

74. JUSCANZ is a grouping of states that works as a loose coalition when there are common goals. At CSW42, JUSCANZ consisted of Japan, the United States, Canada, Australia, Norway, and New Zealand.

75. Commission on the Status of Women, "Report on the Forty-Second Session," 2–13 March 1998, 20. E/CN.6/1998/12-E/1998/27.

76. Commission on the Status of Women, "Draft Conclusions, Human Rights of Women," E/CN.6/1998/L.2 and Add.1, 9 March, para. III,10 quart.

77. Commission on the Status of Women, "Report on the Forty-Second Session," 20. "The treaty bodies within their mandates should continue to promote a better understanding of the rights contained in international human rights instruments and their particular significance to women."

78. Commission on the Status of Women, "Draft Conclusions," para. II.2.

79. Commission on the Status of Women, "Report on the Forty-Second Session," 17.

80. Ibid., 20 (last para.).

81. See, for example, PFA, Beijing (1995), para. 59.

82. Commission on the Status of Women, "Draft Conclusions," para. III.5bis.

83. Commission on the Status of Women, "Report on the Forty-Second Session," 19.

84. Mary Robinson, "Statement" (author's notes).

85. Dianne Otto, "Everything Is Dangerous: Some Poststructural Tools for Rethinking the Universal Knowledge Claims of Human Rights Law," *Australian Journal of Human Rights* 5 (1998): 17.

86. Martin Scheinin, "Women's Enjoyment of their Economic and Social Rights: Conceptual Framework for the Discussion," UN DAW, EGM/WESR/1997/BP.1.

87. Simma, "Bilateralism."

88. Philip Alston, "The 40th Anniversary of the Universal Declaration of Human Rights: A Time More for Reflection than for Celebration," in *Human Rights in a Pluralist World: Individuals and Collectivities,* ed. Jan Berting et al. (Paris: UNESCO, 1990), 1; Katherine Cox, "Should Amnesty International Expand Its Mandate to cover Economic, Social, and Cultural Rights?" *Arizona Journal of International and Comparative Law* (1999): 261. But note, Human Rights Watch Report, *Indivisible Human Rights: The Relationship of Political and Civil Rights to Survival, Subsistence and*

Poverty (New York: Human Rights Watch, 1992), arguing that the enjoyment of economic and social rights is often dependent on civil and political rights.

89. Dianne Otto, "A Post-Beijing Reflection on the Limitations and Potential of Human Rights Discourse for Women," in Askin and Koenig, *Women and International Human Rights Law*, vol. 1, 115.

Chapter 4. Human Rights Mean Business

1. Ernest Mahaim, "The Principles of International Labor Legislation," *Annals of the American Academy of Political and Social Science* 166 (1933), as cited in Michael Tonya, "Baby Steps Towards International Fair Labor Standards," *Case Western Reserve Journal of International Law* 24 (1992): 631.

2. See UN Centre Against Apartheid, *The Sullivan Principles: No Cure for Apartheid: A Public Statement*, Notes and Documents 16/80 (1980), 5.

3. See Renate Pratt, *In Good Faith: Canadian Churches Against Apartheid* (Waterloo, Ont.: Wilfred Laurier Press 1997), 101.

4. Richard Hull, *American Enterprise in South Africa* (New York: New York University Press), 245. There is compelling evidence that in the absence of investor loans, the apartheid regime would have faced a debilitating economic crisis after the Sharpeville massacre. Similar difficulties may have been encountered during the oil crisis of the early 1970s and in the aftermath of the Soweto massacre but for U.S. private sector support. See ibid., 301, for a discussion of the role of U.S. businesses in providing support to the regime after Soweto.

5. Ibid., 334. U.S. firms controlled 44 percent of foreign direct investments in oil, 33 percent in automobiles, and 70 percent in computers.

6. Ibid., 271.

7. UN Centre Against Apartheid, *The Sullivan Principles*, 3.

8. Hull, *American Enterprise*, 337.

9. Exec. Order 12,532, 50 Fed. Reg. 36,861 (1985).

10. Hull, *American Enterprise*, 337.

11. See Michael Trebilcock and Robert Howse, *The Regulation of International Trade* (New York: Routledge, 1995), 4.

12. See OECD, *Open Markets Matter: The Benefits of Trade And Investment Liberalization* (Paris: OECD 1998), 9–10, ⟨www.oecd.org/ech/events/⟩.

13. See Trebilcock and Howse, *The Regulation of International Trade*, 20. See also League of Nations, *Commercial Policy in the Interwar Period: International Proposals and National Policies* (Official No. 1942.II.A.6), 22, as reported in Robert Hudec, *The Gatt Legal System and World Trade Diplomacy* (Salem: Butterworths, 1990), 6–7.

14. Hudec, *Gatt Legal System*, 5–7.

15. George Bermann, *European Community Law* (St. Paul, Minn.: West Publishing, 1993), 5–6.

16. Thomas d'Aquino, CEO of the BCNI, in International Centre for Human Rights and Democratic Development (ICHRDD), Summary Report, *Globalization: Trade and Human Rights, the Canadian Business Perspective* (Montreal: ICHRDD, February 1996), 2.

17. Department of Foreign Affairs and International Trade (DFAIT), *Canada in the World* (Ottawa: Government of Canada, 1995), 34.

18. Lloyd Axworthy, Notes for an address to the International Conference on Universal Rights and Human Values, Department of Foreign Affairs and International Trade, "A Blueprint for Peace, Justice and Freedom" (Ottawa: Government of Canada, 1998).

19. See discussion in Diane Orentlicher and Timothy Gelatt, "Public Law, Private Actors: the Impact of Human Rights on Business Investors in China," *Journal of International Law and Business* 14 (1993): 98.

20. Ibid., 99.

21. USA*Engage, *Economic Engagement Promotes Freedom*, ⟨www.usaengage.org/studies/engagement.html⟩.

22. For a similar discussion from a Canadian source, see Senate Standing Committee on Foreign Affairs, *Crisis in Asia: Implications for the Region, Canada, and the World* (Ottawa: Senate Standing Committee, December 1998), 104–5.

23. OECD, *Open Markets Matter*, ⟨www.oecd.org/ech/events.open.html⟩.

24. Samuel Huntington, *The Third Wave: Democratization in the Late Twentieth Century* (Norman: University of Oklahoma Press, 1991).

25. Ibid., 65.

26. Ibid., 59.

27. Michael Leicht, "Trade Policy and Human Rights," *Intereconomics* 33 (1998): 4.

28. For statistical studies, see John Lonfregan and Keith Poole, "Does High Income Promote Democracy?" *World Politics* 49 (1996): 29: "We find that even after correcting for many features of the political and historical context, the democratizing effect of income remains as a significant factor promoting the emergence of democratic political institutions. However, the small magnitude of our estimated income effect suggests the democratizing effects of high income are modest. . . . Our findings indicate that policies that seek to increase the economic development of countries with authoritarian governments as a means of changing them into democracies, such as the current policy of many democracies towards China, may take more years to have an effect than current policymakers imagine"; and Adam Przeworski and Fernando Limongi, "ModernizationTheories and Facts," *World Politics* 49 (1997): 177: "The emergence of democracy is not a by-product of economic development. Democracy is or is not established by political actors pursuing their goals, and can be initiated at any level of development."

29. The Freedom House survey ranks countries from one to seven, with "1" representing the most and "7" the least freedom. In assigning numerical labels under "civil rights," Freedom House considers, inter alia, freedom of assembly, freedom of political organization, equality before the law, protection from political terror, the presence of free trade unions and free businesses, and personal freedoms such as property rights. See Freedom House, *Freedom in the World* (New York: Freedom House, 1996), 531.

30. Pearson product moment correlations can be used for interval data. The data sets analyzed in this study can be characterized as such a sort of data. The test produces a coefficient, r, that ranges from -1.0 to 1.0, inclusive, and reflects the extent of a linear relationship between two data sets. Negative figures reflect a negative relationship while positive figures suggest a positive relationship between variances in the data sets. The correlations demonstrate covariance in the data sets, not causality. The coefficient, r, can be squared to arrive at a coefficient of determination. The coefficient of determination, r^2, represents "the proportion of the variance in Y that may be accounted for by its linear relationship with X, or vice versa." Don Ary and Lucy Jacobs, *Introduction to Statistics* (Montreal: Holt, Rinehart and Winston, 1976), 186.

31. Tests: r for FDI as percent of GDP/Freedom House scores for 133 countries for which 1996 data were available: 0.0144; same, without OECD countries (except Mexico and South Korea), -0.0478; r for change in FDI as percent of GDP between 1980–96/1996 Freedom House scores for 102 countries for which data were available -0.1289; same, without OECD countries: -0.1872; r for change in FDI as

percent of GDP between 1980–96/change in Freedom House scores between 1980–96 for the 102 countries for which data were available, −0.0507; same, without OECD countries, −.0637.

32. Mahmood Monshipouri, *Democratization, Liberalization, and Human Rights in the Third World* (Boulder, Colo.: Lynne Rienner Publishers, 1995), 174.

33. For example, the human rights situation in China has not improved, despite billions of dollars in increased investment. For a discussion, see Miro Cernetig, "China: Dragons and Doves," *Globe and Mail*, 16 January 1999, D1. In 1999 Human Rights Watch, in its *World Report 1999*, ⟨www.hrw.org/hrw/worldreport99/⟩, reported that "Despite some encouraging developments, China's human rights practices remained cause for concern. . . . Western governments seized on tentative signs of tolerance to strengthen calls for engagement, a desirable goal, but one that in policy terms all too often meant silence on China's egregious human rights record." See also "US: China Human Rights a Farce," Associated Press, 6 March 1996 and Rod Mickleburgh, "China Relentless in Pursuit of Critics," *Globe and Mail*, 28 October 1996, A12.

34. See Richard Howitt, *Report on EU Standards for European Enterprises Operating in Developing Countries*, European Parliament, PE228.198/DEF.

35. A key element of international labor rights, freedom of association, is protected by ILO Conventions 87 (1948) and 98 (1949). The Universal Declaration of Human Rights, UNGA Res. 217(III), UN GAOR, 3rd Sess., Supp. 13, at 71, UN Doc. A/810, at 71 (1948), art. 20, also deals with rights of association and, in Art. 23, protects the right to form and to join trade unions for the protection of one's interests. The International Covenant on Civil and Political Rights (1966), 999 UNTS 171, 1976 Can. T.S., no. 47, defines a right to "freedom of association with others, including the right to form and join trade unions for the protection of one's interests," in art. 22. See also art. 8 of the International Covenant on Economic, Social, and Cultural Rights (1966), 999 UNTS 3, 1976 Can. T.S., no. 46.

36. Rights to nondiscrimination permeate international legal instruments. See, for example, UDHR, art. 23, ICESR, art. 7, and ILO 111 (Discrimination [Employment and Occupation] Convention) (1958).

37. ILO 182 (Worst Forms of Child Labour) (1999).

38. Under the first ILO forced labor treaty, Convention 29 of 1930, forced labor is outlawed. The UDHR, arts. 4 and 23, ICCPR, art. 8, and the ICESCR, art. 6, also contain relevant language.

39. OECD, *Trade and Labour Standards*, COM/DEELSA/TD(95)5 (1995), 14.

40. As of April 2000, Convention 29 on forced labor had 153 ratifications; Convention 98 on the rights to organize and bargain collectively had 146; Convention 100 on equal pay, 146, Convention 111 on nondiscrimination, 142; Convention 105 on forced labor, 146; Convention 87 on freedom of association, 128; Convention 138 on child labor, 89; Convention 182 on exploitative child labor, 13. See the ILO homepage, ⟨www.ilo.org⟩.

41. For example, according to the International Confederation of Free Trade Unions, *Annual Survey of Violations of Trade Union Rights 1998* (June 1998), in 1997 "nearly 300 trade unionists were killed for standing up for their rights, 1681 were tortured or illtreated, 2329 were detained, there were 3369 cases of intimidation and there was blatant interference in union affairs in 79 countries." See the ICFTU web page, ⟨www.icftu.org⟩.

42. OECD, *Trade and Labour Standards*, 40: "there is some evidence that over the short-run, episodes of improvements of freedom of association can be associated with a loss of competitiveness."

43. OECD, *Trade, Employment, and Labour Standards: A Study of Core Workers' Rights and International Trade*, COM/DEELSA/TD(96) 8/FINAL (1996), 36, 47.

44. Ibid., 46–47.

45. Ibid., 49.

46. See United Nations Conference on Trade and Development (UNCTAD), *World Investment Report: Globalization, Integrated International Production, and the World Economy* (New York: United Nations, 1994). For a discussion of labor conditions in EPZs, see International Confederation of Free Trade Unions, *Behind the Wire: Anti-Union Repression in the Export Processing Zones*, ⟨www.icftu.org⟩.

47. For a discussion of these controversies, see Craig Forcese, *Commerce with Conscience?* (Montreal: International Centre for Human Rights and Democratic Development 1997), and Craig Forcese, *Putting Conscience into Commerce* (Montreal: International Centre for Human Rights and Democratic Development 1997).

48. See Human Rights Watch, *World Report, 1997* and *World Report, 1999*, ⟨www.hrw .org/worldreport99/special/corporations.html⟩. See also Dan Atkinson, "BP Denies MEP's Colombia claims," *Guardian*, 23 October 1996; Amnesty International, *Colombia: British Petroleum Risks Fuelling Human Rights Crisis Through Military Training* (30 June 1997); Project Underground, "Oil Companies Buying Up Colombian Army to Fight Pipeline Violence," *Drillbits and Tailings* (1 September 1996).

49. Pratap Chatterjee, "The Mining Menace of Freeport McMoRan," *Multinational Monitor* (April 1996): 11. For a detailed description of the military role in the events and their aftermath, see also Amnesty International, *Indonesia: Full Justice? Military Trials in Irian Jaya*, AI Index: ASA 21/17/96 (March 1996).

50. Jessie Banfield, "The Corporate Responsibility Debate," *African Business* (November 1998): 30–31.

51. Human Rights Watch, *World Report, 1999*.

52. Ibid.

53. Human Rights Watch, *The Enron Corporation: Corporate Complicity in Human Rights Violations* (January 1999), ⟨www.hrw.org/hrw/reports/1999/enron/⟩.

54. See EarthRights International and Southeast Asian Information Network, *Total Denial: A Report on the Yadana Pipeline Project in Burma* (July 1996), ⟨metalab.unc .edu/freeburma/docs/totaldenial/td.html⟩; and Lucien Dhooge, "A Close Shave in Burma: Unocal Corporation and Private Enterprise Liability for International Human Rights Violations," *North Carolina Journal of International Law and Commercial Regulation* 24 (1998): 2.

55. See "Petrocan Ending Drilling in Myanmar," *Globe and Mail*, 3 November 1992.

56. Indochina Goldfields, "Start of Copper Production at Monywa Project," press release, 2 November 1998; Indochina Goldfields, "Indochina Goldfields Completes Financing to Construct Myanmar Copper Mine," press release, 24 September 1997.

57. Mindoro Resources, "Mindoro Increases Interest and Identifies New Gold Potential in Myanmar Project," press release 12 January 1998.

58. Paul Watson, "How Burma's Junta Defies World," *Toronto Star*, 16 March 1997: A12. Interview with Christine Harmston, then-coordinator, Canadian Friends of Burma, July 1997.

59. Lou Wilking, "Should US Corporations Abandon South Africa?" in *The South African Quagmire*, ed. S. Prakash Sethi (Cambridge, Mass.: Ballinger, 1987), 390. See also Jeanne Stephens, "MNCs and Change in South Africa" (master's thesis, Carleton University, Ottawa, 1983), 38.

60. Canadian Friends of Burma, *Dirty Clothes* (Ottawa: Canadian Friends of Burma, 1996), 12.

61. Human Rights Watch, *World Report, 1997*, 360.

62. Project Underground, "Unocal Looks to Afghanistan's Taliban for New Profits," *Drillbits and Tailings* (2 August 1997).

63. Senate Standing Committee on Foreign Affairs, *Crisis in Asia*, 105.

64. Lloyd Axworthy, Minister of Foreign Affairs, notes for an address, "Human

Rights and Canadian Foreign Policy: Principled Pragmatism," McGill University, Montreal, October 1997 (emphasis added).

65. Ibid.

66. See Steve Charnovitz, "The Influence of Labor Standards on the World Trading Regime," *International Labor Review* 126 (1987): 565.

67. Tonya, "Baby Steps," 641–42.

68. Art. 7, chap. 2 of the Havana Charter, E/CONF.2/78 (24 March 1948), UN Doc. ICITO/1/4 (1948).

69. Tonya, "Baby Steps," 642.

70. The U.S. position during the Uruguay round of trade talks in 1986 was to include labor rights in the negotiating round. See Erika de Wet, "Labor Standards in the Globalized Economy: The inclusion of a social clause in the General Agreement on Tariffs and Trade/World Trade Organization," *Human Rights Quarterly* 17 (1995): 445.

71. WTO minutes, ministerial conference, Singapore, 18 December 1996 (WT.MIN[96] DEC).

72. OECD, *Trade, Employment, and Labor Standards*, 61, has described the limited functions of the ILO on core labor rights as follows: "the ILO has an important role as a focal organization where universal agreement on core labor standards can be reached. It can also persuade countries that it is in their own interest to promote basic labor rights and to avoid workers' exploitation, while also informing the international community on cases of non-respect of core labor standards. In poor countries, the ILO technical assistance may also contribute to the eradication of child labor exploitation."

73. It is notable that where trade measures under the U.S. General System of Preferences (see discussion below) have been used to penalize poor labor practices, trade unionists from developing countries have reported that their governments have "responded to the criticism in the GSP petition more seriously than they [have] ever reacted to a negative judgement by the ILO's Committee on Freedom of Association or Committee of Experts." See Pharis Harvey, *U.S. GSP Labor Rights Conditionality: "Aggressive Unilateralism" or a Forerunner to a Multilateral Social Clause* (International Labor Rights Fund, 1995), 6.

74. Elisabeth Cappuyns, "Linking Labor Standards and Trade Sanctions: An Analysis of Their Current Relationship," *Columbia Journal of Transnational Law* 36 (1998): 684.

75. Department of Foreign Affairs and International Trade, *Canada and the Future of the World Trade Organization: Government Response to the Report of the Standing Committee on Foreign Affairs and International Trade* (November 1999), ⟨www.dfait-maeci.gc .ca/tna-nac/Canwto-e.asp#Labour⟩.

76. House of Commons Standing Committee on Foreign Affairs and International Trade, *The Free Trade Area of the Americas: Towards a Hemispheric Agreement in the Canadian Interest* (October 1999), ⟨www.parl.gc.ca/infocomdoc/ 36/ 2/ fait/studies/ reports/faitrp01-e.htm⟩.

77. Government Response to the Report of the Standing Committee on Foreign Affairs and International Trade (15 March 2000), ⟨www.dfait-maeci.gc.ca/tna-nac/ FTAAreport-full-e.asp⟩.

78. Clyde Summers, "NAFTA's Labor Side Agreement and International Labor Standards," *Small and Emerging Business Law* 3 (1999): 187.

79. Senate Standing Committee on Foreign Affairs, *Asia in Crisis*, 105.

80. Ibid., 110.

81. Ibid., 107, citing Forcese, *Putting Conscience into Commerce*. On the issue of government procurement, the European Union and Japan brought a now-suspended trade complaint against the United States for a Massachusetts-Burma selective pur-

chasing law barring dealings with companies operating in Burma. It remains to be seen, however, whether the Massachusetts law in fact violates trade law. For a recent discussion of issues surrounding the Massachusetts law, see Jennifer Loeb-Cederwall, "Restrictions on Trade in Burma: Bold Moves or Foolish Acts?" *New England Law Review* 32 (1998). For a discussion of selective purchasing laws at the municipal level, see Craig Forcese, "Municipal Buying Power and Human Rights in Burma: The Case for Canadian Municipal Selective Purchasing Policies," *University of Toronto Faculty of Law Review* 56 (1998).

82. For the position of the NGO coalition working on the EDC, see *Race to the Top: How to Make the Export Development Corporation Responsible to People and the Environment*, ⟨www.web.net/~halifax/edc/pubs/policy.htm⟩. The Report of the House of Commons Standing Committee on Foreign Affairs and Trade, *Exporting in the Canadian Interest: Reviewing the Export Development Act*, is at ⟨www.parl.gc.ca/ infocomdoc/36/ 2/fait/studies/reports/faitrp02-e.htm⟩, while the government position on the issue is at ⟨www.dfait-maeci.gc.ca/english/news/development act-e.htm⟩.

83. See European Parliament, *European Breakthrough In Combating Multinational Abuses*, news release, 15 January 1999. See also European Parliament, *Resolution on EU Standards for European Enterprises Operating in Developing Countries*. Minutes (EN) A4–0508/98 (15 January 1999), ⟨www.europarl.eu.int/ ⟩.

84. See Frank Bradley, "Prepare to Make a Moral Judgement," *People Management* (4 May 1995).

85. See Douglass Cassel, "Corporate Initiatives: A Second Human Rights Revolution?" *Fordham International Law Journal* 199 (1996): 1974.

86. The Franklin pollsters focused on major U.S. retailers and brand-name goods manufacturers. Telephone Interview with Simon Billenness, Franklin Research and Development (February 1997).

87. U.S. Department of Labor, *The Apparel Industry and Codes of Conduct: A Solution to the International Child Labor Problem?* (Washington, D.C.: U.S. GPO, 1996), 370. The Department of Labor survey focused on the largest apparel manufacturers, department stores and mass merchandisers as measured by 1995 annual sales figures.

88. Council on Economic Priorities, *International Sourcing Report* (New York: Council on Economic Priorities, March 1998).

89. KPMG, *KPMG Ethics Survey –2000: Managing for Ethical Practice*, ⟨www.kpmg.ca/ english/news/n ethicssurvey2000.html⟩.

90. This 1996 CLAIHR/ICHRDD survey is reported in Forcese, *Commerce with Conscience?*

91. In a survey of forty-eight companies having operations outside Canada or the United States, KPMG found that 14.6 percent had policies on supplier child and forced labor practices, 25 percent on supplier discrimination practices, and 16.7 percent on supplier freedom of association/collective bargaining practices. As concerned their own overseas operations, 16.7 percent of the companies had policies on child and forced labor, 41.7 percent on discrimination, and 33.3 percent on freedom of association/collective bargaining. Some 29.2 percent of companies had formal policies on the "human rights status of host countries" in countries in which they operated. See KPMG, *KPMG Ethics Survey*.

92. See discussion in Lance Compa and Tashia Hinchliffe-Darricarrére, "Enforcing International Labor Rights Through Corporate Codes of Conduct," *Columbia Journal of Transnational Law* 33 (1995): 674; and Robert Liubicic, "Corporate Codes of Conduct and Product Labeling Schemes: The Limits and Possibilities of Promoting International Labor Rights Through Private Initiatives," *Law and Policy of International Business* 30 (1998): 123, 124.

93. See Forcese, *Putting Conscience into Commerce*.

94. Personal communication with Al Cook, former deputy director of the Interna-

tional Defence and Aid Fund for South Africa, former executive director of the Canada-South Africa Cooperation (May 1996).

95. See comments in Compa and Hinchliffe-Darricarrére, "Enforcing International Labor Rights"; Jeremy Lehrer, "Trading Profits for Change," *Human Rights* 25 (1998): 21; and Debora Spar, "The Spotlight and the Bottom Line," *Foreign Affairs* (March/April 1998): 7. Similarly, codes of conduct introduced to govern business domestic operations reflect the emergence of external pressures. As one study examining U.S. codes has noted, "during the period 1960 to 1994, many of the Fortune 1000 companies have voluntarily enacted corporate codes of conduct, and . . . this activity coincides with the growth in regulatory, prosecutorial, and judicial incentives for corporate self-regulation during this period." John Ruhnka and Heidi Boerstler, "Governmental Incentives for Corporate Self-Regulation," *Journal of Business Ethics* 17 (1998): 3.

96. In 1984, Congress added labor conditions on the extension and renewal of the General System of Preferences tariff benefit to potentially eligible nations. An infringement of "internationally recognized worker rights" would remove a nation from eligibility under the system. "Generalized System of Preferences, 19 U.S.C. § 2461, the Caribbean Basin Economic Recovery Act, 19 U.S.C. § 2701, and the Andean Trade Preference Act, 19 U.S.C. § 3201. Removal of these benefits might prove highly disruptive to corporate activities if imposed on nations in which businesses have invested or from which they are sourcing. See Forcese, *Putting Conscience into Commerce*. For the relationship between these measures and codes, see Compa and Hinchliffe-Darricarrére, "Enforcing International Labor Rights," 675.

97. Compa and Hinchliffe-Darricarrére, "Enforcing International Labor Rights," 674.

98. Ibid. For a discussion of a recent lawsuit on human rights grounds, see Dhooge, "A Close Shave in Burma."

99. For a more detailed discussion of these campaigns, see Forcese, *Putting Conscience into Commerce*. U.S. surveys suggest that a sizable majority of Americans prefer to buy from a retailer they know is not sourcing products or materials from sweatshops. See John McClain, "Government Fingers Retailers that Sell Sweatshop Made Clothing," Associated Press 5 December 1995: "69 percent of Americans are more likely to shop at stores on the list" of non-sweatshop-using business prepared by the U.S. Department of Labor." See also Vivian Marino, "Garment Workers Get Attention," Associated Press, 18 June 1996: "A recent poll by Marymount University in Arlington, Va., said 84 percent of 1,008 individuals questioned would pay a dollar more for a garment that cost $20, if it were guaranteed to be made at a legitimate factory. Seventy-eight percent would avoid shopping at stores that sell garments made in sweatshops." For a discussion of how such figures motivate code development, see Liubicic, "Corporate Codes of Conduct," 114, 115. In Canada, a 1998 CROP survey commissioned by Toronto-based Ideation Conferences suggests that a majority of Canadians consider conditions of production when buying consumer goods. Further, a majority of Canadians are prepared to pay higher prices for ethically produced products. In fact, given a choice between two products of equivalent price, almost one-third of Canadians would prefer to purchase a product made by a human rights-respecting U.S. company over a product simply produced by a Canadian company.

100. See Forcese, *Putting Conscience into Commerce*.

101. Government of Canada, *Voluntary Codes: A Guide for Their Development and Use* (Ottawa: Office of Consumer Affairs, 1998), 8–9.

102. Ibid., in preface.

103. Ruhnka and Boerstler, "Governmental Incentives."

104. Ibid.

105. U.S. Department of Labor, *The Apparel Industry*, 9.

106. For a discussion of independent monitoring, see Forcese, *Putting Conscience into Commerce*. See also discussion by Liubicic, "Corporate Codes of Conduct," 136.

107. U.S. Department of Labor, *The Apparel Industry*, v, 9.

108. Ibid., 101.

109. Ibid., 107.

110. Of 48 companies with non-U.S. or Canadian operations surveyed by KPMG, the following proportion of companies actively monitored their own practices: child labor (12.5 percent); forced labor (10.4 percent); freedom of association/collective bargaining (16.7 percent); discrimination (29.2 percent). The following proportion actively monitored supplier practices: child labor (14.6 percent); forced labor (12.5 percent); freedom of association/collective bargaining (6.3 percent); discrimination (18.8 percent). See KPMG, *KPMG Ethics Survey*.

111. ⟨www.uottawa.ca/hrrec/busethics/codeint.html⟩.

112. Senate Standing Committee on Foreign Affairs, *Crisis in Asia*, 108.

113. Department of Foreign Affairs and International Trade, "Canada Appoints Facilitator to Encourage Private Sector Discussion of Voluntary Business Codes of Conduct," press release, 11 May 1999.

114. See ETAG webpage, ⟨www.web.net/~msn/3code.htm#Update_on_code_ negotiations⟩.

115. Transcript of Minister Axworthy's statement on the Harker mission to Sudan, 14 February 2000. Can be obtained by contacting the Department of Foreign Affairs and International Trade.

116. Liubicic, "Corporate Codes of Conduct," 149.

117. Howitt, *Report on EU Standards*.

118. For an illustration of restrictions on shareholder activism under the Canada Business Corporations Act, R.S.C. 1985, c. C-44, as amended, see *Re Varity Corp. v. Jesuit Fathers of Upper Canada* (1987), 59 O.R. (2d) 459 (Ont. H.C.) aff'd (1987) 60 O.R. (2d) 640 (Ont. C.A.). For discussion, see Forcese, *Putting Conscience into Commerce*. At the time of this writing, the government has proposed amendments to the Act that do relatively little to liberalize ethical shareholder activism.

119. See Forcese, *Commerce with Conscience?* for a discussion of the Levi's country guidelines. Levi Strauss, "Global Sourcing and Operating Guidelines. Part II: Country Assessment Guidelines."

120. On U.S. sanctions see Exec. Order 13,047, Fed. Reg. 28,301 (1997). The European Commission decided in March 1997 to suspend trading benefits to Burma (Myanmar) under its Generalized System of Preferences program. See Human Rights Watch, *World Report, 1999*. The Canadian government had withdrawn Burma's (Myanmar) General Preferential Tariff eligibility under the Custom Tariff, R.S.C. c. 41 (3rd Supp.), as amended, (see General Preferential Tariff Withdrawal Order-Burma (Myanmar), SOR/97-398) and placed the country on the Area Control List under the Export and Import Permits Act, S.C. 1991, c. 28, as amended (see Order Amending the Area Control List, SOR/97-397).

121. Department of Foreign Affairs and International Trade, "Canada Announces Further Actions on Burma," press release, 7 August 1997.

122. Ibid.

123. In January 1997 Aung San Suu Kyi, Burma's leader for democracy and winner of the 1991 Nobel Peace Prize, asked students at American University to "please use your liberty to promote ours" and to "take a principled stand against companies which are doing business with the military regime of Burma," a nation she characterized as "the shadowlands of lost rights." G. Kramer, "Suu Kyi Urges U.S. Boycott," Associated Press, 27 January 1997. See discussion of the Canadian-Burmese ventures above.

124. Quoted in Canadian Friends of Burma, *Dirty Clothes*, 51. Estimates suggest that roughly one-sixth of earnings from clothing exports is used to purchase armaments for the military government. Ibid., 8.

125. Claudia Cattaneo, "Talisman Drawn into Sudanese Conflict: Sudanese Rebels Say Calgary Company's Properties, People Are Targets," *National Post*, 5 May 1999, C1, C2.

126. See discussion in Steven Edwards, Claudia Cattaneo, and Sheldon Alberts, "Calgary Firm Tied to Sudan 'Atrocities'," *National Post*, 17 November 1999.

127. *Human Security in Sudan: The Report of a Canadian Assessment Mission*, 15, ⟨www.dfait-maeci.gc.ca/foreignp/menu-e.asp⟩.

128. Ibid., 48, 64.

129. Amnesty International, *Sudan: The Human Price of Oil*, AFR 54/04/00 3 May 2000, ⟨www.amnesty.org/news/2000/15400400.htm⟩.

130. See discussion in Edwards, Cattaneo and Alberts, "Calgary Firm." See also CEO James Buckee's letter to shareholders (23 November 1999).

131. Jennifer Ditchburn, "Codes of Conduct Needed in Deals with Sudan: Axworthy," *Canadian Press*, 17 March 1999.

132. *Human Security in Sudan*, 16.

133. Department of Foreign Affairs and International Trade, "Canada Announces Support to Sudan Peace Process," press release, 26 October 1999.

134. Transcript of press conference given by Minister Axworthy, 14 February 2000.

135. See the comments by M.P. Bill Graham, chair of the House of Commons Standing Committee on Foreign Affairs, in the Committee's minutes, Tuesday, 28 April 1998, ⟨www.parl.gc.ca/infocomdoc/36/1/fait/meetings/evidence/faitev47-e.htm⟩: " . . . the only legal mechanism for [imposing sanctions] in Canada would be under the legislation, which permits us to apply United Nations organized sanctions. I don't think there's anything we can do on a unilateral basis."

136. S.C. 1992, c. 17, s. 4.

137. For example, on second reading of the act, Barbara McDougall, then minister of external affairs, indicated that "the purpose of the Bill C-53 is to enable Canada to impose a broad range of economic sanctions against a state or part of a state whose actions pose a serious threat to international peace and security or fail to conform to commonly accepted standards of behaviour. . . . Bill C-53 does not dictate the policy considerations that would determine whether or not to apply sanctions in any particular situation, nor does it dictate the types of measures to be used when the government decides to apply sanctions." House of Commons, *Debates*, 20 February 1992), 7403, 7405.

138. Income Tax Act, R.S.C. 1985, 5th Supp., s. 126(2). See discussion in Vern Krishna, *The Fundamentals of Canadian Income Tax*, 5th ed. (Toronto: Carswell, 1995), 1166.

139. See Pratt, *In Good Faith*, 189.

140. Senate Standing Committee on Foreign Affairs, *Crisis in Asia*, 106.

141. Sir Leon Brittan, "Globalization: Responding to New Political and Moral Challenges," World Economic Forum, Davos (30 January 1997), cited in Leicht, "Trade Policy."

142. See discussion in Eleanor Fox, "Globalization and Its Challenges for Law and Society," *Loyola University of Chicago Law Journal* 29 (1998).

143. Ethan Kapstein, "Workers and the world economy," *Foreign Affairs* 75 (1996): 16, 18.

144. OECD, *Open Markets Matter*, 62.

145. Ibid.

146. Spar, "The Spotlight," 110.

147. See discussion concerning Shell in Nigeria in Banfield, "The Corporate Responsibility," 30–31.

148. Paraphrased from Lehrer, "Trading Profits," 21.

149. Roy Culpepper, president of the North-South Institute, cited in Bruce Cheadle, "Busy Year in Foreign Policy Ends to Mixed Reviews," *Canadian Press*, 16 December 1997.

Chapter 5. Feminism After the State

1. Robert Boyer and Daniel Drache, eds., *States Against Markets: The Limits of Globalization* (London: Routledge, 1996).

2. World Bank, *The State in a Changing World*, 1997 World Development Report (New York: Oxford University Press, 1997).

3. World Bank, *Development and Human Rights: The Role of the World Bank* (Washington, D.C.: World Bank, 1998).

4. Guy Standing, "Labor Insecurity Through Market Regulation: Legacy of the 1980s, Challenge for the 1990s," in *Poverty, Inequality, and the Future of Social Policy: Western States and the New World Order*, ed. Katherine McFate, Roger Lawson, and William Julius Wilson (New York: Russell Sage, 1995), 153–96.

5. Nancy Fraser and Linda Gordon, "A Genealogy of 'Dependency': Tracing a Keyword of the U.S. Welfare State," in *Justice Interruptus: Critical Reflections on the "Postsocialist" Condition*, ed. Nancy Fraser (New York and London: Routledge, 1997), 121–49.

6. *Forward-Looking Strategies for the Advancement of Women to the Year 2000*, UN Doc. A/CONF.11/28 (15 September 1985).

7. Beijing Declaration and Platform for Action, adopted 15 September 1995, United Nations, *Report of the Fourth World Conference on Women*, Beijing, 4–15 September 1995, UN Doc. A/CONF. 177/20 (1995).

8. World Bank, *Toward Gender Equality* (Washington, D.C.: World Bank, 1995); World Bank, *Development and Human Rights*.

9. See World Bank, *The State in a Changing World*.

10. See, for example, World Bank, "Legal Institutions and the Rule of Law" in *From Plan to Market*, 1996 World Development Report (Washington D.C.: World Bank, 1996).

11. Ibid., 87–88.

12. World Bank, *From Plan to Market*, 48–49.

13. Joseph Stiglitz, "More Instruments and Broader Goals: Moving Toward the Post-Washington Consensus," WIDER Annual Lectures 2, 7 January 1998, ⟨www .wider.unu.edu/publications/publications.htm⟩; Joseph Stiglitz, "Whither Reform? Ten Years of Transition," in World Bank, *Annual Bank Conference on Development Economics*, 28–30 April 1999, ⟨www.worldbank.org⟩.

14. Vienna Declaration and Program of Action, World Conference on Human Rights, adopted 25 June 1993, reprinted in 32 ILM, 1661 (1993), *Human Rights Law Journal* 14, 143 (1993): 352.

15. This claim, as well as its counterclaim, is a central subject of critical legal studies, critical race theory and some feminist theory. See Fran Olsen, "The Family and the Market: A Study of Ideology and Legal Reform," *Harvard Law Review* 96 (1983): 1497; Karen Engle, "Beyond the Public/Private Divide" in *Reconceiving Reality: Women and International Law*, ed. Dorinda Dallmeyer (Washington, D.C.: American Society of International Law, 1993).

16. Suzanne Berger and Ronald Dore, eds., *National Diversity and Global Capitalism* (Ithaca, N.Y. and London: Cornell University Press, 1996), 3.

17. Shelley Wright, "Economic and Social Justice: A Feminist Analysis of Some International Human Rights Conventions," *Australian Yearbook of International Law* 12 (1991): 242.

18. Karen Engle, "International Human Rights and Feminism: When Discourses Meet," *Michigan Journal of International Law* 13 (1992): 517.

19. Convention on the Elimination of All Forms of Discrimination Against Women, 18 December 1979, GA Res. 180, UN GAOR, 34th Sess., Supp. (No. 46), at 193, UN Doc. A/34/46 (1979), reprinted in 19 ILM 33 (1980).

20. ILO, Declaration on Fundamental Principles and Rights at Work, 86th Session, Geneva, June, 1998, ⟨www.ilo.org/public/english/10ilc/ilc86/com-dtxt.htm⟩.

21. Ibid., 5.

22. World Bank, *Workers in an Integrating World*, 1995 World Development Report (New York: Oxford University Press, 1995).

23. Ontario Human Rights Code, R.S.O. 1990, c. H. 19; *Griggs v. Duke Power Co.*, 401 U.S. 424 (1971), 91 S. Ct. 849 (U.S.S.C.); Civil Rights Act of 1964, Pub. L. 88–352, ss. 706, 78 Stat. 253 (codified in 42 U.S.C. ss. 2000e to 2000e-17) (1982).

24. Kalima Rose, *Where Women Are Leaders: The SEWA Movement in India* (London: Zed Books, 1992).

25. World Bank, *Development and Human Rights*.

26. See World Bank, *The State in a Changing World*.

27. Sally Baden, "The Impact of Recession and Structural Adjustment on Women's Work in Developing and Developed Countries," working paper, ILO, Geneva, 1993; United Nations, *World's Women 1995: Trends and Statistics* (New York: United Nations, 1995).

28. Liba Paukert, "Economic Transition and Women's Employment in Central European Countries, 1989 to 1994," *Labor Market Papers* 7, Employment Department and International Labor Office (Geneva: ILO, 1995).

29. Norene Pupo, "Always Working, Never Done: The Expansion of the Double Day" in *Good Jobs, Bad Jobs, No Jobs: The Transformation of Work in the 21ˢᵗ Century*, ed. Ann Duffy, Daniel Glenday, and Norene Pupo (Toronto: Harcourt Brace, 1997).

30. World Bank, *Toward Gender Equality*.

31. Guy Standing, "Global Feminisation Through Flexible Labour," *World Development* 17, 7 (1989): 1077; Standing, "Labor Insecurity."

32. Canadian Human Rights Act, R.S.C. 1985, c. H-6.

33. *P.S.A.C. v. Canada (Treasury Board) (No.3)* (1998), 32 C.H.R.R. D/349 (Can. Trib.). In this case 200,000 federal public service employees alleged that the Treasury Board had breached the Canadian Human Rights Act by maintaining differences in wages between male and female employees who were performing work of equal value. The human rights tribunal ruled in their favor, awarding past and present employees approximately $4 billion in back pay. The federal court subsequently dismissed the application for review.

34. "Time to Pay Equity's Piper," *Globe and Mail* (Toronto), 19 November 1998: A28; Jeffrey Simpson, "Dances with Taxpayers," *Globe and Mail*, 30 July 1998, A16.

35. Special issue, "Gender, Adjustment, and Macroeconomics" *World Development* 23, 11 (1995).

36. United Nations Development Program, *Human Development Report 1995* (New York: Oxford University Press, 1995).

37. Standing, "Labor Insecurity," 153.

38. World Bank, *Workers in an Integrating World*.

39. Karl Polanyi, *The Great Transformation: The Political and Economic Origins of Our Time* (Boston: Beacon Press, 1957).

Chapter 6. Advancing Safe Motherhood Through Human Rights

I am grateful to Susan Scarrow and Andrew Wilson, graduates of the Faculty of Law, University of Toronto, for their research assistance.

1. World Health Organization and UNICEF, *Revised 1990 Estimates of Maternal Mortality: A New Approach by WHO and UNICEF* (Geneva: WHO, 1996).

2. United Nations Population Fund, *The State of the World Population 1999, 6 Billion: A Time for Choices* (New York: UNFPA, 1999), 30.

3. Ann Starrs, *The Safe Motherhood Action Agenda: Priorities for the Next Decade, Report on the Safe Motherhood Technical Consultation, Colombo, Sri Lanka, 1997* (New York: Family Care International, 1998).

4. Ibid., 1.

5. Mahmoud Fathalla, "The Long Road to Maternal Death," *People* 14, 3 (1987): 8–9.

6. Ibid.

7. World Health Organization, *Mother-Baby Package: Implementing Safe Motherhood in Countries* (Geneva: WHO, 1996).

8. UNICEF, *Guidelines for Monitoring the Availability and Use of Obstetric Services*, 2nd ed. (New York: UNICEF, 1997).

9. See Women's Human Rights Resources website, ⟨www.law-lib.utoronto.ca/diana⟩.

10. United Nations, *Report of the International Conference on Population and Development*, A/CONF.171/13 (New York: United Nations, 1994) [hereinafter, Cairo Program].

11. United Nations, *Key Actions for the Further Implementation of the Programme of Action of the International Conference on Population and Development*, UN Doc. A/s-21/5/Add.1 (1 July 1999), ⟨www.unfpa.org/icpd/icpdmain.htm⟩ [hereinafter, *Cairo Plus Five*].

12. United Nations, *Report of the Fourth World Conference on Women*, UN Doc. A/CONF.177/20 (1995).

13. United Nations, *Further Actions and Initiatives to Implement the Beijing Declaration and Platform for Action*, unedited final outcome document as adopted by the plenary of the special session, 23rd Special Session of the General Assembly, 10 June 2000 [hereinafter, *Beijing Plus Five*] ⟨www.un.org/womenwatch/daw/followup/beijing+5.htm⟩.

14. GA Res. 217 A (III), UN Doc. A/810 (1948).

15. 18 December 1979, 34 UN GAOR Supp. (No. 21) (A/34/46) at 193, UN Doc. A/Res.34/180.

16. GA Res. 2200 (XXI), 21 UN GAOR Supp. (No. 16) at 52, UN Doc. A/6316 (1966).

17. Ibid., 49.

18. GA Res. 25 (XLIV), UN Doc. A/Res/44/25 (1989), reprinted in 28 ILM 1448 (1989).

19. 213 UNTS 221 (1959).

20. Organization of American States Treaty Series at 1 (1969).

21. OR OEA/Ser. L/V/II.23/Doc. 211 rev. 6 (1949).

22. Organization of African Unity Doc. CAB/Leg/67/3/ Rev. 5 (1981).

23. CEDAW General Recommendation 24, UN Doc. A/54/38/Rev.1 (1999), pp. 3–7.

24. Ibid., para. 14.

25. Ibid.

26. Ibid., para. 15.

27. Ibid.

28. Ibid., para. 17.

29. *Tavares v. France*, application no. 16593/90, decision 12 September 1991, European Commission of Human Rights (unreported).

30. Human Rights Committee, UN Doc. CCPR/C/21/Rev.1 (1989), para. 5.

31. Ibid.

32. Cairo Program (1994), para. 7.2.

33. *Paschim Banga Khet Mazdoor Samity v. State of West Bengal* (1996), 4 SCC 37.

34. *Cruz Bermudez et al. v. Ministerio de Sanidad y Asistencia Social (MSAS)*, case no. 15789, ⟨www.csj.gov.ve/sentencias/SPA/spa15071999–15789.html ⟩; *Cruz del Valle Bermúdez y otras v. MSAS*, no. 15789.

35. Inter-American Commission on Human Rights, Annual Report, 1980–81 at 125, cited in Annual Report, 1989–90, 187.

36. Human Rights Committee, 11/18/96, UN Doc. CCPR/C/79/Add.72, para. 15.

37. Ibid., para. 22.

38. *D v. United Kingdom*, 24 E.H.R.R. 423 (1997).

39. *Williams v. Jamaica*, Comm. No. 609/1995, UN Doc. CCPR/C/61/D/609/1995 (17 November 1997).

40. World Health Organization, *Obstetric Fistulae: A Review of Available Information*, WHO/MCH/MSM/91.5 (Geneva: WHO, 1991).

41. Ibid., 3.

42. Ibid.

43. Maggie Bangser, Balthazar Gumodoka, and Zachary Berege, "A Comprehensive Approach to Vesico-Vaginal Fistula: A Project in Mwanza, Tanzania," in *Safe Motherhood Initiatives: Critical Issues*, ed. Marge Berer and Sundari Ravindran, special edition, *Reproductive Health Matters* (1999): 157–65, esp. 158.

44. See generally, Brigit Toebes, *The Right to Health as a Human Right in International Law* (Antwerpen: Intersentia-Hart, 1999).

45. Inter-American Commission on Human Rights, Annual Report, 1984–85, Resolution 12/85, Case 7615.

46. *Open Door Counselling and Dublin Well Women Centre v. Ireland*, 15 E.H.R.R. 244 (1992), para. 77.

47. Committee on Economic, Social, and Cultural Rights, 4 July 2000, E/C.12/2000/4, para. 12.

48. *Soobramoney v. the Minister of Health, Kwazulu Natal*, 1998 (1) SA 765 (CC).

49. Starrs, *The Safe Motherhood Action Agenda*, 17.

50. Committee on Economic, Social, and Cultural Rights, 31 May 1994, UN Doc. E/C.12/1994/9, para. 16.

51. Committee on the Elimination of Discrimination Against Women, UN Doc. A/52/38 (Part I) 24 June 1997, para. 68.

52. Hani K. Atrash, Sidney Alexander, and Cynthia J. Berg, "Maternal Mortality in Developed Countries: Not Just a Concern of the Past," *Obstetrics and Gynecology* 86 (1995): 700–705.

53. Ibid.

54. Rebecca Cook and Deborah Maine, "Spousal Veto over Family Planning Services," *American Journal of Public Health* 77 (1987): 339–44.

55. Corinne Packer, " Preventing Adolescent Pregnancy: The Protection Offered by International Human Rights Law," *International Journal of Children's Rights* 5 (1997): 46–76.

56. Rebecca Cook and Bernard M. Dickens, "Recognizing Adolescents' 'Evolving Capacities' to Exercise Choice in Reproductive Health Care," World Report on Women's Health, 2000, *International Journal of Gynecology and Obstetrics* 70, 1 (2000): 13–21.

57. Virginia Leary, "Justiciability and Beyond: Complaint Procedures and the Right to Health," *The Review* 55 (1995): 105–22.

58. *Paschim Banga Khet Mazdoor Samity* (1996).

59. Leary, "Justiciability and Beyond."

60. CEDAW General Recommendation 24.

61. UN Doc. A/50/38, 31 May 1995.

62. World Health Organization, *Monitoring Reproductive Health: Selecting a Short List of National and Global Indicators*, WHO/RHT/HRP/97.26 (Geneva: WHO, 1997).

63. Ibid., 3.

64. World Health Organization, *Coverage of Maternity Care: A Listing of Available Information*, WHO/RHT/MSM/96.28 (Geneva: WHO, 1997).

65. *Cairo Plus Five* (1999), para. 47. See note above.

66. Alicia Yamin and Deborah Maine, "Maternal Mortality as a Human Rights Issue: Measuring Compliance with International Treaty Obligation," *Human Rights Quarterly* 21 (1999): 563–607.

67. Ibid., 576, 591–601.

68. UNICEF, *Situation Analysis of Children and Women in Mali: A Conceptual Framework in Programming for Children's and Women's Rights: UNICEF's Mali Experience* (UNICEF Bamako, November 1996), 18.

69. Maria Isabel Plata, "Reproductive Rights as Human Rights: The Colombian Case," in *Human Rights of Woman: National and International Perspectives*, ed. Rebecca J. Cook (Philadelphia: University of Pennsylvania Press, 1994).

70. Upendra Baxi, "From Human Rights to the Right to Be Human: Some Heresies," *Indian International Law Quarterly* 13 (1986): 185.

Chapter 7. Canada's New Child Support Guidelines

I would like to thank Raj Gandesha, Nikki Gershbain, and Carita Pereira for their very able research assistance. Thanks also to Janet Mosher, Carol Rogerson, and Craig Scott for their extremely helpful comments on aspects of this essay.

1. Divorce Act, R.S.C. 1985 (2nd Supp.), c. 3. Many of the provinces have enacted similar guidelines for children receiving support under provincial legislation.

2. For a discussion of the previous method of calculating child support, see below notes 22–25 and accompanying text.

3. Federal/Provincial/Territorial Family Law Committee, Department of Justice, Canada, *Child Support: Public Discussion Paper 3–4* (Ottawa: Government of Canada, 1991).

4. Convention on the Rights of the Child, 12 December 1989, art. 27, UN Doc. A/Res/44/25.

5. I will refer to parents who pay child support as fathers since most noncustodial parents (those who will be making child support payments) are men.

6. For a discussion of the Children's Convention that emphasizes this feature, see Stephen J. Toope, "The Convention on the Rights of the Child: Implications for Canada" in *Children's Rights: A Comparative Perspective*, ed. Michael Freeman (Brookfield, Vt.: Dartmouth, 1996), 33–64.

7. In particular, arts. 2, 3, 6, 16, 19, 37.

8. In particular, arts. 14, 15, 37(d).

9. Arts. 23, 24, 25.

10. Art. 26.

11. Arts. 28, 29.

12. Convention on the Rights of the Child, art. 27. Art. 27 should be read in light of arts. 2, 3(1), 3(2), 6(2), 18(1), 26.

13. Family Law Act, R.S.O. 1990, c. F.3.

14. *Larocque v. Larocque*, 195 N.B.R. (2d) 161 (N.B.Q.B. Fam. Div. 1998).

15. It is also consistent with art. 4 of the Children's Convention, which provides in part that "States Parties shall undertake all appropriate legislative, administrative, and other measures for the implementation of the rights recognized in the present Convention."

16. Divorce Act, s. 2(2).

17. Family Law Act, s. 1. The provision makes an exception for arrangements "where the child is placed for valuable consideration in a foster home by a person having lawful custody" of the child.

18. *Chartier v. Chartier*, 1 S.C.R. 242 (S.C.C. 1999).

19. According to Statistics Canada, in 1997 there were 222.6 divorces for every 100,000 population in Canada. See Statistics Canada, "Divorces," *Daily*, 18 May 1999, ⟨www.statcan.ca:80/Daily/English/990518/d990518b.htm⟩. However, Anne-Marie Ambert suggests that a more informative figure is that of the number of divorces among those actually eligible to divorce, which in 1995 was 1,222 divorces per 100,000 married couples. Furthermore, Canada has the third highest divorce rate in the Western world, ranking below the United States and the United Kingdom. See Anne-Marie Ambert, "Divorce: Facts, Figures and Consequences," Vanier Institute of the Family Home Page, ⟨www.vifamily.ca/cft/divorce/divorce.htm⟩.

20. See, for example, the Ontario Children's Law Reform Act, R.S.O. 1990, c. C.12.

21. Section 13 of the regulations to the Ontario Works Act, S.O. 1997, c. 25, places an obligation on social assistance recipients to make "reasonable efforts to obtain compensation or realize a financial resource or income that the person may be entitled to." This is the authority under which social assistance applicants may be required to apply for child support (as well as spousal support and property division, if applicable).

22. These reforms were contained in Bill C-41, an act to amend the Divorce Act, the Family Orders and Agreements Enforcement Assistance Act, the Garnishment, Attachment and Pension Diversion Act and the Canada Shipping Act, 2nd sess., 35th Parl., 1996–97 (S.C. 1997, c. 1).

23. Family Orders and Agreements Enforcement Assistance Act, R.S.C. 1985 (2nd Supp.), c. 4.

24. The full extent of the expanded powers of the Family Responsibility Office are set out in the Family Responsibility and Support Arrears Act, S.O. 1996 (explanatory note), c. 31.

25. *Paras v. Paras*, 1 O.R. 130-136 (Ont. C.A. 1971).

26. For a discussion of the problems with the *Paras* method, see Carol J. Rogerson, "Judicial Interpretation of the Spousal and Child Support Provisions of the Divorce Act, 1985 (Part I)," *Canadian Family Law Quarterly* 7 (1991): 155; Carol J. Rogerson, "Judicial Interpretation of the Spousal and Child Support Provisions of the Divorce Act, 1985 (Part II)," *Canadian Family Law Quarterly* 7 (1991): 271.

27. Child support orders made since the guidelines came into effect in 1997 are not taxable in the hands of the parent receiving the payment.

28. In assessing the success of the guidelines, it is worth noting, however, that immediately prior to their enactment courts had begun to award higher levels of child support under the *Paras* formula. There is some speculation that the guidelines may actually result in lower child support awards for certain income levels than awards that would have been made under this more generous *Paras* approach.

29. Campaign 2000, "1999 Federal Report Card," ⟨www.Campaign2000.ca/national.htm⟩.

30. In its report to the UN Committee on Economic, Social, and Cultural Rights in November, 1998, Low Income Families Together (LIFT) points to 1988 as the begin-

ning of the dismantling of Canada's social safety net. In that year the federal government imposed a limit on its funding under the Canada Assistance Plan. See *The Ontario People's Report to the United Nations*, ⟨www.lift.to/unreport2.htm⟩.

31. CAP was created in 1966. For a good comparison of CAP and CHST see Martha Jackman, "Women and the Canada Health and Social Transfer: Ensuring Gender Equality in Federal Welfare Reform," *Canadian Journal of Women and the Law* 8,2 (1995): 371.

32. Ibid., 375.

33. Ibid.

34. In 1997 Ontario repealed its existing social welfare legislation and introduced the Ontario Works Act. CAP prevented provinces from requiring work for welfare.

35. LIFT, "Introduction," *Ontario People's Report to the United Nations*.

36. Ibid.

37. LIFT, *Ontario People's Report to the United Nations*. Ontario also brought in workfare legislation that premised the receipt of social assistance benefits by ablebodied persons on the ability to work.

38. LIFT, "Introduction."

39. Campaign 2000, "1999 Federal Report Card," ⟨www.Campaign2000.ca/national.htm⟩. These organizations include the Canadian Academy of Child Psychiatry, the Canadian Mental Health Association, and the Canadian Association of Social Workers.

40. The statistics for Ontario come from Campaign 2000, 1998 Ontario Report Card, ⟨www.Campaign2000.ca/provincial.htm⟩.

41. United Nations Committee on Economic, Social, and Cultural Rights (CESCR),- *Concluding Observations to Reports Submitted by Canada to the Committee on Economic, Social, and Cultural Rights*, 10 December 1998, ⟨www.unhchr.ch/tbs/doc .nsf/ Document# E/C.12/1/Add.31⟩ ⟨www.lift.to/images/UNrespond.pdf⟩ p. 2. The UNDP has since ranked Canada first again for the sixth consecutive year. See John Barber, "Canada Again Tops Survey as Best Place to Live," *Globe and Mail* (Toronto), 12 July 1999, A3.

42. CESCR, *Concluding Observations*, 2.

43. Ibid., 3.

44. The committee's comments on this point (ibid., 4–5) are particularly insightful and bear quoting in their entirety:

The replacement of the Canada Assistance Plan (CAP) by the Canada Health and Social Transfer (CHST) entails a range of adverse consequences for the enjoyment of Covenant Rights by disadvantaged groups in Canada. The Government informed the Committee in its 1993 report that the CAP set national standards for social welfare, required that work by welfare recipients be freely chosen, guaranteed the right to an adequate standard of living, and facilitated court challenges to federally funded provincial social assistance programs which did not meet the standards prescribed in the Act. In contrast, the CHST has eliminated each of these features and significantly reduced the amount of cash transfer payments provided to the provinces to cover social assistance. It did, however, retain national standards in relation to health under CHST, thus denying provincial "flexibility" in one area, while insisting upon it in others. The delegation provided no explanation for this inconsistency. The Committee regrets that, by according virtually unfettered discretion in relation to social right to provincial Governments, the Government of Canada has created a situation in which Covenant standards can be undermined and effective accountability has been radically reduced.

45. Ibid., 5. The committee discussed its concerns regarding the living conditions of aboriginal persons (4). In terms of women, the committee noted "with grave concern" that with "the repeal of CAP and cuts to social assistance rates, social

services and programmes have had a particularly harsh impact on women, in particular single mothers" (5) and that over 90 percent of single mothers under 25 live in poverty (7).

46. National Anti-Poverty Organization, "UN Human Rights Committee Cites Canada for Violating Rights of the Poor," 12 April 1999, ⟨povnet.web.net/NAPOpr-apr12.html⟩.

47. See, for example, Ontario Ministry of Community and Social Services, "Canada, Provinces Launch New National Benefit Program for Children in Low-Income Families," 18 June 1998, ⟨www.gov.on.ca:80/CSS/page/news/nr97-98/june1898.html⟩.

48. Felicite Stairs, "The Canada Child Tax Benefit: Income Support and the Tax System," *Journal of Law and Social Policy* 14 (1999): 123.

49. New Brunswick and Newfoundland.

50. CESCR, *Concluding Observations*, 2.

51. Ibid., 8.

52. Campaign 2000, 1999 Federal Report Card, ⟨www.Campaign2000.ca/national.htm.

Chapter 8. Implementing Economic, Social, and Cultural Rights

This chapter is adapted from Barbara von Tigerstrom, "The Role of the Ombudsman in Protecting Economic, Social and Cultural Rights," *International Ombudsman Yearbook* 2 (1998): 3. The initial research for this project was conducted during an internship at the International Ombudsman Institute (IOI) with the support of the University of Toronto Faculty of Law International Human Rights Programme. The author gratefully acknowledges the support and assistance of the Programme, the IOI, Professors Linda Reif (University of Alberta), Rebecca Cook (University of Toronto), and Anne Gallagher (UN Office of the High Commissioner for Human Rights).

1. Mario Gomez, "Social Economic Rights and Human Rights Commissions," *Human Rights Quarterly* 17 (1995): 155, 162ff.

2. The word "ombudsman" is borrowed from the Swedish and is generally considered to be gender neutral, although it is occasionally modified to "ombudswoman" or "ombudsperson." In this chapter the word ombudsman will be used to refer to officials of both genders and both female and male pronouns will be used to reflect this. For convenience the anglicized plural "ombudsmen" will be used.

3. Similar models existed in China and India, for example, as far back as 3000 B.C.: Judge Anand Satyanand, *The Ombudsman Concept and Human Rights Protection*, Occasional Paper 68 (Edmonton, Alberta: International Ombudsman Institute, January 1999), 1.

4. This list is based on Donald C. Rowat, *A Worldwide Survey of Ombudsmen*, Occasional Paper 60 (Edmonton, Alberta: International Ombudsman Institute, March 1997), 1–2.

5. See, e.g., Donald C. Rowat, "Why a Legislative Ombudsman Is Desirable," *Ombudsman Journal* (1993): 127, 129.

6. Daniel Jacoby, *The Development of the "Ombudsmediator" on a Global Scale*, Occasional Paper 69 (Edmonton, Alberta: International Ombudsman Institute, March 1999), 1. Jacoby counts 220 general legislative ombudsman offices and 102 "specialty" ombudsmen that act in specific areas, 5–6.

7. See, e.g., Linda C. Reif, "The Promotion of International Human Rights Law by the Office of the Ombudsman" in *The Ombudsman: Diversity and Development*, ed. Linda Reif, Mary Marshall, and Charles Ferris (Edmonton, Alberta: International

Ombudsman Institute, 1993), 87; Linda C. Reif, "Building Democratic Institutions: The Role of National Human Rights Institutions in Good Governance and Human Rights Protection," *Harvard Human Rights Journal* 13 (2000): 3; National Ombudsman of the Netherlands, ed., *Ombudsman and Human Rights* (The Hague: National Ombudsman of the Netherlands, 1995).

8. See, e.g., von Tigerstrom, "Role of the Ombudsman"; Jorge Madrazo Cuellar, "The Ombudsman and His Relationship with Human Rights, Poverty and Development," *International Ombudsman Yearbook* 2 (1998): 129.

9. Committee on Economic, Social, and Cultural Rights (CESCR), General Comment 10, "The Role of National Human Rights Institutions in the Protection of Economic, Social, and Cultural Rights," 3 December 1998, UN Doc. E/C.12/1998/25, para. 1, 2. International Covenant on Economic, Social, and Cultural Rights, 16 December 1966, 993 UNTS 3; Can. T.S. 1976 No. 46.

10. CESCR, General Comment 10, paras. 3, 4.

11. For a discussion of these factors, see Reif, "Promotion of International Human Rights Law," 89.

12. Ibid., 89–90.

13. See CESCR, General Comment, para. 3, for a list of activities that may be undertaken by national human rights institutions in relation to economic, social, and cultural rights.

14. Philip Alston, "International Law and the Human Right to Food" in *The Right to Food*, ed. Philip Alston and Katarina Tomasevski (Boston: Martinus Nijhoff, 1984), 9, 58.

15. Florence Mumba, "The Ombudsman and Human Rights in Africa" in *Ombudsman and Human Rights*, 10, 12.

16. Mary A. Marshall, "The Ombudsman: Challenges and Opportunities" in *The Ombudsman Concept*, ed. Linda C. Reif (Edmonton, Alberta: International Ombudsman Institute, 1995), 241, 245.

17. Satyanand, *The Ombudsman Concept and Human Rights Protection*, 5.

18. I. E. Nebenzahl, "The Direct and Indirect Impact of the Ombudsman," in *International Handbook of the Ombudsman: Evolution and Present Function*, ed. Gerald E. Caiden, vol. 1 (Westport, Conn.: Greenwood Press, 1983), 59, 60–63.

19. Stephen Owen, "The Expanding Role of the Ombudsman in the Administrative State," *University of Toronto Law Journal* 40 (1990): 670, 675.

20. Ibid., 677, 679.

21. See, e.g., Roberta Jamieson, "The Ombudsman and Human Rights: The Canadian/North American Experience" in *Ombudsman and Human Rights*, 28, 33.

22. See, e.g., the Namibian Ombudsman Act, 1990 (Act No. 7 of 1990); section 391(a) provides that the Ombudsman shall inquire into, inter alia, "alleged or apparent instances or matters of violations or infringements of fundamental rights and freedoms," defined in section1 as "any fundamental right or freedom as defined in Chap. 3 of the Namibian Constitution." In Honduras, the law establishing the national commissioner of human rights (Ley orgánica del Comisionado Nacional de los Derechos Humanos, decree no. 153-95, 24 October 1995) provides that the Commissioner has the power to monitor observance of "rights and guarantees established in the Constitution of the Republic and the present Law, the Universal Declaration of Human Rights and other treaties and conventions ratified by Honduras" (art. 9[1], author's translation). The scope of rights protected by the Guatemalan human rights ombudsman is similar (see Ley de la Comision de los Derechos Humanos del congreso de la República y del Procurador de los Derechos Humanos, decree no. 54-86 and 32-87, art. 8). The provisions establishing the Ombudsman offices in Bosnia and Herzegovina (Annex 6 to the General Framework Agreement for Peace Agreement for Peace in Bosnia and Herzegovina, Agreement on Human

Rights, chap. 2, art. 2.2; *Rules of Procedure*, Official Gazette of Bosnia and Herzegovina, 18 September 1997, Title II, Rule 5); Latvia (Law of 5 December 1996 r. on the Latvian National Human Rights Office, arts. 1, 2); Georgia (Law on the Public Defender of Georgia, 16 May 1996, art. 13); and Ukraine (Law of Ukraine on the Authorized Human Rights Representative of the Verkhovna Rada of Ukraine, 23 December 1997, arts. 1, 3) all expressly confer upon the office the responsibility to protect rights guaranteed in international agreements. These provisions are reproduced in *National Ombudsmen: Collection of Legislation from 27 Countries* (Warsaw: Commissioner for Civil Rights Protection of Poland, 1997).

23. For example, the rights and freedoms in chap. 3 of the Constitution of the Republic of Namibia (1990), which are within the jurisdiction of the ombudsman, include the right to "enjoy, practise, profess, maintain and promote any culture, language, tradition or religion" (art. 19) and the right to education (art. 20). The rights set out in the Constitution of Honduras (Constitucion de la República de Honduras, decree no. 131 of 11 January 1982, amended by decree no. 5-91 of 30 January 1991) and protected by the national commissioner include social rights (chap. 3), children's rights (chap. 4), worker's rights (chap. 5), social security (chap. 6), health (chap. 7), education and culture (chap. 8) and housing (chap. 9). The jurisdiction of the Honduras commissioner also includes economic, social, and cultural rights contained in international instruments ratified by Honduras. The international conventions over which the human rights ombudsman of Bosnia and Herzegovina has jurisdiction include the International Covenant on Economic, Social, and Cultural Rights (*Rules of Procedure*, Title 2, Rule 5(2)(i)).

24. Ewa Letowska, "The Commissioner for Citizens' Rights in Central and Eastern Europe: The Polish Experience," *St. Louis-Warsaw Transatlantic Law Journal* (1996): 1, 6.

25. See generally Edelberto Torres-Rivas and Mirta González-Suárez, *Obstacles and Hopes: Perspectives for Democratic Development in El Salvador* (Montreal: International Centre for Human Rights and Democratic Development, 1994), 11ff.

26. Inter-American Commission on Human Rights, *Report on the Situation of Human Rights in El Salvador* (Washington, D.C.: Organization of American States General Secretariat, 1994), 18.

27. Howard Elcock, "Making Bricks Without Straw?: The Polish Ombudsman and the Transition to Democracy," *International Journal of the Sociology of Law* 20 (1992): 173.

28. Act of 15 July 1987 on Commissioner for Civil Rights Protection, reprinted in Commissioner for Civil Rights Protection, *Annual Report 1995* (Warsaw: Bureau of the Commissioner for Civil Rights Protection, 1996), 169–76; and in *St. Louis-Warsaw Transatlantic Law Journal* (1996): 85. Subsequent citations will be to the former (the translations differ slightly).

29. Letowska, "Commissioner for Citizen's Rights," 1.

30. Ibid.

31. Constitution of the Republic of Poland, 2 April 1997, arts. 208–12.

32. See Elcock, "Bricks Without Straw," 178; Howard Elcock, "The Polish Ombudsman and the Transition to Democracy" *International and Comparative Law Quarterly* 45 (1996): 684–85.

33. Letowska, "Commissioner for Citizen's Rights," 5.

34. Ibid., 6.

35. Elcock, "Polish Ombudsman," 686.

36. See, e.g., art. 35 (minority language and cultural rights), art. 59 (trade union rights), art. 65 (work), art. 66 (working conditions), art. 67 (social security), art. 68 (health), art. 70 (education), art. 73 (artistic, scientific and cultural activity), art. 75 (housing).

37. Letowska, "Commissioner for Citizen's Rights," 9; Elcock, "Polish Ombudsman," 690.

38. Elcock, "Polish Ombudsman," 686.

39. Act of 15 July 1987, art. 14.

40. Ibid., art. 16.

41. Commissioner for Civil Rights Protection, *Annual Report, 1995*, 9–16.

42. Ibid., 9.

43. See Ian Johnstone, *Rights and Reconciliation: UN Strategies in El Salvador* (Boulder, Colo.: Lynne Rienner, 1995), esp. 65–67; Alvaro de Soto and Graciana del Castillo, "Implementation of Comprehensive Peace Agreements: Staying the Course in El Salvador" *Global Governance* 1 (1995): 189.

44. De Soto and del Castillo, "Implementation," 189.

45. Letter dated 8 October 1991 from El Salvador transmitting the text of the Mexico Agreement and annexes signed on 27 April 1991 by the Government of El Salvador and the FMLN, UN Doc. A/46/553-S/23130, 9 October 1991, Annex, art. 2(1)(c).

46. Letter dated 27 January 1992 from El Salvador transmitting the entire text of the Peace Agreement between the Government of El Salvador and the FMLN, signed at Chapultepec Castle in Mexico City on 16 January 1992, UN Doc. A/46/864-S/23501, 30 January 1992, Annex, c.3, art.2.

47. Constitution of the Republic of El Salvador, as amended by Decree No. 64, art. 194.

48. Law of the Human Rights Ombudsman, Decree No. 163. The decree was made on 20 February 1992 and came into force in March.

49. Johnstone, *Rights and Reconciliation*, 66.

50. Law of the Human Rights Ombudsman, art. 11.

51. Ibid., art. 34.

52. Ibid., art. 30.

53. Ibid., art. 32.

54. See Johnstone, *Rights and Reconciliation*, 66; Letter from Victoria Marina de Avilés to Linda Reif, 8 July 1997, on file with the International Ombudsman Institute.

55. Law of the Human Rights Ombudsman, art. 33.

56. Ibid., art. 42.

57. Ibid., art 2.

58. Ibid., arts. 40–41, 12(3).

59. Quoted in Inter-American Commission on Human Rights, *Report*, 7.

60. Constitution of the Republic of El Salvador, c. 2.

61. Additional Protocol to the American Convention on Human Rights in the Area of Economic, Social and Cultural Rights, 17 November 1988, OAS Treaty Series 69.

62. Procuraduría para la Defensa de los Derechos Humanos, *Informe de Labores, junio 96–mayo 97*, 11.

63. Ibid., 38ff; letter from Victoria Marina de Avilés, 1997.

64. Johnstone, *Rights and Reconciliation*, 66; letter from Victoria Marina de Avilés, 1997.

65. Procuraduría para la Defensa de los Derechos Humanos, *Informe de Labores, junio 96–mayo 97*, 45.

66. See de Soto and del Castillo, "Implementation," 197.

67. Gustavo G. Giraldo, "Latin America: Challenges in Economic, Social and Cultural Rights," *International Commission of Jurists Review* 55 (1995): 59, 62.

68. Danilo Turk, Special Rapporteur, *The Realization of Economic, Social, and Cultural Rights: Final Report*, 3 July 1992, UN Doc. E/CN.4/Sub.2/1992/16, para. 89.

69. Joseph Oloka-Onyango, "Beyond the Rhetoric: Reinvigorating the Struggle

for Economic and Social Rights in Africa" *California Western International Law Journal* 26 (1995): 1, 67.

70. In Ontario, for example, the Ombudsman Act, R.S.O. 1990, c. O.6 (as amended) states that the Ombudsman shall make a report if she or he "is of the opinion that the decision, recommendation, act or omission which was the subject matter of the investigation, (a) appears to have been contrary to law" (s. 21).

71. Ibid., s. 18(6): "If, during or after an investigation, the Ombudsman is of the opinion that there is evidence of a breach of duty or of misconduct on the part of any officer or employee of any governmental organization, the Ombudsman may refer the matter to the appropriate authority." In some jurisdictions, there are provisions requiring the ombudsman, if she or he becomes aware of an allegedly criminal act, to refer the matter to the attorney general or prosecutor; e.g., Ley Orgánica del Comisionado Nacional de Los Derechos Humanos (Honduras), art. 40.

72. See Charles Maino, "Investigating Corruption in Institutions: The Legislative Mandate" in Reif, Marshall and Ferris, ed. *The Ombudsman,* 123; Charles Maino, "Ethical Considerations: The Leadership Code of Papua New Guinea" in Reif, *Ombudsman Concept,* 53.

73. Sections 218 and 219 of the Constitution set out the powers of the commission. See Maino, "Investigating Corruption," 133–34, 141ff.

74. Ibid., 134.

75. Ibid., 147.

76. John Hatchard, "The Ombudsman in Africa Revisited," *International and Comparative Law Quarterly* 40 (1991): 937, 939.

77. Constitution of the Republic of Uganda, 1995, s. 230(1), (2).

78. Joseph Oloka-Onyango, "The Dynamics of Corruption Control and Human Rights Enforcement in Uganda: The Case of the Inspector General of Government," *East African Journal of Peace and Human Rights* 1 (1993): 23, 33.

79. Ombudsman Act, 1990, s. 3(1)(a), (e).

80. Jacoby, *Development of the "Ombudsmediator",* 13.

81. See, e.g., Jorge Luis Maiorano, "An Institution Adaptable to Every Community" *International Ombudsman Institute Newsletter* 21(1) (1999): 1: "In the Asian and African countries, the Ombudsman's mission is closely related to the struggle against corruption and, in order to fight it, they have not hesitated to resort to this renowned Ombudsman institution which had not originally been designed to fulfill this function, but . . . has become an effective means against corruption." See also World Bank (Poverty Reduction and Economic Management), *Helping Countries Combat Corruption: The Role of the World Bank* (Washington, D.C.: World Bank, September 1997), 44; this report cautions that ombudsman and similar institutions can only be effective if they are sufficiently independent. The Lima Declaration Against Corruption states that, "The Office of Ombudsman . . . can make a major contribution to the elimination of bureaucratic obstruction and corruption, and so countries without this necessary post should examine its adoption as an independent office of its elected congress." *Lima Declaration Against Corruption,* 1997, reprinted in *Economic Perspectives* 3 (1998): 47, para. 25.

82. See Elcock, "Polish Ombudsman," 688.

83. Commission for Civil Rights Protection, *Annual Report, 1995,* 91–94, 101–6.

84. Law of the Human Rights Ombudsman, art. 11.

85. Law of 5 December 1996, art. 2(7).

86. Law of Ukraine, art. 3(4).

87. Malfrid G. Flekkoy, "The Children's Ombudsman as Implementer of Children's Rights," *Journal of Transnational Law and Contemporary Problems* 6 (1996): 353, 368–69.

88. See, e.g., Parliamentary Commissioner for Data Protection and Freedom of

Information, *First Report (Summary)* (Budapest: Office of the Parliamentary Commissioner for Data Protection and Freedom of Information, 1996). For references to a selection of such offices, see Department of Justice Canada, "International Access and Privacy Laws and Commissions," ⟨canada.justice.gc.ca/en/ps/atip/index .html⟩.

89. Inspection Panel, *Operating Procedures* (19 August 1994), ⟨wbln0018.worldbank .org/ipn/ipnweb.nsf⟩, para. 1.

90. See Inspection Panel, *Panel Register,* ⟨wbln0018.worldbank.org/ipn/ipnweb .nsf⟩. For a brief but very useful overview of the Inspection Panel's activities in its first three years, see Richard E. Bissell, "Recent Practice of the Inspection Panel of the World Bank," *American Journal of International Law* 91 (1997): 741.

91. See, e.g., Notices of Registration: IPN Request RQ94/1 (Nepal: Arun III Hydroelectric Project); Notice of Registration: RQ96/2 (Argentina/Paraguay: Yacyretá Hydroelectric Project); RQ97/1 (Brazil: Itaparica Resettlement and Irrigation Project); RQ97/2 (India: NTPC Power Generation Project); RQ99/1 (Brazil: Land Reform and Poverty Alleviation Pilot Project), at ⟨wbln0018.worldbank.org/ipn/ ipnweb.nsf⟩.

92. See Ibrahim F. I. Shihata, *The World Bank Inspection Panel* (Oxford: Oxford University Press, 1994), 92–93.

93. Katarina Tomasevski, "The Influence of the World Bank and IMF on Economic and Social Rights," *Nordic Journal of International Law* 64 (1995): 385.

94. Larry B. Hill, "The Self-Perceptions of Ombudsman: A Comparative Survey," in Caiden, *International Handbook,* vol. 1, 43, 47.

95. Owen, "Expanding Role," 672.

96. Reif, "Promotion of International Human Rights Law," 98.

97. Parliamentary Commissioner for Civil Rights, *The First One and a Half Year Experiences of the Parliamentary Commissioner and of the Deputy Commissioner for Civil Rights* (Budapest: Parliamentary Commissioner for Civil Rights, 1997), 8 (emphasis in original).

98. Ibid., 9.

99. Ibid.

100. See e.g., ICESCR, art. 2(2), 3.

101. The Limburg Principles on the Implementation of the International Covenant on Economic, Social and Cultural Rights, UN Doc. E/CN.4/1987/17, Annex, reprinted in *Human Rights Quarterly* 9 (1987): 122, paras. 25–28.

102. Elcock, "Polish Ombudsman," 686.

103. Ombudsman Act, s. 21 (1)(b).

104. Owen, "Expanding Role," 675.

105. Letter from Victoria Marina de Avilés.

106. United Nations Centre for Human Rights, *National Human Rights Institutions: A Handbook on the Establishment and Strengthening of National Institutions for the Promotion and Protection of Human Rights* (New York and Geneva: United Nations, 1995), 10.

107. See Mary A. Marshall and Linda C. Reif, "The Ombudsman: Maladministration and Alternative Dispute Resolution," *Alberta Law Review* 34 (1995): 215, 223–24.

108. Katarina Tomasevski, "Justiciability of Economic, Social, and Cultural Rights," *International Commission of Jurists Review* 55 (1995): 203, 214–15.

109. E.g., Ley orgánica del Comisionado Nacional de los Derechos Humanos (Honduras), art. 23; Ley orgánica de la Defensoría del Pueblo, no. 26520 (Peru), art. 10.

110. United Nations Centre for Human Rights, *National Human Rights Institutions,* 34.

111. Ibid., 14–15.

112. Maino, "Investigating Corruption," 127; World Bank, *Helping Countries Combat Corruption,* 44.

113. Diego Garcia-Sayan, "New Path for Economic, Social, and Cultural Rights" *International Commission of Jurists Review* 55 (1995): 75, 79.

114. United Nations Centre for Human Rights, *National Human Rights Institutions*, 10–12.

Chapter 9. Bringing Economic, Social, and Cultural Rights Home

Thanks to David Wiseman for editing this essay and to Soraya Farha, Miloon Kothari, and Joseph Schechla for comments on an earlier version.

1. See Scott Leckie, "Another Step Towards Indivisibility: Identifying the Key Features of Violations of Economic, Social and Cultural Rights," *Human Rights Quarterly* 20 (1998): 81.

2. Palestine Housing Rights Movement [hereinafter PHRM], "Living in Jerusalem: An Assessment of Planning Policy, Housing and Living Conditions in Light of the Palestinians' Right to Adequate Housing" (East Jerusalem: PHRM, May 1996), 8.

3. Mayor Ehud Olmert, *Jerusalem Post*, 26 November 1994. See United Nations Commission on Human Settlements, HS/C/14/2/Add.1 at 7 (1992), "Housing Requirements of the Palestinians," which states: "The military occupation and colonial policy of the occupying power which is aimed at the Judaization of the land had extremely adverse effects on the Palestinian housing sector."

4. Report of the Kubersky Committee of the Ministry of Interior for Investigating the Annexation of Territory East of Jerusalem (Government of Israel, 1992).

5. See Palestine Human Rights Information Centre [hereinafter PHRIC], "Clever Concealment" (East Jerusalem: PHRIC, February 1994).

6. This essay does not address other means by which the Israeli government is Judaizing Jerusalem, such as the revocation of residency rights, absentee property laws, and discriminatory taxation policies. See PHRM, "Living in Jerusalem" and Miloon Kothari and J. Abu Shakrah, *Planned Dispossession: Palestinians, East Jerusalem and the Right to a Place to Live*, Occasional Paper (Utrecht: Centre on Housing Rights and Evictions, 1995).

7. PHRIC, "Israeli Human Rights Violations Against Palestinians: Summary Data Totals, December 1987–March 1997" (East Jerusalem: PHRIC, 1997). It should be noted that house sealings are now uncommon. They were imposed when an Israeli official suspected that a house was being used as a base for an attack against the State of Israel and involved physically barring access to the residence, blocking access points. See M. Carroll, "The Israeli Demolition of Palestinian Homes" *Michigan Journal of International Law* 11 (1990): 1195, 1196.

8. PHRM, "Living in Jerusalem," 18.

9. Emily Playfair, *Demolition and Sealing of Houses as Punitive Measure in the Israeli-Occupied West Bank*, al-Haq Occasional Paper 5 (Ramallah: Al-Haq, 1987), 6.

10. In the past, antitank missiles and high level explosives were used to force "wanted" Palestinians hiding inside to come out and surrender to the Israeli authorities. See al-Haq, *Missiles and Dynamite* (Ramallah: Al-Haq, 1993).

11. A. Vitullo, "War by Bureaucracy" (manuscript on file with PHRIC, 1989), 11. See UN Commission on Human Settlements, "Housing Requirements."

12. Al-Haq, *Urban Planning in the West Bank Under Military Occupation* (Ramallah: Al-Haq, 1991), 6.

13. Israelis have been able to register land since 1967. Palestine Human Rights Information Centre, "Whose Jerusalem?" *From the Field: A Monthly Report on Selected Human Rights Issues* (6 January 1994).

14. Ibid., 2.

15. Rose-Marie Barbeau, "No Room Left to Build," *Palestine Report* (April 1997).

16. Michael Dumper, "Israeli Settlement in the Old City of Jerusalem" *Journal of Palestine Studies* 21 (1992): 32.

17. Under international principles governing bilateral agreements such as the Oslo Accords, neither party should set up obstacles that could alter the current status of issues to be resolved in further negotiations. See Kothari and Shakrah, "Planned Dispossession," 2.

18. Palestinian Society for the Protection of Human Rights and the Environment [hereinafter LAW], "Settlement Expansion " (on file with author of this essay).

19. Isabel Kershner and Tom Sawicki, "The Battle for Jerusalem," *Jerusalem Report* (July 1994): 11.

20. PHRM, "Living in Jerusalem," 9.

21. Ibid.

22. Ibid., 17.

23. S. Kaminker, "Housing and Community Development Through Land Reclamation: A Proposal for Planning and Building New Communities in East Jerusalem" (manuscript on file with PHRIC, 1994), 2.

24. Uri Davis, "The Legal Status of the World Zionist Organization (WZO), Jewish Agency for the Land of Israel (JA) and the Jewish National Fund (JNF) and Their Role in Planning and Financing Land Use and Housing Inside the State of Israel," report submitted to the Committee on Economic, Social, and Cultural Rights, 19th Sess. (November 1998)

25. Ibid., 3–4.

26. Arab Association for Human Rights [hereinafter HRA], "Discrimination in Housing Rights: Issues Concerning the Palestinian Arab Community in Israel," report submitted to the Committee on the Elimination of Racial Discrimination, 52nd Sess. (Nazareth: HRA, March 1998), 2.

27. Arab Co-ordinating Committee on Housing Rights [hereinafter ACCHR], "Housing for All? A Report for the UN Committee on Economic, Social, and Cultural Rights, on the Implementation of Article 11(1) of the United Nations ICESCR" (Nazareth: ACCHR, 1996), 32.

28. Ibid., 42. See Association for Support and Defence of Bedouin Rights in Israel [hereinafter Association for Support], "The Situation of the Bedouin in the Negev," report submitted to the Committee on Economic, Social, and Cultural Rights (on file with author) (July 1995), 10.

29. Ibid.; ACCHR, "Housing for All," 30.

30. Association for Support, "Situation of the Bedouin," and ACCHR, "Housing for All," 48–54.

31. ACCHR, "Housing for All," 35–36.

32. "The Association of Forty," memorandum on the recognition of the Arab unrecognized villages (on file with author of this essay, 1994), 13.

33. Ibid., 12.

34. HRA, "Discrimination in Housing Rights," 6.

35. Ibid., 5, and ACCHR, "Housing for All," 66–81.

36. Habitat International Coalition is an international body representing grassroots, community- based and nongovernmental organizations in over seventy countries that work on a range of issues related to housing.

37. International Covenant on Economic, Social and Cultural Rights, adopted 16 December 1966, GA Res. 2200 (XXI), 21UN GAOR, Supp. (No. 16), UN Doc. A/6316 (1966), 993 UNTS 3 (entered into force 3 January 1976).

38. Committee on Economic, Social, and Cultural Rights, General Comment 4 on the right to adequate housing, article 11(1)), 6th Sess. (1991), UN Doc. E/C.12/1991/4.

39. Ibid., para. 7.

40. Ibid., para. 8.

41. See Scott Leckie, "Housing as a Human Right," *Environment and Urbanization* 1, 2 (1989): 90; and Scott Leckie, "The UN Committee on Economic, Social and Cultural Rights and the Right to Adequate Housing: Towards an Appropriate Approach," *Human Rights Quarterly* 11, 4 (1989).

42. Under art. 16 of the ICESCR, signatories to the covenant undertake to submit such reports.

43. International Human Rights Internship Program, *Ripple in Still Water* (Washington, D.C.: IHRIP, 1997), 50.

44. Miloon Kothari, "The Global Struggle for the Right to a Place to Live," *Development in Practice* 7, 1 (1997): 5, 13.

45. British Broadcasting Corporation, "Arafat's Authority," SBS Television, Australia, 5 May 1999.

46. E-mail communication from Miloon Kothari, 22 March 1999 (on file with the author).

47. Telephone interview with Mohammed Zeidan, coordinator of the Arab Coordinating Committee on Housing Rights and of the HRA, 25 June 1998.

48. Joseph Schechla, member of HIC and coordinator of training and information at the UN Office for the High Commissioner for Human Rights, Gaza, interview, 25 November 1998 and e-mail communication, 23 March 1999 (on file with the author).

49. Telephone interview with Miloon Kothari, convener of the HIC Housing and Land Rights Committee, 10 June 1998.

50. Telephone interview with Anne Kindrachuk, consultant, Canadian International Development Agency (Ms. Kindrachuk spoke to me about her experiences working with the PHRM), 30 August 1998.

51. Telephone interview with Mohammed Zeidan, 25 June 1998. See ⟨www.arabhra .org⟩.

52. Conversation with Jihad Abu Zneid of PHRIC, 18 February 1998.

53. YUVA is an NGO based in Mumbai, India.

54. Telephone interview with Miloon Kothari, 10 June 1998.

55. See Miloon Kothari, "The Global Struggle," 9–12.

56. Representatives from the PHRM and HIC have also testified at the UN Special Committee to Investigate Israeli Practices in the Occupied Territories, a body that was established to allow Palestinians and experts with relevant knowledge to testify before the committee. The committee's findings are transmitted to the General Assembly.

57. Participation in this group has been an essential aspect of ACCHR's work. For the first time, the Palestinian struggle inside Israel has been compared with ethnic minority and indigenous peoples' struggles throughout the world.

58. See Committee on Economic, Social, and Cultural Rights, 8th Sess., UN Doc. E/1994/23, para. 354 (1994).

59. The urgency of the situation was due to the fact that the Israeli government was building settlements for Jews and demolishing Palestinian homes at such a rapid rate that Palestinian residents of East Jerusalem feared that the government of Israel would successfully Judaize Jerusalem and hence render moot the need for final status talks on Jerusalem. This remains a major concern.

60. PHRM, "The United Nations Condemns Israel's Housing Policies Towards Palestinians in East Jerusalem and Calls for Immediate Action" (East Jerusalem: PHRM, 1996).

61. Telephone interview with Mohammed Zeidan, 25 June 1998.

62. Committee on Economic, Social, and Cultural Rights, "List of Issues," UN Doc. E/C.12/Q/ISR/1 (June 1998).

63. Ibid., para. 31.

64. Ibid., para. 33.

65. Committee on Economic, Social and Cultural Rights, "Concluding Observations," 19th Sess., UN Doc. E/C.12/1/Add.27 (December 1998), para. 21.

66. Ibid., para. 22.

67. Ibid., paras. 26, 28.

68. Ibid., para. 41.

69. Ibid.

70. Of course, it is possible to use international human rights covenants and jurisprudence to support domestic litigation and social movements and/or campaigns.

71. Telephone interview with Miloon Kothari, 10 June 1998.

72. Ibid.

73. Telephone interview with Mohammed Zeidan, 25 June 1998.

74. For a summary of this case in English see ⟨www.court.gov.il/mishpat/html/en/home/index.html⟩.

75. As of October 2000 this information had not been received.

76. CESCR, "Concluding Observations," para. 32.

77. Ibid., para. 11.

78. E-mail communication from Joseph Schechla, 23 March 1999 (on file with the author).

79. Ibid.

80. Telephone interview with Mohammed Zeidan, 25 June 1998.

81. There are many other purposes of monitoring and documenting the actions and activities of governments, organizations, and institutions, including education and mobilization, providing immediate assistance during a crisis or problem, litigation, legislative advocacy and policy reform, preparing submissions to intergovernmental agencies, and so on. See International Human Rights Internship Program, *Ripple in Still Water.*

82. Telephone interview with Anne Kindrachuk, 30 August 1998.

83. Telephone interview with Mohammed Zeidan, 25 June 1998. While the UN has passed a number of resolutions indicating that Israel is in breach of international law, few resolutions have directly addressed everyday living and housing conditions for Palestinians.

84. E-mail communication from Joseph Schechla, 23 March 1999.

85. Telephone interview with Miloon Kothari, 10 June 1998.

Chapter 10. The Maya Petition

1. For a description of Belize and its tourist industry, see ⟨www.travelbelize.org⟩.

2. See John D. Ivanko, "On the Chopping Block: Logging in Belize, Earth Action Network," 21 November 1997, available in Lexis-Nexis Library.

3. See Inter-American Commission on Human Rights, *Report on the Situation of Human Rights in Ecuador*, OEA/Ser.L./V/II.96, Doc. 10 rev. 1, 24 April 1997, 77–117.

4. Another notable case involves a petition by the Mayagua indigenous community of Awas Tingni against Nicaragua. That case similarly challenges government-authorized logging on indigenous traditional lands and the failure of the government to adequately recognize and secure indigenous lands. The Inter-American Commission issued a report in favor of the petitioner indigenous community in May of 1998 and subsequently submitted the case to the Inter-American Court of Human Rights, a judicial body of the OAS with jurisdiction to issue legally binding decisions against Nicaragua and other OAS member states that have accepted the Court's jurisdiction. The case is still pending before the Court. For information on the *Awas Tingni* Case, see ⟨www.indianlaw.org/central_america.html⟩.

5. See generally, S. James Anaya, *Indigenous Peoples in International Law* (New York and Oxford: Oxford University Press, 1996); Siegfried Wiessner, "The Rights and Status of Indigenous Peoples: A Global Comparative and International Legal Analysis," *Harvard Human Rights Journal* 12 (1999): 57.

[1]. See Toledo Maya Cultural Council and Toledo Alcaldes Association, *Maya Atlas: The Struggle to Preserve Maya Land in Southern Belize* (Berkeley, California: North Atlantic Books, 1997) (Appendix A) (hereinafter *Maya Atlas*).

[49]. See ss.16(1), *Petroleum Act, 1991,* 8/1991 (Belize).

[50]. See ss.19(4), *Petroleum Act, 1991,* 8/1991 (Belize).

[52]. See Inter-Am. C.H.R., *Report on the Situation of Human Rights in Ecuador*, OEA/Ser.L./V/II.96, Doc. 10 rev. 1, April 24, 1997, 77–117 [hereinafter *Ecuador Report*].

[57]. See ss.2 and 6, *National Lands Act, 1992,* 6/1992 (Belize).

[87]. See *Velasquez Rodriguez*, Judgment of July 29, 1988, Inter-Am. Ct. H.R. (Ser. C) no. 4, at para. 63 (1988).

[88]. Case 10.636 (Guatemala), Inter-Am. C.H.R., OEA/ser. L/V/II.91, doc.7 rev., at 125, 133 (1996).

[89]. See Case 10.580 (Ecuador), Inter-Am. C.H.R., OEA/ser. L/V/II.91 doc.7 rev., at 76, 86 (1995).

[90]. *See Velasquez Rodriguez*, para. 67.

[91]. Case 10.897 (Guatemala), Inter-Am. C.H.R., OEA/ser. L/V/II.95, doc. 7 rev., at 394, para. 31 (1997).

[92]. Ibid., para. 68.

[93]. Ibid., paras. 75 to 77.

[94]. See ibid., para. 77.

[95]. Case 11.411 (Mexico), Inter-Am. C.H.R., OEA/ser. L/V/II.95 doc. 7 rev. at 476, para. 31 (1997). See also Case 10.636, Inter-Am. C.H.R., OEA/ser. L/V/II.91 doc.7 rev. at 125, para. 44 (1996).

[96]. *Velasquez Rodriguez*, Preliminary Objections, Judgment of June 26, 1989, Inter-Am. Ct. H.R. (ser. C) no. 1, at para. 93 (1994).

[97]. See *Interpretation of the American Declaration of the Rights and Duties of Man in the Framework of Article 64 of the American Convention on Human Rights*, Advisory Opinion OC-1089 of July 14, 1989, Inter-Am. Ct. H.R. (1989), paras. 42, 43.

[98]. The relevant general principle of law is reflected in art. 21.1 of the American Convention on Human Rights, which states: "No one shall be deprived of his property except upon payment of just compensation, for reasons of public utility or social interest, and in the cases and according to the forms established by law." Additionally, the commission has understood property to refer to "the right to dispose of a thing in any legal way, to possess it, to use it and to exclude everyone else from interfering with it." Report No. 47/97, *Tabacalera Boquerón Petition* (Paraguay), Inter-Am. C.H.R., OEA/Ser.L/II.98, doc. 7 rev., at 230 (1998) (quoting *Black's Law Dictionary* (West Publishing Co.), p. 1382).

[99]. See ibid., paras. 12–22.

[100]. See, e.g, *Mabo [No. 2] v. Queensland* (1992), 175 C.L.R. 1, 69 (Austl.); *Delgamuukw v. British Columbia* (1997), 153 D.L.R (4th) 193 (S.C.C.) (Can.); *R. v. Van Der Peet* (1996), 137 D.L.R. (4th) 289, 109 C.C.C. (3d) 1 (S.C.C) (Can.); *U.S. v. Shoshone Tribe of Indians*, 304 U.S. 111, 116–118 (1938); *Amodu Tijani v. Secretary, Southern Nigeria*, 2 A.C. 399, 3 N.L.R. 21 (P.C. 1921); *Adong bin Kuwau & ors v. Kerajaan Negeri Johor & Anor*, [1997] 1 M.L.J. 418 (H.C.) (Malaysia). See generally Kent McNeil, *Common Law Aboriginal Title* (Oxford: Oxford University Press, 1984); Felix S. Cohen, *Original Indian Title*, 32 Minn. L. Rev. 28 (1947); Brian Slattery, *Understanding Aboriginal Rights*, 66 Can. B.Rev. 727 (1987).

[101]. See, e.g., *R. v. Adams* (1996), 110 C.C.C. (3d) 97, 32 W.C.B. (2d) 91 (S.C.C.) (Can.) (Mohawks of St. Regis Reserve found to have right to fish in waters not within the reserve); *Antoine v. Washington*, 420 U.S. 194 (1975) (upholding off-reservation right to fish). See also *Amodu Tijani v. Secretary, Southern Nigeria*, 2 A.C. 399 (P.C. 1921) (holding native rights of a tribe include usufructuary occupation or right).

[102]. (1992), 175 C.L.R. 1 (Austl.).

[103]. Ibid., 58, 61.

[104]. See generally Belize Constitution, art. 134 (1981) (incorporating British law existing prior to independence).

[105]. See, e.g., *San Jose Farmers' Coop. Soc'y Ltd. v. Attorney-General*, 43 W.I.R. 63, 77 (Belize C.A. 1991) (citing a Canadian case applying the doctrine of severance law); *Caribe Farm Indus. v. British Am. Cattle Co.*, 49 W.I.R. 39, 46–47, 49 (Belize C.A. 1995) (considering Australian and New Zealand title cases in land registration case). See generally Velma Newton, *Commonwealth Caribbean Legal Systems: A Study of Small Jurisdictions* 52–53 (1988) (noting that Caribbean judges have treated other Commonwealth and American court decisions as persuasive authorities); A.D. Burgess, *Judicial Precedent in the West Indies*, 7 Anglo-Am. L. Rev. 113, 130 (1978) (noting that English cases, while not binding, are of high persuasive authority in the West Indies).

[106]. This conclusion is supported by a full analysis of the common law doctrine of aboriginal rights and its specific application to the Maya of the Toledo District in Anaya, *Maya Aboriginal Land and Resource Rights*, see n. 80.

[107]. Cf. *Mabo [No.2]*, 175 C.L.R. at 42 (regarding as "unjust and discriminatory" the earlier failure of the Australian common law to recognize property rights of indigenous peoples on the basis of customary land tenure). See *infra*, paras. 121–125.

[108]. Proposed American Declaration on the Rights of Indigenous Peoples, art. XVIII, approved by the Inter-Am. C.H.R. at its 1333rd sess. on Feb. 26, 1997, in OEA/Ser.L/V/II.95.doc.7, rev. 1997, at 654–676 (hereinafter "Proposed American Declaration").

[109]. Draft United Nations Declaration on the Rights of Indigenous Peoples, art. 26, adopted by the U.N. Sub-Commission on Prevention of Discrimination and Protection of Minorities, 26 August 1994, E/CN.4/Sub.2/1994/45, at 105 (hereinafter "Draft U.N. Declaration").

[110]. International Labour Organisation Convention (No. 169 of 1989) concerning Indigenous and Tribal Peoples in Independent Countries, art. 14.1 (entered into force Sept. 1991) (hereinafter "Convention No. 169").

[111]. See ibid., paras. 12–22.

[112]. Ibid., paras. 23–25.

[113]. Ibid., paras. 14–20.

[114]. *Ecuador Report* (1997), 103 (commenting on the implications of analogous provisions of the American Convention on Human Rights).

[115]. See, e.g., Case 11.137 (Argentina), Inter-Am. C.H.R. Report 55/97, OEA/Ser.L/V/II.98 doc. 7 rev., at 271, para. 157, *et seq.* (applying international humanitarian law). The Commission's practice of applying sources of international law, other than the American Convention or the American Declaration has been viewed with approval by the Inter-American Court of Human Rights. See *"Other Treaties" Subject to the Advisory Jurisdiction of the Court (Art. 64 of the American Convention on Human Rights)*, Advisory Opinion OC-1/82 of September 24, 1982, Inter-Am Ct. H.R. (Ser. A) no. 1, para. 43 (1982).

[116]. See, e.g., Case 7964 (Nicaragua), Inter-Am. C.H.R., *Report on the Situation of a Segment of the Nicaraguan Population of Miskito Origin*, OEA/Ser.L/V/II.62, doc. 10 rev 3, at 76–78, 81 (1983) (hereinafter "Miskito Case"); Case 7615 (Brazil), Inter-Am. C.H.R., OEA/Ser.L/V/II.66, doc. 10 rev 1, at 24, 31 (1985) (concerning the Yamonami of Brazil); *Ecuador Report* (1997), 103–04.

[117]. Miskito Case (1983), 81.

[118]. Proposed American Declaration on the Rights of Indigenous Peoples, (1997), art. VII.

[119]. Human Rights Committee, General Comment No. 23 (50) (Art. 27), adopted April 6, 1994, para. 7 (hereinafter "HRC General Comment on art. 27").

[120]. See, e.g., *J. E. Länsmann v. Finland*, Communication No. 671/1995, CCPR/C/58/D/671/1995, paras. 2.1–2.4, 10.1–10.5 (*Länsmann II*) (Saami reindeer herding in certain land area is protected by art. 27, despite disputed ownership of land; however, article 27 not violated in this case). See also *B. Ominayak, Chief of the Lubicon Lake Band v. Canada*, Communication No. 167/1984, Hum. Rts. Comm., A/45/40, vol. II, annex IX.A. para 32.2 (economic and social activities linked with territory are part of culture protected by art. 27); *Länsmann et al. v. Finland*, Communication No. 511/1992, Hum. Rts. Comm., CCPR/C/52/D/511/1992 (1994) (*Länsmann I*) (reindeer herding part of Saami culture protected by art. 27); *Kitok v. Sweden*, Communication No. 197/1985, Hum. Rts. Comm., A/43/40, annex VII.G (1988) (art. 27 extends to economic activity "where that activity is an essential element in the culture of an ethnic community").

[121]. Communication No. 167/1984, see above, no. 120.

[122]. Ibid. at para. 33.

[125]. *Ecuador Report* (1997) 106.

[126]. Ibid., paras. 14–22.

[127]. Declaration of the U.N. Conference on Environment and Development, principle 1, U.N. Doc. A/CONF.151/26 (1992) (hereinafter "Rio Declaration").

[128]. Ibid., principle 22.

[129]. U.N. Conference on Environment and Development: Agenda 21, ch. 26, U.N. Doc. A/CONF.151/26 (1992), ch. 26.1 (hereinafter "Agenda 21").

[130]. Proposed American Declaration on the Rights of Indigenous Peoples (1997), art. XIII.1.

[131]. Draft U.N. Declaration (1994), art. 28.

[132]. Ibid., paras. 26–35.

[133]. *Ecuador Report* (1997), 89.

[134]. Ibid., paras. 41–45.

[135]. See HRC General Comment on art. 27 (1994), para. 7.

[136]. Cf. Committee on the Elimination of Racial Discrimination, General Recommendation XXI on self-determination, CERD/48/Misc.7/Rev.3, paras. 3, 5 (1996) (hereinafter "CERD general recommendation on self-determination") (linking the right of self-determination with the right to take part in public affairs and the right of ethnic groups to lead lives of dignity and to preserve their culture).

[137]. See S. James Anaya, *Indigenous Peoples in International Law* (Oxford University Press, 1996), 85–88.

[138]. Proposed American Declaration on the Rights of Indigenous Peoples (1997), art. XVI.1.

[140]. Convention No. 169 (1991), art. 15.1.

[141]. Ibid., art. 7.1.

[142]. Ibid., art. 6.2.

[143]. The situation here is in stark contrast to those in which the U.N. Human Rights Committee has found that the state concerned complied with its obligation to consult with indigenous peoples over development activities that could affect their traditional land or resource use. For example, in *Länsmann II*, Comm. no. 671/1995, the committee examined the impact of logging activities on reindeer herding by the indigenous Saami people of Finland. In addition to finding minimal impact on the reindeer herding, the committee determined that sufficient consultation had taken

place. The Committee observed that a reindeer herders' committee had participated in developing plans for the logging, and it found that Finland had gone
through a process of weighing the interests of the Saami herders. Id. at para. 10.5.

[144]. Ibid., para. 25.

[145]. Ibid., paras. 37–38.

[146]. Ibid., paras. 46–63.

[147]. Ibid., paras. 41–45.

[148]. Committee on the Elimination of Racial Discrimination, General Recommendation XXIII, on indigenous peoples, adopted at the Committee's 1235th meeting, 18 August 1997, CERD/C51/Misc. 13/Rev. 4 (1997), para. 3 (hereinafter
"CERD General Recommendation on indigenous peoples").

[149]. *Report of the United Nations Seminar on the Effects of Racism and Racial Discrimination on the Relations Between Indigenous Peoples and States*, E/CN.4/1989/22, HR/
PUB/89/5, at 5 (1989).

[150]. Ibid.

[151]. See Belisle Affidavit (Appendix B.48); Cardona Affidavit (Appendix B.49);
Gardiner Affidavit (Appendix B.50) (countering Maya claims of aboriginal property
rights by recounting a history of colonial conquest and land administration that
excluded legal recognition of traditional indigenous land tenure).

[152]. CERD General Recommendation on indigenous peoples, para. 5.

[153]. (1992), 175 C.L.R. 1, 41–43 (Austl.).

[154]. (1988), 166 C.L.R. 186 (Austl.)

[155]. Ibid., 218.

[156]. The obligation of effectiveness is implicit in the obligation to uphold human rights. See Theodor Meron, *Human Rights and Humanitarian Norms as Customary
Law* (Oxford University Press, 1989), 139. The obligation of effectiveness is made
explicit in arts. 1 and 2 of the American Convention on Human Rights, in relation to
the rights affirmed in that Convention.

[157]. See *Velasquez Rodriguez Case,* Judgment of July 29, 1988, Inter-Am. Ct. H.R.
(ser. C) No. 4, para. 166 (1988) (with particular regard to the obligations under the
American Convention on Human Rights).

[158]. See *International Responsibility for the Promulgation and Enforcement of Laws in
Violation of the Convention (Articles 1 and 2 of the American Convention on Human Rights),*
Advisory Opinion OC-14/94 of December 9, 1994, Inter-Am. Ct. H.R. (ser. A) No.14
(1994).

[159]. Miskito Case, (1983), 76.

[160]. *Ecuador Report* (1997), 106 (quoting F. Caportorti, *Study on the Rights of
Persons belonging to Ethnic, Religious and Linguistic Minorities* (U.N. Center for Human
Rights, 1991), para. 585).

[161]. HRC Comment on art. 27, *supra* note 39, para. 7.

[162]. See *Ecuador Report* (1997), at 106.

[163]. Convention No. 169, (1991), art. 14.2–3.

[164]. Proposed American Declaration, art. XVIII.4

[165]. Ibid., art. XVIII.8

[166]. Agenda 21 (1992), ch. 26.3(a).

[167]. Ibid., paras. 46–63.

[168]. Ibid., paras. 64–77.

[169]. This right also is found in the U.N. Universal Declaration of Human Rights
in its art. 8 in the following terms: "Everyone has the right to an effective remedy by
the competent national tribunals for acts violating the fundamental rights granted
him by the constitution or by law." Universal Declaration of Human Rights, G.A. Res.
217 (III 1948).

[170]. *"Judicial Guarantees in States of Emergency", Arts. 27(2), 25 and 8 American Convention on Human Rights,* Advisory Opinion OC-9/87 of October, 1987, Inter-Am. Ct. H.R., Paras. 27 & 28.

[171]. See Case 11.233 (Peru), Inter-Am. C.H.R., OEA/Ser.L/VII.98, Doc.7 rev. at 799, para. 98 (particularly articles 25 and 8 of the American Convention).

[172]. Section 20 (1) & (2) of the Belize Constitution (1981) provides:
(1) If any person alleges that any of the provisions of sections 3 to 19 inclusive of this Constitution has been, is being or is likely to be contravened in relation to him (or, in the case of a person who is detained, if any other person alleges such a contravention in relation to the detained person), then without prejudice to any other action with respect to the same matter which is lawfully available, that person (or that other person) may apply to the Supreme Court for redress.

(2) The Supreme Court shall have original jurisdiction
(a) to hear and determine any application made by any person in pursuance of subsection (1) of this section . . .
and may make such declarations and orders, issue such writs and give such directions as it may consider appropriate for the purpose of enforcing or securing the enforcement of any of the provisions of sections 3 to 19 inclusive of this Constitution.

[178]. Case 10.606 (Guatemala), Inter-Am. C.H.R., OEA/Ser.L/VII.98, Doc. 7 rev. at 619, para. 52 (1998).

[179]. See Case 11.218 (Nicaragua), Inter-Am. C.H.R., OEA/Ser.L/VII.98, Doc. 7 rev. at 692, para. 106 (1998) ("judicial protection entails . . . the right . . . to a simple and swift remedy").

[180]. Ibid., paras. 133–134.

[181]. See Case 10.580 (Ecuador), Inter-Am. C.H.R., OEA/Ser.L/VII.91, Doc. 7 at 76, paras. 5–6 (1996) (Commission found failure of domestic court to respond to petition for over a year as evidence of unresponsiveness and unwarranted delay).

[182]. See Case 11.577 (Nicaragua), *Annual Report of the Inter-American Commission on Human Rights,* OEA/Ser.L/VII.98, Doc. 7 rev. at 46 (1998).

Contributors

S. James Anaya, B.A. (University of New Mexico) 1980, J.D. (Harvard) 1983, is Samuel M. Fegtly Professor of Law at the University of Arizona. One of the attorneys for the Toledo Maya Cultural Council of southern Belize, he is the principal author of the Maya petition to the Inter-American Commission on Human Rights and author of *Indigenous Peoples in International Law.* He also serves as Special Counsel to the Indian Law Resource Center, a U.S.-based nongovernmental organization with consultative status at the United Nations.

Rebecca J. Cook, A.B. (Barnard) 1970, M.A. (Tufts) 1972, M.P.A. (Harvard) 1973, J.D. (Georgetown) 1982, LL.M. (Columbia) 1988, J.S.D. (Columbia) 1994, Fellow, Royal Society of Canada, is a professor in the Faculty of Law, the Faculty of Medicine, and the Joint Centre for Bioethics at the University of Toronto, specializing in the international protection of human rights and in health law and ethics, and is founding director of the International Human Rights Programme at the Faculty of Law. She is editor of *Human Rights of Women: National and International Perspectives* (University of Pennsylvania Press) and co-author of *Considerations for Formulating Reproductive Health Laws.*

Leilani Farha, B.A. (Toronto) 1990, LL.B./M.S.W. (Toronto) 1995, is a lawyer and human rights consultant in the area of economic, social, and cultural rights. Her research focuses on women's rights and land and property issues. Recent publications include *Women's Rights to Land, Property, and Housing During Situations of Armed Conflict: A Global Overview,* "Contextualizing Violence Against Women: Forced Evictions in Situations of Armed Conflict," *Canadian Woman Studies* 19, 4 (2000); and "Women and Housing," in *Women and International Human Rights Law,* vol. 1, ed. Kelly D. Askin and Dorean Koenig.

Nora Flood, B.A. (Kenyon) 1997, is an LL.B. candidate (2001) at the Faculty of Law, University of Toronto. She is a member of the Senior Editorial Board of the University of Toronto Faculty of Law Review for the 2000–2001 academic year. Her area of interest is law and development.

Craig Forcese, B.A. (McGill) 1992, M.A. (Carleton) 1997, LL.B. (Ottawa) 1997, is an LL.M. candidate (Yale) of the Bars of New York and Ontario. At the time of writing he was a Visiting Professor, University of Ottawa, Faculty of Law (1998–2000), and a Project Manager, Business and Human Rights Project, Canadian Lawyers Association for International Human Rights (CLAIHR), 1996–2000.

Isfahan Merali, B.A. (Toronto) 1990, LL.B. (Toronto) 1995, is Legal Counsel with the Ontario Human Rights Commission. Former director of the International Human Rights Programme and a Human Rights Fellow with the Programme on Reproductive and Sexual Health Law, Faculty of Law, University of Toronto, she was co-chair of the 1998 conference, "Linking the Domestic and the International: Human Rights into the 21st Century." Her publications include, with Rebecca Cook, "The Interpretation and Application of Human Rights by Commonwealth Courts to Reproductive and Sexual Health," *Commonwealth Law Bulletin* (1999) and "Advancing Women's Reproductive and Sexual Health Rights: Effectively Using the International Human Rights System," in Oxfam's *Development in Practice.*

Valerie Oosterveld, B.Soc.Sc. (Ottawa) 1990, LL.B. (Toronto) 1993, LL.M. (Columbia) 1999, J.S.D. candidate (Columbia), is a legal officer with the Canadian Department of Foreign Affairs and International Trade. Former director of the International Human Rights Programme at the Faculty of Law, University of Toronto, she was co-chair of the 1998 conference "Linking the Domestic and the International: Human Rights into the 21st Century." Her publications include "Women and Employment," in *Women and International Human Rights Law,* vol. 1, ed. Kelly D. Askin and Dorean Koenig, and, with Gabriela Mastaglia, "Women's Rights Under Labor Law: A Comparative Study of Argentina and Canada," *Loyola of Los Angeles International and Comparative Law Journal* 19, 4 (1997).

Dianne Otto, B.A., 1973, LL.B., 1992, LL.M. (Melbourne) 1996, LL.M. (Columbia) 1998, J.S.D. candidate (Columbia) is a senior lecturer in law at the University of Melbourne and co-convener of the Women's Rights Action Network, Australia. Her research interests include using feminist, postcolonial, and queer theory to reveal the voices and interests that are marginalized or silenced by mainstream international legal discourse. Her publications include "A Post-Beijing Reflection on the Limitations and Potential of Human Rights Discourse for Women," in *Women and International Human Rights Law,* vol. 1, ed. Kelly D. Askin and Dorean Koenig, "Rethinking the 'Universality' of Human Rights Law," *Rights Law Review* 29 (1997), and "Holding Up Half the Sky But for Whose Benefit? A Critical Analysis of the Fourth World Conference on Women," *Australian Feminist Law Journal* 6 (1996).

Chisanga Puta-Chekwe, B.A. (Oxford) 1979, M.A. (Oxford) 1984, LL.B. (Birmingham) 1975, LL.M. (King's College, London) 1977, is a solicitor of the Supreme Court (England and Wales), and an Advocate of the High

Court for Zambia. He attended Sir William Borlase School in Marlow, Buckinghamshire, before studying law at the University of Birmingham in England. A Rhodes scholar, he received graduate degrees in law from the University of London and in philosophy, politics, and economics from the University of Oxford. He is the author of *An Election to Remember: Recollections of a United Nations Observor to the 1994 South African Election.*

Kerry Rittich, LL.B. (Alberta) 1992; S.J.D. (Harvard) 1998, is an assistant professor in the Faculty of Law and Women's Studies, University of Toronto. She teaches and researches in the areas of international law and human rights, labor law, critical legal theories, and feminist theory. Her current research centers around gender and labor market regulation, and the distributive effects of market reform projects. Her publications include "Transformed Pursuits: The Quest for Equality in Globalized Markets," *Harvard Human Rights Journal* 13, 232 (2000) and "Distributive Justice and the World Bank: The Pursuit of Gender Equity in the Context of Market Reform," in *The Legitimacy of International Organizations,* ed. Veijo Heiskanen and Jean-Marc Coicaud.

Craig Scott, B.A. (McGill) 1984, B.A. (Oxford) 1986, LL.M. (London/London School of Economics) 1987, LL.B. (Dalhousie) 1988, is an associate professor at Osgoode Hall Law School, York University, Toronto. His research interests converge around the theory and legal doctrine of international human rights regulation. Recent publications include Craig Scott, ed. *Torture as Tort: Comparative Perspectives on the Development of Transnational Human Rights Litigation,* "Multinational Enterprises and Emergent Jurisprudence on Violations of Economic, Social and Cultural Rights," in *Economic, Social and Cultural Rights: A Textbook,* 2nd ed., ed. Asbjørn Eide, Catarina Krause, Allan Rosas, and Martin Scheinin, and, with Philip Alston, "Adjudicating Constitutional Priorities in a Transnational Context: A Comment on Soobramoney's Legacy and Grootboom's Promise," *South African Journal of Human Rights* 16, 2 (2000).

Martha Shaffer, A.B. (Harvard) 1983, LL.B. (Toronto) 1987, LL.M. (Harvard) 1990, is an associate professor of law at the Faculty of Law, University of Toronto. In her research and teaching she concentrates on family law, criminal law, and equality issues.

Barbara von Tigerstrom, M.A. (Toronto) 1993, LL.B. (Toronto) 1997, Ph.D. (Cand.) (Cambridge), was the project coordinator for the Health Law Institute at the University of Alberta Faculty of Law. She is coeditor with Timothy Caulfield of *Meeting the Challenge: Health Care Reform and the Law* and author of a number of articles and book chapters on human rights, environmental law, and health law issues, including "Health Care Reform and Human Rights" (in von Tigerstrom and Caulfield) and "The Role of the Ombudsman in Protecting Economic, Social and Cultural Rights," *International Ombudsman Yearbook* 2, 3 (1998).

Index

Numbers in square brackets refer to notes in the Maya petition. United Nations agencies are listed under UN.

Acknowledgments

This book was inspired by a conference celebrating the tenth anniversary of the International Human Rights Programme at the Faculty of Law, University of Toronto. The 1998 conference, entitled "Linking the Domestic and the International: Human Rights into the 21st Century," brought together a diverse group of international scholars, advocates, and activists to generate valuable reflection on a number of pressing international human rights issues. Out of this discussion came the idea of a book examining different approaches to taking economic, social, and cultural rights "out of their box," so to speak, so they could be realized in a meaningful way. In this sense, this book is the offspring of that gathering of ideas. We would like to thank everyone who participated in the conference, especially the authors who contributed to this collection, for helping to bring about this book.

A special thank you to Dean Ronald Daniels of the Faculty of Law, University of Toronto for originally suggesting the idea of a book to celebrate the Programme. As well, we would like to thank Professor Rebecca J. Cook, the founder of the International Human Rights Programme, for her forward-looking vision from the moment the idea for this book was conceived right to the end of the process. We are greatly indebted to Tracey Pegg for her unfailing good humor and incredible organizational skills, and for going well beyond the call of duty throughout the process. Our deep appreciation to our editorial assistants, without whose help this book would not have been completed: Anne Carbert, Heather Gamester, and Kevin Janus. On a personal note, we wish to express our deepest thanks to our families (Walter, Sergio, and Jonah) for their encouragement and patience. Finally, a special recognition for the authors of this collection, a most professional group with which to work, who continue to contribute to the advancement of economic, social and cultural rights in their daily lives in many ways. This is their book, but any errors are strictly our own.